D1599802

URBAN SOCIETY IN AN AGE OF WAR: NÖRDLINGEN, 1580-1720

Urban Society in an Age of War: Nördlingen, 1580–1720

CHRISTOPHER R. FRIEDRICHS

PRINCETON UNIVERSITY PRESS
PRINCETON, NEW JERSEY

Published by Princeton University Press, Princeton, New Jersey
In the United Kingdom: Princeton University Press, Guildford, Surrey

Library of Congress Cataloging in Publication Data will be found on the last printed page of this book

Publication of this book has been aided by a grant from the Andrew W. Mellon Foundation and by the Whitney Darrow Publication Reserve Fund of Princeton University Press

This book has been composed in linotype Janson

Clothbound editions of Princeton University Press books are printed on acid-free paper and binding materials are chosen for strength and durability.

Printed in the United States of America by Princeton University Press, Princeton, New Jersey

To my father
Kurt Otto Friedrichs
My first and best teacher

CONTENTS

List of Tables and Figures		ix
Preface		xi
A Note About Money and Dates		xvi
Abbreviations		xvii
One	The Setting: An Imperial City in Peace and War	3
Two	The People of Nördlingen: Demographic Patterns	35
Three	A City at Work: Occupational Patterns	73
Four	Rich Man, Poor Man: The Wealth of Nördlingen	95
Five	The Burden of War: Municipal Finance	144
Six	An Urban Elite: The City Council	170
Seven	In Search of Order: The Politics of Paternalism	198
Eight	To Make Them Fear the Lord: Church and School in a Lutheran Community	222
Nine	Capitalism and Its Enemies: The Wörner Family and the Weaving Industry of Nördlingen	239
Ten	Conclusion	288
Appendixes		
I.	Population Statistics for Nördlingen, 1579-1720: Baptisms, Marriages, Burials	298
II.	Distribution of Occupations Among Male Citizens in Five Selected Years	312
III.	Citizens of Nördlingen, 1579-1724: Mean, Median and Total Wealth (fl.)	321
IV.	Price Index for 1579-1724	322

V. Calculation of Wealth Distribution for 1579 — 324
VI. Wealth Mobility Tables — 326
VII. Members of the City Council of Nördlingen, 1580-1720 — 330
Select Bibliography — 335
Index — 343

TABLES AND FIGURES

Tables *page*

2.1. Nördlingen Marriages, 1581-1720: Origins of Spouses 65
2.2. Marital Status of Spouses 67
2.3. Ages of Men and Women at First Marriage 69
3.1. Ten Most Common Occupations (Among Male Citizens) in Five Selected Years 80
3.2. Male Citizens in Each General Occupational Category in Five Selected Years 82
3.3. Heritability of Occupations 86
3.4. Occupational Mobility Patterns, 1580-1700 91
4.1. Shoemakers Who Became Citizens in 1580-85: Their Wealth at Six-Year Intervals 96
4.2. Distribution of Wealth, 1579 104
4.3. Seven Most Common Occupations in 1579 (Male Citizens): Median and Mean Wealth 107
4.4. Distribution of Wealth Among Male Citizens in the Seven Major Occupational Groups, 1579 108
4.5. Wealth Mobility of Men Who Became Citizens in 1580-1585 126
4.6. Summary of Wealth Mobility Patterns 127
4.7. Percentage of the Total Wealth Owned by Members of Each Occupational Group 136
5.1. Receipts and Expenditures of the City Treasury, 1579 146
5.2. Receipts and Expenditures of the City Treasury, 1634 154
5.3. Debts Owed to and Owed by the City Treasury 160
5.4. Receipts and Expenditures of the City Treasury, 1700 162
5.5. Amounts Owed to and Owed by the Anlagskasse 163
5.6. Receipts and Expenditures of the Anlagskasse for Selected Years 164
6.1. Occupations of Council Members Upon Appointment, 1581-1700 175
6.2. Family Backgrounds of Council Members, 1580-1720 188

Figures *page*

Frontispiece. Merian's View of Nördlingen (1643) 2
1.1. Map of Nördlingen and the Ries (c. 1600) 5
1.2. Andreas Zeidler's Plan of Nördlingen (1651) 8
2.1. Total Number of Citizen Households in Nördlingen, 1579-1724 42
2.2 Baptisms, Burials and Marriages of Nördlingen Residents, 1581-1720 (Five-Year Averages) 46
2.3. Baptisms, Burials and Marriages of Nördlingen Residents, 1633-1636 50
2.4. Number of Alien Males Admitted to Citizenship During Each Six-Year Period 56
2.5. Percentage of Aliens Among All Males Admitted to Active Citizenship, 1580-1700 58
3.1. The Geissler Family (Males Only) 74
4.1. Total Wealth of the Citizenry, 1579-1724 112
4.2. Total Wealth of the Citizenry, 1579-1724, Adjusted for Real Value 113
4.3. Mean and Median Wealth of the Citizenry, 1579-1724 118
4.4. Mean and Median Wealth of the Citizenry, 1579-1724, Adjusted for Real Value 119
4.5. Percentage of the Total Wealth Owned by Selected Segments of the Citizenry, 1579-1724 122
4.6. Median Wealth of Wool Weavers and Tanners 130
4.7. Median Wealth of Four Production Crafts 132
4.8. Median Wealth of Major Food and Drink Trades 134
4.9. Proportion of the Total Wealth (of All Male Citizens) Owned by Merchants, 1579-1724 138
5.1. Average Annual Expenditures of the City Treasury and Anlagskasse 150
5.2. Average Annual Expenditures of the City Treasury and Anlagskasse, Adjusted for Real Value 151
6.1. Proportion of the Total Wealth (of All Citizens) Owned by Council Members, 1579-1724 180
6.2. The Frickhinger Family (A Selective Genealogy) 186
6.3. Interrelationships of Citizens Who Were Council Members in 1695 192
9.1. The Wörner Family (A Selective Genealogy) 242

PREFACE

THE traditional map of European history is dotted with place names like London and Paris, Florence and Amsterdam, Geneva, Versailles and Waterloo—the great commercial centers, seats of government, or scenes of intellectual and military history whose names will be familiar to every reader of this book. Among social historians, however, there has begun to emerge a new map of European history—a map designed not to supplant the traditional one, but to be superimposed upon it. This new map is less densely covered than the older one, and the terrain is inscribed with unfamiliar names—names like Colyton and Crulai, Beauvais and Carmaux, Upper Hesse and Heidenreichstein. Such places, unremarkable though they seem, have become significant because social historians have used their records to explore in depth the fabric of social life in premodern times—to create, as it were, a sociology of the past.

The little German city of Nördlingen has always occupied a place on the traditional map of European history, for two great battles of the Thirty Years War were fought there. This book hopes, however, to add Nördlingen to the second map as well, by using the remarkable records of this community to reconstruct the nature of its society during a century and a half of early modern history.

One sometimes encounters the attitude that local studies are, in some way, the second-class citizens of historical literature, useful only as building blocks upon which broad comparative studies or works of historical synthesis can be constructed. This is an attitude, however, which I firmly reject. No doubt there are some local studies, suffused with antiquarian detail or brimming over with statistical output, which take on meaning only when their findings are woven into some broader framework. But the best local studies can stand by themselves as contributions to our understanding of the past. When I look back at my own training as an historian, it is easy to identify the two works which impressed me most deeply: Pierre Goubert's *Beauvais et le Beauvaisis de 1600 à 1730* and William Sheridan Allen's *The Nazi Seizure of Power: The Experience of a Single German Town, 1930-1935*. Works like these convinced me—as they should convince any reader—that local history can illuminate some aspects of the past in ways that few works of broad historical synthesis can ever hope to equal.

Like Allen's book, this study examines the people and problems of a small German city during a troubled era. In spirit and methodology, however, this book owes more to the example of Goubert. Although I have obviously conceived my study on a much more modest scale, I have at least attempted something approximating an *histoire totale* of one German community during the seventeenth century.

To whatever extent I may have succeeded, I was able to do so because of the extraordinary quality of the records preserved in the municipal and parish archives of Nördlingen. Although I have drawn on many different kinds of sources, two series in particular—the tax registers and the parish registers—have proved invaluable. Remarkably enough, though a number of fine German dissertations have been written about specific aspects of Nördlingen's history, no historian has ever systematically exploited these two crucial sources. I have made them, however, the linchpins of my study. This book opens in 1579, the year the parish registers begin, and closes in the 1720's, shortly before the tax registers end. In between these dates I could work with two complete and concurrent series which made it possible to offer a solid statistical foundation for my conclusions about the society of early modern Nördlingen.

These conclusions will become clear in the course of this book. It may be useful here, however, to alert the reader to two topics of historical discussion to which this book hopes to make some contribution. One of these questions is a familiar—indeed, quite venerable—subject of German historiography: the effects of the Thirty Years War. For a century, historians have argued whether or not the war of 1618 to 1648 resulted in an economic, social and demographic disaster for the German people. My own work on Nördlingen has convinced me, however, not so much that either side in this debate is correct as that the question itself has been incorrectly posed. For the Thirty Years War was only the first in a long cycle of wars which affected the Holy Roman Empire for a century after 1618. If we look at Nördlingen a decade or so after the Thirty Years War ended, we get one answer to the question about the impact of war on such a community. But if we look at Nördlingen fifty years later—after half a century of further warfare—we get quite different answers. And these answers are relevant for more than just the history of one city.

The second question is an even more basic, and more elusive, one. For it has to do with the very nature of the community in premodern society. Most historians agree that there was something about "traditional" societies that made them different from those of the modern world. What that something was, however, and when, why and how it changed, are matters that historians still but scarcely understand. Obviously a study like this can provide no definitive answers. But it can hope to offer some insights into the factors involved in the transformation from a traditional to a modern way of life in European communities. For it was during the period covered by this book that some elements of this transformation—new forms of capitalism, for example, and new patterns of social mobility—began to emerge in Nördlingen.

Yet while much changed in this community between 1580 and 1720, much else remained the same. For Nördlingen at the end of this period was still essentially what it had been at the beginning: a community of the *ancien régime*, rooted in traditions and assumptions quite alien to those of our own time. To explore and reconstruct this distant world is what really challenges the historian of early modern Europe. No one can ever fully succeed in making the world of the past as immediate as our own, but I hope that these pages will bring at least some of its people and some of its patterns back to life.

IN some ways, my greatest debt in preparing this book has been to the seventeenth-century clerks and clerics of Nördlingen, whose painstaking methods yielded records of exceptional completeness and clarity. Among those I can thank in person, however, the first place belongs to the current custodian of most of these records, Dr. Dietmar-H. Voges, director of the Stadtarchiv Nördlingen. Without his generous cooperation and assistance I could not have completed nearly as much research as I did during two long visits to Nördlingen. I am also indebted to the distinguished former archivist of Nördlingen, Dr. Gustav Wulz, who offered much valuable assistance and advice during my first visit to the city.

I am grateful to officials of the Evangelische Kirchengemeinde of Nördlingen and the Pfarrei Nähermemmingen for permission to use the parish registers in their care. Sincere thanks are also due to Frau Maria Weiss and Fräulein Irmgard Donner of the Stadtbibliothek Nördlingen.

This book, like many others, began as a doctoral dissertation. By now it bears little resemblance to that earlier form, but I am still deeply grateful for both the encouragement and the criticism I received from two of my Princeton University teachers: Theodore K. Rabb, my doctoral supervisor, and Lawrence Stone. For assistance in my computer analysis of the Nördlingen tax data, I owe thanks to Judith Rowe, Irene Goldfarb and Nita Rome of the Princeton University computer center.

I am grateful to the Canada Council for the financial support which underwrote my second trip to Nördlingen, during which most of the demographic research was undertaken.

Along the road from dissertation to book I have benefited

from the advice of many scholars. To Myron Gutmann, Donald Paterson and Gerald Soliday I am especially indebted for careful readings of part of or all of the manuscript—and for many suggestions, of which I adopted most but (perhaps unwisely) not all. Many other friends and colleagues, particularly at Princeton University and at the University of British Columbia, have also been generous with advice, assistance and commentary.

Parts of this book have already appeared in print. I am grateful to the editor of the *Business History Review* for permission to include as part of Chapter Nine a slightly revised version of my article, "Early Capitalism and its Enemies: The Wörner Family and the Weavers of Nördlingen," which first appeared in the *Review*, vol. 50, no. 3 (Autumn 1976). Some sections of Chapters Two and Three first appeared in my article, "Marriage, Family and Social Structure in an Early Modern German Town," in the Canadian Historical Association's *Historical Papers* for 1975. Finally, I am grateful for permission to publish as Appendix I some demographic tables which have also been accepted for publication in the *Jahrbuch des historischen Vereins für Nördlingen und das Ries*.

But above all I must express deep appreciation to my wife, Rhoda Lange Friedrichs, not only for assistance in research but also for a constant and generous supply of editorial advice and historical judgment throughout the eight years that have gone into the making of this book.

C.R.F.

Vancouver, B.C.
September, 1978

A NOTE ABOUT MONEY AND DATES

THE normal coin of account in seventeenth-century Nördlingen was the gulden (abbreviated fl., for an earlier variant, the florin). One gulden consisted of 60 kreuzer (krz.). Many different currencies circulated in the city, but when it came to drawing up records or accounts, these currencies were normally converted to their equivalent value in fl. and krz.

Until the 1620's, some accounts were rendered in "fl. münz." One fl. münz was equal to 252 pfennige, and since a pfennig was worth 4/17 of a kreuzer, simple arithmetic will show that the fl. münz was worth only .988 of a regular fl. But the difference is so slight that it need not seriously concern us in this book.

THE Gregorian calendar was introduced in the Catholic countries of Europe in 1582. But Nördlingen, as a Lutheran community, remained loyal to the old calendar until 1700, when the new system was finally adopted by the Protestant states of the Holy Roman Empire. Thus, all dates in this book which fall before 1700 are given in Old Style. Among other things this will explain why the battle of Nördlingen, which most textbooks date as September 6, 1634, is recorded here as having happened on August 27.

ABBREVIATIONS

AR	Anlagsrechnungen
ER	Eheregister, St. Georg
KR	Kammerrechnungen
OB	Ordnungsbücher
Pfb.	Pfandbücher
RP	Ratsprotokolle
SpR	Spitalrechnungen
SR	Sterberegister, St. Georg
StR	Steuerregister
TR	Taufregister, St. Georg
JHVN	*Jahrbuch des historischen Vereins für Nördlingen und das Ries*

(For full citations, see Bibliography)

Note: Except for the parish registers, all manuscript sources cited in the footnotes are located in the Stadtarchiv Nördlingen.

URBAN SOCIETY IN AN AGE OF WAR: NÖRDLINGEN, 1580-1720

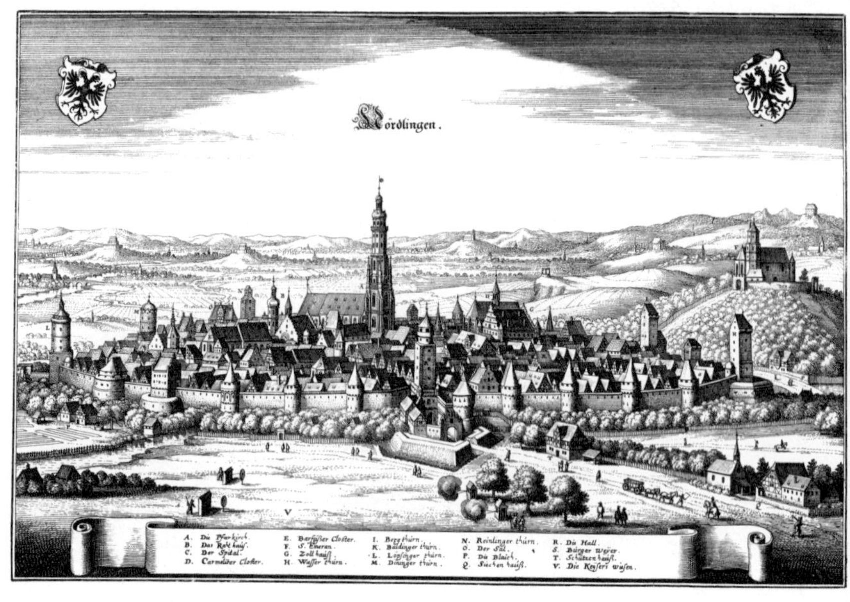

FRONTISPIECE. Merian's View of Nördlingen (1643). From Matthaeus Merian, *Topographia Sueviae* (Frankfurt am Main, 1643).

One

The Setting: An Imperial City In Peace and War

TAKE any map of Germany and draw a line from Frankfurt am Main to Munich. Two-thirds of the way from Frankfurt to Munich your pencil will land on the town of Nördlingen. Until 1803 Nördlingen was a free city of the Holy Roman Empire, but today it is just a modest provincial town of western Bavaria, made prosperous by light industry and a bustling tourist trade. Nördlingen's population today is over 15,000, but as late as 1938 the town had only 8,400 inhabitants—roughly equal to the number that can be estimated for the late sixteenth century.[1] The city's retarded growth is precisely what makes it attractive to the modern tourist, for Nördlingen has succeeded in retaining much of its medieval appearance. The fourteenth-century walls, with their covered parapets and imposing sixteenth-century towers, form an unbroken ring which sharply separates the old city from its modern suburbs. And inside the walls, the street pattern and location of buildings conform almost exactly to what was recorded in the seventeenth century.[2] Almost every house in the old city still displays strong traces of its

[1] Gustav Adolf Zipperer, "Nördlingen nach 1945," in *Nördlingen: Porträt einer Stadt* (Oettingen/Bayern, 1965), p. 146, gives the city's population in 1964 as 15,086. More recent population figures are even higher, but they are misleading because in the meantime a number of rural villages have been incorporated into the city. For Nördlingen's population in the late sixteenth century, see the discussion in Chapter Two.

[2] The location of streets and buildings in contemporary Nördlingen can be compared with the detailed plan of the city by Andreas Zeidler, published in 1651 with the title "Delinatio Vera Imperialis Civitatis ad Aras Flavias Sive Nördlingen," reproduced below in this chapter.

medieval facade. In few European cities is the past still so visible as it is today in the city of Nördlingen.[3]

I

Nördlingen lies near the center of the Ries, a fertile agricultural basin about fifteen miles in diameter (see Figure 1.1). Today this district straddles the border between Bavaria and Württemberg, but in sixteenth-century terms the Ries is better identified as lying in the northernmost part of the larger region, or imperial circle, of Swabia. The district is almost entirely enclosed by a ring of low hills, broken only where the river Wörnitz cuts through on its progress southward to the Danube. Nördlingen itself is situated on a minor tributary of the Wörnitz, the Eger—not a navigable river, but enough of a stream to activate the water wheels on which in preindustrial times the city's mills depended.

The rich soils of the Ries yielded a variety of crops, but the area was known above all as a source of grains; indeed, the Ries was a major supplier of grain for the city of Nu-

[3] No comprehensive history of Nördlingen has been written. The best introduction is provided by Gustav Wulz, "Historischer Einleitung," in Karl Grober and Adam Horn, eds., *Die Kunstdenkmäler von Schwaben und Neuburg, II: Stadt Nördlingen* (Munich, 1940), pp. 1-45, which also includes a detailed bibliography. This essay was reprinted, with some revisions and without the bibliography, in *Nördlingen: Porträt einer Stadt.* Another useful survey, emphasizing economic history, is provided by Heinz Berger, *Nördlingen: Die Entwicklung einer Stadt von den Anfängen bis zum Beginn der sechziger Jahre des 20. Jahrhunderts* (Dissertation, Erlangen, 1969). These works completely supersede the three earlier published histories of the city, all essentially chronicles: Johannes Müller, *Merkwürdigkeiten der Stadt Nördlingen, nebst einer Chronik* (Nördlingen, 1824); C. Beyschlag, *Geschichte der Stadt Nördlingen bis auf die neueste Zeit* (Nördlingen, 1851); and Christian Mayer, *Die Stadt Nördlingen: ihr Leben und ihre Kunst im Lichte der Vorzeit* (Nördlingen, 1876). Of these three works, that of Beyschlag, with its critical approach, is the most useful.

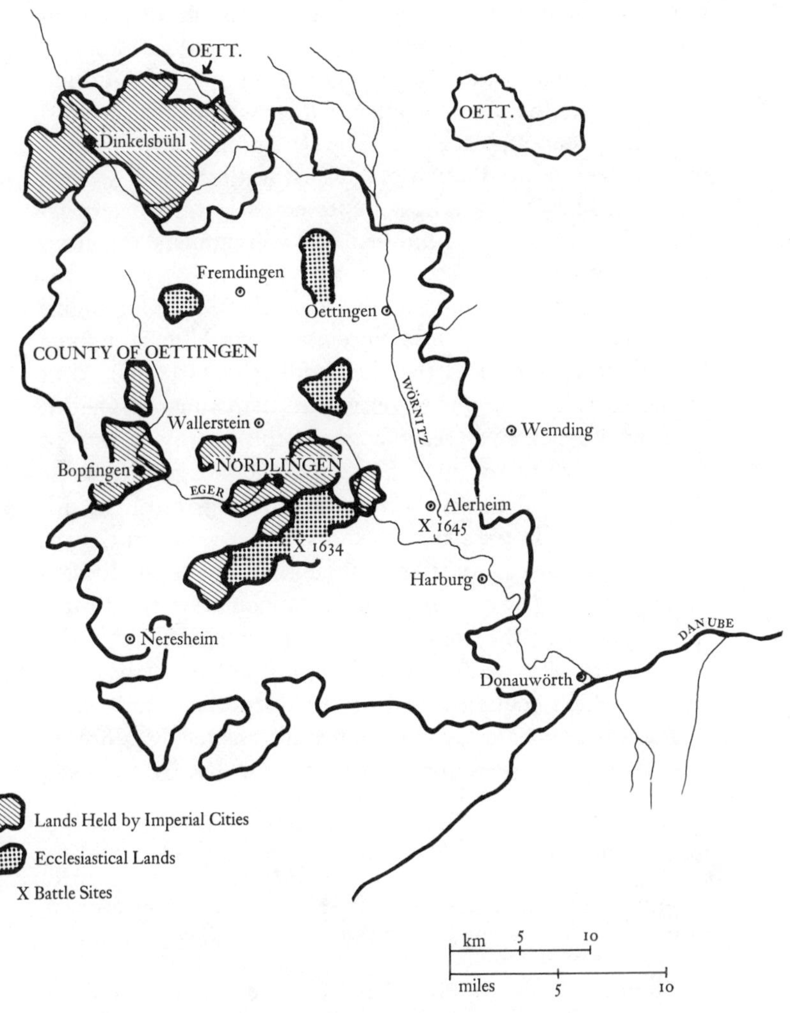

FIGURE 1.1. Map of Nördlingen and the Ries (c. 1600).

remberg, some fifty miles away.[4] Flax was the major non-food crop, while sheep were the most important kind of livestock raised in the region. Within the city of Nördlingen, the manufacture of woolen textiles was by far the most important economic activity. The second industry was tanning, while the production of finished leather goods—shoes, purses, saddles and the like—represented a third major activity. Linen, ropes and finished furs were among the city's minor manufactures.

Nördlingen was the metropolis of the Ries, but unlike some imperial cities, such as Nuremberg and Ulm, it enjoyed little political power in the surrounding countryside. Most of the Ries, in fact, was governed by the counts of Oettingen, whose principal seats were in the nearby towns of Wallerstein and Oettingen. Since the middle ages the house of Oettingen had rivaled Nördlingen for control of the district, although in the sixteenth and seventeenth centuries the threat it posed was somewhat diminished by its subdivision into two, three, or even four ruling branches.[5] A third force in the Ries was the constellation of ecclesiastical organizations—especially the Teutonic Knights and the Knights of Malta—which occupied lands in the district.

Two great medieval trade routes intersected in Nördlingen. One followed a northeast-southwest axis, from Bohe-

[4] Rudolf Endres, *Die Nürnberg-Nördlinger Wirtschaftsbeziehungen im Mittelalter bis zur Schlacht von Nördlingen, Ihre rechtlich-politischen Voraussetzungen und ihre tatsächlichen Auswirkungen* (Schriften des Instituts für fränkische Landesforschung an der Universität Erlangen-Nürnberg, 11: Neustadt/Aisch, 1962), pp. 188ff.

[5] For the complex dynastic history of the house of Oettingen, which was further complicated after the Reformation by a division into Catholic and Protestant branches, see the summary in Arnulf Häffner, "Forst- und Jagdgeschichte der fürstlichen Standesherrschaft Oettingen-Wallerstein," *JHVN*, 16 (1932), 8-21; and Georg Grupp, "Aus der Geschichte der Grafschaft Oettingen," in *Rieser Heimatbuch* (Gesellschaft für Volksbildung, Nördlingen, Munich, 1922), pp. 154-77.

mia and Nuremberg via Nördlingen to Ulm and the Lake of Constance. The other route moved from Frankfurt am Main and Würzburg southward via Augsburg to Italy. Much of the traffic along these medieval routes was in textiles: fine cloth from the Netherlands traveled via Frankfurt to southern Germany and the Alps; coarser textiles produced in southern Germany moved to Switzerland and Italy; linen from southern Swabia went northward toward Nuremberg. But other products were transported along these routes as well: spices were conveyed northward, furs and metals southward, livestock in both directions.[6] The city's advantageous location at the junction of these routes undoubtedly contributed significantly to the development of the annual Pentecost fair in Nördlingen. In its prime, during the early fifteenth century, the fair had played a crucial role in the regional economy, attracting merchants and their wares from all over southern Germany and beyond; textiles, wool, furs, hides, metals and dyes headed the list of products that were exchanged.[7] Already in the course of the fifteenth century, however, both the trade routes and the Pentecost fair had begun to decline in importance, although it was not until the nineteenth century that the fair would dwindle to purely local significance.

To many inhabitants of early modern Nördlingen, however, the broader economic and geographic setting was probably less important than the immediate physical realities of their community. The 1651 plan of the city, reproduced in Figure 1.2, provides a detailed impression of what Nördlingen looked like in the seventeenth century. The city formed a rounded oval, roughly two-thirds of a mile in diameter; no hills or bodies of water had been significant

[6] For more detail on the late-medieval trade patterns, see Heinrich Steinmeyer, *Die Entstehung und Entwicklung der Nördlinger Pfingstmesse im Spätmittelalter, mit einem Ausblick bis ins 19. Jahrhundert* (Dissertation, Munich, 1960), pp. 71-83, 132-44; and Endres, *Wirtschaftsbeziehungen*, pp. 122-91.

[7] Steinmeyer, *Pfingstmesse*, pp. 132-44 and passim.

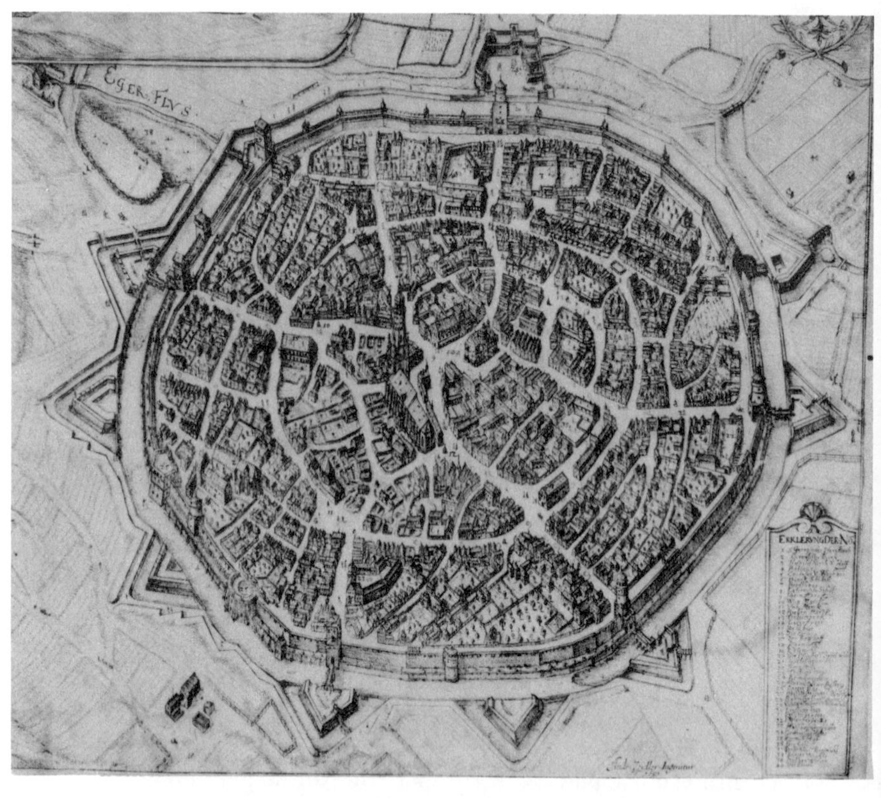

FIGURE 1.2. Andreas Zeidler's Plan of Nördlingen (1651). Reproduced by permission of the Stadtarchiv Nördlingen.

enough to prevent the city from expanding almost equally in every direction. A careful inspection of the plan will disclose that the city was divided into two concentric rings. The circular road separating these two rings approximates the location of Nördlingen's earliest wall. Already in the fourteenth century, however, the second wall was constructed to enclose the suburban houses and gardens that had grown up around the original city.[8] The new boundary proved ample for the city's medieval and early modern population; indeed, in the seventeenth century, the city was still dotted with numerous orchards and gardens, especially in the less densely occupied outer ring.[9]

Near the center of town, the plan shows Nördlingen's most prominent building—the fifteenth-century church of St. Georg, whose spire is still visible throughout the Ries. Slightly to the right, standing somewhat apart, is the turreted city hall; the area between church and city hall formed the principal marketplace of Nördlingen. On the road curving leftward from the church is the stately Hallgebäude, the chief municipal warehouse; and at the very top of the plan one can see the two courtyards of the hospital complex. Yet the most imposing physical elements in Nördlingen were not buildings at all: they were the massive walls and fortifications which enclosed the city and separated it—physically, politically, even spiritually—from the world outside. Physically, the walls not only set apart the built-up city from the open fields and villages of the countryside, but they also enabled the authorities to control access to the town: passage in and out of Nördlingen was possible only through one of the five carefully supervised gates, and at

[8] Gustav Wulz, "Bauchronik der Nördlinger Stadtbefestigung," *JHVN*, 21 (1938/9), 50-56.

[9] However, the vacant lots which are evident on the plan within the inner ring (to the left of the church) should not be mistaken for gardens. These lots are the sites of houses which had been destroyed during a heavy bombardment of the city in December 1647. (Since this portion of the city faced a small hill, it was particularly vulnerable to attack.)

night even these were kept shut.[10] Politically, the walls separated the area where the magistrates' authority was unchallenged from the areas in which, if they maintained sovereignty at all, it was shared with or disputed by other powers. The walls even represented a religious barrier: within them, Lutheran uniformity prevailed; beyond them, however, lay the complicated patchwork of the Ries with its mixture of Catholic, Protestant and even Jewish inhabitants.[11]

Although many of Nördlingen's citizens owned fields outside the city, virtually all of them lived within the space enclosed by the walls—an area of about one-fifth of a square mile.[12] The location of their houses within the city was to some extent determined by their status or occupations; leading citizens tended to live in the center of town, near the church and the city hall; wool weavers were mostly clustered in the northeastern section; tanners' homes were strung out along either side of the river. Yet there was no formal

[10] All five gates were closed at night, although two of them might be opened to admit latecomers upon payment of a special fee: Beyschlag, *Geschichte*, p. 33.

[11] Only a tiny number of Catholics—less than a dozen at any given time—lived in Nördlingen, in order to administer certain church-owned properties. They were not citizens, and they were required to worship in strictest privacy: even Catholic travelers were forbidden to join in their services and had instead to visit nearby villages in order to attend mass. (Anton Steichele, *Das Bisthum Augsburg, historisch und statistisch beschrieben*, vol. 3 [Augsburg, 1872], p. 1051.) As for Jews, they had been expelled from Nördlingen at the beginning of the sixteenth century, but continued to live in villages in the Ries. (L. Müller, "Aus fünf Jahrhunderten. Beiträge zur Geschichte der jüdischen Gemeinden im Riess [1. Teil]," *Zeitschrift des historischen Vereins für Schwaben und Neuburg*, 25 [1898], 75-99.)

[12] There appear to have been no habitations clustered outside the walls. (The only citizens of Nördlingen who lived outside the city proper were a few millers who occupied mills along the Eger, and clergymen or officials who lived in other communities while retaining the right of citizenship in Nördlingen with the permission of the council.) The area inside the walls amounts to about 52 hectares, or approximately one-fifth of a square mile.

articulation into neighborhoods. In the first place, except for the hospital complex, the entire city comprised a single parish. In addition, when citizens had to be organized for administrative purposes—in order to hear a new decree, for example, or when paying their taxes—they were grouped not by neighborhoods but by occupations. There is nothing, moreover, to suggest that citizens identified themselves in terms of the streets on which they lived. It seems likely, then, that the geographical consciousness of Nördlingen's inhabitants was dominated less by a sense of differences within the community than by the far more obvious distinctions between the city within the walls and the countryside beyond.

II

THE constitutional history of Nördlingen is punctuated by three crucial dates: 1348, 1552 and 1803.[13] The first of these dates refers to the time when, as in many German cities in the mid-fourteenth century, the guilds of Nördlingen acquired political power. Until then, the city had been governed by a council whose members were drawn from a small group of leading families; in 1348, however, the guilds obtained political parity with the patricians, and the council was reorganized to include an equal number of guild representatives and members of the old council families. In the course of time the distinction between these two groups became less rigid: the "old council" began to include "new" families and eventually even some guild masters as well.

[13] A brief introduction to the constitutional history of Nördlingen is provided by Wulz, "Einleitung," pp. 8-12. An excellent survey of the constitutional and institutional structure of the city on the eve of the Bavarian takeover in 1802-03 (substantially similar to, although not identical with, conditions prevailing in the sixteenth and seventeenth centuries) is provided in Andreas Meier, "Der Reichsdeputationshauptschluss und das Ende der freien Reichsstadt Nördlingen," *JHVN*, 3 (1914), 87-127. Where not otherwise cited, the factual framework for the following section is based on these two sources.

Yet the basic system lasted until the middle of the sixteenth century. It was then, in the wake of the Reformation and the Schmalkaldic War, that Charles V attempted to reduce popular participation in urban government and to this end imposed new constitutions on most of the imperial cities of southern Germany, including Nördlingen.

In 1552, therefore, the guilds of Nördlingen were abolished and replaced by apolitical craft associations, while the city council was both reduced in size (from twenty-four to fifteen men) and reconstituted in its principles of membership: all citizens, including craftsmen, would still be eligible, but now they would sit as individuals rather than as representatives of any corporate associations. The initial membership of the reorganized council was dictated by the Emperor's commissioners; thereafter, however, as vacancies arose they were to be filled under a complex electoral system which in fact the council completely controlled. In short, while membership on the council was not restricted to specific occupations or families, the new constitution ensured that no councilman would be bound by commitments to any subgroup of the citizenry.[14]

[14] For the events of 1552, see J. Kammerer, "Die Nördlinger Verfassungsveränderung vom Jahre 1552," *JHVN*, 14 (1930), 44-64. The council perpetuated itself in the following manner: at the beginning of each year, a group of seven councilmen known as the Ratswähler confirmed the existing council in office and when necessary filled vacancies that had arisen during the previous year. The only concession to "popular" participation was that the city court and the "large council" (which themselves had been appointed by the city council) were each entitled to designate one city council member as a Ratswähler; the remaining five Ratswähler were named *ex officio* on the basis of their status on the council. (These five were normally the five members of the "secret council"; when there were only four secret councillors, as happened occasionally before the middle of the eighteenth century and permanently thereafter, the fifth place was taken by the senior ordinary councilman.) This system can be seen in operation from the council minutes, almost always under the entry for the first session in January. (For particularly clear ex-

The imperial decree also specified the internal structure of the council: of the fifteen members, ten would be ordinary councilmen, and five would belong to the "privy council," or executive committee. Three of the privy councillors would share the title of Bürgermeister, rotating the position of presiding mayor every four months. In this form the council persisted with only minor changes until Nördlingen lost its imperial status and became part of the Kingdom of Bavaria in Napoleonic times.[15]

Directly beneath the city council, not in power but in status, was the city court, a body of ten men chaired by an official known as the Ammann.[16] The court was very circumscribed in its powers, for its jurisdiction was limited to certain types of civil cases, particularly disputes over debts. The city council, in fact, was the real court of Nördlingen, deciding not only criminal cases but also disputes over property rights, inheritances, marriage portions and the like.[17] Even less powerful than the city court was the 25-member "large council," which was convoked occasionally by the city council as a consultative body. This appears, however, to have happened only rarely, and—in contrast

amples, see RP 2 Jan. 1600 and 3 Jan. 1648.) The system is described by Meier as being in effect around 1800: Meier, "Reichsdeputationshauptschluss," p. 112.

15 In the middle of the eighteenth century, the number of councilmen was reduced from fifteen to twelve, with the number of Bürgermeister (and hence of secret councillors) reduced by one. See Wilhelm Friedrich Lettenmeyer, *Der Niedergang der reichsstädtischen Finanzwirtschaft Nördlingens und die Tätigkeit der kaiserlichen Subdelegationskommission (XVIII. Jahrhundert)* (Dissertation, Munich, 1937), pp. 194-98, 201-06.

16 In the middle ages the Ammann had been the imperial administrator of the town, but centuries of determined effort by the citizenry had succeeded in whittling the powers of this office down to insignificance. By the sixteenth century the Ammann was simply a citizen selected by the council to perform certain symbolic functions and to preside over the city court. See Wulz, "Einleitung," pp. 8-9.

17 Ibid., p. 12.

to the city court—members of this body did not enjoy the expectation of later promotion to councilman.[18]

A small bureaucracy aided the council in administering the city. The principal civil servants were the city counsel and the city clerk. Beneath them came thirty or forty other officials: lesser clerks, tax- and toll-collectors, inspectors, watchmen, messengers, beggar-wardens and the like. In addition, the city employed a number of skilled persons—generally on a seasonal or part-time basis—ranging from the municipal physician and the official clock setter through various craftsmen, masons, street pavers, musicians and midwives down to the well-paid but socially degraded executioner.[19]

Despite such assistance, however, the city council itself was deeply involved in day-to-day administration. Specific councilmen were designated to supervise the city treasury, the educational system, charitable foundations, market activities and other areas of responsibility. The council as a

[18] That membership on the city court was seen as a stepping-stone toward membership on the council is clear not only from the patterns of council recruitment, to be discussed in Chapter Six, but also from specific evidence. For example, in 1602 the council decided that persons who would later be barred from the council for being too closely related to living members should not normally be chosen for the court. (RP 5 Jan. 1602.)

[19] The distinction between "civil servants" and other persons—e.g., craftsmen—who were employed by the city is, of course, not a sharp one. The former term is used here to refer to people whose employment involved either administrative or supervisory tasks or direct service to persons engaged in such administrative functions (e.g., *Ratsknecht*, *Gerichtsknecht*, etc.). Taken in this sense, the number of civil servants (including those in the hospital bureaucracy) was roughly 30 toward the beginning of our period and roughly 40 toward the end of it. (See the occupational breakdowns provided in Appendix II.) The executioner received 1½ fl. per week in 1579, the same amount paid to the Zahlmeister, a position involving the collection of indirect taxes which was normally filled by a member of one of the city's leading families. (See KR 1579: Ausgaben.)

whole supervised all criminal investigations: two members would be delegated to conduct the actual hearings and, if necessary, to oversee the torture of recalcitrant suspects, but after each session the council as a whole would review the transcript and give instructions for the next round.[20] Altogether, it must be emphasized that the council not only made all policy, decided great issues and supervised the administrative machinery; it also handled countless petitions from individual members of the community. Could a citizen change his status from craftsman to merchant? Should an immigrant be admitted to citizenship? Could an old widow be granted wood for the winter? Might someone take up residence in another town? Hundreds of questions like these were carefully weighed and decided by the council each year.[21]

The fifteen members of the city council, then, exercised not only supreme authority but also direct personal supervision over the lives of thousands of people in Nördlingen. To say this, however, is not to suggest that these fifteen magistrates enjoyed a dictatorial control over the community. A later chapter will examine the paternalistic attitudes and practical difficulties which acted to restrain the council in the exercise of its powers. Here, then, it is necessary only to enumerate the constitutional or institutional factors which exercised a similarly moderating influence.

In the first place, the magistrates were ultimately subject to the will of the Emperor. In 1552, as we have seen, Charles V imposed a new constitution on the community. Throughout the sixteenth and seventeenth centuries the imperial authority was invoked to arbitrate disputes between Nördlingen and neighboring principalities. And in the eighteenth

[20] For a description of the council's procedure in criminal cases, see Alfons Felber, *Unzucht und Kindsmord in der Rechtsprechung der freien Reichsstadt Nördlingen vom 15. bis 19. Jahrhundert* (Dissertation, Bonn, 1961), pp. 25-31.

[21] Examples of how the council dealt with such questions will be found in Chapters Seven and Nine.

century imperial authorities intervened to overhaul the city's financial system and introduce administrative reforms.[22] For years or even decades at a time, the Emperor's ultimate authority over the city might lie dormant, but it always remained in reserve as a potential corrective to the council's activities.

A second moderating factor was the absence of a rigidly defined patriciate. In a larger city like Nuremberg, membership on the council might be limited strictly to members of specific long-established patrician families.[23] Such restrictions, however, applied to Nördlingen neither in principle nor in practice, at least not in the sixteenth and seventeenth centuries. A detailed examination of recruitment to council membership will come in Chapter Six; here it need only be emphasized that a system of formal barriers between governed and governing—the kind of system likely to turn magistrates into a closed, oppressive oligarchy—did not exist in Nördlingen.

A third factor that limited the powers of the council was institutional—the existence of religious, welfare and economic organizations which created a kind of buffer zone between the magistrates and the individual citizen. By collectively representing the interests of certain groups, by interceding on behalf of individuals, or simply by creating an additional layer of authority or bureaucracy to diffuse the direct power of the magistrates, such organizations could play a significant role in moderating the power of those in control of the community. In Nördlingen their effectiveness in doing so was limited, but the part they played was at least significant enough that no sketch of the city's institutional structure would be complete without identifying the most important of these buffering organizations.

22 The imperial intervention in the eighteenth century is described in detail by Lettenmeyer, *Finanzwirtschaft*.

23 See Gerhard Hirschmann, "Das Nürnberger Patriziat," in Hellmuth Rössler, ed., *Deutsches Patriziat 1430-1740* (Limburg/Lahn, 1968), pp. 257-76.

To start with, there was the church. As in other Lutheran polities, ultimate control of the ecclesiastical establishment rested with the political leadership. Moreover, the size of the ministry was very small—there were normally only five or six clergymen active within the city. Nevertheless, the church represented an additional structure of moral authority, and one which, while normally in harmony with that of the magistrates, was still clearly derived from a source higher than mere delegation from the political leadership.

A very different kind of institution was the city hospital. Founded as early as the thirteenth century (if not before), by the late sixteenth century the hospital had developed into a complex institution with care of the aged or infirm as only one of its many activities. Above all, the hospital had become one of the major landowners of the Ries. Within the city itself, the hospital buildings and grounds included not only housing for the inmates but also a chapel, a brewery, a mill, administrative facilities, stables, a workyard and barns for the storage of crops.[24] Like the church, the hospital of Nördlingen was subject to control by the city council, but with its separate bureaucracy, records and bookkeeping, it retained a considerable degree of administrative autonomy.

The institutions which most frequently mediated between the magistrates and the individual, however, were the craft organizations—the *Handwerke*. Like every other aspect of life in the city, the crafts were regulated by the magistrates, yet the collective body of masters in each trade enjoyed a considerable degree of self-government. The council, for example, had to approve any changes in the craft bylaws—the rules regarding working conditions, quality control, treatment of apprentices and journeymen, or standards of admission for new masters. But the initiative for such changes often as not came from the craft organizations

24 For a description of the hospital's origins and a more complete enumeration of its buildings within the city, see Hermann Frickhinger, "Die Stiftungen der Stadt Nördlingen (1. Teil)," *JHVN*, 9 (1922/24), 33-42.

themselves, and the administration of the rules was normally left to them.[25]

The Handwerke were quite distinct from the guilds—the *Zünfte*—whose political power had been broken in 1552. There had been twelve guilds in Nördlingen, most of them encompassing a number of different crafts, and the elected heads of these twelve organizations had sat as *ex officio* members of the city council before the constitutional change. After 1552, however, all that remained of the old guild structure was the division of the citizenry into twelve "quarters"—convenient administrative groupings whose members were summoned from time to time to hear decrees from the council or pay their taxes on appointed days.[26] But though the political power of the guilds had thus been eliminated, the role they had played was to some extent absorbed by the scores of craft organizations which succeeded them as the principal interest groups in the community.[27]

[25] By the end of the sixteenth century, the leaders of the crafts were no longer elected by their fellow masters, but chosen by the council. See, for example, Heinz Dannenbauer, "Die Leinenweberhandwerk in der Reichsstadt Nördlingen," *Zeitschrift für bayerische Landesgeschichte*, 3 (1930), 283-84. But there is ample evidence from the city's ordinance books that craft bylaws (*Handwerks-Ordnungen*) were inspired by requests from the craft masters themselves. As only one example, we may cite the series of Ordnungen issued for the saddlers at their request in the late sixteenth century: first in 1566 (OB 1553-67, fols. 164b ff.); then shortly thereafter in 1567 (ibid., fols. 175b ff.), and a third time in 1580 (OB 1567-87, fols. 143b ff.).

[26] Neither the number of guilds nor the number of "Viertel" appears to have been rigidly fixed at twelve in the sixteenth century, but it had certainly stabilized at that number by the eighteenth century. A thirteenth "quarter" included the council members and civil servants. Meier, "Reichsdeputationshauptschluss," pp. 107-08. For an example of the Viertel functioning as the administrative unit for payment of taxes, see the tax oath of 1651 (OB 1641-88, fols. 105a-106a); for an example of the twelve Viertel as units for hearing of decrees, see OB 1688-1706, fol. 276b ff. (16 Jan. 1700).

[27] The exact number of craft organizations cannot be given. Strictly

The fourth and final type of inherent limitation on the power of the council was imposed by the territorial organization of the Ries. Within the walls, the legal autonomy of the city and thus the supremacy of its council remained unchallenged. Outside the walls, however, although the city had hundreds of rural tenants, its powers were generally much restricted. By the middle of the sixteenth century, the hospital of Nördlingen—and thus, in effect, the city—owned property in dozens of surrounding villages. But the hospital was normally only one of the many landowners in any given community. Over the farmsteads it owned, the city enjoyed the so-called *Grundherrschaft*—the rights of a landowner, mostly including jurisdiction over noncapital crimes. Yet the *Landeshoheit*, or political supremacy over the entire village, which normally included jurisdiction over capital crimes, might be in other hands. It was usually claimed by the largest landowner in the village: sometimes Nördlingen, but more often one of the counts of Oettingen or some other authority. Disputes repeatedly erupted over who was entitled to exercise Landeshoheit over certain villages, or what rights Landeshoheit actually conferred, while local traditions and privileges made the situation in each village slightly different from that of the next.[28]

---

speaking, this number would equal the total number of crafts practiced in the city, but it seems unlikely that crafts with only two or three masters could sustain a viable organization. On the other hand, in 1663 the craft of hatmakers, with only five masters (but nine journeymen) was granted the kind of ordinance which implied a complete organization ("Huetmacher Ordnung, Gebrauch und Gewohnheit," in OB 1641-88, fol. 222a). The number of adult male citizens in each craft—essentially the same as the number of masters—is given for five selected years in Appendix II.

[28] For an introduction to the relationship between Nördlingen and its extramural districts, see Meier, "Reichsdeputationshauptschluss," pp. 87-107. Detailed though unsystematic information on the situation in the villages of the Ries can be found under the heading for each village in: Ludwig Mußgnug, "Die Rieser Siedlungen," in *Rieser Heimatbote*, nos. 11-90 (1925-33); Steichele, *Bisthum Augsburg*, vol. 3; and *Beschreibung des Oberamtes Neresheim* (Königliches statis-

In some cases, village administration might be conducted rather smoothly. Take, for example, the village of Nähermemmingen, some two miles west of Nördlingen. About two-thirds of the farmsteads and buildings in Nähermemmingen were owned by the hospital of Nördlingen, with the rest divided among the counts of Oettingen-Wallerstein, the abbey of Kaisheim and some other authorities. Nördlingen was clearly the dominant landowner, and the other landlords conceded to the city—in practice if not in theory—virtually complete control over village affairs.[29]

The nearby village of Pflaumloch, however, illustrates the almost anarchic mixture of rights which could also prevail in a rural community. According to a tabulation made in 1760, there were 36 farmsteads in Pflaumloch, of which Nördlingen owned 16 and Oettingen-Wallerstein owned 10, while three abbeys, one ecclesiastical chapter and the imperial city of Bopfingen accounted for the remainder. Each landowner maintained lower jurisdiction over his own ten-

---

tisch-topographisches Bureau von Württemberg, Stuttgart, 1872), pp. 169-454. For villages within present-day Bavaria, however, the information provided by Mußgnug and Steichele is largely superseded by the massive compilation of data available in Dieter Kudorfer, *Nördlingen* (Historischer Atlas von Bayern, Teil Schwaben, Heft 8; Munich, 1974). It should be added here that the acquisition of Landeshoheit by the principalities of the Empire was a gradual development which (especially in the case of imperial cities) was not completed until the Peace of Westphalia in 1648. Nevertheless, for all practical purposes, the situation described here was already in effect in the sixteenth century.

29 Steichele, *Bisthum Augsburg*, vol. 3, p. 1264; Mußgnug in *Heimatbote*, no. 68, p. 2; Kudorfer, *Nördlingen*, pp. 517-18. Mußgnug gives a total of 45 "Anwesen" in Nähermemmingen in 1760, of which 27 belonged to Nördlingen, while Kudorfer records a total of 74 farmsteads and buildings in the 1790's, of which 51 belonged to the city. The difference is accounted for by different practices in counting farm plots; in actual fact landownership in the village had stabilized centuries before. (A farmstead might change hands from one peasant family to another, of course, without affecting who had ultimate title to the land.)

ants—subjects of Nördlingen, for example, were referred to the village court of Nähermemmingen, from which cases could be appealed to the city council. The counts of Oettingen-Wallerstein, however, maintained the Landeshoheit and higher jurisdiction over Pflaumloch, while the villagers themselves enjoyed a certain degree of self-government. Religious matters were a source of bitter disagreement. Since Nördlingen had originally held the advowson of the parish, it had introduced the Reformation into Pflaumloch. In 1597, however, the count of Oettingen-Wallerstein took belated issue with this step and installed a Catholic priest. When the city sent an armed detachment to restore the Protestant preacher, a bloody skirmish ensued. The issue was eventually turned over to the high imperial court, the Reichskammergericht; but as to the villagers, they were left without any pastor at all and had to rely upon the services of clergymen from the neighboring communities.[30]

In only two villages of the Ries—Goldburgshausen and Schweindorf—did the city own every or almost every farmstead, and only there could it claim a virtually complete Landeshoheit. In addition, the city had exclusive rights to a few square miles of forest lands and to a belt of roughly three square miles which surrounded the city—the so-called *Stadtmarkung*, which consisted of fields largely owned by individual citizens. Yet even in these areas the city's legal rights were challenged by the house of Oettingen, whose claims to territorial supremacy extended right up to the walls of Nördlingen.[31]

The total number of the city's rural dependents at any

[30] Mußgnug in *Heimatbote*, no. 78, p. 4; *Oberamt Neresheim*, pp. 399-401. The religious dispute dragged on in the imperial courts for years; when or how it was finally resolved—if at all—is not clear.

[31] Meier, "Reichsdeputationshauptschluss," especially pp. 88-92. The size of the Stadtmarkung around 1800 is estimated by Meier, p. 89, at slightly over 800 hectares, which equals roughly 3 sq. mi. For the two villages mentioned, see also *Oberamt Neresheim*, pp. 316, 414; and Mußgnug in *Heimatbote*, nos. 44 and 84.

one time does not appear ever to have been recorded, presumably because the legal relationship between the city and its peasants, the *Untertanen*, varied so much from one village to the next. Some villagers were both tenants and subjects of Nördlingen, others were only tenants, and still others were neither subjects nor tenants but were nevertheless members of the city's hospital parish.[32] Probably the number of Nördlingen's subjects (in the broadest sense) before the Thirty Years War came to a few thousand, and certainly the dues and rents that they owed the hospital were a major source of income for the city. Yet the villages—or rather, the rivalry of landowners in the villages—proved a constant source of political irritation, and a constant reminder to every citizen of Nördlingen that the world outside the city walls was a very different one from the world within.

III

At the time this study opens, around 1580, the Reformation was still a living memory for Nördlingen's oldest citizens, particularly since the advent of Protestantism in the city had been a gradual process, spread out over three decades. As early as 1522, the city council had summoned a preacher of distinctly Lutheran bent to the pulpit of St. Georg's,[33] but as German Protestants moved closer and closer to an absolute break with the Emperor and pope, both the city council and its appointed minister hesitated to follow suit. Throughout the 1530's and 1540's, the council of Nördlingen attempted

[32] The last-mentioned situation applied to the inhabitants of Baldingen, a village in which Oettingen owned most property and exercised both higher and lower jurisdiction, yet which belonged to the hospital parish of Nördlingen. Steichele, *Bisthum Augsburg*, vol. 3, pp. 1002-03.

[33] The fact that the council summoned the minister is itself significant. It was precisely in this period that the advowson of the parish church of Nördlingen ceased to be exercised by a distant monastery, the Kloster Heilsbronn in Franconia, and was assumed by the city council. Ibid., pp. 950-54.

to satisfy the increasingly Protestant orientation of its citizens—even the city's monks and nuns had almost all converted—without overtly antagonizing the emperor. But the failure of this policy became fully evident during the Schmalkaldic War, which began in 1546. The city had refused to join the Schmalkaldic league of Protestant estates, but in 1546 it did allow the league to garrison the town. This action, in turn, exposed the town to reprisals from an imperial army which occupied Nördlingen in 1547, and brought in its train an unidentified epidemic disease which claimed hundreds of lives. Only after the Peace of Augsburg was established in 1555 did it become possible for the city to reconcile its by now firm Lutheranism with its traditional loyalty to the Emperor.[34]

The year 1555 is significant in another respect as well, for after the religious settlement Nördlingen, like most of Germany, was left in peace for two-thirds of a century. And nothing is more important in understanding what happened to the city between 1580 and 1720 than to recognize the great divide between these peaceful years before 1618 and the epoch of prolonged warfare which followed.

Certainly these decades did witness occasional military adventures, generated by the city's perpetual state of conflict with the counts of Oettingen-Oettingen and Oettingen-Wallerstein. In 1566, for example, there was the "lark war," which began when soldiers from Wallerstein tore down nets in which citizens of Nördlingen were catching larks outside the town. From 1569 onward there was a new cycle of flare-ups—mill burnings, skirmishes, economic retaliations. In 1575 the intervention of an imperial commission brought about a reduction in the violence, yet the hostilities simmered on. In fact, during a quarrel over hunting rights in 1614, one of the counts of Oettingen himself was shot by a group of soldiers from Nördlingen.[35] Dramatic and alarming

[34] For the Reformation era in general, ibid., pp. 950-77; Wulz, "Einleitung," pp. 6, 19.

[35] Beyschlag, *Geschichte*, pp. 91-95, 108-09; "Johann Christoph

as all this may have seemed at the time, however, none of these episodes had any real impact on the city. Precisely because the Empire as a whole was at peace, higher authorities—the Swabian Circle or the Emperor—were always available to intervene when things got out of hand. In the long run there was no significant loss of lives or property.

The most significant episode in Nördlingen's history during these years, in fact, was an internal affair: the witch-craze that gripped the city between 1589 and 1594.[36] The episode began with the trial of a woman who was accused of causing the deaths of three children by witchcraft, and who evidently believed this accusation herself. Under torture, however, she also implicated other women as witches, thus triggering a chain reaction of accusation, interrogations, torture and more accusations, which eventually led 32 women and one man to their deaths.[37] The cycle only ended in 1594 when one remarkable victim withstood being tortured 62 times without making a confession. Since she had avoided accusing any new victims, the cycle of persecutions came to an abrupt halt.[38]

In the course of these five years, women of every social station had been burnt as witches, including four widows of

---

Mötzels Chronik von Nördlingen" [c. 1734], *Heimatbote*, nos. 31-37 (1927), passim. The shooting is also referred to in the OB 1612-40, fol. 33b.

36 For the entire witch-craze, see the articles by Gustav Wulz: "Nördlinger Hexenprozesse," *JHVN*, 20 (1937), 42-72, and 21 (1938/9), 95-120, which offer a vivid description of four major cases; and "Die Nördlinger Hexen und ihre Richter," *Heimatbote*, nos. 142-45 and 147 (1939), which provides an excellent biographical summary of each accused witch.

37 Twenty-nine of these women and the one man were executed; three additional women died during their imprisonment and their bodies were burnt. In addition, a number of other women were imprisoned and interrogated but then released.

38 The witch-craze was briefly revived in 1598, when two additional women were executed. This time, however, there was no chain-reaction of further executions, and these were the last burnings of witches in Nördlingen's history. Wulz in *Heimatbote*, no. 145.

council members. The spectacle of some of Nördlingen's most prominent women disappearing for months of incarceration, and then emerging to publicly confess themselves witches and die at the stake, must have had a significant emotional impact on their fellow citizens. Yet it must be emphasized that, as far as can be determined, the pattern of witch accusations did not reflect any social divisions within the community, nor did the witch-craze leave the community divided into hostile groups. We shall return to this entire subject in greater detail in Chapter Seven. At this point, then, only one point need be emphasized: despite whatever emotions it may have evoked at the time, the witch-craze had no long-term impact on the social functioning of the community. Like the intermittent feud with the house of Oettingen, it was a violent and memorable experience, but not one which upset the community's basic equilibrium during the peaceful years before the Thirty Years War.

This equilibrium was upset, however, by two events which affected Nördlingen in the early 1620's: the severe wave of inflation throughout Germany known as the *Kipper- und Wipperzeit*, and the beginning of the Thirty Years War. In the long term the war was to have by far the greater impact on the community of Nördlingen. Yet in the early 1620's it was the inflation more than the war which obsessed the citizens of Nördlingen.[39]

The rise of prices in southern Germany during the early 1620's was not related to the factors which were normally associated with short-term price rises in early modern Europe; there were, for example, no bad harvests in Swabia in the early 1620's, nor had the Thirty Years War started to

[39] Gustav Schöttle, "Die grosse deutsche Geldkrise von 1620-23 und ihr Verlauf in Oberschwaben," *Württembergische Vierteljahrshefte für Landesgeschichte*, N.F. 30 (1921), 36-57 provides an excellent introduction to the history of the Kipper- und Wipperzeit in southern Germany, on which many of the following general observations are based.

make significant inroads into the regional economy.[40] Instead, the inflation was caused by strictly monetary factors: the acceleration and culmination of a long trend in which the various cities and states privileged to mint coins increasingly debased the currency they issued. Certain rare coins such as the *Taler* and the *Dukat*, denominations which were used principally in large-scale commercial transactions, remained stable in their metal content. But the so-called *Scheidemünzen*, the widespread currency used for everyday transactions, were often subjected to gross debasement. The obvious consequence, of course, was that wealthy individuals whose assets included real property or hard currency like the Taler remained largely protected from the effects of the inflation, while people who owned little real property and were dependent on the Scheidemünzen for wages or income faced severe disadvantages—especially since, as a rule, while prices soared wages tended to remain constant.[41]

The distress engendered by the inflation was fully evident in Nördlingen. Throughout the early 1620's, municipal authorities were engaged in a futile attempt to regulate rates of exchange and prevent debased coins from being circulated in the city.[42] By 1622, the city was repeatedly obliged to make grain available to its citizens at prices far below the inflated market prices.[43] A decree of August 1622 attempted to set maximum prices for grain—yet nine months later the price of wheat was almost double the legal maximum.[44]

High prices, moreover, were not the only problem created by the inflation. The city's accounting system collapsed as income and, even more so, expenditures soared out of the

[40] Ibid., p. 38.

[41] Ibid., pp. 44-46.

[42] OB 1612-40, fols. 83-125 passim, e.g., fol. 98a-b (6 April 1621); fol. 107a (22 Feb. 1622); fol. 120a (19 Sept. 1622); etc.

[43] E.g., KR 1622, fol. 86a.

[44] The decree of August 1622 set a maximum of 24 fl. per Malter for *Kern*, the principal form of wheat: OB 1612-40, fols. 120a-124a. Yet by May 1623 Kern was selling in Nördlingen for 42 fl. per Malter: KR 1623, fol. 88b.

order of magnitude to which the clerks were accustomed.[45] The inflation also wreaked havoc upon traditional economic relationships within the city. Like any inflation, the Kipper- und Wipperzeit favored the interests of debtors over creditors. Among the creditors in Nördlingen were numerous orphans who (through their guardians) had lent parts of their inheritances out at interest, to provide a steady income for themselves. Now, of course, their debtors attempted to take advantage of the total debasement of the coinage to pay back the capital at its nominal value—a practice which the civic authorities attempted vigorously to prevent.[46]

By the middle of 1623, however, the inflation had run its course. By now the Scheidemünzen had become so thoroughly worthless that even the minting authorities which had profited most from recycling coins and reissuing them with less metal content no longer benefited from the spiral of debasement. This made it possible for the south German states to agree on a complete reform of the currency: the hopelessly debased coins then in circulation were simply abandoned, and a reformed standard of currency was established. The coins in the gulden system—in effect, all of the Scheidemünzen—were henceforth to be issued with a metal content of slightly under three-quarters the pre-inflation standard.[47]

[45] Item-by-item entries continued to be made in the city account books, but from 1621 on it proved impossible to calculate totals for each heading in the books, let alone the annual totals of income and outgo; see Kammerrechnungen 1621-29. The books for 1620-33 are missing entirely; only in 1634 do the Kammerrechnungen resume, restored to their original level of accuracy.

[46] OB 1612-40, fol. 124a-b (11 Oct. 1622). See Schöttle, "Geldkrise," pp. 97-99, for similar measures in other cities.

[47] Gustav Schöttle, "Münz- und Geldgeschichte von Ulm in ihrem Zusammenhang mit derjenigen Schwabens," *Württembergische Vierteljahrshefte für Landesgeschichte*, N.F. 31 (1922-24), 91-94, and Schöttle, "Geldkrise," 52-54. Strictly speaking, reform efforts had already begun in 1622, but apparently only the final currency reform of 1623 had a significant effect in arresting the inflation in southern Germany.

In Nördlingen, as elsewhere, attempts were immediately made to liquidate the effects of the inflation. Decrees were issued reordering the value of all coinage, and prices were rolled back to bring them into line with the newly restored value of the currency.[48] On the other hand, the council decided, with considerable misgivings, that people who had made contracts during the inflation and registered them with the city would have to observe to the letter whatever obligations they had entered into. This decision, of course, could be disastrous to a debtor, since the real value of the debt he owed would now be vastly greater than what he would have anticipated during the inflation. But the council was evidently sincere in its concern that any tampering with the 200-year-old procedures for registering contracts and giving them the force of civil law could "open the doors and the gates" to countless disputes about the validity of *any* registered contracts.[49]

Certainly the Kipper- und Wipperzeit left its mark on the economic structure of Nördlingen. Yet it is impossible to determine just how thoroughly the inflation disrupted the city's economic life or how quickly the community might have recovered after 1623. For the impact of the inflation was rapidly overshadowed by the effects of an even more important event: the beginning of the Thirty Years War.

The war began in 1618.[50] Located as it was at the intersection of two major routes, Nördlingen felt its impact from the start. Both Protestant and Catholic troops passed through the city, demanding money, food or the right to quarter soldiers. By the mid-1620's such episodes seem to

[48] E.g., OB 1612-40, fols. 128a-129a (4 June 1623); fol. 129a-b (9 June 1623); fol. 131a-b (14 July 1623).

[49] Ibid., fols. 136a-137b (18 Feb. 1624).

[50] For the basic chronology of the Thirty Years War in Nördlingen, I have relied chiefly on "Mötzel," *Heimatbote*, nos. 36-40 (1927-28); Beyschlag, *Geschichte*, pp. 110-25; and Johann Friedrich Weng, *Die Schlacht bei Nördlingen und Belagerung dieser Stadt in den Monaten August und September 1634* (Nördlingen, 1834), a more comprehensive work than its title implies.

have become increasingly frequent, and they certainly became more one-sided: by the end of the decade, it was almost always imperial troops who established themselves in the city. In 1630 Wallenstein himself visited Nördlingen, and by the following year the city had become formally established as an imperial garrison.

This situation was sharply reversed in 1632. As Gustavus Adolphus approached the region, the imperial troops abandoned Nördlingen, only to be replaced by a Swedish garrison soon thereafter. The new troops were more welcome to the Protestant citizenry—Gustavus Adolphus himself was given rousing receptions on his two visits to Nördlingen[51]—but the essential conditions of life remained the same: like the imperials, the Swedes demanded a constant flow of financial contributions, not to mention labor services by the inhabitants to strengthen the city's fortifications. By the middle of 1634 the need for such efforts had become acute: the region was gradually becoming an imperial stronghold again, but the Swedes insisted on maintaining a garrison in Nördlingen and holding the city for the Protestant cause.

Imperial troops, soon to be joined by their Bavarian allies, laid siege to Nördlingen on August 8, 1634. Crowded with refugees from the countryside and beset by severe food shortages and an incipient epidemic of the plague,[52] the city was subjected to repeated bombardments and assaults. But, sustained by hopes of relief from a Swedish army encamped

[51] Ludwig Mußgnug, "Gustav Adolf in Nördlingen," *Heimatbote*, nos. 83-84 (1932).

[52] The eyewitness account of Johannes Mayer, an oration delivered in 1638, described the disease as "lues et pestilentia." (*M. Johannis Mayeri Historia Caesareae Obsidionis et Expugnationis Liberae S.R.I. Civitatis Nördlingensis in Bello Tricennali Ao MDCXXXIV* [Göttingen, 1746], p. 24. This account has been translated by Ludwig Mußgnug as *Die Belagerung von Nördlingen 1634, Erinnerungsrede des Magisters Johannes Mayer* [Nördlingen, 1927].) A municipal ordinance of October 15, 1634 described the disease as a "Seuch der hochschädlichen Pestilenz" (OB 1612-40, fol. 283a). There is no reason to doubt that the disease was an epidemic of the bubonic plague.

behind imperial lines to the west, Nördlingen held out for three weeks. Finally, on August 26, the Swedish army broke camp and swung around to challenge the Catholic forces in the hilly area south of the city. But the imperial army, reinforced by Spanish troops, vastly outnumbered them, and the battle of Nördlingen which took place the next day was a crushing defeat for the Swedes.[53]

The city itself had no choice but to open its gates to the victorious imperial army. Although its political autonomy and religious freedom were left intact, the months that followed were among the most difficult in Nördlingen's history. The plague continued to rage throughout the autumn, while the imperial army quartered hundreds of soldiers in citizens' homes and imposed taxes of unprecedented severity. The recollections of one eyewitness, if somewhat exaggerated, nevertheless vividly suggest the mood of the community in the fall of 1634: "It was considered a blessing in these times to die of the plague. Many might have been healed of this evil if they had taken steps against it at its onset, but they preferred to take on the sickness than to live such lives of punishment."[54]

By the end of the year, the plague had abated, and eventually the imperial occupation was lifted as well. But the battle of Nördlingen had eliminated the Swedes from southern Germany for years to come, and for the next decade the city remained in the imperial orbit, sometimes harboring large contingents of soldiers, at other times subject only to financial levies. In 1645, while a Bavarian garrison was occupying the town, a French army engaged imperial and Bavarian forces at Alerheim, a few miles to the east. This

[53] The literature on the battle itself is enormous; a generally reliable and accessible account is that of Erich Leo, *Die Schlacht bei Nördlingen im Jahre 1634* (Hallesche Abhandlungen zur neueren Geschichte, 39 [Halle, 1900]). Emphasis on events in the city is provided by the works of Weng and Mayer, cited above. An excellent chronology of events was prepared by Gustav Wulz: "Chronik der Kriegsereignisse des Sommers 1634," *Heimatbote*, nos. 101-02 (1934).

[54] Mayer, *Historia*, p. 41.

engagement—often identified as the second battle of Nördlingen—was one of the fiercest of the war. Its results were inconclusive; the French, however, retained possession of the battlefield and received Nördlingen's surrender before marching out of the region.[55]

After another interval of Bavarian occupation, the city underwent one more reversal of control when, in the summer of 1646, a Swedish garrison was established in Nördlingen. Although the war was drawing to a close, this final period of occupation witnessed two dramatic episodes. In December 1647 a Bavarian bombardment directed from a nearby hill succeeded in destroying 98 houses and another 43 stables and other auxiliary buildings in the city. And the following summer the city was defeated in the humiliating "cow war," which began when the municipal herd of cattle was stolen by a troop of armed rustlers. A posse of citizens rode out to give chase, but their attempt ended in a fiasco, with seventeen inhabitants killed—including one of the Bürgermeister—and another seven captured by the bandits and held for ransom.[56]

The signing of the Peace of Westphalia was solemnly celebrated in Nördlingen on January 1, 1649. But it was only in the summer of 1650 that the Swedish garrison marched out of the city, signaling the real end of the Thirty Years War for the inhabitants of Nördlingen.

[55] The standard account of this battle is that of Sigmund Riezler, "Die Schlacht bei Alerheim, 3. August 1645," *Sitzungsberichte der philosophischen-philologischen und der historischen Classe der königlichen bayerischen Akademie der Wissenschaften* (1901), 477-548, which describes the result as a standoff. (The major modern French account of the war, however, records the battle as an unqualified French victory: G. Pagès, *The Thirty Years War*, trans. David Maland and John Hooper [London, 1970], p. 208.)

[56] Ludwig Mußgnug, "Nördlingen unter Oberst von Bülow (1646-1650)," *Heimatbote*, no. 78 (1931); "Mötzel," *Heimatbote*, nos. 39-40 (1928); Weng, *Schlacht bei Nördlingen*, pp. 211-16. In addition to 141 buildings destroyed, 68 buildings were described as having been severely damaged by the bombardment of 1647.

It must be emphasized, however, that the epoch that opened for the city in 1618 did not come to end in 1648, or even in 1650. For the Thirty Years War was only the first in a series of wars which continued to afflict the city until well into the eighteenth century. During the 1650's, it is true, Nördlingen experienced a decade of peace. But, beginning in the 1660's, the Empire was confronted with the double threat of Turkish and then French aggression, and the repercussions of what evolved into war on two fronts were severely felt in Nördlingen for the next half-century. The main effect of these wars was financial: the sophisticated system which developed within the Swabian Circle for obtaining soldiers and money from the estates of southwestern Germany caused an ever-increasing drain on Nördlingen's resources.[57] In 1664 Nördlingen contributed 87 soldiers for an emergency expedition against the Turks.[58] In the 1670's the city was again required to recruit and outfit a contingent of soldiers, this time to serve for some years in the war against France.[59] And by the 1680's the Swabian militia was evolving into a standing army to which Nördlingen had to provide a contingent of soldiers on a permanent basis.[60] These recruits did not necessarily come from the city, but the money to pay them did; and funds to support the

[57] See Chapter Five. For a general introduction to the workings of the Swabian Circle in this period, see James Allen Vann, *The Swabian Kreis: Institutional Growth in the Holy Roman Empire, 1648-1715* (Studies Presented to the International Commission for the History of Representative Institutions, 53 [Brussels, 1975]). The evolution of the military system of the Swabian Circle is discussed by Vann, pp. 61-66 and 267-84, and by Peter-Christoph Storm, *Der Schwäbische Kreis als Feldherr: Untersuchungen zur Wehrverfassung des schwäbischen Reichskreises in der Zeit von 1648 bis 1732* (Schriften zur Verfassungsgeschichte, 21 [Berlin, 1974]), especially pp. 71-111.

[58] Storm, *Der Schwäbische Kreis*, pp. 304-05.

[59] OB 1641-88, fols. 318b-319a (25 Sept. 1672); 319a-320a (20 June 1673). Cf. Storm, *Der Schwäbische Kreis*, pp. 306-14.

[60] See Storm, *Der Schwäbische Kreis*, pp. 314-41, passim, for the changing size of the Nördlingen contingent between 1683 and 1732.

"Nördlingen contingent" came to represent one of the city's most constant and pressing financial obligations. In addition to this, Nördlingen was often required to provide food and lodgings for troops quartered in the region. From 1675 to 1679, for example, Nördlingen served as winter quarters for various imperial troops participating in the war against France, and the same pattern was repeated during the war of 1688-1697. On top of the city's formally stipulated payments for provisioning the troops, citizens were frequently subjected to informal pressure from soldiers to provide additional food or cash.[61]

For fifty years, however, except for one French incursion in 1688, the Ries remained free of any actual fighting. But this changed once the War of the Spanish Succession broke out in 1701. Once again France was pitted against the Empire, but this time Bavaria also took arms against the Emperor, and as a result the Danube basin became a major seat of the war. Nördlingen soon found that its customary obligations to the Emperor and the Swabian Circle were supplemented by demands for supplies or money to support hostile Bavarian troops in the region. By the end of 1703 the French and Bavarian armies controlled the north bank of the Danube, although Nördlingen itself was garrisoned by imperial troops. The following year, however, brought a dramatic reversal of events, beginning with Marlborough's march to the Danube and ending with his victory at the Battle of Blenheim (to Germans, the Battle of Höchstädt) on August 13, 1704. The battlefield lay scarcely fifteen miles from Nördlingen, and as soon as the fighting ended thousands of wounded soldiers were brought to the city. For months they lay in public and private buildings in

[61] "Mötzel," *Heimatbote* nos. 41-45 (1928), passim. The financial demands made on the city during the French war of 1672-79 are vividly reflected in OB 1641-88, fols. 332-70 (1674-79), passim. The kind of pressure that citizens faced from quartered soldiers is illustrated by OB 1688-1706, pp. 127-29 (24 Oct. 1694) and 245-49 (30 June 1698).

Nördlingen; not until the following spring did the last of the English and imperial soldiers march off.[62]

The battle of Blenheim did have the advantage for Nördlingen of ending hostilities in the Danube region. Bavaria was completely eliminated as a belligerent, and the contest between the Empire and France was transferred to more traditional locations: the Rhineland and the Low Countries. Yet military and financial obligations to the Empire and the Swabian Circle continued to burden the city throughout the war. Indeed, even after the war ended in 1714 the community had to provide quarter to imperial troops: the "Nördlingen contingent" was sent to the city some months after peace was made and remained there until it could be posted on to garrison duty along the Rhine.[63]

Certainly Nördlingen's experiences in the late seventeenth and early eighteenth century cannot be compared, in terms of the severity of their immediate impact, with the Thirty Years War. But, as we shall see, the great war had depleted the city's demographic, economic and financial strength, and thus the constant recurrence of lesser wars from 1660 onward was to have a very critical impact on the fragile resources of the community. The Thirty Years War does stand out as the single most dramatic experience of the community in the years between 1580 and 1720. But in attempting to understand what happened to Nördlingen during these years, one must divide the history of the community into two phases: an epoch of peace before 1618, followed by a century during which warfare frequently occupied the foreground and always loomed in the background of Nördlingen's history.

[62] Hans Albrecht, "Die freie Reichsstadt Nördlingen und der Spanische Erbfolgekrieg bis zum Ausgang des Jahres 1704," *JHVN*, 2 (1913), 32-185, esp. pp. 130-39.

[63] "Mötzel," *Heimatbote* no. 53 (1929), p. 3.

Two

The People of Nördlingen: Demographic Patterns

In the year 1459, the magistrates of Nördlingen conducted a census of the city's inhabitants. Enumerators went from house to house to determine the names of each man, woman and child residing in the city. This census established a total of 5,295 inhabitants, including 80 clerics (mostly monks) and 8 Jews.[1] Why the city fathers wanted to enumerate the city's inhabitants in that year is not known, but whatever the circumstances were, they never recurred. The census of 1459 was the first and last such enumeration in Nördlingen's history until the early nineteenth century.

Thus, we have no direct data about the number of Nördlingen's inhabitants during the period of this study: the late sixteenth to the early eighteenth century. Nevertheless, information about the city's population in these years is anything but scarce. In fact, Nördlingen is endowed with a uniquely rich body of demographic source material for the years under consideration. By way of illustration, let us see what we can find out about Nördlingen's size and demographic structure in a single year at the beginning of our period.

The year selected is 1579—a noteworthy point in Nördlingen's demographic history, since it was in that year that

[1] The census may omit some persons living in institutions, such as the city hospital or journeymen's hostels, but in other respects it appears to be highly reliable. The contents of the census are summarized and evaluated in Friedrich Dorner, *Die Steuern Nördlingens zu Ausgang des Mittelalters* (Dissertation, Munich, 1905), pp. 94-100. See also Christopher R. Friedrichs, "Nördlingen, 1580-1700: Society, Government and the Impact of War" (Ph.D. Dissertation, Princeton University, 1973), pp. 88-91.

the church officials began to maintain parish registers. We shall begin, however, with evidence from the tax books. Every year on St. Martin's Day (November 11) the head of each citizen family in Nördlingen had to pay the annual citizen tax. In 1579, a total of 1,541 citizens owed the Martin's day tax.[2] Of these citizens, 21 lived outside the town serving as clergymen or administrators in some other community; the remainder, however, all lived within the city walls, along with their families, journeymen, apprentices and servants. In addition, the city harbored 143 noncitizen households.[3] Thus, we find a total of 1,663 households within the walls of Nördlingen in 1579.

Some of these households consisted of a single person, usually a woman (one-sixth of the citizen householders were widows); most, of course, were larger. It is not yet possible to determine the average household size in sixteenth-century Nördlingen, but it is scarcely plausible that this number could have been less than four.[4] Using four, then, as the lowest likely multiplier, we would arrive at a minimum of 6,652 persons living in the households of Nördlingen. To this number one would want to add at least 300 persons who did not live in households. There were, of course, no monks in 1579, and no longer any Jews—but well over 100 persons lived in the city hospital, numerous journeymen lived in special hostels, and the city tolerated a limited number of licensed beggars and other transients.[5]

[2] StR 1579.

[3] KR 1579 (Einkommen von Pakt- und Beysassen).

[4] The census of 1459, discussed above, gives a total of 5,207 persons (family members and servants) living in 1,264 households. This yields a multiplier of 4.12.

[5] The Jews had been banished from Nördlingen in 1507 (Müller, "Aus fünf Jahrhunderten [1. Teil]," pp. 75ff.), and the regular clergy had, of course, disappeared during the Reformation. The number of hospital inmates in 1579 cannot be determined; but in January 1587 the hospital housed 133 poor inmates, and possibly a few additional richer ones. (SpR 1587, fol. 133a.) Information about the number of journeymen living in hostels and beggars in the city is even harder to

Thus, a minimum population estimate for Nördlingen in 1579 would lie close to 7,000.

Even this minimum estimate would imply a substantial increase in the number of inhabitants since 1459. In actual fact, however, the population of Nördlingen was probably considerably higher than 7,000 in 1579. This becomes apparent once we turn to the evidence of the parish registers.

Burial registers, unfortunately, were not started until 1618, but registers of baptisms and of marriages (or, to be more precise, of betrothals) were maintained with great precision from the beginning of 1579.[6] In the course of that year, a total of 104 betrothals was announced from the pulpit of St. Georg's church. Three couples manifestly settled down elsewhere, but the remaining 101 couples appear to have established households in Nördlingen. In almost half of the cases, however, one spouse came from outside the city: Nördlingen was certainly not a closed community in 1579.

During the course of the same year, 223 boys and 214 girls—a total of 437 infants—were baptized in St. Georg's church. None of these children was illegitimate, although two were conceived in sin (the pastors were careful to note when a child was born less than nine months after the wedding). The total of 437 baptisms is slightly misleading, since 46 of these infants were the children of villagers or travelers who did not live in Nördlingen. This still leaves us, however, with a total of almost 400 births to Nördlingen's own families in 1579. (Nor was this an exceptionally fertile year; in fact, the average number of baptisms for Nördlingen families during the seven-year period 1579-85 was 398.)

Demographers tend to assume that an annual rate of 35 to

---

establish. (For example, the hostel for journeymen in Nördlingen's largest craft, wool weaving, is described in W. H. Konrad Ebert, *Die Lodweberei in der Reichsstadt Nördlingen* [Nördlingen, 1919], p. 53, but there is no indication of the number of residents.) An estimate of about 100 in each category, however, does not seem excessive.

[6] Evangelische Kirchengemeinde, Nördlingen: Tauf- und Eheregister, 1579ff.

45 births per thousand inhabitants was the norm for communities in preindustrial Europe.[7] Since we know the number of births in 1579, it is possible to estimate the size of Nördlingen's population in that year: a birth rate of 35 per thousand would imply a total of 11,400 inhabitants, while a rate of 45 per thousand would indicate a total of 8,900. Within this range, however, the higher figures seem rather dubious; for example, a population of 11,400 would imply that Nördlingen's 1,663 households had an average of 6.8 members each—an implausibly high figure. By contrast, a population of only 8,900 would imply a household size of 5 members each, which seems more likely. In short, we can say that Nördlingen's population in 1579 was somewhere between 8,900 and 11,400—and probably toward the lower end of this scale.

A similar attempt to estimate Nördlingen's population could be made for any year between 1579 and the early eighteenth century. But in fact it may be best to leave aside such attempts to determine indirectly Nördlingen's total size at any given point. Instead, we shall let the records speak for themselves. The tax records will tell us about the changing number of citizen households, and also about the occupations and wealth of the householders. The parish registers will disclose not only the frequency of births, marriages and deaths in Nördlingen but also much about the families, origins and ages of the people whose lives they record. From data like these we shall be able to examine both the short-term crises and long-term trends in Nördlingen's demographic history, and we can begin to assess the impact of a century of warfare on the people of this one city.

I

WE can start by looking at the changing number of citizen households in Nördlingen between 1579 and 1720. To ap-

[7] See E. A. Wrigley, *Population and History* (New York, 1969), p. 62; Pierre Guillaume and Jean-Pierre Poussou, *Démographie historique* (Paris, 1970), pp. 168-171.

preciate these figures, however, it is necessary to understand a crucial feature of Nördlingen's social system: the division of its inhabitants into citizens and noncitizens. The citizens, or *Bürger*, were the permanent, legally protected members of the community. In order to engage in commerce, practice a skilled trade, or participate in the political life of the community, it was almost always necessary to be a citizen. This does not mean, however, that the citizenry as a whole was a privileged elite. Included in its ranks were merchants, professionals, skilled artisans—but also day-laborers, street sweepers, chalk cutters, even gravediggers. Many of the citizens, as we shall see, were very wealthy—but others lived in grinding poverty. The reason for this is simple: citizenship was an inherited right which did not depend on economic circumstances. Every citizen's son who had not disqualified himself (by committing a crime, for example, or by emigrating without permission) was entitled to exercise the right of citizenship when he reached adulthood. The same applied to any citizen's daughter.

It would be well, however, to draw a distinction between what might be called "active" and "passive" citizenship.[8] An "active" citizen was an independent adult head of a household. The wife and children of an active male citizen were "passive" citizens. When a citizen's son reached young adulthood, he normally assumed active citizenship; when a citizen died, his widow—now the head of the household—exchanged her passive citizenship for an active one until she remarried or died. But the system was fluid. Not all sons remained in the city: some left, often as journeymen, and proceeded to marry and settle down elsewhere. At the same time, outsiders could obtain active citizenship by purchase. Often they, too, were journeymen who married citizens' daughters or widows and set up a trade in Nördlingen.[9]

[8] The terms "active" and "passive" citizenship do not appear in the sixteenth- and seventeenth-century records of Nördlingen, but they describe a distinction that was clearly recognized by contemporaries.

[9] Passive citizenship could be lost, either by marrying a noncitizen or by assuming the citizenship of another community. Thus, a man

The transition from passive to active citizenship was part of a complex of crucial events in the life of a young man. In most cases, all of these events occurred at the same time: he received some property from his parents and ceased to be a dependent, which made it possible for him to marry, to establish a household and to set up a trade. At the same time, he became an active citizen, an event signaled by his entry into the tax registers, for now that he owned property he was obliged to pay taxes. His name would continue to appear in the tax rolls year after year, until he died, or he relinquished or lost his citizenship and left the city, or (in some cases) he was admitted as an old man to the hospital.

An outsider, by contrast, would have to meet stringent financial and moral qualifications before he was admitted to citizenship. In the first place, he had to demonstrate that he owned an adequate amount of property. Second, he would have to satisfy the magistrates as to his character and qualifications for practicing a trade. If admitted, he then had to pay for the right of citizenship for himself and (unless she was already the daughter or widow of a citizen) for his wife. And for the first five years after his arrival, the newcomer's conduct was subject to annual review before his status as a citizen was made permanent.[10]

The citizens, then, formed a clearly demarcated segment of the inhabitants of Nördlingen. But what about the noncitizens? In addition to the citizens of Nördlingen and their families, we can identify three other types of inhabitants.

The first such group consisted of noncitizens of inde-

---

who married an outsider would normally purchase on her behalf the right of passive citizenship. In the case of outsiders who purchased citizenship, only children born after that time would automatically receive passive citizenship; for children born before that time, passive citizenship would have to be purchased if they were later to enjoy active citizenship.

[10] See RP 16 Apr. 1607, and "Der Stadt Nördlingen Statuta und Satzungen" [1650], in D. August Friedrich Schott, *Sammlungen zu den Deutschen Land- und Stadtrechten*, vol. 1 (Leipzig, 1772), pp. 210-11. (Hereafter cited as: Schott, *Sammlungen*.)

pendent status—*Paktbürger* (or *Einwohner*) and their families. Like the citizens, these Paktbürger headed separate households and enjoyed a distinct legal status. Some were well-to-do outsiders who presumably preferred to remain citizens of their native communities. The majority, however, appear to have been poorer persons who could not meet the property requirements or did not wish to pay the purchase price of citizenship. For the period before the Thirty Years War, we can obtain accurate indications of the number of such Paktbürger: they show that the ratio between citizens and Paktbürger stood at roughly 10:1 in the late sixteenth and early seventeenth centuries.[11] Similar information is available for the year 1802, and shows a ratio of 8:1.[12]

The second category of noncitizens consisted of individuals who lived in a dependent relationship to citizens (or, in a few cases, to wealthy Paktbürger): journeymen, apprentices and servants. It is impossible to estimate the number of such persons during the period of our study. In the mid-fifteenth century, however, we find a ratio of 4:7 between dependent serving persons and the total number of households in Nördlingen.[13]

The third group consisted of beggars, vagrants, travelers and other transients. They enjoyed virtually no legal privileges and the references to them in the surviving records, while not sparse, are inevitably scattered and unsystematic.

[11] The number of Paktbürger at six-year intervals between 1579 and 1621 is as follows—1579: 143; 1585: 194; 1591: 158; 1597: 175; 1603: 165; 1609: 153; 1615: 121; 1621: 115. (KR Einkommen von Pakt- und Beysassen, for the indicated years.) These figures for the heads of Paktbürger households can be compared to the figures provided in Appendix III for the total number of active citizens (i.e., heads of citizen households) in the same years.

[12] In 1802 Nördlingen had 1,221 citizen households and 152 noncitizen households, which yields a ratio of 8:1. Meier, "Reichsdeputationshauptschluss," p. 108.

[13] The census of 1459 reports a total of 1,264 households and 746 dependent serving-persons living in them.

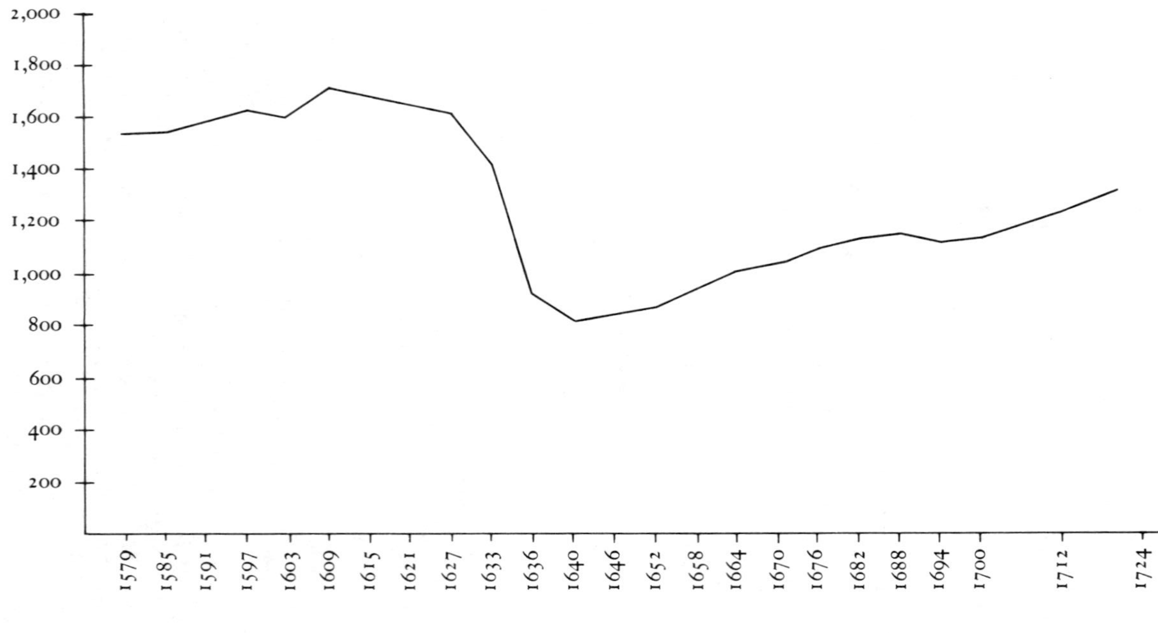

FIGURE 2.1. Total Number of Citizen Households in Nördlingen, 1579-1724.

There is no basis for even attempting an estimate of their numbers.

Thus, although it is possible to determine for any year the number of "active" citizens—or, to put it another way, the number of citizen households—it is not possible to establish with precision the ratio between this number and the total population of the city.[14] But whatever it is, there is no reason to assume that it changed very substantially between the late sixteenth and the early eighteenth century. The changing curve of citizen households, to which we can now turn our attention, provides at least a rough indicator of overall population trends in Nördlingen during the years under study.

This curve is presented in Figure 2.1.[15] The fundamental pattern is immediately evident. During the first 40 years of our era, the number of citizen households remained essentially stable. Then, between 1627 and 1640, this number underwent a catastrophic reduction. Between 1627 and 1640, the community lost 793 citizen households—very nearly half the total number. To be sure, beginning in the 1640's

[14] Even for 1459 this ratio cannot be established. The census of that year gives the total number of households and the total number of inhabitants. But it is not always clear whether the household was headed by a citizen or noncitizen.

[15] This figure records the total number of citizen households in Nördlingen, which is slightly less than the total number of "active" citizens in any given year, since it does not include the citizens of Nördlingen who were temporarily resident in other communities. The proportion of such active citizens (mostly clergymen) who lived elsewhere ranged between a high of 2.5% (in 1633) and a low of 0.8% (in 1724). All of the data presented in Figure 2.1 are based on the Steuerregister for 1579-1724. The tax registers are extant for every year of this period except 1639 and 1647-51. For this study, the tax registers have been analyzed at six-year intervals, except for the crucial 1630's, where a shorter interval was used, and the period after 1700, where the data was taken at twelve-year intervals. For a complete description of the techniques used in recording and analyzing the data from these registers, see Friedrichs, "Nördlingen," Chapter 4 and Appendix III; see also the discussions below in Chapters Three and Four.

and continuing for half a century thereafter, the number of households did increase again, but the rate of recovery was slow, averaging out to less than seven additional households a year. During the pan-European famine of the early 1690's, the number of citizen households dropped once again. The recovery rate between 1694 and 1724 was again slightly less than 7 households per year.[16] And even this slow growth rate must have petered out in the course of the eighteenth century: in 1724 there were 1,323 citizen households; in 1802 there were only 1,221.[17]

Altogether, this curve illustrates eloquently the importance of the Thirty Years War—in particular, the period from the late 1620's onward—in the city's demographic history. It is quite possible that the population of Nördlingen was declining slightly before the war; certainly the number of citizen households had reached its peak around 1609. But the contrast between the gentle downward slope before 1627 and the drastic collapse thereafter is too obvious to need emphasis. As elsewhere in southern Germany, the war had only a limited impact during most of the 1620's. But when the seat of war shifted from the north German plains and the Baltic shore toward the south, Nördlingen came to feel the effects. The sharpest drop in population occurred between 1633 and 1636, as a result of the great crisis of 1634, when Nördlingen underwent first a prolonged siege and then a military occupation, accompanied by a devastating outbreak of the plague. As we shall see below, Nördlingen did experience some of the classic signs of demographic recovery in the months following the crisis. But these developments proved inadequate to restore the community to anything like its earlier size, especially since the war, with its

[16] The exact figures on which these statements are based are as follows—in 1627: 1,619 citizen households; in 1640: 823; in 1688: 1,154 (i.e., a net increase of 331 over 48 years, or 6.9 per year); in 1694: 1,104; in 1724: 1,313.

[17] The figure for 1802 is provided by Meier, "Reichsdeputationshauptschluss," p. 108.

debilitating sequence of military occupations and financial exactions, dragged on for another fifteen years.

In short, the community never fully recovered from the crisis of the 1630's. Why was this so? To answer this question, even in part, will require a much closer examination both of the demographic data for Nördlingen and of the pattern of immigration as it changed during the period under study.

II

THE parish registers of Nördlingen were maintained with exemplary precision, even during periods of crisis, and we can be sure that they contain as complete a record of vital events as will be found in any preindustrial European community.[18] There are, however, two problems involved in using the data they provide. In the first place, while baptisms and marriages were recorded from 1579 onward, burials were recorded only from the middle of 1618. This means that we lack any information about mortality in Nördlingen before the Thirty Years War. In the second place, the

[18] All baptisms and most marriages and burials in Nördlingen were recorded in the parish registers of the Hauptkirche St. Georg, which are preserved by the Evangelische Kirchengemeinde, Nördlingen. The baptismal and marriage registers (Tauf- und Eheregister, hereafter: TR and ER) are complete from 1579 onward, with the exception of one year, 1640, in which marriages are missing. The burial register (Sterberegister, hereafter: SR) is complete from April 1618. A very small number of additional marriages and a substantial number of additional burials conducted in Nördlingen (along with all marriages and burials for the nearby village of Baldingen) are recorded in the Trau- und Sterberegister of the Spitalkirche Nördlingen; these registers, which are complete from 1602 onward, are now preserved in the nearby parish of Nähermemmingen. It should be noted that the St. Georg marriage register actually records betrothals, which took place three weeks before the wedding. The occasional cases in which a wedding was canceled after the betrothal was recorded are marked in the registers, and I have, of course, eliminated these cases in from the totals. A more complete description of the parish registers will be found in Appendix I.

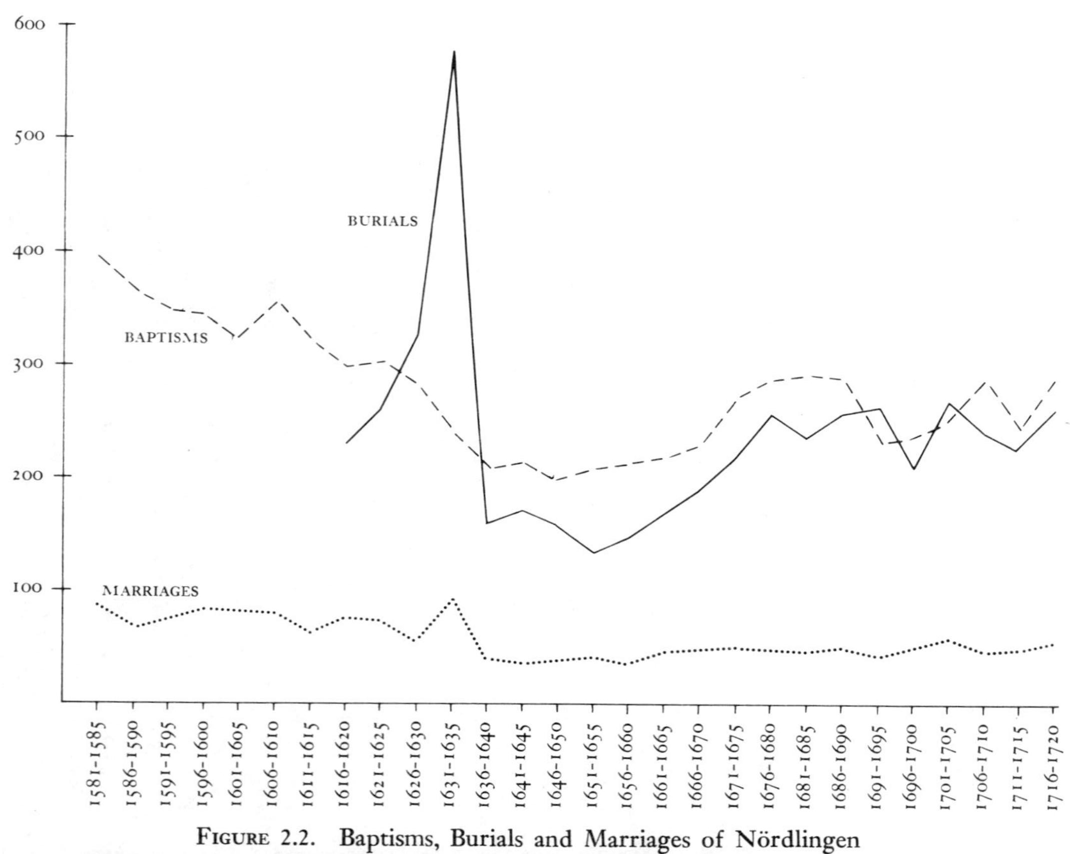

FIGURE 2.2. Baptisms, Burials and Marriages of Nördlingen Residents, 1581-1720 (Five-Year Averages)

entries in the parish registers were not confined to residents of Nördlingen alone. Instead, the registers are studded with entries for inhabitants of the surrounding villages and for travelers and transients who gave birth, married or died in Nördlingen—especially during times of war, when the city swelled with refugees.

In order to correctly assess the demographic trends for Nördlingen itself, it is necessary to eliminate the information for outsiders. Fortunately this can almost always be done, since the place of residence of the individual or family concerned is normally indicated. In the case of marriages, however, it often happened that one spouse came from Nördlingen and one did not. Later on we shall see what these cases of "mixed marriages" can tell us about patterns of immigration in seventeenth-century Nördlingen. But in determining the basic number of marriages among Nördlingen residents in any given year, what matters is not where the spouses came from but where they settled down after the wedding. Thus, any couple which can be assumed to have established a household in the city has been counted among the residents of Nördlingen. By contrast, whenever a couple appears from the record to have settled down elsewhere—when, for example, a Nördlingen man is recorded as having moved to his bride's community after the wedding—their marriage has not been included in the tabulation.[19]

Figure 2.2, then, presents the changing level of baptisms, marriages and burials among residents of Nördlingen, expressed as five-year averages.[20] It is immediately apparent

[19] For a fuller description of the way in which residents and outsiders were distinguished from each other in recording data from the parish registers, as well as year-by-year tables of the total number of baptisms, marriages and burials for both residents and outsiders, see Appendix I.

[20] In two cases the data plotted are not five-year averages. Since the marriage register for 1640 is missing, the number of marriages indicated for 1636-40 is really a four-year average for 1636-39. And since the first complete year for burials is 1619, the number of burials plotted for 1616-20 is a two-year average for 1619-20.

that between 1580 and 1620 the number of births in Nördlingen was on the decline—a development which was accentuated during the Thirty Years War but then began to reverse itself during the 1640's. Even more obvious is the huge excess of deaths over births in the years 1631-35, which is attributable chiefly to the plague of 1634. From 1636 onward, however, the level of deaths dropped substantially below that of births, and continued to remain so for over half a century—not only until the 1670's, while baptisms were steadily rising, but even during the 1680's, when baptisms began to level off. This clearly corresponds to the trend of demographic recovery which we have already observed in the increase of citizen households during the same period. On the other hand, even at its peak in 1681-85, the number of baptisms had not attained the levels achieved before the Thirty Years War or even in the early 1620's. And in any case, from the 1690's on, the pattern of recovery was interrupted: the number of baptisms plunged, and deaths exceeded births for the first time since the 1630's. In the years 1701-05, when major operations of the War of Spanish Succession were being waged in the region around Nördlingen, deaths once again exceeded births; although baptisms surged ahead of burials in 1705-10, they dropped sharply in the following five years. Clearly the pattern of regular, steady, demographic growth that had been established after the Thirty Years War was interrupted around 1690 and had not yet been reestablished by 1720.

In the cases of marriages, the most obvious turning-point came during the crisis years of the early 1630's. In 1631-35 there was, in fact, a great increase in the number of marriages, which can be attributed specifically to the regrouping of households when widows and widowers remarried after the plague of 1634. But after 1635 the level of marriages dropped below the prewar level, where it remained for the rest of our period.

The crisis years of the early 1630's appear to represent a watershed in the demographic history of Nördlingen. It will be instructive to examine this period in greater detail. Figure 2.3 records the demographic data for each four-month period between 1633 and 1636.[21] The staggering mortality of the plague months—September to November 1634—is immediately evident. During 1633 and the first two-thirds of 1634, the average number of deaths for any four-month period was 146. In the last four months of 1634, this figure rose ninefold; the deaths of 1,273 men, women, and children of Nördlingen are recorded—easily one-sixth of the entire community.[22]

The normal rhythms of community life came to a virtual standstill. During the last four months of 1634, only three weddings took place. Sexual activity as a whole must also have diminished at the height of the plague, as suggested by the drastic drop in baptisms exactly nine months later.[23] By December 1634, however, the plague had abated, and with the new year the tempo of social activity changed. Some households had been wiped out entirely in the plague, but many others had only been left incomplete, and scores of widows and widowers started looking for new partners. The result was a massive increase in marriages: a total of 121 weddings are recorded for the first four months of 1635. One year later, quite predictably, we see a sudden up-

[21] Demographers customarily divide the year into quarters, not thirds. I have chosen, however, to use four-month periods in order to draw attention to the impact of the plague, which occurred during the last four months of 1634. Dividing the year into three-month periods would have split the two peak plague months, September and October, between two separate quarters.

[22] There were 1,441 "active" citizens of Nördlingen in 1633. Taking 5.5 as the highest plausible multiplier would yield a population of 7,926, of which 1,273 represent one-sixth. If a more cautious multiplier is used, e.g., 5.0, the death toll would represent an even higher proportion of the inhabitants.

[23] The peak months of the plague were September and October 1634. In June 1635 there were no Nördlingen baptisms and in July there were only three, even though for 1635 as a whole the average number of baptisms per month was 10.9.

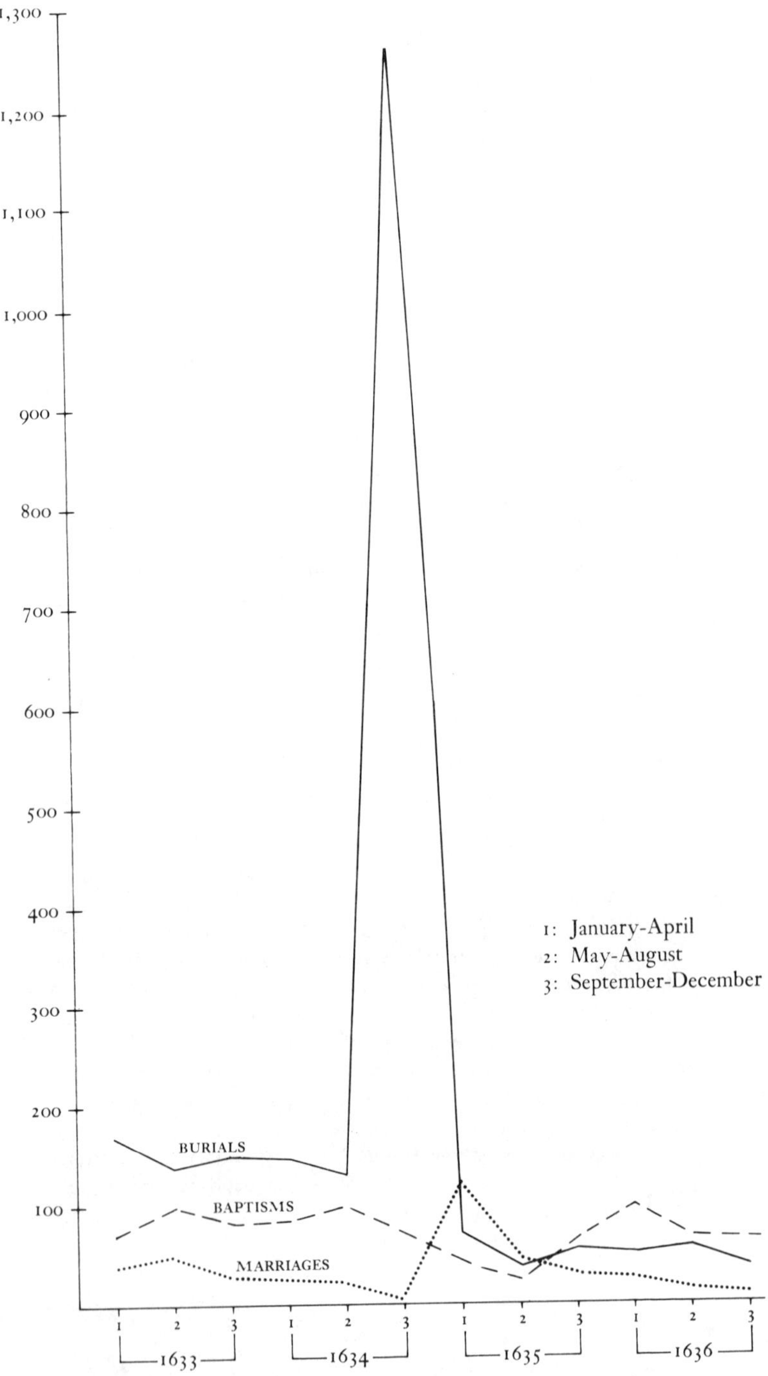

FIGURE 2.3. Baptisms, Burials and Marriages of Nördlingen Residents, 1633-1636.

surge of baptisms. In short, Nördlingen exhibited distinct signs of the kind of recovery which normally followed a demographic crisis in the *ancien régime*.[24]

Yet this recovery was hardly adequate to reverse the overall trend of population loss in the 1630's. Between 1633 and 1636, the number of citizen households dropped by over one-third. In the following four years, the number of households continued to fall—as did the number of baptisms. In fact, the plague of 1634 was only the most spectacular incident in an overall trend of population loss which was not arrested until the 1640's and which was not reversed until after the war.

But when did this trend begin? Did the war cause the decline in population, or did it merely accentuate a trend that was already underway? Unfortunately the two main sources of evidence we have consulted so far suggest rather different answers. The parish records show a pronounced decline in baptisms during the forty years before the war. Between 1580 and 1620, despite one interruption in 1606-10, the average annual number of births dropped by 25 percent, from about 400 a year to about 300. The tax registers, however, suggest a different picture. The number of citizen households rose until 1609 and then only barely declined before 1627.

There are two ways to explain this apparent contradiction. In the first place, it must be remembered that new households were formed by young adults, generally in their twenties when they got married. Possibly the 1580's represented the beginning of a downward slope of baptisms; and if so, it would be logical for the downward slope of households to follow only twenty or thirty years later, as is in-

[24] For a classic discussion of the phases of demographic crises in the *ancien régime*, see Pierre Goubert, *Beauvais et le Beauvaisis de 1600 à 1730: contribution à l'histoire sociale de la France du XVII*[e] (Paris, 1960), pp. 45-59. See also Jean Meuvret, "Demographic Crisis in France from the Sixteenth to the Eighteenth Century," in D. V. Glass and D.E.C. Eversley, eds., *Population in History: Essays in Historical Demography* (London, 1965), pp. 507-22.

deed the case. In the second place, one must take into account the possibility of immigration. Even if the supply of local youths were on the decline, their absence might be compensated for by an adequate supply of immigrants—young men and women from other communities who married and settled down in Nördlingen.

In a moment we shall examine the question of immigration. But on the basis of the demographic data considered so far, we can already outline the basic pattern of Nördlingen's demographic history. Between the mid-fifteenth and mid-sixteenth centuries, Nördlingen experienced a very substantial growth. But this trend had ended by the turn of the sixteenth century, and the population was, if not declining, at least stagnating in the decades before the Thirty Years War. The war years themselves—especially the catastrophic 1630's—brought about a drastic reduction in the number of inhabitants. After the war, however, the city experienced a gradual but steady demographic recovery. Had it continued without interruption, this growth might eventually have restored Nördlingen to its prewar level, but instead it came to end in the 1690's. Throughout northern Europe the years 1690-1715 were a period of bad weather and bad harvests, notably during the years 1693-94 and 1709. And for Nördlingen this was also a period of intensified exposure to the effects of war, especially during the opening campaign of the War of the Spanish Succession. In fact, the climatic and military events of the 1690's and early 1700's evidently ushered in a century of demographic stagnation, for the population of Nördlingen was no greater in 1800 than it had been in 1720.

It is well known that the sixteenth and eighteenth centuries were periods of tremendous demographic growth in Europe, including Germany. In the sixteenth century, Nördlingen conformed to the European pattern; in the eighteenth century it did not. The explanation for this, however, cannot be found in Nördlingen's internal history; it must be sought instead by looking at changes in the relationship—in particular, of course, the demographic relationship —between Nördlingen and the outside world.

III

THIS brings us to the most complex aspect of Nördlingen's demographic history: immigration. After all, a community's population is determined not only by the births and deaths among the resident population, but also by immigration and emigration. Unfortunately there are no ways to systematically study patterns of emigration from Nördlingen. Nor can all forms of immigration be studied—many people drifted into Nördlingen to work as servants or journeymen and then left town without finding a permanent place in its records. What we can study, however, is by far the most important group of immigrants from the demographic point of view: the people who came to the city and established themselves there on a permanent basis.

In fact there are two different sources for the study of immigration to Nördlingen. First there is the Bürgerbuch, which records the name of each alien who was admitted to citizenship in Nördlingen. Second, there are the marriage registers, from which one can determine how many spouses came from outside the city. To a large extent, the data in these two sources overlap, since in order to marry into a citizen family the foreigner would first have to be granted citizenship himself. Nevertheless, the two sources do not completely coincide. For one thing, many of the foreigners who became citizens of Nördlingen were already married and admitted as couples. Thus, they never appear in the marriage registers. Conversely, many of the foreigners who married there never became citizens; in order to marry even a noncitizen in Nördlingen, a foreigner would need the permission of the authorities, but his status would be that of a Paktbürger and his name would not appear in the Bürgerbuch. Thus, we shall have to look at these two sets of data separately. It will become evident, however, that although they differ in some details, the fundamental trends they disclose are the same.

The Bürgerbuch[25] contains a wealth of entries, for it records not only the names of alien men who were admitted as active citizens, but also the names of alien women and children who were admitted as passive ones, not to mention former citizens who had lost their rights but were now readmitted. For our purposes, however, it is most important to tabulate the first of these groups: the alien males who were granted the right of citizenship. Between 1580 and 1724, a total of 1,097 alien men received this privilege. In fact not all of these men were immigrants. In 221 cases, no place of origin is given, or the person concerned is identified as living in Nördlingen. Many of these men were certainly Paktbürger who were upgrading their status and cannot, of course, be considered as immigrants. Others, however, appear to have been foreigners or recent arrivals whose place of origin the clerk simply did not know. In any case, 876 men—almost four-fifths of the total—are definitely recorded as having immigrated to Nördlingen from outside the city.

Most of the immigrants came to Nördlingen as bachelors and married the daughters or widows of local citizens, often taking over a father-in-law's or an earlier husband's shop. About one-fifth, however, came with their wives in tow, and some even with entire families. The immigrants were engaged in the entire spectrum of occupations, although the

25 There are actually two sources for the information on which the following statistics are based: first, the Bürgerbuch 1513-1672; and second, the Kammerrechnungen (city treasury accounts) for 1579 to 1724, under the heading: Einnehmen von neueinverkaufften Bürgern. For the most part the entries in these two sources overlap; however, from mid-1594 to mid-1609 and from 1673 onward the Bürgerbuch was not maintained. It is clear that after 1672 the Kammerrechnungen were consciously used as a substitute for the discontinued Bürgerbuch, since they include even the names of individuals who were admitted gratis, and thus made no payment. I have counted individuals whether they appeared in both sources or only one.

city's chief industry, wool weaving, is somewhat underrepresented, probably because it was essentially a local form of production. The manufacture of heavy "Loden" was a skill more likely to be acquired in Nördlingen than to be brought in by an outsider.

The number of alien males admitted during each six-year period from 1580 to 1724—divided into those men specifically identified as immigrants and the remaining aliens—is indicated in Figure 2.4. Clearly the number of immigrants accepted by the city was far from constant. Fluctuations in the number of outsiders admitted to citizenship could, of course, reflect changes both in the supply of aliens and in the community's demand for them. In the case of Nördlingen, however, the latter factor clearly predominated. The council closely regulated the number of newcomers who were allowed to become citizens, for the rigidly structured economy of the city could not tolerate the indiscriminate admission of all who applied. In 1585, for example, the council reached the conclusion that too many impoverished persons were being admitted to citizenship, and, as a consequence, the number of citizens was excessive and native craftsmen were faced with unbearable competition. In addition, the council charged, many of the poorer newcomers promptly abandoned their wives and children, causing an intolerable burden on the welfare facilities of the community. In order to reduce the number of new citizens and to ensure that those admitted would be of a more responsible character, the council toughened the requirements for admission: whereas hitherto male newcomers had been required to prove that they owned at least 50 fl. in cash, now they would have to own at least 100 fl.[26]

The immediate effectiveness of this policy is reflected in

[26] OB 1567-87, fols. 229b-231b (15 Nov. 1585). The same decree also introduced a property requirement for women. (Previously any woman who married into the citizenry would be admitted to citizenship upon payment of a fee; henceforth, however, she would also have to prove ownership of 50 fl. in cash.)

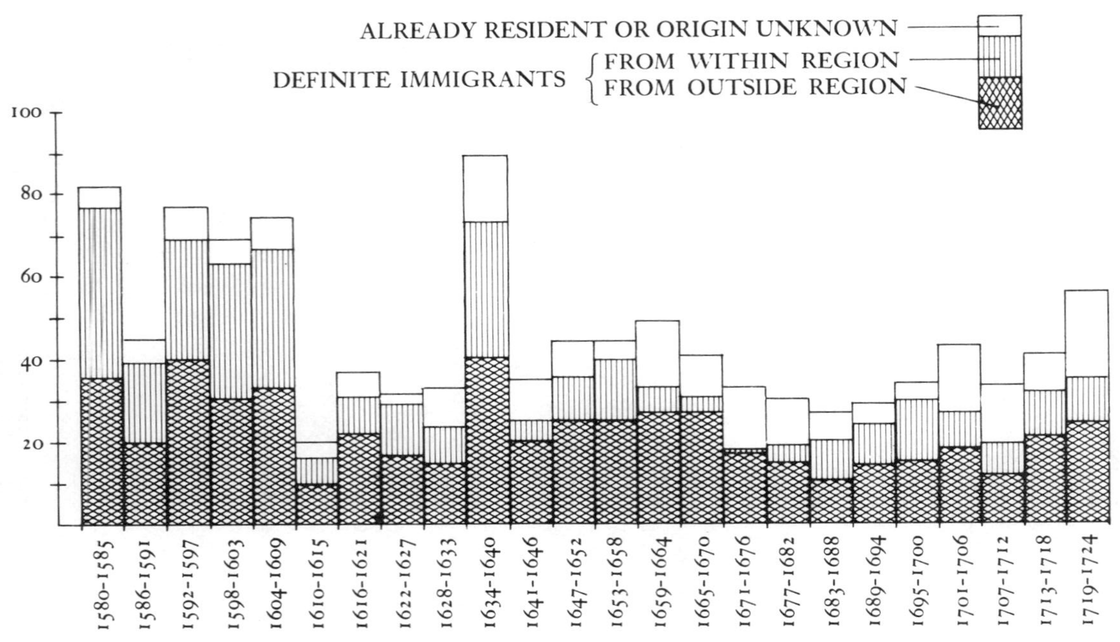

FIGURE 2.4. Number of Alien Males Admitted to Citizenship During Each Six-Year Period.

the reduced number of admissions in 1586-91. Thereafter, however, the number of outsiders admitted to citizenship rose again. By 1607, in fact, the council felt constrained to tighten the requirements even further: the minimum cash requirement for males was again doubled, from 100 fl. to 200 fl.[27] This represented a very substantial toughening of the rules, and the effectiveness of the council's restrictive policy is suggested by the sharp reduction in admissions in the following periods, extending into the unsettling opening years of the Thirty Years War.

The years 1634-40, however, witnessed a sudden, sharp increase in the number of aliens admitted. Even if the total number is reduced by one-seventh, to account for the extra year included in this period,[28] the huge increase would still stand out. This increase coincided, of course, with the tremendous drop in population associated with the plague of 1634, or, more precisely, with the great number of marriages which took place immediately after the plague. Hundreds of households in Nördlingen had been broken, and although many remarriages took place between citizen families, the opportunities for outsiders were vastly increased.

The postwar years show some fluctuations. From a high point around 1660, the number of aliens admitted tended to drop for two decades, only to start rising again from the 1680's on. At no time after the war, however, did the number of immigrants reach the level which had been normal before 1609.

But how much of a role did immigration play in the total recruitment of Nördlingen's citizenry? The answer to this question has been determined with some precision for the period up to 1700. Between 1580 and 1700, about 4,700 men were inscribed as active citizens of Nördlingen—an average

[27] RP 16 Apr. 1607. The minimum requirement for women was also increased, from 50 fl. to 100 fl., plus clothing and a bedstead.

[28] This is a seven-year period because the tax was not levied and the tax register was not maintained in 1639, making it necessary to use the register for the following year.

FIGURE 2.5. Percentage of Aliens Among All Males Admitted to Active Citizenship, 1580-1700.

of about 39 per year. Most of these men were enrolled as citizens by right of heredity. But 924 of them, or about 20 percent, were aliens, and of these aliens 760—or 16 percent of the total number—can definitely be identified as immigrants. Men of foreign origin, then, made up something under one-fifth of the citizenry of Nördlingen.

This proportion, however, remained far from constant over the years. Figure 2.5 records the changing proportion of aliens among the 4,525 citizens whose names were recorded and tabulated for this study.[29] Again one can note a sharp decline in alien admissions after 1609, as well as an unusually high proportion of immigrants during the crisis years of the 1630's. In the postwar years, one can see a pronounced decline in the proportion of aliens admitted from the 1650's to the 1670's, followed by a rise in this proportion toward the end of the century.

It is suggestive to compare the data for 1650-1700 presented here with the demographic data for the same period presented in Figure 2.2. For the downswing of alien admissions coincides precisely with a sharp spurt in baptisms; conversely, the upswing from 1683 onward coincides with a leveling-off and decline in the number of births. Clearly, immigration was not positively correlated with population growth. If anything, the opposite is more likely: when, as in the 1630's and the 1690's, the community faced a period of demographic crisis, immigrants were more freely admitted; but when the community was growing, immigration was discouraged. The attitude that had motivated the mag-

[29] As noted above, data were taken from the tax registers at six-year intervals up to 1700. The names of 1,266 men appear in the tax registers in 1579. An additional 4,525 men appear for the first time in one of the selected years between 1585 and 1700. It was not possible to search out and include each man who appeared and then disappeared from the records within a six-year interval, e.g., someone who started paying taxes in 1581 and died already in 1584. Careful sampling, however, suggests that the total number of such cases between 1579 and 1700 amounted to about 175, leading to the total of approximately 4,700 cited earlier.

istrates in 1607—that the interests of the existing members of the community must be preferred to indiscriminate growth—continued to predominate in the century that followed.

The degree to which immigration patterns reflected the intentions of the city's policymakers becomes even more apparent when we look at the newcomers' places of origin. To this end, those aliens who can specifically be identified as immigrants have been divided into two groups: men of regional and of distant origin. The regional area has been broadly defined; it covers, of course, the surrounding Ries district with its agricultural villages, but also extends slightly beyond the boundaries of the Ries to include the nearest small towns in each direction.[30]

Figure 2.4 indicates how many of the definite immigrants admitted during each six-year period came from within the nearby region and how many were of more distant origin. Until 1609, the two groups retained a rough parity; thereafter, however, the number of distant immigrants consistently outweighed the number from nearby communities. Most of these distant immigrants came from somewhere in southern Germany—from within Swabia, or from Bavaria, Franconia, or the Upper Rhine Valley. Over 10 percent, however, came from even further away—especially during and after the Thirty Years War. In fact the toll of new citizens is interspersed with immigrants from every corner of the German-speaking world: Switzerland, Bohemia, Hessen, Lower Saxony, Brandenburg, even far-off Prussia.

The "close" immigrants came from both towns and small peasant villages; the distant ones, however, appear to have come primarily from cities and only rarely from peasant

[30] This region has been defined as the area formed by straight lines connecting the communities of Bopfingen, Fremdingen, Oettingen, Wemding, Harburg, Neresheim and Bopfingen again (with these communities included). All of the Ries except for its extreme northeastern corner (the part farthest away from Nördlingen) falls within these boundaries. Cf. map above, Chapter One.

communities.[31] This means, of course, that already before 1610 and even more so thereafter, immigrants to Nördlingen tended to come not from peasant villages, but from urban communities. In fact, the same conclusion could be reached simply by observing the occupational backgrounds of the immigrants. The overwhelming majority of them came to Nördlingen equipped with training in some trade or craft, and while such training was occasionally available to villagers, it was usually far more accessible to men who had grown up in an urban environment.

Figure 2.4 does indicate that before about 1609 the community showed a greater willingness to accept villagers. Thereafter, however, the city became more stringent about the background and training of those it admitted. The stiffer financial requirements introduced in 1607 certainly reduced the number of peasant villagers qualified for citizenship. And once the Thirty Years War had started, even fewer villagers could meet the city's requirements. For much as Nördlingen and other cities suffered in the war, the surrounding villages usually suffered even more: where a walled city had to pay tribute, the unprotected village was often totally destroyed. Desperate and dispossessed, countless peasants flocked into Nördlingen in times of crisis, but this hardly made them acceptable candidates for citizenship. Indeed, the severe economic setbacks suffered by the villages of the Ries clearly diminished the total number of villagers who could ever rise sufficiently in wealth and status to obtain the hand of a citizen's daughter or widow.

In short, the city fathers were highly selective when it

[31] At least four-fifths of the "distant" immigrants are identified as coming from specific towns or cities. It might be argued that when an immigrant came from a distant village, the clerk in Nördlingen merely wrote down the name of the nearest sizable community instead of the obscure village, but this is unlikely, since the normal practice when a villager immigrated was to identify his village *and* the nearest town (e.g. "Monheim bei Gunzenhausen") or to identify the newcomer's place of origin as being within a certain region or territory ("Ulmisches Gebiet," "Pfälzische Herrschaft," etc.).

came to admitting outsiders to full membership in the community. Had the growth of the community been their goal, it would have been easy enough to recruit additional citizens from among the villagers of the Ries, many of whom were already in the city as unmarried domestics. But the magistrates' sense of their responsibility never encompassed such crudely mercantilist notions. Instead, they felt it their duty to protect the community by limiting citizenship to those who met the traditional standards of wealth and skill. One competent artisan, able to contribute his wealth and his skills to the common weal, was worth more to the community than any number of sturdy peasant sons.

Thus, it is clear that the aliens who were admitted to citizenship in Nördlingen were drawn from all over Germany—and increasingly so after the beginning of the Thirty Years War. The city's standards of admission were high, and if the surrounding villages were less able than before to produce men with the requisite training and wealth, then men from more distant regions would be admitted instead. But this would scarcely have been possible were it not for an extensive amount of geographical mobility throughout Germany—mobility perhaps accelerated by the upheavals of the Thirty Years War, but something which must have been a normal feature of German life already long before 1618.

Much of this mobility involved itinerant peddlers and craftsmen, who spent their lives wandering from one community to the next, selling their wares or performing services. Typical of this group were the Italian chimney sweeps who for a century and a half were commissioned to clean the chimneys of city-owned buildings in Nördlingen.[32] But

[32] Gustav Wulz, "Italienische Kaminkehrer und Südfrüchtehändler in Nördlingen," *Schwäbische Blätter für Heimatpflege und Volksbildung*, 10 (1959), pp. 122-28. Originally these Italian chimney sweeps were itinerant, but during the seventeenth century some of them came to live permanently in Nördlingen. (They were not, however, granted citizenship.) It was only after the beginning of the eighteenth century that this work was given to natives.

even more mobile were the journeymen, young men who after completing their apprenticeships moved from town to town seeking work before settling down somewhere as craft masters. As a result of this constant movement, they often built up a far-flung network of personal relationships and friendships among members of their craft throughout Germany; indeed, long after settling down in one place, a craftsman often felt a double loyalty—to his community and to his craft in general.[33] Typical of this phenomenon was the so-called bakers' school of Venice; essentially a hostel for German journeymen bakers seeking work in northern Italy, this institution also functioned as a registry of agreements and a court of honor, even for bakers who had returned to their homeland. In 1589, the warden of this lodge was a native of Nördlingen.[34]

In fact, the proportion of Nördlingen's citizens who were immigrants does not reflect the true extent of geographical mobility affecting the city, since for every alien who was fully accepted into the community there were probably many whose stay was only temporary. In 1663, for example, there were nine journeymen working for the five hatmaker-masters of Nördlingen. Of these nine, two were native-born. The remaining seven came, one each, from Dinkelsbühl, Heilbronn, Styria, Brunswick, Pomerania, Courland and Sweden.[35] But none of these seven foreigners is recorded as ever having become a citizen of Nördlingen. Like the overwhelming majority of journeymen, these seven men moved on after six months or a year.

There was certainly no shortage of potential immigrants in Nördlingen. But even trained craftsmen, while more at-

[33] For a discussion of the extraterritorial organization of trades (and imperial efforts in the eighteenth century to limit the same) see Mack Walker, *German Home Towns: Community, State and General Estate, 1648-1871* (Ithaca, N.Y., 1971), pp. 93-97.

[34] Gustav Wulz, "Nördlingen von A bis Z: Beckenschule," *Der Daniel*, 1967, Heft 4, p. 9.

[35] OB 1641-88, fol. 222a.

tractive than peasants, were not always welcome, for they might pose unwelcome competition to the existing masters. When immigration declined, it was due to limitations on demand, not supply.

IV

THE right to grant or deny citizenship was only one of the means available to the magistrates to regulate the demographic evolution of the community. An equally significant means of control lay in their regulation of marriage. From the point of view of the magistrates, it was important that each head of a household have the maturity and economic capacity to sustain a trade and to meet his obligations to the community. Special permission was required for a man to marry under the age of 23 or a woman under the age of 20.[36] Both partners, moreover, were supposed to bring adequate financial resources into the marriage. In fact it was impossible to impose this provision systematically on citizens. But when outsiders wanted to marry into the community, the magistrates were likely to insist on maintaining the property qualification. In 1587, for example, the city council postponed one citizen's marriage to a foreign woman "because he has not produced sufficient documentation concerning his bride's property"; only when the evidence was submitted could the marriage go forward.[37] In 1601 a Nördlingen widow planned to marry a foreign weaver, but after the banns had been read the magistrates stepped in and forbade the wedding "because he is a dirt-poor journeyman."[38]

After the first decade of the seventeenth century, such requirements were even more strictly enforced. As we have seen, the citizenship records reveal a sharp decline in immi-

[36] ER May 1591. See also Schott, *Sammlungen*, vol. 1, p. 224.
[37] ER Mar. 1587.
[38] ER Jan. 1601.

TABLE 2.1. Nördlingen Marriages, 1581-1720: Origins of Spouses

Years	*Total No.*	*(1) Local Groom and Local Bride (%)*	*(2) Local Groom and Immigrant Bride (%)*	*(3) Immigrant Groom and Local Bride (%)*	*(4) Immigrant Groom and Immigrant Bride (%)*
1581-1590	(779)	57	22	16	5
1591-1600	(784)	53	23	20	4
1601-1610	(814)	59	21	17	3
1611-1620	(706)	72	18	8	2
1621-1630	(677)	74	16	8	2
1631-1640	(629)	80	15	5	1
1641-1650	(377)	64	21	13	3
1651-1660	(391)	63	20	14	3
1661-1670	(500)	68	21	9	1
1671-1680	(518)	71	20	9	2
1681-1690	(511)	69	17	13	2
1691-1700	(473)	72	15	11	2
1701-1710	(549)	73	19	7	0
1711-1720	(521)	70	16	13	2

gration following the restrictive ordinance of 1607. The marriage data, which are summarized in Table 2.1, show the same trend. Up to 1610, the proportion of endogamous marriages (column 1) never exceeded 59 percent—that is to say, 41 percent or more of all Nördlingen marriages included at least one outsider. After 1610, however, the percentage of outsiders suddenly dropped, and in later decades, despite some fluctuations, the proportion of marriages which included immigrants always remained substantially below the pre-1610 level. In short, after 1610 Nördlingen became an increasingly closed, endogamous community. It should be noted, however, that the main reason for this increasing trend toward endogamy lies in a reduction in the number of immigrant men. Even before 1610, the number of immigrant brides always exceeded that of immigrant grooms, and after 1610, the proportion became even more uneven: in many decades, more than twice as many women as men from outside married in Nördlingen.

The reasons for this imbalance are complex. They will become more evident, however, when we have taken a closer look at some more detailed evidence about marriage patterns in Nördlingen. To this end, three samples have been taken. The first two consist of all marriages recorded in the parish registers for 1601-02 and 1701-03 respectively.[39] The third and largest sample is yielded by a family reconstitution project in which the families of all men whose surnames began with the letter G were reconstructed; in addition, whenever possible the life-histories of the spouses of these men were traced. The letter-G sample, which represents 84 different surnames, covers about 4 percent of the Nördlingen population between 1579 and 1720.[40]

Data on the marital status of marriage partners in the three sample groups is presented in Table 2.2. All three groups report essentially the same pattern. In more than half of all marriages, both spouses were single. Among the remaining cases (in which at least one spouse was marrying for the second or later time), the proportion of widowers getting married was always much higher than that of widows. This conspicuous difference in the remarriage rates for men and women did not occur because there was a steady surplus of widowers—on the contrary, from the letter-G reconstitu-

[39] ER 1601-02, 1701-03. Sixteen Nördlingen marriages recorded in the Spitalkirche register for 1701-03 are not included.

[40] The arguments in favor of this form of sampling in family reconstitution studies are presented by Jacques Dupâquier, "Problèmes de répresentativité dans les études fondées sur la reconstitution des familles," *Annales de démographie historiques 1972*, pp. 83-91. Because of the existence of superb alphabetical indexes to the Nördlingen parish registers, the major difficulty mentioned by Dupâquier—the problem of tracing the births of women who married into the sampled families—was easily overcome. The letter G was selected as a sample of reasonable size which contained none of Nördlingen's largest surname-groups (e.g. Mair, Beck), in which the likelihood of inaccurate linkages would have been higher.

TABLE 2.2. Marital Status of Spouses (percent)

	Brides: Single	Brides: Widows	Total Grooms
Sample 1: All Weddings, 1601-1602 ($n = 142$)			
Grooms			
Single	54.9	5.6	60.5
Widowers	32.4	7.0	39.4
Total Brides	87.3	12.6	100.0
Sample 2: All Weddings, 1701-1703 ($n = 136$)			
Grooms			
Single	55.1	8.8	63.9
Widowers	33.1	2.9	36.0
Total Brides	88.2	11.7	100.0
Sample 3: Letter-G Weddings, 1579-1720 ($n = 388$)			
Grooms			
Single	58.9	8.7	67.6
Widowers	23.0	9.3	32.3
Total Brides	81.9	18.0	100.0

tions it can be established that a slightly greater number of marriages ended with the death of the husband than the other way round.[41] In other words, the explanation for this differential in remarriage rates must be sought in terms of social practice. Quite possibly, widows found it easier than widowers to run a household without the help of a spouse. But in addition, the figures presented here suggest that when his wife died, a man was more inclined to marry a single woman than a widow. Economic factors may have played some part in this: a spinster, by definition, could not be burdened with children and debts as a widow might be. But such arguments cannot be pushed too far, for after all, poor spinsters often married and wealthy widows often did not.

[41] Of the 272 marriages in the sample group for which this information can be obtained, 51.8% were terminated by the death of the husband and 48.2% by the death of the wife.

Widowers may have preferred to marry single women not so much for economic reasons as for social ones: perhaps a virgin was simply a more attractive candidate.

It was not only widowers who were more inclined to marry spinsters; to an even greater extent bachelors preferred to marry single women. One need only consider, after all, the selection of spouses made by the single men in our three sample groups:

Sample	*% Single Men Who Married:*	
	Spinsters	*Widows*
1601-1602	90.7	9.3
1701-1703	86.2	13.7
Letter-G (1579-1720)	87.1	12.9

Clearly, marriage to a widow was not the standard route by which a journeyman or other bachelor established himself as a householder; like the widower, he preferred to take a never-married woman to wife.

In a closed community, the consequences of all this would be easy to predict. The heavy demand for spinsters would tend to push the ages of women at first marriage downward. And, since bachelors had to compete with widowers for the available spinsters, one would expect their ages at first marriage to be driven upward. In short, a significant differential would emerge between the ages of men and women at first marriage: low for women and high for men. But was this actually the case in Nördlingen?

On the basis of the letter-G reconstitutions, it has been possible to determine the age at first marriage for over 400 men and women, and these findings are recorded in Table 2.3. The figures show a general increase in the age of marriage between the early seventeenth and the early eighteenth century, a development to which we shall turn shortly. At the moment, however, it is more important to compare the ages of men and women, and here the results run directly

TABLE 2.3. Ages of Men and Women at First Marriage

Period	*Men*	*Women*	*(Size of sample)*[a]
1611-1650			
Mean	25.1	25.1	(48 Men, 89 Women)
Median	25.1	25.1	
1651-1690			
Mean	26.2	26.0	(47 Men, 93 Women)
Median	25.3	25.6	
1691-1730			
Mean	29.2	30.2	(54 Men, 81 Women)
Median	28.6	30.9	

[a] The sample includes men whose surnames begin with G, their daughters and their brides (if spinsters at first marriage).

counter to what one might expect: during most of the seventeenth century the ages of men and women at first marriage were, on average, equal—and by the early eighteenth century the average age of women at first marriage was actually *higher* than that of men.

How was this possible? A number of different explanations might be adduced, but by far the most convincing one is derived from the fact that Nördlingen was, in fact, not a closed community, especially with regard to women. As Table 2.1 showed, the immigration of women always exceeded that of men. In fact, it is possible to suggest that the immigration of women was not only more readily tolerated, but in fact served a vital function: for it provided a useful source of brides for men—both single and widowed —who clearly preferred to marry spinsters than to find spouses among Nördlingen's surplus widows.

The more frequent acceptance of women into the community was, in fact, a matter of social policy. After all, the marriage of foreigners to citizens of Nördlingen was closely regulated by the magistrates. And throughout our period, the property requirements and the fees imposed on women who sought admission to the citizenry were substantially lower than those imposed on men.[42] The immigration of too many men—potential rivals to Nördlingen's own merchants and craftsmen—tended to be discouraged. But the immigration of women, to meet the constant demand for brides, was a process to which the community's leaders gave their sanction and support.

The pattern outlined here had, of course, one inevitable consequence: Nördlingen in the seventeenth and early eighteenth centuries had a perpetual surplus of widows. Throughout our period, in fact, one-sixth to one-fifth of all citizen households were headed by widows. And this, in turn, suggests that more women than men lived in the city. In the absence of census data, there is no way to establish the sex ratio of Nördlingen's inhabitants, but the burial registers do suggest strongly that there was always a surplus of women. Of the adult inhabitants of Nördlingen who were buried between 1621 and 1720, only 42 percent were men, while 58 percent were women.[43] Such an imbalance can only be accounted for by one thing: the fact that immigration by women was encouraged to a much greater extent than immigration by men.

V

THERE is no doubt that the Thirty Years War, and especially the events of the 1630's, constituted the most dramatic episode in the demographic history of early modern Nörd-

[42] Cf. notes 26 and 27 above. In addition, the entry fee for women was always 5 fl. less than that for men.

[43] Adults are defined here as persons aged thirteen and up at the time of death. Between 1621 and 1720, there were 9,694 adult burials: 4,082 (42.1%) were males and 5,612 (57.9%) were females. It is true that among children (up to age 12) buried during the same years, males exceeded females, but by a much smaller proportion: of 14,108 children buried, 7,328 (51.9%) were males and 6,780 (48.1%) were females. See Appendix I.

lingen. The immense mortality of the plague of 1634 and the reduction in the number of Nördlingen's inhabitants during the 1630's made an unforgettable impression on contemporaries. The importance of these events has continued to impress local historians to the present day—and rightly so. There is no need to underplay their impact. Nevertheless, the demographic data presented in this chapter suggest that one must not look too exclusively to the Thirty Years War in attempting to understand Nördlingen's demographic history, and, in particular, in attempting to explain the permanent reduction of the city's population which took place during the period studied in this book.

In the first place, elements of demographic decline are clearly evident in the period before the war. The striking fall in the number of baptisms between 1580 and 1620 certainly presaged a drop in the city's population level. This drop must have been associated with the city's increasingly restrictive policy toward immigration, at least immigration by men. Some steps in this direction were taken in 1585; more decisive and more effective steps were taken in 1607. Thus, it seems likely that even if the war had not intervened, the population of seventeenth-century Nördlingen would have dropped substantially below the sixteenth-century level.

Secondly, although the war and the huge mortality it brought in its train obviously reduced the population to a much greater extent than would have happened otherwise, the city did experience a steady, if gradual, demographic recovery after the war. Had it continued unchecked, in fact, this trend might eventually have merged into the general demographic upswing that characterized most European communities in the eighteenth century. But it did not continue. For, beginning around 1690, we can observe both an increase of deaths and a decrease of births in Nördlingen. These trends were no doubt responses to the military and climatic crises of the years 1690 to 1715. But another equally striking development must have heightened the effect of these trends. As Table 2.3 showed, the years 1691-1730 were characterized by a dramatic increase in the age of men and women at first marriage. As such this is not inconsistent with what we know of the "European marriage pattern."[44] Why it occurred in Nördlingen at precisely this time is difficult to say, but some plausible explanations do present themselves. As we shall see in the next chapter, this was a period of economic contraction, diminished upward mobility and increasingly uneven distribution of wealth in Nördlingen. In this atmosphere it must have taken longer for young women to accumulate their dowries and for young men to find the means necessary for founding a household. Inevitably the age at first marriage would be pushed upward.

Whatever the reasons, the effects of this development are obvious. Women were getting married, on average, four years later than they had during most of the seventeenth century. This would have reduced fertility in any community, but especially in a community where, once a woman was widowed, she was unlikely to marry for a second time. It is scarcely surprising, then, that the population of Nördlingen failed to increase in the course of the eighteenth century.

The changing size of Nördlingen's population was significantly affected by events over which the people of this city had no control: warfare, disease, climatic disasters. But to concentrate only on such factors in explaining Nördlingen's demographic history would be a mistake. For it was also shaped by strictly human factors—by individual attitudes about the choice of marriage partners and by communal policies about the admission or rejection of strangers. Helpless as they stood before the invasions of soldiers and diseases with which they were beset in early modern times, the people of Nördlingen never completely lost the capacity to shape their own demographic destiny.

[44] See J. Hajnal, "European Marriage Patterns in Perspective," in Glass and Eversley, *Population in History*, pp. 101-43.

Three

A City at Work: Occupational Patterns

AMONG the twelve immigrants who became citizens of Nördlingen in 1597 was one named Caspar Geissler, a rope-maker from the village of Pfefflingen in the Ries. Let us take a brief look as Caspar's career and those of his descendants (Figure 3.1) in seventeenth-century Nördlingen.[1]

Caspar was admitted to citizenship in September 1597, and the following month he married Elisabeth Aislinger, the daughter of a prosperous tanner. In 1606, after Elisabeth's death, Caspar got married again, this time to the daughter of the municipal grain inspector. And in 1629 he married for the third time, taking as his bride an immigrant to Nördlingen, a butcher's daughter from Lauingen on the Danube. Four years later Caspar died, leaving his widow as well as three daughters and four sons who had survived to adulthood.

Caspar remained a ropemaker all his life, but only one of his four sons followed in his footsteps. That was his third son, Caspar junior, who married a ropemaker's daughter and became a ropemaker himself. The oldest son, Johann, went into weaving; his wife was the daughter of a wealthy Nördlingen weaver. The second son, Georg, started out as a journeyman baker. In 1628, he got a tanner's daughter pregnant and was obliged to marry her. After this initial

1 The following is based principally on information in the parish registers and tax registers, and represents findings from the family reconstitution project described in Chapter Two. Additional details are from Karl Kern, "Die Söhne der Reichsstadt Nördlingen auf hohen Schulen," *JHVN*, 5 (1916), 43; and Gustav Wulz, *Die Nördlinger Wirtschaftsgerechtigkeiten* (Nördlingen, 1956), passim.

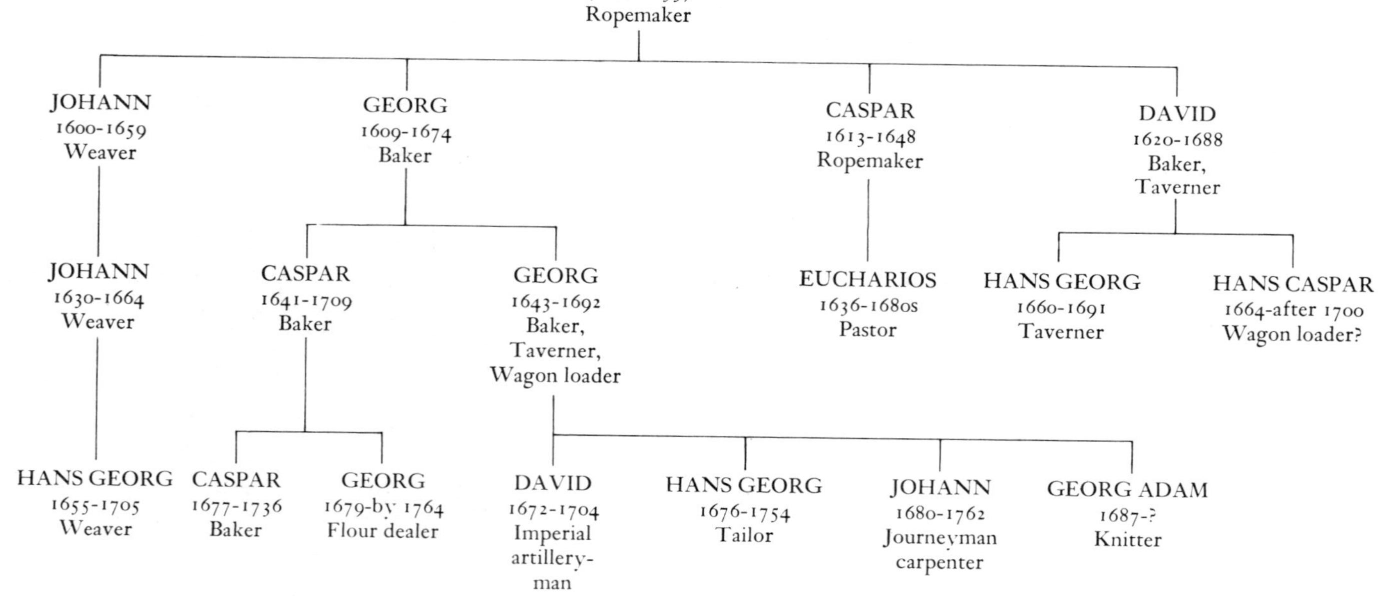

FIGURE 3.1. The Geissler Family (Males Only).

disgrace, however, he settled down to a successful career as a baker and rose in time to become an overseer of his guild.

The youngest of Caspar's four sons, David, had a more complicated career. Like his brother Georg, David started out as a baker. But his second wife, Margareta Jauffert, was the widow of a beer-taverner, and David took over the tavern when he married her in 1659. Fifteen years later David rebuilt and reopened the Gasthaus zum goldenen Löwen, an inn which had been destroyed by the bombardment of 1647. His third wife, Apollonia, whom he married in 1683, was the widow of the innkeeper "zum Strauss," but it is not clear whether David acquired this inn as well; when he died in 1688, he was listed only as the innkeeper "zum Löwen."

Three of Caspar's four sons, then, branched out into other occupations. Some of their own children, however, pursued their fathers' trades. Johann's only surviving son followed him into weaving, as did his son in turn. Georg, the baker, had two sons. The older one, Caspar, was also a baker, as was his own older son in the next generation. Georg's younger son, also named Georg, started out as a baker but later became a taverner and still later a simple wagon loader; his four sons drifted into four unrelated trades. David's older son inherited the inn "zum Löwen" from his father; for David's younger son the record is unclear, although he appears in one source as a wagon loader. Finally there is Caspar junior's son, Eucharios. He did not continue rope-making into a third generation but instead attended the University of Altdorf, married a clergyman's daughter and returned to the Ries to serve as pastor in the village of Hürnheim.

The Geisslers were not a "typical" family; no family ever is. But their history does illustrate the complexity of occupational patterns in seventeenth-century Nördlingen. A man's career might be determined by his family background, by his marriage, by his education, or by some accident we can no longer trace. One man would remain fixed for life in a single line of work, a second would move restlessly from one activity to another. Some men—like David Geissler—moved up the social ladder; others—like his obscure younger son—moved down. Seen on the individual level, these developments appear so random and complicated as to defy any reasoned analysis. But when we add the data about different individuals and different families together, some basic characteristics of Nördlingen's social and economic life will become apparent. For, in the last analysis, the occupational structure of Nördlingen was simply the end product of the ambitions, frustrations and fortunes of thousands of individuals like Caspar Geissler and his descendants.

I

In examining the occupational structure of Nördlingen, one must begin by looking at the community as a whole, or, to be more exact, at that part of the community about whose economic activities we have the most precise information: the male citizens. Certainly these men did not encompass the entire adult male working force, which also included Paktbürger, journeymen, apprentices and servants. And, of course, there were women who worked in Nördlingen—a few in independent capacities, such as midwives, many as domestics, most as assistants to their husbands or fathers. Nevertheless, if we conceive of Nördlingen's economic structure in terms of households rather than individuals, we will find that the figures presented here cover a very large part of the community, since about 90 percent of all households in the city were headed by citizens.

The most comprehensive source of information about Nördlingen's occupational structure is the series of annual tax registers. For any given year, the occupations of 96 to 99 percent of the male citizens can be determined.[2] As for the

[2] StR 1579-1724. In a few cases no occupation is given for a partic-

small remaining number for whom no occupation is given, at least some were men who simply had no occupation—often wealthy rentiers or men of property whose membership on the city council or court represented their only formal activity.

For women, too, occupations are normally listed—almost always in the form of "baker's widow," "butcher's widow," or the like. Many of these widows continued to carry on their husbands' trades with the assistance of journeymen. But there were undoubtedly also many who lacked the resources or assistance to carry on a trade actively. In fact there is no way to establish which women did and which did not continue to engage in their husbands' occupations. For males, on the other hand, one can assume that virtually all were actively engaged in the occupations with which they are designated. The male citizens, then, will receive the main share of our attention in the chapters to come.

About one-eighth of these male citizens underwent a change of occupation once or more during their lifetime—an important phenomenon which will be studied below. For present purposes it is enough to specify that in breaking the citizens down into occupational groups for any single year, the occupation for each citizen in that particular year—not one he formerly had or would later acquire—is the one that is taken into account. (About 6 percent of all citizens are listed as holding two occupations simultaneously at some point or other during their careers. But as a rule such double designations refer to situations in which a citizen had retained his old trade identification or membership in his craft while actually devoting his energy to some new activity. Certainly, in most cases the second-listed occupation reflects the more recent and up-to-date activity. Accordingly, in cases of double designations the practice has been adopted of always recording the second occupation for the year in question.)

ular year, but the individual's occupation can be determined from an earlier tax book.

II

WHAT, then, do the tax records reveal about the occupational structure of Nördlingen? We can begin by looking at the situation toward the beginning of our period, before proceeding to find out how—or whether—things changed over the following century and a half.

Nördlingen had 1,541 active citizens in 1579. Virtually all of them headed independent households. This is certainly true of the 1,266 men in the group; it is also true of most, though perhaps not all, of the women: 268 widows and 7 spinsters. In most of these households a craft or trade was being carried out, for Nördlingen in 1579 was preeminently a community of artisans. Well over sixty different crafts were plied in the city, and they absorbed the energies of four-fifths of the citizenry; the remaining fifth were engaged in variety of commercial, professional, administrative and other noncraft occupations.[3]

By far the most important single craft in the city was the production of the coarse woolen cloth known as "Loden." The 269 male wool weavers represented fully one-fifth of the total number of male citizens. Yet even this does not completely reflect the central role of wool production in the city's economic structure, for there were also 66 wool weavers' widows, at least some of whom continued to produce cloth through journeymen; and the city's 11 cloth shearers, 3 dyers, 2 carders and 1 bleacher were closely involved in the production of Loden at various stages. Thus, over 300 households participated in the city's chief industry.

Nor was wool weaving the city's only textile trade. Of the male citizens, 64 were *Geschlachtwander*, or fine-cloth weavers, and 15 were involved in the rather small industry of linen weaving. There were 24 tailors, 11 hatters and 4 craftsmen engaged in other aspects of cloth manufacture or

[3] For a complete breakdown of the male citizens by occupation in 1579, see Appendix II.

finishing. Altogether, the production of textiles and cloth occupied 31.9 percent of the male citizenry in 1579.

Leather and leather goods represented the second great sphere of production of Nördlingen. Tanning, in fact, was the second largest craft, with 108 representatives in 1579. Almost an equal number of craftsmen were engaged in derivative leather trades: above all in shoemaking, but also in the manufacture of purses, belts, saddles and straps. In addition, 29 citizens were furriers.

Textiles, clothing, leather, leather goods, furs—653 male citizens were engaged in the production of these items, which included among them the principal export goods of the community. Certainly, not every one of these individuals was himself linked economically to the world outside; many of the tailors and many of the shoemakers, for example, may have catered largely to local needs. But it is safe to say that about half of the citizens in 1579 were participating in production for the export-oriented sphere of the city's economy.

And what about the other half? Construction trades, wood- and metalworking, ropemaking, and a variety of other crafts occupied an additional 18.7 percent of the male citizens. Straddling the division between crafts and distributive trades were the food and drink trades; if taverners are included, these trades account for 13 percent of the total. The remaining citizens were devoted to occupations with no craft connotations: commerce and retailing, learned professions, city administration, carting, menial work and a host of other service occupations. For 2.8 percent of the male citizens, no occupation is given in 1579.

In a community devoted so substantially to textile production, the number of textile merchants recorded in 1579—only five—appears to be tiny. In fact this figure is probably somewhat deceptive. Wealthy men were occasionally listed without occupations, even though they had appeared in earlier tax registers as cloth merchants. And even a few of the wealthiest wool weavers may have engaged in some

TABLE 3.1 Ten Most Common Occupations (Among Male Citizens) in Five Selected Years

	1579		*1615*		*1652*		*1700*		*1724*	
	Rank	*No.*	*Rank*	*No.*	*Rank*	*No.*	*Rank*	*No.*	*Rank*	*No.*
Wool Weavers	1	(269)	1	(344)	1	(113)	1	(138)	1	(134)
Tanners	2	(108)	2	(137)	2	(59)	2[a]	(75)	4	(69)
Fine-Cloth Weavers	3	(64)	8	(32)	—	—	—	—	—	—
Shoemakers	4	(60)	4[a]	(61)	5	(34)	7	(35)	7	(41)
Butchers	5	(54)	3	(68)	3	(51)	2[a]	(75)	2	(101)
Bakers	6	(48)	4[a]	(61)	4	(48)	4	(50)	5	(55)
Taverners	7	(36)	6	(51)	6	(33)	5	(41)	6	(46)
Furriers	8	(29)	7	(44)	7	(21)	10	(14)	10	(24)
Tailors	9[a]	(24)	9	(30)	8	(18)	8[a]	(21)	8	(36)
Carpenters	9[a]	(24)	—	—	—	—	—	—	—	—
Ropemakers	—	—	10	(29)	10	(15)	8[a]	(21)	—	—
Shopkeepers	—	—	—	—	9	(16)	—	—	—	—
Linen Weavers	—	—	—	—	—	—	6	(38)	3	(65)
Cloth Weavers	—	—	—	—	—	—	—	—	9	(26)
(Total No. of Male Citizens)	(1,266)		(1,456)		(715)		(952)		(1,113)	

[a] Tied.

commerce in cloths. But no matter how the number of merchants is augmented, the huge numerical preponderance of production crafts over commercial trades remains one of the striking characteristics of the community in 1579.

III

In industrial and postindustrial societies, massive changes in the economic structure of a community are normal in the course of a century. In preindustrial societies the tempo of change is less swift. Textiles, leather goods, victualing—these were the main sectors of Nördlingen's economy in 1720 as they had been in 1580. Within this broadly stable framework, however, some striking shifts in the city's occupational structure can be observed.

These changes can be traced in detail in Appendix II, which provides the complete occupational breakdown for five selected years between 1579 and 1724. Some industries virtually disappeared. The number of citizens engaged in the manufacture of weapons and armor, for example, dwindled from twenty in 1579 to only two in 1724. By contrast, the book industry expanded: whereas in 1579 the city had no printers and only two bookbinders, by 1724 it had four of each.

Table 3.1 summarizes the data for the city's most important occupations. Here, too, some striking changes are apparent. The wool weavers, for example, although they were always the most important craft, declined from 21.2 percent of the total in 1579 to only 12 percent in 1724. Tanners and shoemakers also declined in importance, and fine-cloth weavers dropped out of the top ten entirely. Butchers, on the other hand, rose dramatically in importance: not only did they advance from fifth place to second, but they more than doubled their proportion between 1579 and 1724.

These examples, in fact, give hint of a more fundamental

TABLE 3.2. Male Citizens in Each General Occupational Category in Five Selected Years (percent)

Category	*1579*	*1615*	*1652*	*1700*	*1724*
Textile and Clothing Crafts	31.9	31.5	22.7	25.7	27.3
Leather and Fur Crafts	19.7	19.3	17.9	14.8	13.1
Other Crafts	18.7	17.8	18.0	19.0	18.1
Food and Drink Trades	13.0	14.9	20.4	19.9	20.4
Commerce and Retailing	1.9	3.4	3.8	3.6	4.4
Learned and Bureaucratic Occupations	6.5	8.1	10.4	9.6	8.6
Other Noncraft Occupations	5.8	4.0	3.8	6.6	6.1
No Occupation Given	2.7	0.9	3.1	0.8	2.0
(Total No. of Cases)	(1,266)	(1,456)	(715)	(952)	(1,113)

development, which can be observed clearly in Table 3.2. Here the entire spectrum of occupations is grouped into eight broad categories of economic or social function.[4] From 1579 to 1615, the proportion of citizens in most categories remained relatively constant. Between 1615 and 1652, however—that is to say, during the period of the Thirty Years War—two major changes occurred: a sharp decline in the number of textile workers and a simultaneous increase in the proportion of citizens engaged in the food and drink trades. The next seventy years saw some further changes, notably a pronounced decline in the importance of the leather and fur sector. But the basic result is the same whether one looks at 1652 or 1724: the proportion of citizens devoted to the production of textiles, clothing, furs and leather—which encompassed the major export products of the community—decreased from about 50 percent before the Thirty Years War to about 40 percent after it. At the same time, the city experienced a substantial increase in the

[4] The occupations which fall into each of these larger categories can be determined from Appendix II.

proportion of citizens devoted to food production, distribution of goods, civic administration and other services—in short, an increase in the number of those oriented to meeting local needs.

These changes in the nature of Nördlingen's economy were reflected in the history of the annual trade fair. For the Thirty Years War not only brought about a reduction in the number of merchants who attended the Pentecost fair, but also contributed to basic structural changes: long-distance trading in textiles, furs and luxury products decreased in importance, while the exchange of food and other basic consumption goods came to play a more central role. Although the postwar years did bring a restoration to earlier levels in the number of visitors, the structural changes that occurred during the war years were never fully reversed.[5]

There was one important development, however, whose origins antedated the Thirty Years War: the decline of fine-cloth weaving. From a total of 64 artisans in 1579, which made this the city's third-ranking occupation, the number of fine-cloth weavers dropped to 32 in 1615 and a single representative in 1652. Although the craft revived slightly in later years, it never regained its former importance. This development is linked to the fine-cloth weavers' dependence on a distant source of supply; in fact, their troubles appear to have begun as early as the 1560's, when the supply of British and Flemish wool which they normally used began to be cut off by political disturbances in the Netherlands.[6] The Thirty Years War, of course, accentuated their difficulties in obtaining the special wool they needed. The place of the fine-cloth weaving in the city's economy, however, was to some extent taken over by the growing importance of linen manufacture, which rose from relative obscurity

[5] By 1668 the number of merchants registered at the fair had again reached the typical prewar level of 300, although the nature of their wares tended to be somewhat different. Steinmeyer, *Nördlinger Pfingstmesse*, pp. 155-57.

[6] See Endres, *Wirtschaftsbeziehungen*, pp. 160-62.

to become the second most important branch of Nördlingen's textile industry by the early eighteenth century. The reason is simple to find. Unlike British and Flemish wool, the flax which linen weavers required was grown in the region and was thus available close to home.

The changing relative importance of these two crafts was part of a broader pattern: the increasingly local orientation of Nördlingen's commerce. A number of long-term developments common to many south German cities certainly contributed to this trend: the general decline in the importance of German trade routes to Italy, for example, and the growing competition to urban production posed by rural craftsmen. But it is also clear, at least in the case of Nördlingen, that the Thirty Years War greatly accelerated these trends. By blocking routes and disrupting commerce, the war inevitably contributed to a decline in the importance of the city's export-oriented production crafts. At the same time, of course, as a result of the wartime situation, those trades which met the most basic needs of the populace —the victualing trades—expanded in their importance. To be sure, there was a substantial revival of commerce in and through Nördlingen after the war. But the changes wrought during thirty years of economic disruption and population loss were too substantial to be reversed, and the new balance of occupations in the community persisted.

IV

So far we have looked at changes in the occupational structure of the community as a whole. But, in order to understand the nature and organization of work in Nördlingen more fully, we must also look at occupational changes on the individual level. After all, long-term shifts in the economic structure were of little moment to the individual citizen of Nördlingen; far more important were the obstacles and opportunities he confronted in his own life. How much flexibility did the individual have in choosing—and changing

—his career? How tightly knit were the different occupational groups, and how hard was it to cross the boundaries between them? The answers to these questions will help us appreciate what the occupational system of Nördlingen meant to the people who participated in it.

One important measure of occupational mobility is intergenerational: how often did sons follow their fathers' occupations? The answer to this question would suggest the degree of solidarity within occupational groups. Closely related to this is the problem of intermarriage: how often did marriages link families of the same occupational background? Both of these questions can be explored by looking at the Nördlingen marriage registers: a groom's occupation, as listed at his first marriage, can be compared both to that of his own father and to that of his bride's father. (If the bride was a widow—which occurred in about one-eighth of all cases—the relevant comparison is to the occupation of her late husband.) The results are most meaningful if occupations are defined in the narrowest sense: among weavers, for example, one must make distinctions between wool weavers, linen weavers, fine-cloth weavers and so on—distinctions that reflect the differences in training and organization among the crafts themselves.

Table 3.3 provides this two-way comparison for three sample groups: men who married in 1601-02 and in 1701-03, as well as all male members of the reconstituted letter-G families.[7] From this Table it will be apparent that almost three-fifths of all men followed their fathers' occupations; heritability of occupations in the paternal line was clearly the norm in Nördlingen. Nevertheless, two out of every five men entered nonpaternal occupations. As the case of the Geisslers showed, it was quite possible for the son of a craftsman to do so; but switching of occupations was even more common among noncraft families. This can be illustrated by some of the largest families in our letter-G sample.

[7] Cf. above, Chapter Two.

TABLE 3.3. Heritability of Occupations

	Occupation of Groom at First Marriage (%)						
	Same as His Father		*Different From Father*				
	and same as bride's father or prev. husband	*but diff. from bride's father or prev. husband*	*but same as bride's father or prev. husband*	*and diff. from bride's father or prev. husband*	*No. Used*	*Incomplete Data*	*Total*
1601-1602 Sample	16.1	41.1	21.4	21.4	56	30	86
Letter G, 1579-1650	18.1	41.9	13.3	26.7	105	40	145
Letter G, 1651-1720	13.0	44.0	13.0	30.0	100	11	111
1701-1703 Sample	15.1	43.0	12.8	29.1	86	1	87

Consider the Geiders: Caspar Geider, a tanner, had twelve male descendants who reached maturity and married in Nördlingen between 1580 and 1720; of these twelve, eight were tanners like Caspar himself. Or the Goschenhofers: sixteen male descendents of Wolf Goschenhofer, a butcher, married during the same 140-year period; thirteen of them were butchers. By contrast, consider the progeny of Veit Genzler, a surgeon who married in 1587. Twenty-six of his descendents married before 1720; seven of them were surgeons or barbers, but there were also seven government officials, three retailers, three tinsmiths, and two each of teachers, painters and weavers.

To what extent, however, did marriages link families who practiced the same occupations? If we return again to Table 3.3, we can see that there was no pronounced tendency to marry within occupational groups. Of the 60 percent who entered their fathers' occupations, substantially less then one-third took brides from the same background. And among the 40 percent of men who abandoned the parental path and entered new careers, in all but the smallest sample group only one-third married women connected with that new occupation. The great majority of marriages, in fact, cut across occupational lines. Of course there were cases—like that of David Geissler, who acquired a tavern along with his second wife—where marriages were specifically linked to occupational change. But as a whole, marriage did not function systematically as a stepping-stone into new careers, nor did it serve as a mechanism to promote occupational solidarity. Occupational background was not a major factor in the selection of marriage partners.

In short, paternity played a much larger role than matrimony in determining a man's career. This reflects, of course, the fact that a man began training for his future occupation long before he got married. This is not to say that men necessarily worked as children: in fact, in Nördlingen's largest industry, wool weaving, the minimum age for apprenticeship was 16 years.[8] But men were not supposed to get married before the age of 23 and, as we have seen, the average age of marriage was always higher than that.[9] Thus, by the time he got married, a man may have spent five or ten years in training for his craft, and his occupation had long since been determined.

V

NOT every man remained fixed in his vocation for life. A second measure of occupational mobility is intragenerational: once a man had got married and established a household, how likely was he to change his occupation? To answer this question, the careers of males who became citizens during the first ninety years of our study have been examined.[10] A total of 3,608 men are recorded as having begun their adult careers between 1580 and 1670.[11] Of these, a total of 550, or 15.3 percent, changed their occupations at some point during their lifetimes; 86 changed more than once, with about a third of these reverting to their original occupations and the remainder moving into still other fields.

There does appear to have been a slight increase in the frequency of occupational mobility after the Thirty Years

[8] Ebert, *Lodweberei*, p. 52.

[9] Cf. above, Chapter Two, esp. Table 2.3.

[10] The findings that follow are based on the tax records at six-year intervals for 1579 to 1700. (Data for 1712 and 1724, although used elsewhere in this study, were not used in this analysis.) The subjects actually considered are confined to those who began their careers by 1670, since those who started after 1670 would include an ever-increasing number of men whose careers could be only partially reconstructed. For those who became citizens before 1670, one has either the whole career or at least the first thirty years.

[11] In fact the total number of men who were enrolled as citizens between 1580 and 1670 was slightly higher, by about 130. As explained in Chapter Two, data were taken at six-year intervals, so that men whose careers began and ended between two such years are not recorded. In light of their short careers, however, very few of them are likely to have undergone any change of occupation.

War: of the men who started out before the war, less than 15 percent changed occupations; of those who started out after the war, 18 percent did.[12] But the basic pattern remained constant: intragenerational occupational mobility was a rarity in Nördlingen. Altogether 85 percent of the citizens retained their original occupations throughout their adult lifetimes.

Yet occupational mobility was not impossible, and something about the opportunities open to citizens in early modern Nördlingen will become apparent if we look at the 15 percent who did make a change. Accordingly, we shall take the 550 men who did so and compare their first and second occupations. It must be pointed out that in about 125 cases—over one-fifth of the total—there is no sharp break between the first and second occupations. Instead, the second one is added and listed side by side with the first, at least for a number of years. For example, a man who had been a baker might now be listed as a "baker and innkeeper." Or a craftsman might be appointed to a city office while still retaining some identification with his old craft; perhaps he would continue to supervise an apprentice or journeyman when he was free from official duties. But such an occurrence reflected a significant change in a man's sphere of activity, and by

[12] This statement can be illustrated by the following Table, in which the first column reports the total number of persons admitted to active citizenship in each period, the second column lists the number of persons within each group who were to undergo one or more changes of occupation during their lifetimes, and the third column reports the percentage that this second group represents in relation to the total group:

	I	II	III (%)
1580-1597	901	134	14.9
1598-1615	843	125	14.8
1616-1633	789	111	14.1
1634-1652	535	83	15.5
1653-1670	540	97	18.0
(Total)	(3,608)	(550)	(15.3)

including these cases in our total we can gain a more realistic and more complete statistical picture of occupational change in Nördlingen.[13]

And now, what changes did these 550 men experience? In the first place, it is clear that for certain occupations the outflow vastly exceeded the inflow. For example, 119 men began as wool weavers and moved into other occupations, while only 9 men moved from other activities into wool weaving. Similarly, in 45 of these cases tanning was the first occupation—but in only 6 cases was it the second one. On the other hand, there were occupations which registered a much higher inflow than outflow. For example, 74 men switched from other activities to become taverners, while only 27 men moved from being taverners into other occupations. In fully 132 cases, men became middle- or low-ranking civic functionaries (including watchmen), but only 8 men moved out of this kind of position into other occupations.

The pattern suggested by these examples becomes even clearer in the mobility matrix presented in Table 3.4, in which all occupations have been grouped into seven broad categories and first and second occupations have been cross-tabulated. A number of facts become immediately apparent.

First, a total of 167 cases involve movement within the same general category. Typical of such cases are the 25 butchers, bakers and brewers who became taverners. In-

[13] For the sake of completeness, it should be added that among the 3,608 men who became citizens in 1580-1670, there were about 70 for whom two occupations were listed simultaneously from the very start. Presumably in most such cases, the individual concerned had been trained for a certain craft or trade (the first-listed occupation), yet from the very beginning of his adult career he actually carried out a different or a more broadly defined occupation (the second-listed one). Or sometimes the individual may even have carried out both occupations at once. But either way, these cases cannot be regarded as instances of mid-career occupational change or mobility, and accordingly they have not been included among the 550 men analyzed here.

TABLE 3.4. Occupational Mobility Patterns, 1580-1700
(Cross-tabulation of 1st and 2nd occupational category of each man who became an adult citizen, 1580-1670, and subsequently changed his occupation)

First Occupational Category	*Total No. in Each 1st Occ. Category*	*Second Occupational Category*						
		Crafts	*Food/ Drink*	*Commerce*	*Learned Occ.*	*City Office*	*Other Occ.*	*No Occ.*
Craftsmen	288	*53*	53	32	11	81	58	0
Food and Drink Trades	84	4	*43*	6	0	18	12	1
Commerce and Retailing	28	5	4	*11*	1	4	2	1
Learned Occupations	46	0	0	2	*33*	8	2	1
City Office	32	1	2	0	4	*13*	2	10
Other Occupations	33	5	4	1	0	8	*14*	1
No Occupation	39	7	2	6	6	11	7	*0*
Total No.	550	75	108	58	55	143	97	14

Italics refer to cases of occupational change within the same general category.

deed, in about one-quarter of these 167 cases, it might be argued that the recorded change actually involved only a change in designations for essentially the same occupation.[14] Nevertheless, this leaves a total of well over 500 cases in which the second occupation was distinctly different from the first, and in well over two-thirds of all cases the new occupation represented a completely different sphere of activity.

Particularly striking in this respect are the craftsmen. Of the 288 craftsmen who changed their occupations, only one-

[14] A characteristic instance would be the situation in which a person was transferred or promoted within the municipal bureaucracy, for example from a lower-ranking clerk to council or hospital clerk.

sixth switched to other crafts. The remaining five-sixths turned to completely different types of endeavor: the victualing trades; commercial, learned and service occupations; or, most frequently of all, middle- or low-ranking civic office. The reason for this is clear: once the commitment to one craft was made, the young man had to pass through long years of training as an apprentice and journeyman, and then overcome the hurdle of demonstrating the proficiency and personal probity that entitled him to admission as a master. Thus, if he failed in or became dissatisfied with his chosen trade, a master would rarely be in a position to learn and enter a different craft. To be sure, it did happen occasionally, although in most such cases the new craft either was closely related to the old one or else was a small and relatively unorganized one: knitting, for example. Normally, however, the unsuccessful, dissatisfied or ambitious master would have to turn outside the closed world of the crafts entirely in order to find a substitute for—or in some cases a supplement to—his original source of income.

Thus, it was noncraft activities which made possible most of what movement occurred between occupations. As we have seen, the most common second occupations were middle- and low-ranking municipal offices—toll collector, inspector, watchman, gatekeeper, hospital servant and the like, all jobs which required little or no specific training. In fact, these were not normally activities in which a citizen would begin his adult life: of the entire group of 3,608 men who became citizens from 1580 to 1670, only 37 began in one of these lower civic functions. On the other hand, as we have seen, 132 men acquired such posts as their second occupation. As indicated above, many of them continued, at least for a while, to be designated in the records with both their old and new occupations simultaneously. In some cases, one must assume, even if they were not personally able to carry out their trades, their shops may have been maintained by their wives or journeymen. But in many other cases, the retention of the craft label probably only connoted a sense of continuing identification with the trade for which a man had been trained. In other words, while the council would almost never permit a citizen to carry on two actual crafts at once, many noncraft activities—especially city offices—were at least formally compatible with continued membership in a craft organization.

What this suggests, of course, is that occupational mobility did not necessarily or even normally involve a change in social status. Nor, in fact, was a minor civic office automatically more lucrative than a craft. Such an office did, however, offer something the craft did not: a steady and reliable income, either as a substitute for or as a supplement to the original source of income. Even if it did not involve movement along a verifiable scale of social status, occupational mobility could play a crucial role in the citizens' lives, for it provided an element of flexibility and permitted individual adjustments to compensate for the overall rigidity of the craft structure.

VI

At first glance, the seventeenth century does not appear to have been a dynamic period in Nördlingen's economic history. Technically, the processes of production remained unchanged: woolens were woven and hides were tanned exactly the same way in 1720 as they had been in 1580. Nor were there any notable changes in the organization of the handicrafts and in the training that young men underwent in order to qualify as masters. Opportunities for occupational mobility were limited: three out of every five men followed their fathers' occupations; more than four out of every five remained fixed for life in the trades in which they started out. Opportunities for immigrants were also limited: as we have seen, only a restricted number received permission to settle down and work in Nördlingen on a permanent basis.

This does not mean, however, that the economic system

of Nördlingen remained static during these years. For in fact the Thirty Years War wrought a pronounced and permanent change in the city's economic structure: the number of households devoted to production for export declined—both absolutely and relatively—while the locally oriented sectors of the economy, above all the victualing trades, expanded in importance.

Nor was this the only important change in Nördlingen's economic system. In fact, when we turn from the distribution and mobility of occupations to the distribution and mobility of wealth, we shall find evidence of considerably more fluctuations, both in the history of the community as a whole and in the careers of individual citizens. Similarly, when we turn from the formal occupational structure to the actual working relationships among different sectors of the community—for example, between merchants and artisans—we shall find profound changes underway by the end of the seventeenth century. Occupational patterns are the indispensable starting-point for any investigation of the city's social and economic system. But only when we have looked at the wealth of Nördlingen—how much people owned, and how they gained or lost it—will we begin to appreciate what it meant to live and work as a citizen of early modern Nördlingen.

Four

Rich Man, Poor Man: The Wealth of Nördlingen

BETWEEN the years 1580 and 1585, fifteen shoemakers were enrolled as adult citizens of Nördlingen. Ten of these men were native-born sons of citizens; the remaining five were immigrants—three from nearby communities, one from Württemberg and one probably from Franconia.[1] Table 4.1 records the wealth of these fifteen shoemakers at six-year intervals, based on their assessments in the city's tax registers.[2] It also indicates, indirectly, their longevity: nine of the fifteen were still alive in 1615 and three were still living in 1627, more than forty years after they had begun their careers. All of them, however, had died by 1633, thus escaping the most dismal phase of the Thirty Years War in Nördlingen.

Take a look at the wealth patterns of these fifteen men. In the first place, one will notice the great inequality of wealth among them, both in the initial year and in subsequent ones. In 1585, for example, Michael Gall and Georg Wasser were assessed at 25 fl. each, while Martin Deffner enjoyed a fortune twelve times as large. In 1609 the distribution of wealth was even less equal, ranging from a minimum of 25 fl. to a maximum of 900 fl. Clearly the shoemak-

1 Bürgerbuch 1513-1672. (I have identified "Dietershofen," the place of origin for Matthias Kienlin, as Dietenhofen in Franconia.) Strictly speaking, the period referred to in the opening sentence runs from November 1579 to November 1585, in accordance with the tax cycle. For convenience, however, I have referred to it as 1580 to 1585, and a similar usage has been followed throughout this chapter and in Appendix VI.

2 StR 1585-1627. See below for a detailed discussion of the tax registers and the way in which data from them has been interpreted.

TABLE 4.1. Shoemakers Who Became Citizens in 1580-85: Their Wealth at Six-Year Intervals (fl.)

	1585	*1591*	*1597*	*1603*	*1609*	*1615*	*1621*	*1627*
Anthoni Anboss[a]	150	100	25	25	25	25		
Friedrich Bachmair	50	100	250	400	600	700	900	800
Caspar Beck	50	25	25	25				
Georg Beck	50	25	50	100	150	150	150	50
Martin Deffner[a]	300	400	400					
Michael Gall	25	25	25	50				
Matthias Kienlin[a]	50	50	50	50	100	200		
Jacob Klein[a]	150	200						
Adam Knoll	50	50	150	150	200	100	50	
Hans Kom[a]	50	100	200	200	300	50		
Thomas Mair	150	100	50					
Hans Ostermair	250	350	450	700	900			
Martin Scherzhemer	50	50	50	50	50	100	200	200
Matthias Sellner	100	100	100	600	800	600		
Georg Wasser	25	25	50	50	50	25		

[a] Immigrant.

ing craft was not homogeneous in terms of the wealth of its members.

At the same time, one can see that most of these men were able to increase their personal wealth in the course of their lifetimes—most spectacularly in the case of Friedrich Bachmair. But there were also men who suffered downward mobility, such as Anthoni Amboss. And there were men who first increased their wealth and then, in mid-career, began to lose it—witness Adam Knoll. The experiences of these fifteen contemporaneous shoemakers certainly varied tremendously.

All this information, of course, pertains to just a handful of citizens. To analyze the distribution of wealth and the extent of wealth mobility in Nördlingen as a whole we shall have to work on a much wider scale: some 6,500 men and 2,500 women are recorded as having been active citizens at some point between 1579 and 1724. Yet the examples of these fifteen shoemakers do illustrate the kind of data from the Nördlingen tax registers on which this analysis will be based. In addition, they suggest two questions which the use of these data will raise. First, there is the problem of reliability: can the tax registers be trusted as an accurate source of information about the wealth of Nördlingen's citizens? Second, there is the problem of money: can these data be used in a way that takes into account fluctuations in the value of the gulden? We shall consider these two problems before we proceed to the main question: what was the structure of wealth in early modern Nördlingen and how did it change during a century and a half of peace and war?

I

THE Steuerregister, or tax registers, of Nördlingen were maintained to record one type of information: the payment by citizens of the annual tax on citizen-owned property. This property tax was, in fact, not a particularly burdensome one: the amount paid by a poor man in 1579, for example, might equal about one-and-a-half days' wages.[3] Yet payment of this tax, no matter how small, was regarded as one of a citizen's principal civic obligations. Among other things, it was through these payments that the authorities kept track of who was and who was not still to be regarded as a citizen. Failure to pay the tax for three or four successive years might easily cause someone to lose his citizenship.

The formula for this property tax was simple, and it remained unchanged throughout the entire period under study: each year each citizen had to pay one two-hundredth, that is, one-half of 1 percent, of the assessed value of his and his wife's real and personal property. For example, if a man owned property worth 100 fl., his tax was

[3] Low-ranking city functionaries, such as Stadtknechte or wardens of beggars, received a weekly wage of 30 krz., or, if we were to assume a six-day week, 5 krz. a day. By comparison, the minimum tax payment in 1579 was either 1 lb. (roughly 7 krz.) or 7½ krz. (See KR 1579: Ausgaben, for wages cited.)

½ fl.; if he owned property worth 200 fl., his tax was 1 fl.; and so on.[4]

What was taxed? Precise lists of items to be taxed are not available before the eighteenth century, but according to decrees and tax oaths of the sixteenth and seventeenth centuries, all property, "immovable and movable, within the city and without," was to be included.[5] Thus, not only were a citizen's house, garden and fields subject to the tax, but also his household furnishings, plate, linen, jewelry, livestock, cash and other tangible assets.[6] Debts were also taken into account in the assessments, with amounts owed to the citizen added to the total assessment and liabilities subtracted from it.[7]

[4] Tax payments were normally rounded off to the nearest ⅛ fl. or (from about 1621 onward) to the nearest ¼ fl., meaning that we can usually calculate the corresponding property value to the nearest 25 fl. or 50 fl. For very wealthy citizens the tax was often rounded off only to the nearest ½ fl., making it possible to calculate property values only to the nearest 100 fl. It should also be mentioned that in any given year a few citizens would be listed as having made no tax payment. But most citizens, even the very poor, were required to pay a minimum amount. At the beginning of our period, this minimum was ⅛ fl., or 7½ krz. (To be quite precise, the very poorest were permitted to pay 1 lb.) By 1621 this minimum had increased to 1/5 fl., or 12 krz., and a few years later it increased to ¼ fl., or 15 krz. In 1700 it was once again reduced to ⅛ fl.

In the computing process for this study, all fractions of a gulden were converted to one-place decimals.

[5] This phrase appears, for example, in StR 1552-54 (under "Stewr Ayd"): only the weapons maintained for defense of the city could be excluded from the assessment. The same phrase, without mention of the weapons, though with certain other qualifications, appears in the municipal ordinance of 1650: Schott, *Sammlungen*, vol. 1, p. 213.

[6] Most of these items are mentioned explicitly only in the eighteenth century, e.g., in the 1732 Steuer-Ordnung and Steuer-Eid, printed in Lettenmeyer, *Finanzwirtschaft*, pp. 219-28. But there is no reason to doubt that such items were also included in the earlier requirement that all movable and immovable property be taxed.

[7] Again, specific formulas for the partial or full assessment of different kinds of debts are only available in the eighteenth century, e.g., in the Steuer Ordnung of 1716 in OB 1706-31, fols. 552-64. But

Real property was normally assessed at its most recent purchase price or (if obtained by inheritance or marriage) at its real value, except that after the Thirty Years War the custom was instituted of assigning a fixed value per unit of size to various kinds of agricultural acreage.[8] The principles governing the assessment of personal property are more difficult to document for most of our period. In the eighteenth century, formulas were laid down for the fractional assessment of such property: livestock to be assessed at one-half its real value, jewelry and household goods at one-third, and so on.[9] During the period of our study, however, it seems probable that most personal property was assessed at its full value. A tax ordinance of 1651, for example, seems to exclude only household items from the provision that a citizen should assess personal property "in the value that it is worth to him."[10]

Uncertainties about the precise methods of assessing personal property, however, must not obscure the importance of the very fact that such property was included in the assessments. For our results are at least substantially spared the bias that ensues when tax data are based on real property alone. Whatever the precise formulas may have been, it is clear that the property tax reflected the wealth of each citizen's household in a very broad sense of the term.

The property tax system was based, during our period, on

---

there can be little doubt that debts were also included in the assessments during the earlier period, and from late seventeenth-century inventories, e.g., those cited below, it would appear that debts were normally assessed at full value.

[8] Rates for assessments of fields outside the city are specified in ordinances of 1651 (OB 1641-88, fol. 106a), 1716 (OB 1706-31, fols. 557ff.), and 1732 (in Lettenmeyer, *Finanzwirtschaft*, p. 228). The principle that houses and other real property within the city should be assessed at the purchase price or, if obtained by inheritance, marriage or gift, at the real value, is explicitly stated only in the 1732 ordinance (ibid.) but presumably had prevailed throughout.

[9] Lettenmeyer, ibid.

[10] Schott, *Sammlungen*, vol. 1, p. 213.

a three-year cycle. In the first year, each citizen swore an oath, assessed his own property, and paid the appropriate tax. During the second and third years, this citizen (or, if he died, his heirs) had to pay the same amount. Then a new cycle would begin, with new oaths sworn and new, up-to-date assessments made.[11] The practice of trienniel revisions means that the amounts quoted in the tax books did not represent outdated, traditional assessments, but instead were brought constantly up to date with the changing circumstances of each citizen's life.

The fact that property was self-assessed, however, raises another important question: were the assessments honest? Certainly there were a few instances of cheating on taxes, but social and legal controls were sufficient to keep such episodes to a barest minimum. The very fact that assessments were accompanied by an oath—in an age when oaths still carried considerable moral authority—certainly contributed to accurate reporting. But the civic authorities also had more practical means at their disposal. In the first place, virtually all property transactions within the city had to be witnessed and registered by the city council.[12] Moreover, when the council suspected that a person had underassessed his property, the city was entitled to buy out that person's property, using his own assessment as the price.[13] No doubt this clause of the tax ordinances served as a deterrent to underreporting.

[11] A detailed description of the workings of this three-year cycle is found in StR 1552-54 (in the section "Wer und wie man Steuern soll" of the "Ordnung der Bürgerlichen Jarsteur").

[12] The Pfandbücher maintained by the city government recorded every transaction in which payments were to be made in installments. In addition, the city stipulated that no contract was valid in the city unless it had been prepared by one of a small handful of city clerks. This stipulation appears in the 1650 statutes (Schott, *Sammlungen*, vol. 1, p. 214), which for the most part codified long-standing legal principles.

[13] See StR 1549-51, "Ordnung der Bürgerlichen Jarsteur"; the ordinance was originally promulgated in 1528.

Sometimes cheating did take place. As a rule, it was discovered only posthumously, but when it was, the magistrates could impose heavy fines on the cheater's heirs. And at least during the Thirty Years War they actually did so to a staggering extent. In 1635, for example, an inventory of the estate of Peter Haaf showed that he had underassessed his property by 1,000 fl.—in other words, he had paid 5 fl. less per year than he owed. For this transgression, the city imposed and actually collected a fine of 10,000 fl. from Haaf's estate.[14] Similarly, in 1641 the wealthy merchant Balthas Adam's estate was fined 5,000 fl. for tax irregularities.[15] Members of the ruling elite, moreover, enjoyed no special favoritism: even the heirs of council members were subject to such penalties. In 1638, an inventory of the estate of councilman Georg Widenmann showed that he had underassessed himself, and a fine of 3,000 fl. was collected.[16] To be sure, the fines cited here were imposed during a time when the city was under enormous pressure to produce revenues. But these episodes do prove that the government felt itself legally empowered to punish tax evasion by levying fines that vastly exceeded the amount withheld. Even if this power normally lay dormant, the fact that it might be exercised suggests that cheating on taxes, while practiced, was a somewhat risky undertaking, and probably a rather uncommon one.

There is another way in which we can see how closely the assessments corresponded to the actual property values. For the later seventeenth century, a number of inventories survive which not only list all property owned by the deceased citizen but also assign an exact value to each item and calculate the totals. By comparing such an inventory with

[14] KR 1635: Einnehmen: Straafgellt. Since this and the next two examples are taken from records of treasury receipts, there can be no doubt that the amounts cited were actually received by the city government.

[15] KR 1641: Einnehmen: Straffgellt.

[16] KR 1638: Einnehmen: Straffgellt.

the tax paid immediately before a citizen's death, we can test the accuracy of that citizen's last assessment.

In 1685, for example, the widow of Conrad Wuesst, a wool weaver, paid a tax of 3 fl. In other words, she assessed her property at 600 fl. A few months later she died, and an inventory of her property was taken.[17] The inventory lists the following:

One house, purchased in 1655 for	500 fl.
About forty items of furniture, linen, metalware and weaving equipment, worth	216 fl. 45 krz.
A debt to her of	50 fl.
Assets:	766 fl. 45 krz.
Debts she owed, i.e., Liabilities:	149 fl. 10 krz.
Total	617 fl. 35 krz.

Or, to take another case: In 1685, the city council member Michael Streitter paid a tax of 12 fl., representing an assessment of 2,400 fl. When he died the following year, an inventory of his estate recorded the total value of his property as 2,540 fl. 16¼ krz.[18] Even for a member of the city council, the assessment did not differ substantially from the actual value of the property.

Altogether, then, we can maintain with confidence that the tax records will provide us with a reliable picture of the wealth of Nördlingen's citizens in any given year. But what if we wish to compare individual or group assessments over time? In order to do this it will be necessary to account for any long-term changes in the real value of the gulden.

Changes in the purchasing power of a given unit of money can be determined, at least approximately, if one has

[17] Inventare 1682-88, fols. 605ff.

[18] Ibid., fols. 633ff. In transcribing the total, the clerk wrote 2,560 fl., but this was clearly a clerical error for 2,540 fl.

sufficient information about the movement of prices. In fact there are some price data for Nördlingen, but they are neither complete in terms of years nor comprehensive in terms of commodities. On the other hand, there is a rich fund of price information for the city of Augsburg, only fifty miles south of Nördlingen and the economic capital of the east Swabian region to which Nördlingen belonged. The Augsburg price lists were published forty years ago by M. J. Elsas; more recently two British economists used these data to devise an annual price index for Augsburg—an estimate of year-to-year changes in the total price of a "basket" of consistently defined commodities.[19] From time to time, especially during wars, there may have been short-term differences in the price levels of Augsburg and Nördlingen. But there is no reason to doubt that the long-term movement of prices in these two cities was very similar. Accordingly, I have used these data to establish a nine-year average price index for Augsburg, which forms the basis for my estimates of the changing real value of the gulden in Nördlingen between 1579 and 1724. This index appears in Appendix IV.

II

AND now, what do the tax records actually tell us about the distribution of wealth in early modern Nördlingen? Once again, it will be useful to begin with a detailed look at the year 1579 before we proceed to determine how—or whether —things changed in the following 140 years.

For the year 1579, we find that the total wealth of the citizenry amounted to 699,922 fl. This averages out to 454 fl. per capita. At first glance this might suggest considerable prosperity among the citizens of Nördlingen—after all, 454 fl. was more than enough to purchase a substantial home.[20]

19 The relevant works are cited in Appendix IV.

20 For example, in 1582 Jörg Sendvogel purchased a house, including a garden, courtyard and water rights at a nearby fountain. The pur-

But in fact this average figure of 454 fl. is deceptive, for the distribution of wealth in Nördlingen was highly uneven. One can see this from the first column of Table 4.2: over

TABLE 4.2. Distribution of Wealth, 1579

Wealth Category (fl.)	*Percentage of Citizens in That Category*	*Estimated Percentage of Total Wealth Held by Members of That Category*
0	1.2	0.0
1-25	26.9	1.5
26-50	13.8	1.5
51-100	10.6	1.7
101-200	11.6	3.7
201-400	12.1	7.9
401-800	9.7	12.7
801-1,600	7.7	20.2
1,601-3,200	4.2	22.1
3,201-6,400	1.7	17.6
6,401-12,800	0.4	8.1
Over 12,800	0.1	3.0
Totals	100.0	100.0
	($n = 1{,}541$)	(699,922 fl.)

a quarter of the citizens paid only the minimum tax amount (⅛ fl.), meaning that their assessments amounted to 25 fl. or less, and three-quarters had assessments under 400 fl.—still considerably under the mean.[21] As for purchasing houses—in fact most citizens lived in houses that were heavily mortgaged.

Table 4.2 divides the citizens of Nördlingen into twelve wealth categories. Knowing as we do how many individuals fall into any one category, we can arrive at a very close approximation of how much of the total wealth the persons constituting each of these groups possessed. This information, which is provided in the second column of Table 4.2,

chase price was 428 fl., of which 100 fl. was paid in cash. Pfandbuch 23, fol. 498.

[21] Nineteen citizens paid no tax at all in 1579.

emphasizes even more clearly the unequal distribution of wealth among the citizens of Nördlingen.[22]

It may be wise to emphasize that this table refers to the distribution of wealth, not income. Many of the poorest citizens may, in fact, have enjoyed adequate incomes to support themselves and their families, while remaining unable to save any significant amounts. But income data are not available for early modern Nördlingen, and even if they were, they could scarcely contradict the impression made by the distribution of wealth: that a huge gulf yawned between the richest and the poorest citizens. The 415 citizens in the bottom category—over one-quarter of the total—possessed only 1.5 percent of the community's wealth; while at the other end of the spectrum, the 7 richest citizens—a mere 0.5 percent of the total—controlled more than 10 percent of the wealth. The richest man of all was Hans Husel, a hard-driving and evidently unpopular textile merchant,[23] whose assessment in 1579 stood at 21,200 fl.—an amount that equaled the collective wealth of over 600 of his poorest fellow citizens.[24] If the same calculation were to be made for the year 1585, it would yield even more dramatic results, for in the course of six years Husel had succeeded in doubling his wealth to 43,000 fl.[25]

Certainly, Table 4.2 makes clear that a small elite con-

22 The calculations on which these results are based are explained in Appendix V.

23 Hans Husel's unpopularity is suggested by the incident of his quarrel with the wool weaver Andreas Wernher, described in Chapter Nine, as well as by the city council's response to the quarrel. Both men were fined by the same amount, and both men petitioned for a modification of the fine. Wernher's plea was heeded, but Husel's plea was rejected and he was, in fact, reprimanded for his "shamelessness." RP 16 and 23 Oct. 1583.

24 Cf. Appendix V, from which it can be seen that the poorest 646 citizens had a total of 20,975 fl.

25 This and all other references to individual tax payments can be traced under the individual's alphabetical listing in the Steuerregister for the year in question.

trolled a huge portion of the town's riches. To provide a basis for later comparisons with other years, however, it may be useful to express the percentages of the citizenry in terms of round figures. By simple arithmetic interpolation, the information in Table 4.2 can be summarized as shown.

% of the Citizenry	*No.*	*% of the Total Wealth*
The Top (richest) 2	31	25.6
The Top 10	154	60.2
The Top 50	771	95.7
Whole Citizenry (100)	1,541	100.0

Of course, it must be remembered that these figures can also be expressed in reverse. Since, for example, the top half of the citizenry owned 95.7 percent of the wealth, this means that the entire bottom half of the citizenry had to share the remaining 4.3 percent.

The basic point need not be further belabored. It is abundantly clear that the distribution of wealth among the citizens was highly unequal. In fact, this would be suggested if one simply compared the mean and median assessments. The median wealth in 1579 was only 100 fl.—less than one-quarter of the mean. In other words, the citizens of Nördlingen, no matter how much they shared a common juridical status, were not even remotely a homogeneous group in terms of economic status.

To say this, however, immediately raises another question: to what extent did the distribution of wealth correspond to the distribution of occupations? Were there "rich" and "poor" occupations? To answer such questions one must first establish average measures for individual occupations—above all the median wealth—and then examine the distribution of wealth within each of these occupations.

We shall concentrate on the seven most common occupations in 1579—trades which among themselves accounted for over half of the male citizens. Table 4.3 provides the

TABLE 4.3. Seven Most Common Occupations in 1579 (Male Citizens): Median and Mean Wealth

Occupations (with No. in each)	*Median Wealth (fl.)*	*Mean Wealth (fl.)*
Taverners (36)	1,200	1,450
Bakers (48)	300	512
Butchers (54)	260	622
Tanners (108)	240	652
ALL MALES	140	438
Shoemakers (60)	100	310
Wool weavers (269)	60	184
Fine-cloth weavers (64)	20	398

median and mean wealth of male citizens in these trades, ranked in descending order of median wealth. The economic superiority of the major victualing trades—above all the taverners—is immediately apparent. Tanning, the city's second-largest craft, also enjoyed both median and mean wealth above the city-wide norms. The three other leading production crafts, however, fall below these norms—including the largest one of all, wool weaving.

But now let us look at the distribution of wealth *within* these leading occupations. Table 4.4 lists the same seven occupations, but indicates for each occupation the percentage of members falling into each wealth category. It is important to observe that none of these occupations is characterized by closely bounded wealth ranges. Bakers and tanners, for example, were generally prosperous, but 15 and 19 percent of them, respectively, still fell into the lowest wealth category. Or, on the other hand, the wool weavers were predominantly poor, yet fully one-fifth of them enjoyed wealth higher than the median level for bakers, butchers and tanners.

The fine-cloth weavers show a particularly broad wealth range. Of the seven leading crafts, the fine-cloth weavers had the lowest median wealth, and over half of them be-

TABLE 4.4. Distribution of Wealth Among Male Citizens in the Seven Major Occupational Groups, 1579

	Percentage in each category of:							
Wealth Category (fl.)	*All Males*	*Wool Weavers*	*Tanners*	*Fine-Cloth Weavers*	*Shoe-makers*	*Butchers*	*Bakers*	*Taverners*
0	1	0	0	0	0	0	0	0
1-25	22	39	19	52	22	4	15	0
26-50	14	16	7	15	13	13	4	3
51-100	12	12	11	3	18	7	10	8
101-200	13	8	11	3	7	19	19	3
201-400	13	11	16	3	16	17	13	11
401-800	11	9	12	8	16	18	15	11
801-1,600	8	3	11	5	7	15	21	28
1,600-3,200	5	1	8	11	2	4	4	28
Over 3,200	2	0	4	0	0	4	0	8
Total No. of Cases	(1,266)	(269)	(108)	(64)	(60)	(54)	(48)	(36)

longed to the bottom wealth category. Yet over 15 percent belonged to the highest wealth groups. In fact, if the distribution of wealth among the fine-cloth weavers were plotted, it would show a strongly bimodal curve, with peaks at both extremes and a depression in the middle.

For some communities of early modern Europe, historians have identified a "threshold" of tax amounts, above which no craftsmen were to be found.[26] In sixteenth-century Nördlingen, however, no such threshold appears to have existed. Among the 190 richest men in the city—the top 15 percent—we can find 25 tanners, 12 bakers, 12 butchers, 11 wool weavers, 10 fine-cloth weavers, 5 shoemakers and a number of other craftsmen. Even the very richest 27 men—the top 2 percent—included 4 tanners and 2 butchers. Clearly, craftsmen were not automatically excluded from membership in the city's wealth elite.

In fact this reflects an important point about sixteenth-century Nördlingen. Sociologists or historians who look at nineteenth- and twentieth-century societies tend to regard occupations in themselves as indicators of an individual's status within his community.[27] And, indeed, in the highly differentiated occupational structures of industrializing and industrialized societies, this assumption may have considerable validity. But to apply such concepts without caution to a traditional social structure like that of preindustrial Nördlingen would be extremely misleading. For, as Table 4.4 has shown, each major occupational group in Nördlingen had its own hierarchy of wealth. The wool weavers of 1579 ranged from the 106 males who paid the bare minimum tax up to well-to-do weavers like Andreas Wernher, who owned

[26] See, for example, Pierre Deyon, *Amiens, capitale provinciale, étude sur la société urbaine au 17e siècle* (Paris, 1967), Chapter 19.

[27] As one example one may cite the comment of Stephan Thernstrom: "Virtually every significant theorist of class sees occupation as a central determinant," *Poverty and Progress: Social Mobility in a Nineteenth Century City* (New York: Atheneum ed., 1971), p. 255, n. 4.

five houses by the time of his death.[28] The tanners similarly ranged from 21 members of the bottom group up to wealthy men like Caspar Schöpperlin, a council member who was worth 4,000 fl. in 1579.

We have already seen that Nördlingen as a whole in 1579 was a community highly stratified by wealth. But now we can see that individual occupations were also highly stratified. Certainly, there were some occupations which almost invariably implied a certain wealth level—obviously merchants were almost all near the top of the scale, and day-laborers were almost always near the bottom. But for the great majority of citizens—the craftsmen—the correlation between occupation and wealth was small. In conceptualizing the social structure of Nördlingen in 1579, we must recognize that the various major occupations represented parallel, though not identical, stratification systems.

The average citizen, then, had not one but two loci of social identity: his craft and his degree of wealth. In actual fact the poor wool weaver may have had more in common with the poor shoemaker or poor tanner than with the richer members of his own craft. Yet the system of craft organization tended to impose upon him a sense—valid or otherwise—of mutual interest with the other members of his own occupation. It was only a century later, as we shall see, that a sense of collective consciousness began to develop among the poorer segment of an individual craft.[29] And not until the nineteenth century, when the craft system was finally dissolved, was it possible for a real lower-class consciousness which crossed occupational lines to emerge.

This, then, was the society of Nördlingen in 1579: a society bottom-heavy with citizens on the lowest levels of wealth, but not a society in which poverty had become

[28] For information on Wernher, see Chapter Nine.

[29] See Chapter Nine for a discussion of the emerging group consciousness among the city's poorer wool weavers in the late seventeenth century and the more fully articulated group consciousness of the linen weavers in the late eighteenth century.

strictly identified with certain occupations or, conversely, in which certain occupations had become strictly identified with poverty. There were, to be sure, "richer" and "poorer" trades, but the range of wealth within each one was sufficient to give each trade—especially among the larger ones—its own internal hierarchy of personal wealth, status and consequent power within the larger community.

III

So much for the situation in 1579. We must now ask what happened to the wealth of Nördlingen in the century and a half that followed. Let us begin by looking at the total collective wealth of the citizenry—that is, of the heads of citizen households—during our period.[30] Figure 4.1 illustrates the changing total wealth of the citizens in nominal terms.[31] In Figure 4.2 the same information is presented again, but adjusted to reflect changes in the real value of

30 In addition to the taxes paid by the adult citizens, which are the basis of the figures presented here, the tax registers also record taxes paid by (a) minor orphans of citizens, through their guardians, and (b) noncitizens (both resident and nonresident) who had been permitted to acquire property formerly owned by citizens and who thus became subject to the "bürgerliche Steuer" on that property. These payments were not included in the present computations. However, in order to indicate the order of magnitude of these two categories, these taxes have been tabulated by hand for five selected years, and the total value of these assessments (rounded off to the nearest 1,000 fl.) is presented below. For purposes of comparison, the total assessments for the adult citizens (also rounded to the nearest 1,000 fl.) are presented too.

Year	*Adult Citizens*	*Orphans*	*Noncitizens*
1579	700,000 fl.	59,000 fl.	13,000 fl.
1615	1,490,000 fl.	84,000 fl.	13,000 fl.
1652	682,000 fl.	65,000 fl.	4,000 fl.
1700	943,000 fl.	60,000 fl.	17,000 fl.
1724	1,058,000 fl.	23,000 fl.	8,000 fl.

31 The figures on which this graph is based appear in Appendix III.

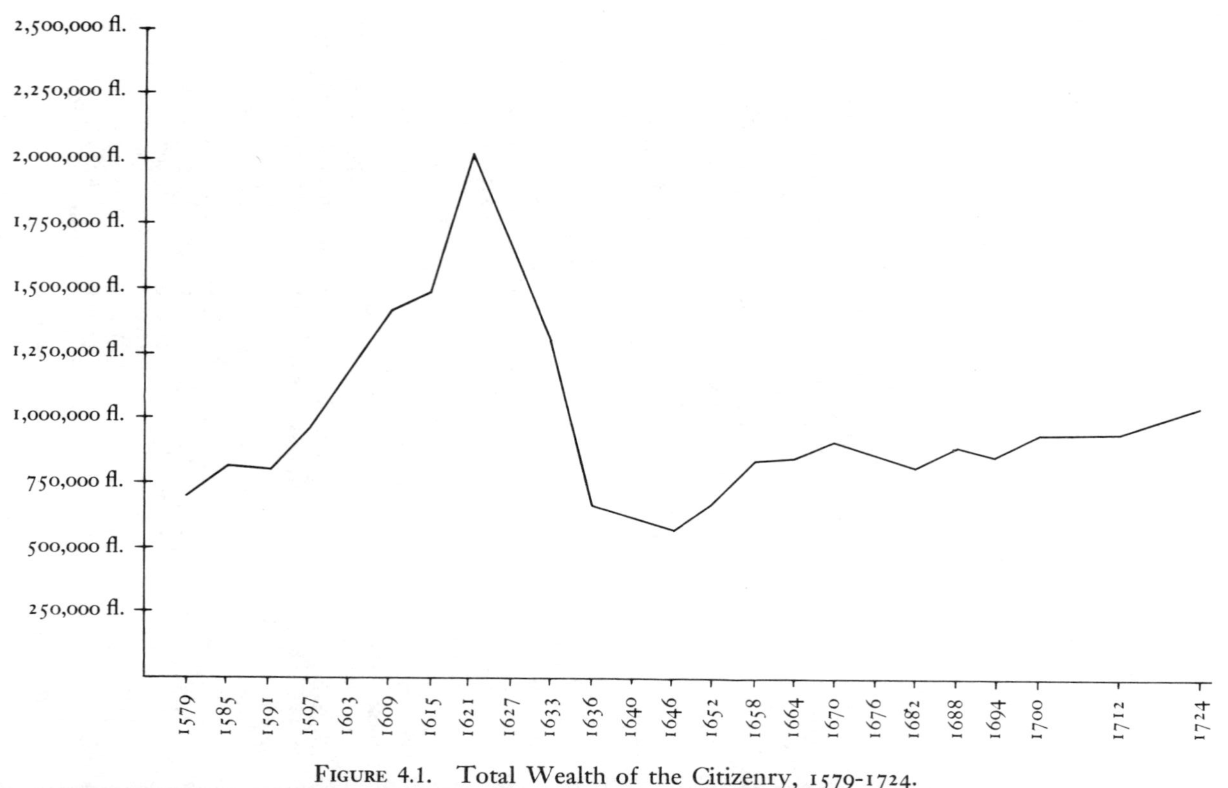

FIGURE 4.1. Total Wealth of the Citizenry, 1579-1724.

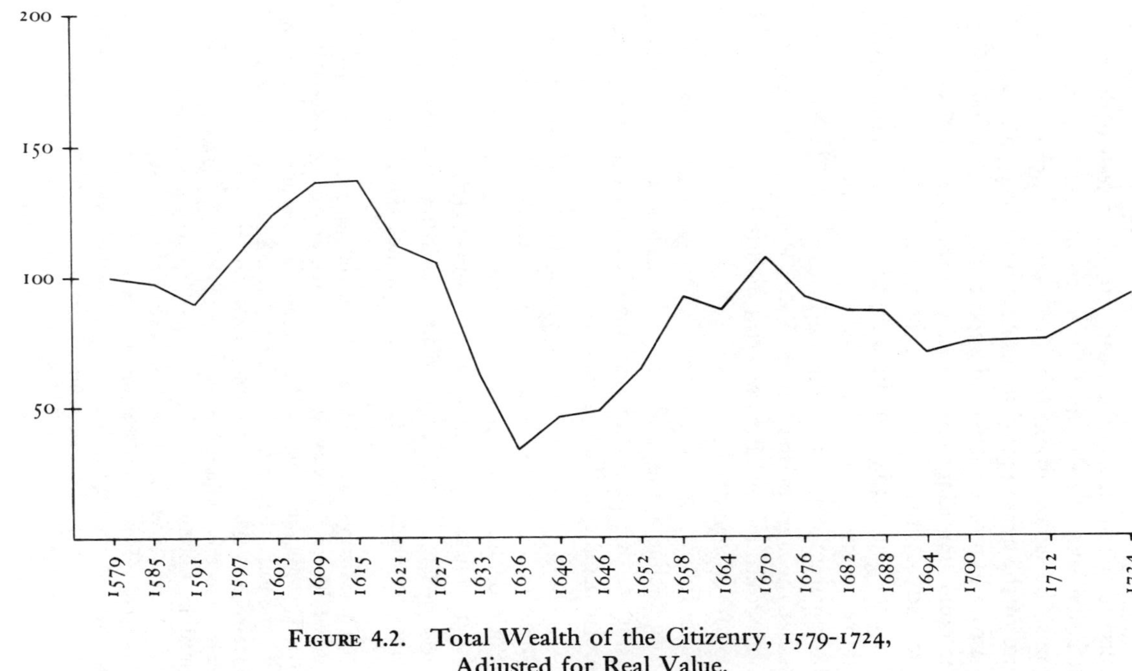

FIGURE 4.2. Total Wealth of the Citizenry, 1579-1724, Adjusted for Real Value.

money and expressed in terms of a base of 1579 = 100.[32] The first curve is a highly distorted one, in particular because of the inflation of the early 1600's as well as the rapid deflation that accompanied the currency reforms of 1623. Thus, the second graph provides a much more reliable picture of the evolution of the community's wealth.

From Figure 4.1 it would appear that the total wealth of the community increased steadily in the first forty years of our study. Actually, however, the real increase in prosperity was confined to the first three decades of this period: from Figure 4.2 we can see that after 1609 inflation accounts for the apparent continued increase in total wealth. Nevertheless, at the start of the Thirty Years War the community's total wealth in real terms was still slightly higher than it had been forty years earlier.

The following years, however, brought with them a dramatic decline in the wealth of the citizenry. Even if we take as our starting point the year 1627, we can observe a spectacular decline in the nominal wealth of the citizenry, from 1,639,000 fl. in that year to only 662,000 fl. in 1636. In real terms, too, a drastic reduction is evident, with the total wealth declining by one-half during the same nine-year period. These years include, of course, the most critical phase of the Thirty Years War in Nördlingen—the period which witnessed the plague of 1634 and the occupation of

[32] These figures were established in the following manner. First, the total wealth for 1579 was expressed as a base of 100 (i.e., 699,900 fl. = 100). Then, all other nominal wealth totals were expressed in terms of the same base. (For example, the total wealth in 1585 was 806,600 fl. Since 699,900 fl. = 100, therefore 806,600 fl. = 115.) These nominal totals were then adjusted in accordance with the price index presented in Appendix IV. (For example, from the price index it is evident that prices have risen from a level of 100 in 1579 to a level of 118 in 1585. This means that the real value of the gulden in 1585 is only 85% of what it had been in 1579. Accordingly, the total wealth for 1585, adjusted for real value, comes out to 85% of 115, i.e., 98. It is this figure that is recorded on the graph.)

the city, first by a Swedish garrison and then, even more onerously, by imperial troops.

Three specific factors can be pinpointed as having contributed to this collapse, although the exact proportion for which each of these factors was responsible cannot be calculated:

(a) The loss of cash, jewels, plate, and other movable property rendered to Swedish and then imperial soldiers as payment of military taxes. An accounting prepared many years later recorded losses of 832,925 fl. during the four-year period from 1632 to 1636—an amount which, if accurate, would account for by far the largest part of the decline in wealth.[33]

(b) Destruction or spoliation of property. There is little evidence of destruction of real property within the city walls, but the gardens and fields outside the walls underwent repeated devastation by enemy troops, especially during the siege of 1634. This could have accounted both directly and (by reducing income from real property) indirectly for reduced property assessments.

(c) Population loss. We have noted above that the number of citizen households was reduced by fully 50 percent during the period from 1621 to 1640. Theoretically this need not have resulted in a reduction of wealth in the city, for (except for the small quantity obtained by heirs outside the city) property would normally be redistributed to heirs among the surviving citizens. In actual fact, however, a reduction by 50 percent in the size of the citizenry must have severely crippled the community's ability to regenerate its wealth.

The Thirty Years War, then, had a dramatic impact on

[33] See Chapter Five, note 10.

the wealth of the citizens. Even more striking than this decline, however, was the recovery of the community's wealth following the war. Signs of recovery, in fact, can already be seen before the war's end, but it is the 1650's which show by far the most impressive rate of increase. After some leveling off, the increase resumed in the late 1660's: by 1670, scarcely twenty years after the end of the war, the total real wealth of the citizenry was roughly equal to that which had been recorded at the end of the sixteenth century. Clearly, then, when both the onerous taxation and the constant political and economic uncertainties associated with the war came to an end, the community recovered its wealth—a particularly impressive feat if we recall that the size of the citizenry had not been increasing at the same rate.

But 1670 was a high watermark. Thereafter, the total wealth of the citizenry once again underwent a precipitous decline—a drop so steep, in fact, that by 1694 the total real wealth of the community was only 70 percent of what it had been in 1579. The explanation for this decline is obvious enough: the renewed warfare of the late seventeenth and early eighteenth centuries. These wars had already begun in the 1660's but their real financial effects were not felt in Nördlingen until the following decade when, for example, the city had to provide winter quarters for imperial troops during five successive years. From that point on, Nördlingen's recovery was undermined by French and Turkish wars which continued almost without interruption until 1714. In fact, it is only after the end of the wars that any noticeable recovery in the level of the community's real wealth can be observed.

This, then, was the pattern of change in the total wealth of the community. But what about the distribution of wealth? To examine this, we must begin by looking for changes in the level of mean and median wealth. Figure 4.3 provides the curves for both of these measures in nominal terms for the entire citizenry between 1579 and 1724. In Figure 4.4 the same measures are again presented, but this time both are adjusted for real value and both are expressed in terms of a base of 1579 = 100.[34]

Let us start with mean, or per capita, wealth. As Figure 4.4 shows, the basic trend for this measure was roughly similar to the trend already noted for the total wealth of the community: an increase until the early seventeenth century; then a decrease until sometime during the Thirty Years War; followed by a renewed increase, especially in the 1650's, and finally, after 1670, a second decline. Yet there are some significant differences between this curve and the curve of total wealth. In the first place, in the late 1620's and the early 1630's the community experienced a severe loss of population: the number of citizens declined at an even faster rate than the total collective wealth. As a consequence, per capita wealth declined less drastically, and began a real upswing even sooner than did total wealth. In the second place, immediately after the war the total wealth of the community was increasing at a faster rate than the number of citizens: accordingly, the initial spurt of post-war recovery rose even higher in terms of mean wealth than in terms of total wealth. This situation, however, did not persist, for the number of citizens continued to grow at a slow rate while total real wealth leveled off and then, after 1670, began to decline: inevitably, by the 1670's mean wealth was dropping, and more sharply than total wealth. By 1724, the real per capita wealth of the citizens of Nördlingen had fallen to a level barely above what it had been in 1579.

In any analysis of wealth distribution, however, even more important than the mean values are the median values. From Figure 4.3 we can see that, as one would expect, the median

[34] These figures were established in precisely the manner used to establish the figures for adjusted total wealth, as detailed in note 32 above. First the mean (or median) for 1579 was expressed as a base of 100, then all other means (or medians) were converted to the same base, and finally these nominal means (or medians) were adjusted in accordance with the price index presented in Appendix IV.

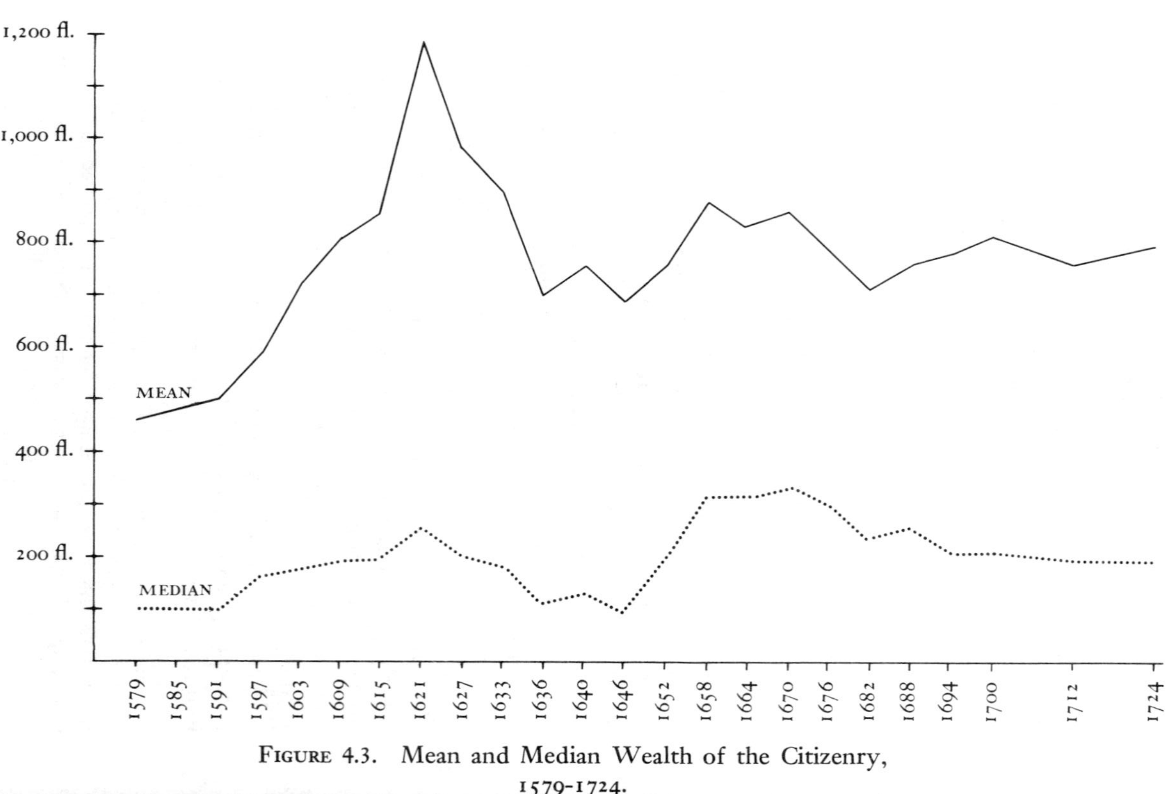

FIGURE 4.3. Mean and Median Wealth of the Citizenry, 1579-1724.

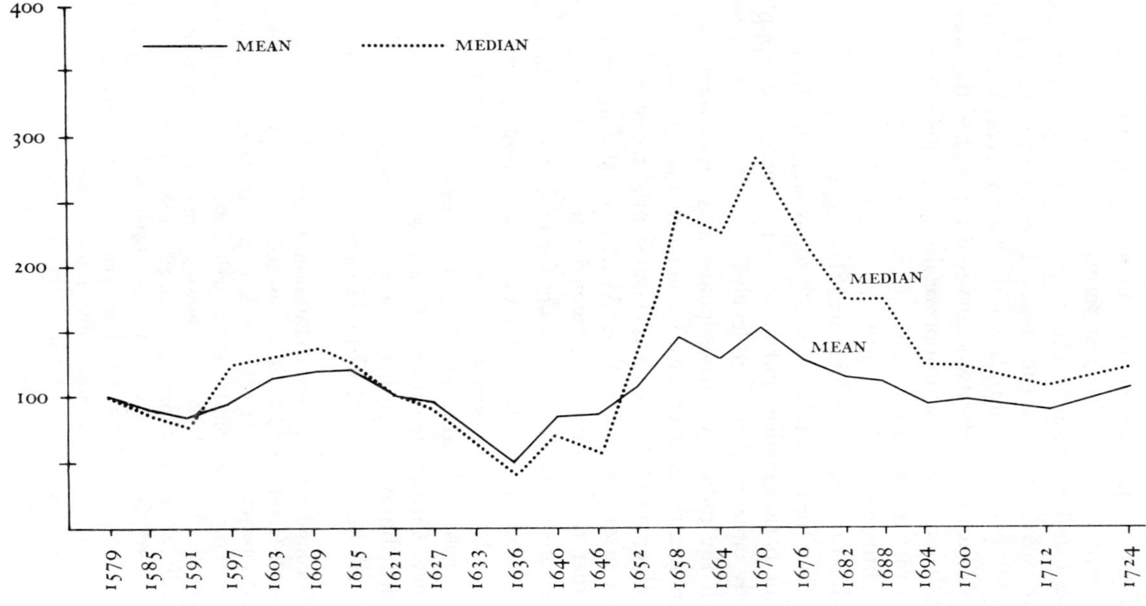

FIGURE 4.4. Mean and Median Wealth of the Citizenry, 1579-1724, Adjusted for Real Value.

wealth was always substantially lower than the mean wealth. In Figure 4.4, however, median wealth, like mean wealth, has been converted to real terms, and both measures are treated as beginning at the same base in 1579. From this figure we can see that the shapes of the two curves remained roughly congruent until late in the Thirty Years War. In the 1650's, however, the two curves diverge, for the median wealth increased at a proportionally much greater rate: by 1670 real mean wealth was 1½ times what it had been in 1579, but real median wealth was almost triple. On the other hand, after 1670 the median wealth declined at a much faster rate than mean wealth—so much so, in fact, that by the end of our period median and mean wealth were both approximately equal to their 1579 levels.[35]

All the indices we have looked at so far—total wealth, mean wealth, median wealth—indicate that the citizens of Nördlingen experienced a very substantial recovery in prosperity after the Thirty Years War, especially in the 1650's, but that the recovery was wiped out from 1670 onward. While answering some questions for us, however, these data immediately pose others. Above all, one must ask why the curves of mean and median wealth behaved so very differently from each other in the second half of the seventeenth century. Clearly, we must take a closer look at changes in the distribution of wealth among the citizens.

It will be recalled that the citizens of 1579 were divided

[35] In considering the mean and median wealth of the citizenry, one additional factor should be taken into account: nonpayment of taxes. During most years in the era studied, the number of citizens who paid no tax remained very small—usually well under 2 percent of the total. During the Thirty Years War, however, this percentage rose considerably, as follows: 1627: 4.6%; 1633: 11.2%; 1636: 18.0%; 1640: 4.1%; 1646: 9.5%. In 1652 it dropped below 2 percent again, and remained there until the end of the century. But in 1700, as a consequence of what was apparently a more liberal attitude by the authorities regarding tax payments by the poor, the percentage of nonpayments rose to 4.2 percent, and by 1724 it had risen to 11.9 percent.

into twelve wealth categories, and it was possible to establish how much of the total wealth of the citizenry was held by each of these twelve groups. Then, by interpolation, the proportion of wealth held by any percentile group of the citizenry could be very closely approximated. The same calculation has been made for eight additional points in time between 1579 and 1724, and the results are presented in Figure 4.5.[36]

Throughout this period, the distribution of wealth clearly remained highly unequal. The richest 2 percent of the citizenry always owned at least a fifth of the wealth; the richest 10 percent always owned at least half. But within this general framework, some significant shifts in distribution are evident. For example, between 1579 and 1646 the top 2 percent increased their proportion of the wealth from 25.6 percent to 40.2 percent, with most of the increase taking place during the second half of the Thirty Years War. After the war, however, this top group suffered a dramatic reversal of its fortunes. Between 1646 and 1670, its share of the total wealth was reduced by almost one-half, from 40.2

[36] In establishing these figures, the same procedure was followed as was used for 1579: first, the known percentage of citizens in each category and the estimated percentage of the total wealth held by members of each category were determined; second, by interpolation, the proportion of the total wealth held by any percentile group could be approximated. This procedure is explained in detail in the text above and in Appendix V. (As indicated there, the validity of this procedure rests largely on the validity of the "midpoint" method for estimating the collective wealth of each wealth category. When the totals for all categories in any given year are added together, they will, of course, yield an approximate total for the wealth of the entire citizenry in that year. If this approximate total wealth differed substantially from what we know to be the real total wealth for that year, this would, of course, raise doubts about the method followed here. But in fact the approximate totals always come out close enough to the real total to inspire confidence in this procedure: in the eleven years studied here, the total wealth as yielded by this method was never more than 2½% larger or 1% smaller than the actual total wealth.)

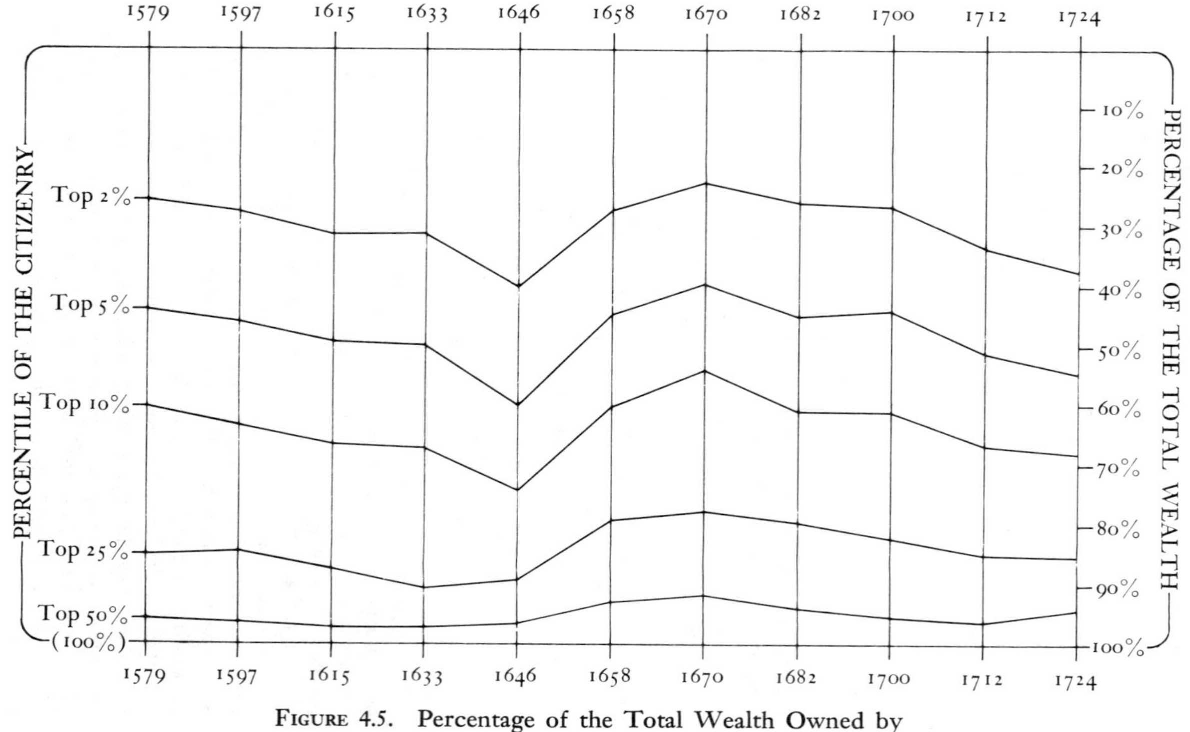

FIGURE 4.5. Percentage of the Total Wealth Owned by Selected Segments of the Citizenry, 1579-1724.

percent down to 22.4 percent. After 1670 this trend was arrested and the top 2 percent again enjoyed a steady increase in their proportion of the wealth, so that by 1724 they once again accounted for 37.2 percent of the total.

The same basic pattern is mirrored by the top 5 percent and the top 10 percent of the citizenry: in each case, there was an increase until 1646, a sharp decrease after the war, and then a steady increase once again after 1670. In fact, much the same pattern is evident for the top 25 percent of the citizenry.

It is crucial to remember that each gain for a "top" group implies a loss for the corresponding "bottom" group, and vice versa. Thus, the proportion of wealth held by the bottom nine-tenths of the citizenry decreased during the Thirty Years War, but increased sharply during the postwar recovery. In fact, an increased proportion after the war is even evident for the bottom 50 percent of the citizens. Admittedly, the share of the total wealth held by this bottom half was always confined to a very small fringe, but the size of this fringe more than doubled between 1646 and 1670, from 3.5 percent to 8.1 percent, before beginning to contract once again.

The overall pattern indicated by Figure 4.5 is clear. From 1579 to 1646 we can observe a slight trend toward a more uneven distribution of wealth, a trend which was sharply accelerated by the Thirty Years War. Although all groups suffered financial losses during the war, in relative terms the burden of military taxation and economic hardship must have fallen much more heavily on the lower and middle groups than on the rich. Immediately after the war, however, the tables were turned: the postwar recovery was accompanied by a great redistribution of wealth. For twenty years, the rich suffered a relative loss of wealth and the poor enjoyed a substantial relative increase. Certainly, not all of the poor partook equally of the postwar redistribution. Although, as we have seen, even the bottom 50 percent shared in some of the benefits, from Figure 4.5 it is clear that the most significant gain in relative position was enjoyed by the group situated between the top 10 and top 25 percent levels. Nevertheless, a redistribution which favored even such middling groups as against the very rich is a significant phenomenon.

We can speculate with some confidence about the reasons for this development. For the middling citizens, predominantly craftsmen, the effect of the war had been constantly to swallow up their earnings: they had suffered because their earnings were immediately collected and carried off to foreign parts by an unending procession of soldiers. Once the war and its ceaseless financial exactions came to an end, however, they were able to hang on to a much greater share of their income. For the richer citizens—among them the merchants—the story was quite different. During the war itself, those with established fortunes had been able to preserve a relatively large share of their wealth from the military commissioners. But in fact the war had cut deeply into the very basis of the merchants' economic lives, for it had shattered patterns of trade and investment all over the region. Thus, the next generation of the elite found it harder to maintain the same level of wealth. Of course, they also shared in the return of prosperity after the war, yet in relative terms their wealth did not increase as quickly as that of the middling citizens during the 1650's and 1660's.

This redistributory trend, however, was not destined to last. It was arrested by the renewal of warfare and the military taxation which accompanied it. From 1670, as we saw earlier, the total real wealth of the community began to decline. But the rich were able to retain a larger share of this declining wealth than the poor. In short, the recovery of prosperity after the Thirty Years War had favored the poor and middling groups of Nördlingen citizens; the return of war once again favored the rich.

The second great cycle of seventeenth-century wars came to an end in 1714. Although our data reach only to 1724,[37]

[37] In fact the tax registers were maintained until 1746. But from

they do suggest some degree of recovery once again: after 1712 there was some increase in communal wealth and, as Figure 4.5 shows, the bottom half of the citizenry enjoyed a slight increase in their share of the total. Yet this improvement in their relative position came at the expense of their nearest neighbors on the scale of wealth. The aggrandizement of wealth by the upper percentiles of the citizenry continued without abatement.

This suggests that the economic recovery after the War of the Spanish Succession did not parallel the recovery that had followed the Thirty Years War: this time there was no redistribution of wealth which favored the middling groups of the citizenry as against the very rich. A number of factors contributed to the difference between these two periods. But the first and most obvious one had to do with a reduction in the extent of wealth mobility. To understand this development, we must look at the entire history of wealth mobility during our period.

IV

WEALTH mobility is difficult to analyze, for the simple reason that so much of it took place. The number of citizens whose assessments remained absolutely constant during their lifetimes was extremely small; almost all adults experienced some increase or decrease in wealth. But it is difficult to establish what degree of upward or downward movement was socially significant, and even when such a determination can be made, it cannot be expressed in terms of absolute numbers. For instance, during the same time span two citizens might both increase their assessed wealth by 500 fl. But suppose one of them increased his wealth elevenfold from 50 fl. to 550 fl., while the other simply increased his capital from 5,000 fl. to 5,500 fl.? Clearly, the same absolute increase

about 1730 they suffered a drastic decline in accuracy and completeness, so that it appeared safer to take 1724 as the terminal date for this study.

in wealth would be much more significant for the first individual than for the second. This consideration has led to the format used here for tabulating mobility in wealth.

In order to determine changes in the frequency and direction of wealth mobility between the late sixteenth and early eighteenth centuries, the experiences of six different cohorts, or generations, of male citizens have been studied. In each case, the wealth of each man at the start of his career has been compared with his wealth 24 years later, if he was still living. The findings take into account changes in the value of money, so that we can establish the extent to which these men lost or gained wealth in real terms.

TABLE 4.5. Wealth Mobility of Men Who Became Citizens in 1580-85

Wealth Level in 1585 (fl.)	*Total No. of Cases*	*No. of Men Whose Real Wealth in 1609 was:*[a]				
		Lower	*Same*	*2×-4×*	*5×-9×*	*10× or more*
Up to 100	128	39	10	39	18	22
101-400	41	13	8	11	6	3
Over 400	18	6	5	6	1	0
Totals (No.)	187	58	23	56	25	25
Totals (%)		31	12	30	13	13

[a] The category "Same" refers to all those whose real wealth in 1609 equaled 1.0-1.99 of their wealth in 1585; the category "2×-4×" includes those whose real wealth in 1609 was 2.0-4.99 of their wealth in 1585, and so on.

Table 4.5 records the experiences of the first of these cohorts: the men who became citizens during the years 1580-85 (including, by the way, the fifteen shoemakers with whom this chapter opened). A total of 353 men were admitted to citizenship during these years; over half of them—187, to be exact—were still alive a quarter of a century later. As the table shows, wealth mobility was overwhelmingly the norm in the lives of these men: only 12 percent of them showed no substantial change in their level of wealth over 24 years. Many of them—31 percent—were unable to sustain the wealth they had inherited and thus were poorer, in real terms, as middle-aged men than they had been when they began their careers. But 56 percent of this cohort at least doubled their wealth between 1585 and 1609; and over 26 percent of them increased their wealth fivefold or more. Those who started out poor shared fully in this upward trend; in fact, of those who started out in the bottom category, 31 percent quintupled their wealth. Clearly, upward wealth mobility could form part of the normal career expectations for all segments of the citizenry before the Thirty Years War.

The same kind of mobility analysis has been made for five additional cohorts of Nördlingen citizens. The complete results will be found in Appendix VI. Table 4.6, however,

TABLE 4.6. Summary of Wealth Mobility Patterns

Starting Years	*End Year*	*Percentage of Men Whose Real Wealth After 24 Years Was:*			
		Lower	*Same*	*2×-4×*	*5× or more*
1580-1585	1609	31	12	30	27
1598-1603	1627	41	21	23	15
1622-1627	1652	28	13	30	29
1647-1652	1676	11	36	31	22
1665-1670	1694	53	24	21	2
1695-1700	1724	16	30	44	11

summarizes the essential data about the wealth mobility of all six groups.

The second cohort—those who started out in 1598-1603—shows more downward and less upward mobility; scarcely surprising, since the end-point falls during the Thirty Years War. Nevertheless, 15 percent of these men managed to quintuple their wealth or more. The third cohort consists of men who began in 1622-27. Due to the war and the plague, the mortality rate of this group was particularly high, and only one-quarter of them were still alive in 1652. Among these survivors, however, the pattern of wealth mobility was almost identical to that of the first cohort. The fourth cohort includes men who became citizens as the Thirty Years War ended, and whose careers coincided with the period of postwar recovery. Only 11 percent of them lost wealth in real terms. Two-thirds of them maintained a stable wealth level or registered a modest increase, while 22 percent quintupled their wealth or more.

The fifth cohort, however—consisting of men whose careers began around 1670—showed a dramatically different pattern. Over half of these men experienced a loss of real wealth; and, even more importantly, only 2 percent of them could as much as quintuple their wealth. For these men, then, substantial upward mobility was almost completely blocked. Nor did the following generation bring a reversal of the situation. It is true that the sixth cohort—those whose careers began in 1695-1700—experienced much less downward mobility. But only 11 percent of them even quintupled their wealth—the second lowest proportion among all six groups.

It is evident that the amount of wealth mobility experienced by the citizens of Nördlingen fluctuated considerably from one period to the next, reflecting the broader economic circumstances of each era. But the patterns of wealth mobility make clear that the 1670's represented a major turning point. We have already noted a sharp decline in wealth after 1670, accompanied by a redistribution of wealth in favor of the richer citizens. It can now be seen that this redistribution coincided with a drastic reduction in upward wealth mobility: over half of the citizens of the 1670 generation lost wealth, less than a quarter experienced any gain and only 2 percent moved substantially upward. This development did not conform to the normal expectations of a citizen of Nördlingen: that he had at least a reasonable chance to augment his wealth. Coming as it did right after a period of considerable upward mobility and a favorable redistribution of wealth, the shock must have been all the greater. Moreover, as we shall see in Chapter Nine, the wealthy stratum included a family of merchants who were fully prepared to exploit the sudden economic distress of Nördlingen's middling and poorer citizens. It is scarcely surprising, then, that the century closed with an explosion of bitter discontent among craftsmen who belonged to the city's largest industry.

Nor was the situation reversed in the early eighteenth century. From 1714 on there was peace in the Empire, but as far as Nördlingen was concerned the decade that followed the Peace of Rastatt did not parallel the decade that had followed the Peace of Westphalia. Opportunities for upward mobility were more limited, and the trend by which the rich increased their share of the total wealth continued without interruption. Even if we could look beyond 1724, it is doubtful that we should find a reversal of these developments. For by the early eighteenth century a number of fundamental changes had taken place in Nördlingen. The first was a basic change in the fiscal structure of the community, which placed a permanently greater burden of taxation on the citizens. The second was a change both in the composition of the city's ruling elite and, more gradually, in the magistrates' perception of their own role. The third and perhaps most important was a change in the economic status of Nördlingen's craftsmen, at least in the critical textile industry. Taken together, these developments all contributed to the same result: a drastic weakening in both the political and the economic position of the middling and poorer citizens of Nördlingen.

V

ALL of these developments will be examined in the chapters to come. But, first, one other aspect of the wealth structure of Nördlingen remains to be examined: the changing levels of wealth among individual occupational groups.

As we have seen from the data for 1579, each major trade included members who varied considerably from one another in their wealth. Nevertheless, a comparison of

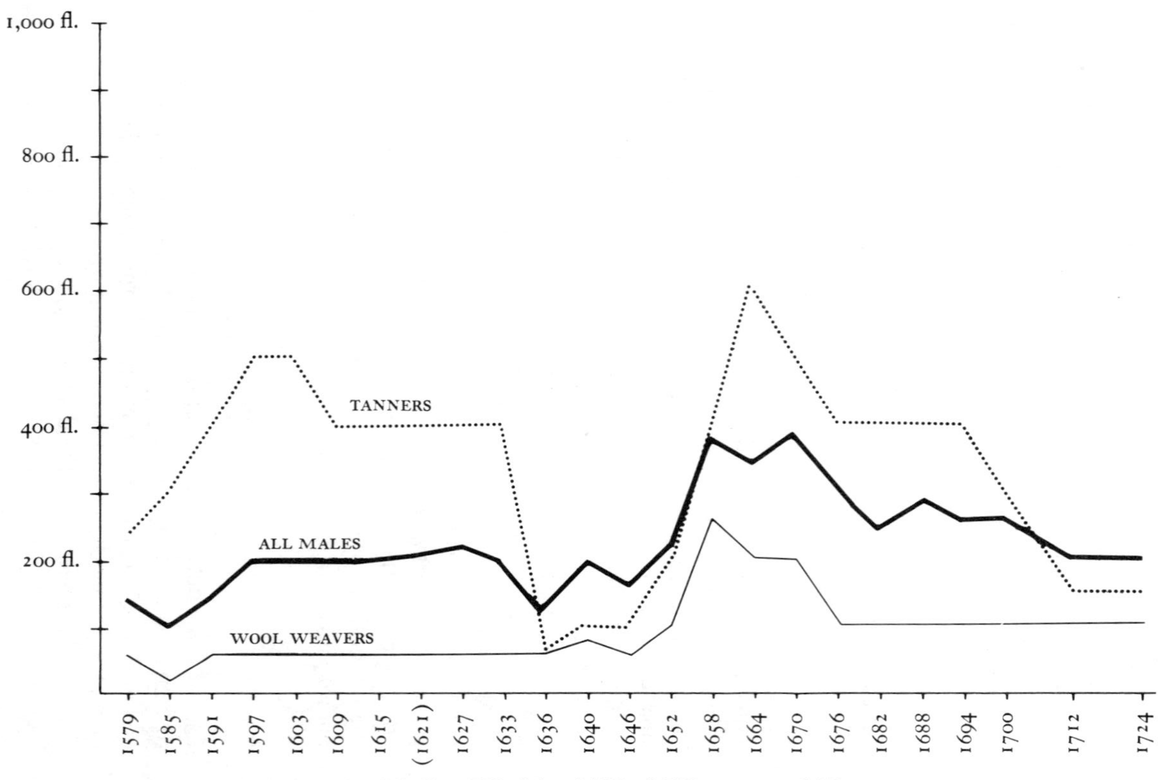

FIGURE 4.6. Median Wealth of Wool Weavers and Tanners.

median wealth levels for the most common occupations will suggest the relative status of these groups. (In looking at the median wealth for any occupation, the crucial point is not so much the median itself as the degree to which this median differs from that for the citizenry as a whole. Thus, a conversion to real values need not be undertaken, as long as a basis for comparison is provided. This has been done in the following pages by giving the median wealth for all male citizens as well as the median wealth for each major occupation. Since the data have been left in nominal terms, the results for 1621—in the midst of the inflationary Kipper- und Wipperzeit—would appear extremely distorted. For this reason the data for 1621, which are unimportant in examining long-term trends, have been omitted.)

The movement of median wealth in the two principal trades of Nördlingen is recorded in Figure 4.6. The median for wool weavers is always substantially lower than that for all male citizens. But it cannot escape notice that one period in which the median for wool weavers did come closer to the norm for all citizens was during the recovery decade of the 1650's, precisely the era when the overall distribution of wealth was most favorable to the poorer segments of the community.

A striking contrast to the weavers is provided by the tanners. Until 1633 they continued to enjoy a status of median wealth far above the norm for the entire city. After 1633, however, the tanners were plunged into crisis, and three years later their median had joined the wool weavers' in what (for 1636) was the lowest normal tax level. Precisely why the tanners were so severely affected by the crisis of the 1630's is difficult to assess. Was the supply of livestock for hides decimated by the events of war? Did the blockage of the River Eger during the siege of 1634 so disrupt tanning operations as to hinder recovery?[38] Or were the tanners so

[38] The tanning industry was dependent on the flow of water in the river. The blocking-up of the river by the enemy is mentioned in various accounts of the siege of 1634, e.g., Johannes Mayer's eyewit-

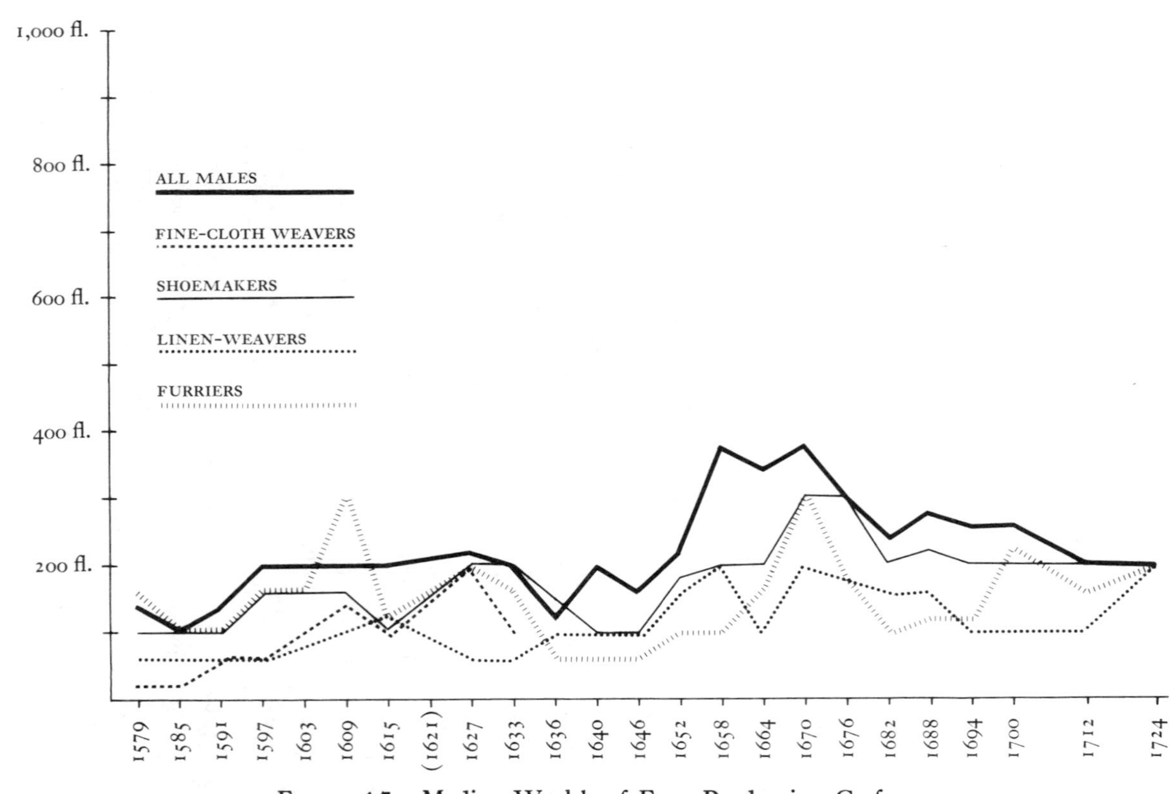

FIGURE 4.7. Median Wealth of Four Production Crafts.

dependent upon export markets that the disruption of trade and the decline of the annual fair proved especially damaging to them? Even if the precise explanation eludes us, the fate of the tanners between 1633 and 1636 illustrates the drastic short-term economic impact of the crisis of the 1630's. Yet the effects were not permanent: during the recovery decade of the 1650's, the tanners swiftly recovered their traditional status of wealth far above the norm, a position they continued to enjoy until the end of the century. About 1700, however, the tanners started to lose wealth once again; by 1712 they had fallen under the general median and in 1724, after a decade of peace, they were still under it. The pattern of swift recovery that had followed the Thirty Years War was not repeated after the second great cycle of wars came to an end.

Figure 4.7 illustrates the movement of medians for four additional production crafts in Nördlingen: the fine-cloth weavers (only until 1633, after which they dwindled into insignificance), the shoemakers, the linen weavers and the furriers. Far more important than the individual fluctuations of each curve, however, is the overall unity they present. With only minor exceptions, the medians for all of these crafts remained permanently below the median for all male citizens. Along with the wool weavers, these production crafts in the aggregate shared a permanently depressed status within the community. Even their participation in the postwar recovery was limited or retarded.

A very different story is provided by the principal victualing trades (Figure 4.8). The taverners stand out as having enjoyed a status of median wealth far above that of most of their fellow citizens. To be sure, their median wealth did undergo considerable fluctuation. Nevertheless, the privi-

---

ness account, translated by Ludwig Mußgnug as *Die Belagerung von Nördlingen anno 1634* (Nördlingen, 1927), p. 16. The river was blocked principally to prevent mills from functioning and to make it hard for fires to be doused, but obviously this would affect tanning as well.

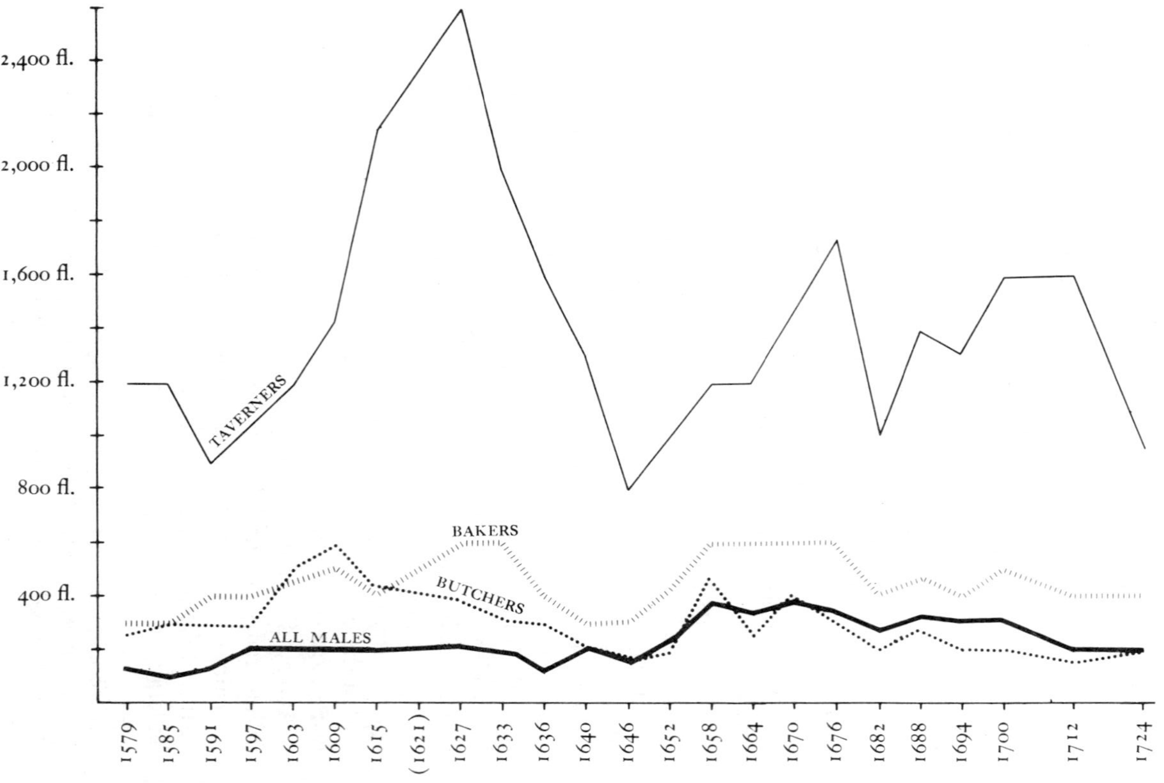
2,400 fl.
2,000 fl.
1,600 fl.
1,200 fl.
800 fl.
400 fl.
TAVERNERS
BAKERS
BUTCHERS
ALL MALES
1579
1585
1591
1597
1603
1609
1615
(1621)
1627
1633
1636
1640
1646
1652
1658
1664
1670
1676
1682
1688
1694
1700
1712
1724

leged status of the taverners is obvious, and it remained secure throughout this era. Much the same applies, on a smaller scale, to the bakers, whose median wealth remained permanently above the norm for all citizens throughout the 140 years under study. The butchers, however, present a more interesting case: after an initial period of approximate parity with the bakers, from about 1620 on they underwent a steady decline and by the end of the century they were permanently below the norm. An explanation for this emerging contrast between the two major victualing trades may lie in their changing numbers: at the beginning of our period, the number of butchers only slightly exceeded that of bakers; by the end, there were half again as many butchers as bakers. The same market was shared by both, but now there were many more butchers than bakers per customer, and the inevitable consequence was a smaller share of the wealth for each individual butcher.

The nine trades analyzed here were the largest ones in Nördlingen: in any given year they accounted for about half the total number of male citizens. But what about the other trades? For smaller occupational groups, the changing level of median wealth is a less meaningful measure: the smaller a group was, the more likely it was that its median wealth would fluctuate erratically due to accidents of marriage, death, inheritance or the like. Thus, in order to study changes in the distribution of wealth among the entire spectrum of occupations, a different measure has been used: the proportion of the total wealth owned collectively by members of each occupational sector. Table 4.7 provides this information for six selected years between 1579 and 1724.

The craftsmen represented by far the largest sector of the citizenry, so their collective experience is of special importance. We saw earlier that the Thirty Years War was the decisive catalyst in reducing their numerical importance: until the war about 70 percent of the citizens were craftsmen, but during the war this proportion dropped to just

TABLE 4.7. Percentage of the Total Wealth Owned by Members of Each Occupational Group

	1579		*1615*		*1652*		*1670*		*1700*		*1724*	
	a	*(b)*	*a*	*(b)*	*a*	*(b)*	*a*	*(b)*	*a*	*(b)*	*a*	*(b)*
Craftsmen	46	(70)	40	(69)	27	(59)	34	(58)	32	(59)	35	(59)
Food and Drink Trades	23	(13)	27	(15)	30	(20)	30	(20)	31	(20)	27	(20)
Commerce and Retailing	10	(2)	15	(3)	18	(4)	11	(4)	8	(4)	13	(4)
Learned and Bureaucratic	6	(7)	13	(8)	14	(10)	13	(10)	23	(9)	17	(9)
Other Noncraftsmen	4	(6)	3	(4)	2	(4)	5	(6)	4	(7)	3	(6)
No Occupation	12	(3)	2	(1)	8	(3)	7	(2)	3	(1)	5	(2)

a: Percentage of total wealth (of all male citizens) owned by members of each occupational group.
(*b*): (Percentage of all male citizens in that group).

under 60 percent. It is not surprising, then, that the craftsmen's share of the total wealth also dropped sharply during the Thirty Years War. But it should be observed that this decline in wealth had already set in before the war began. Postwar developments are equally noteworthy: from 1652 on, the proportion of craftsmen among the citizenry remained stable, yet between 1652 and 1670—during the years of economic recovery and redistribution of wealth—their share of the total wealth increased substantially. Only after 1670 did it level off. Seen from this point of view, the Thirty Years War was not uniquely decisive in affecting the position of Nördlingen's artisans. In the first place, the war only accentuated a decline in wealth which was already underway. In the second place, the losses of the war years were followed by two decades of improvement in the craftsmen's position—improvement which, however, was interrupted by that second great cycle of warfare whose effects are apparent in Nördlingen from the 1670's on. In short, between 1580 and 1650 the craftsmen of Nördlingen were losing wealth relative to their numbers and, despite the improvement of the 1650's and 1660's, they never fully regained the position they had enjoyed at the beginning of our period.[39] But who *was* gaining wealth at the expense of the craftsmen? Certainly not members of the victualing trades, whose increase in wealth could not even keep pace with their increase in numbers. Nor was it members of the noncraft service occupations, whose experiences roughly paralleled those of the craftsmen. Instead our attention must turn to two other sectors of the citizenry: the commercial-retailing sector and the professional-bureaucratic sector. We shall look at each in turn.

At first glance the experiences of the merchants and re-

[39] This is evident if we look at the ratio between (a) the proportion of the total wealth owned by craftsmen and (b) the proportion of the citizens who were craftsmen. In 1579 this ratio was 0.46/0.70, or 0.657. In 1652 it had fallen to 0.458. By 1670 it had risen to 0.586, and it was at approximately the same level (0.593) in 1724.

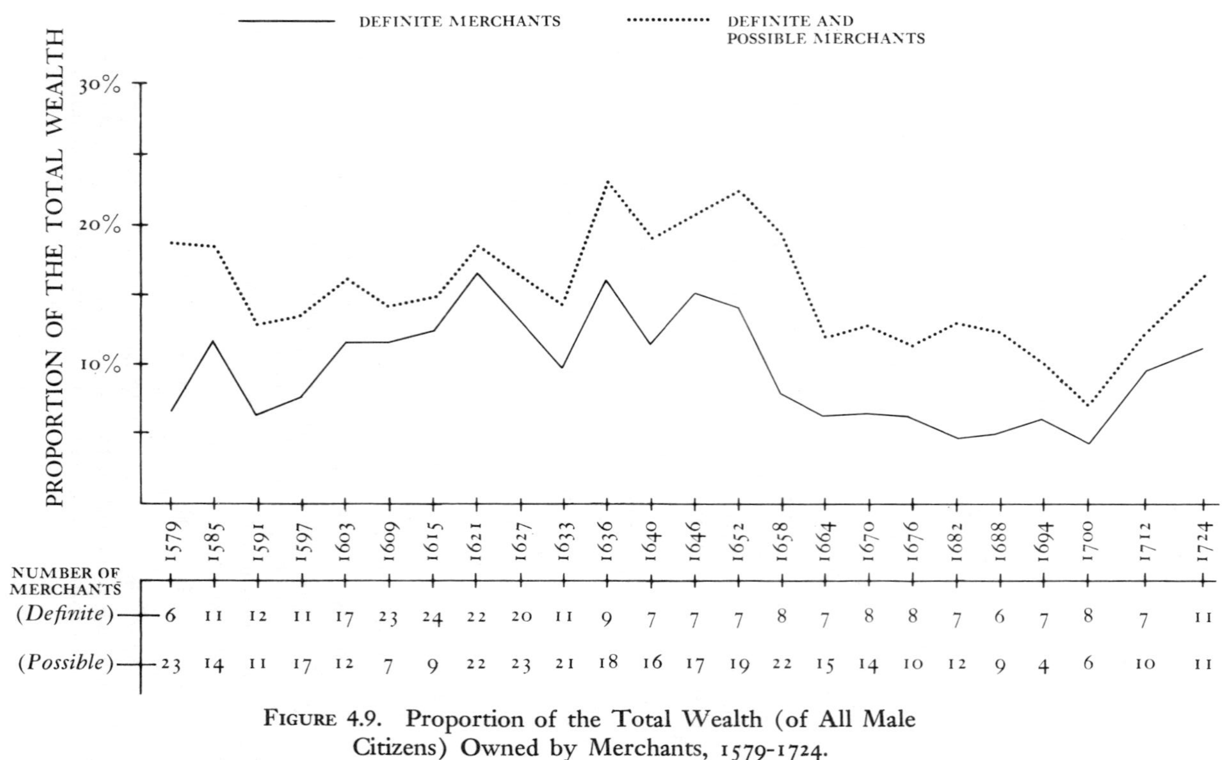

FIGURE 4.9. Proportion of the Total Wealth (of All Male Citizens) Owned by Merchants, 1579-1724.

tailers appear easy to interpret: a dramatic increase in their share of the wealth up to 1650, then a sharp decrease to 1700, followed by a renewed increase. But in fact these findings are complicated by the fact that some citizens listed as having no occupation were, in fact, engaged full-time or part-time in commerce, especially during the early years of this study. Thus, although the general trend suggested by these figures is no doubt accurate, the extreme changes in wealth indicated here may be somewhat misleading.

Let us take a closer look at the most important members of the commercial-retailing sector: the large-scale merchants, men who engaged in long-distance trade, primarily in cloths.[40] In doing so, we must first look at the data for those men who can definitely be identified as merchants, and then ask whether these results can be upheld in light of the information about men who were possibly merchants.[41] Thus, Figure 4.9 records data about the numbers and wealth of both the "definite" and the "possible" merchants in Nördlingen.

From the beginning of our period until the middle of the Thirty Years War, we can observe a constant, rapid expansion in both the number and the wealth of definite merchants. Even disregarding the data for 1579 (when it is especially clear that the number of merchants is underreported), the increase in number from 1585 until the 1620's

[40] All or virtually all of the merchants in Nördlingen were dealers in cloth. The more general term for merchant (Handelsmann) was actually used interchangeably with the more specific terms for cloth merchant (Tuchhändler, Tuchschneider and Gewandschneider).

[41] In a number of cases, persons are listed as merchants in one or more tax register and then cease to have any occupational designations. In accordance with the guidelines cited in Chapter Three, note 2, I continued to code such persons as merchants unless a change of occupation was specifically recorded. By the same token, however, it must be assumed that a few of the persons listed with no occupation from the first entry I recorded onward may actually have been merchants, especially during the earlier years of this study, since many careers began before the first year taken here (1579).

is strikingly evident. Meanwhile, the merchants' share of the total wealth also grew correspondingly larger. The Thirty Years War ended this expansion in the number of merchants. Already between 1627 and 1633—even before the great crisis—the number of definite merchants was almost halved, and it continued to decline slightly thereafter. In a few cases, men listed as merchants in one tax register appear in more modest occupations six years later: two become shopkeepers, one an ironmonger.[42] For the most part, however, the reduction is a product of attrition—old merchants died or moved away and few new ones took their place. It is easy to surmise that, as the war increasingly emptied the citizens' pockets and destroyed the opportunities for long-distance trade, young men who in better times might have joined the citizenship rolls as merchants now selected occupations involving fewer risks and smaller financial outlays. Thus, the merchants became a smaller and more exclusive group. These men, however, continued to retain their wealth. The seven definite merchants of 1646 owned almost as large a share of the total wealth as the twenty-two merchants of 1621.

The postwar years brought a sudden reversal of this situation. The number of definite merchants remained stable, but their share of the wealth did not. Between 1646 and 1664, their proportion dropped by over one-half: clearly, the merchants did not benefit from the economic recovery of the postwar years. Their share remained under 7 percent until the end of the century; it was only after 1700 that we can see a substantial improvement in their position.

Now it must be asked whether these conclusions are contradicted by evidence about persons of indeterminate occupation, of whom at least some were certainly merchants. The upper curve in Figure 4.9 adds the data for these men

[42] The cases are those of Albanus Scheler, Hans Georg Hail and Christoph Wucherer. In the first case the change came between 1627 and 1633, and in the latter two cases between 1621 and 1627.

to the data for definite merchants.[43] Of course, one can never know for sure how many of these "possibles" really were merchants. But it is clear that the addition of data from this group, at least from 1600 on, does not materially contradict the conclusions we have already reached about the merchants' changing position. In 1646, the definite merchants *alone* accounted for 15 percent of the total wealth; by 1700, all of the definite and possible merchants *together* accounted for only 7 percent of the total. Nothing could demonstrate more clearly to what extent the merchants' share of the total wealth declined sharply in the half-century after the Thirty Years War.

Thus, during the war itself, the merchants' relative position within the citizenry had undergone some improvement. As we have seen, the rich were less affected by wartime depredations than the poor; and enough of the old mercantile fortunes lasted during the war to keep the aggregate wealth of the merchants high until the 1640's.[44] But, as these men died out, economic problems ushered in by the war made it harder for younger men to generate the same kinds of fortunes anew, and the collective wealth of the merchants of Nördlingen registered a prolonged decline.

After 1670, as we have seen, the relative position of the richest stratum of citizens began to improve once again. But the merchants no longer figured as prominently among this wealthy elite as they had earlier in the century. For the declining collective importance of merchants in Nördlingen coincided with the growing size and wealth of another sector of the citizenry: the members of learned professions and

[43] Included in this group are all persons for whom no occupation is known, except for those who at no point during their careers were assessed at more than 200 fl.; it is scarcely possible that someone whose wealth remained permanently at or below this level could have been a merchant.

[44] Characteristically, the two wealthiest merchants in 1640 (Balthas Adam and Adam Frickhinger) were both men who had entered the tax rolls before 1604.

the civic bureaucracy.[45] As Table 4.7 showed, between 1579 and 1700 this sector underwent a moderate increase in its size, and a very substantial increase in its wealth.

This development reflected the growing tendency of wealthy German urban families to train their sons for administrative and professional careers; certainly, the contributions of Nördlingen's merchant families to the city's professional and administrative sector can be amply illustrated, starting with the most prominent family of all, the Frickhingers.[46] It is not entirely clear whether declining economic opportunities caused such families to direct their sons into alternative careers, or whether the social pressure to push sons into professional careers resulted in the rejection of potential economic opportunities. What is clear, however, is that the declining number and wealth of merchants in Nördlingen reflects not so much a decline in the leading role of these families as a shift in their fields of activity.

Between 1700 and 1724 there was a reversal of this trend: the merchants' share of the wealth rose and the professional-bureaucratic share declined. A closer inspection, however, would show that this increase in the merchants' wealth was caused by the fortunes of just one family: the Wörners. By the late seventeenth century the Wörners had already become Nördlingen's richest family, but in the early eighteenth century their wealth continued to grow. In 1724 eleven definite merchants owned a total of 99,360 fl., but five-sixths of this amount was held by the brothers David and Daniel Wörner alone. In fact, these two men and their sister accounted for more than one-tenth of the total wealth of Nördlingen's male and female citizens in 1724. This concentration of wealth in the hands of one family helps to account for the increasingly unequal distribution of wealth

[45] For a detailed treatment of one member of this occupational group, see Rudolf Lenz and Gundolf Keil, "Johann Christoph Donauer (1669-1718): Untersuchungen zur Soziographie und Pathographie eines Nördlinger Ratskonsulenten aufgrund der Leichenpredigt," *Zeitschrift für bayerische Landesgeschichte*, 38 (1975), 317-55.

[46] See Chapter Six.

which we have already observed taking place in the early eighteenth century.

How the Wörners achieved their commanding position in the city's economy is the subject of a later chapter. But it is important to emphasize the extent of their economic power, for it helps to explain why the years of peace which followed the War of the Spanish Succession were so different from those which had followed the Thirty Years War. In the 1650's, no single merchant family had dominated the city's economy. It is not surprising, then, that the reduction in taxation and revival of trade during those years had benefited a wide stratum of the citizenry. The situation after 1714, however, was very different. Not only was the economic recovery of those years more limited, it was also more restricted in its benefits. For the ordinary craftsmen of Nördlingen, peace had been good news in the 1650's. In the 1710's and 1720's, however, it made hardly any difference.

Five

The Burden of War: Municipal Finance

So far we have looked at Nördlingen primarily as a collection of individuals and social or occupational groups. In the next three chapters, however, we shall look at the city as a corporate entity, for our attention now turns to the government of Nördlingen. The present chapter will discuss the aspect of civic affairs most directly affected by the century of warfare that began in 1618: municipal finances. The next chapter will examine an aspect of the city government in which long-term change, though also significant, was less directly linked to the vicissitudes of war: the composition of the magistracy. Chapter Seven will treat one feature of civic affairs which remained remarkably stable, at least until the early eighteenth century: the nature and exercise of political authority.

We begin, then, with finances. It should be stressed, however, that an exact chronicle of the city's financial history would be almost impossible to assemble. For one thing, monies were received and disbursed by a variety of different municipal agencies, and these agencies frequently transferred or lent funds to each other: thus, what appears to be an expenditure of funds may often simply represent a shift of cash from one municipal account to another. At the start of the seventeenth century, there were two principal financial agencies—the city treasury and the city hospital—and about half a dozen minor ones, consisting of various charitable foundations. During the course of the century, there emerged an important new agency, the Kriegs- or Anlagskasse, devoted chiefly to the collection and distribution of military-oriented funds. These funds—the *Anlagen*—were initially handled by the city treasury itself, but eventually their management was concentrated under a separate administration. The process of transition, however, remains somewhat unclear: the Anlagen were first collected in the 1630's, but it was only in the 1670's that the Anlagskasse emerged as a clearly defined, separate municipal institution, with its own permanent account books.[1]

Thus, for some crucial decades in the middle years of the seventeenth century, it is difficult to determine just what transactions were taking place. Such complications are compounded by the absence of some financial records and the incompleteness of others. Altogether, then, the sources do not encourage any exhaustive attempt to disentangle the seventeenth-century finances of Nördlingen. They are adequate, however, to draw our attention to two significant developments: the growing financial demands generated by the wars of the seventeenth and early eighteenth centuries, and the consequent transition of Nördlingen from a creditor to a debtor municipality.

I

LET us start with a close look at the financial picture in Nördlingen at the beginning of our period. As noted above, the two major financial agencies were the city treasury and the city hospital. The hospital's revenues were derived largely from dues, rents, tithes and other income from rural lands; its expenditures were devoted chiefly to the administration both of the hospital itself and of the city's rural properties. Unfortunately the hospital accounts of this

[1] The series of regular, bound Anlagsrechnungen (AR) in the Stadtarchiv Nördlingen begins with vol. no. 1 for 1673. From a reference in the Kammerrechnungen for 1664 (Einnahmen: Anlagsgelter) it appears that the Anlagskasse was already in existence by then, but at that point it was evidently just a subordinate bureau of the city treasury.

TABLE 5.1. Receipts and Expenditures of the City Treasury, 1579

Receipts	*fl.*	%	*Expenditures*	*fl.*	%
Taxes from Citizens	4,900	(20.8)	Salaries, Wages and Fees of Municipal Officeholders	3,500	(16.7)
Wine and Beer Taxes (Umgelder von Wein & Bier)	8,500	(36.0)	Construction and Repairs (Wages)	1,900	(9.0)
Tolls and All Other Indirect Taxes	1,700	(7.2)	Purchase of Supplies and Commodities	7,600	(36.2)
Sales of Supplies and Commodities	2,400	(10.2)	Interest Payments and Annuities	1,700	(8.1)
Loans Repaid to the Treasury	3,000	(12.7)	Loans Granted by the Treasury	1,500	(7.1)
All Other Sources	3,100	(13.1)	Imperial and Circle Dues	500	(2.4)
			All Other Expenditures	4,300	(20.5)
Total Receipts in 1579	23,600	(100.0)	Total Expenditures	21,000	(100.0)
Balance from previous year	11,900				
Total receipts plus balance	35,500				

All amounts given in Tables 5.1-5.6 are rounded off to the nearest hundred gulden.

period, while replete with details, do not provide the annual totals of expenditure and income, so an overall evaluation would be difficult to provide.[2]

The city treasury accounts, however, were meticulously kept, and enable us to provide very exact information. Table 5.1 summarizes data from the treasury accounts in 1579, to provide a clear picture of the treasury's sources of revenue and of the distribution of its expenditures in a representative year at the start of our period. Note, for example, that indirect taxes were a far more important source of revenue than direct taxes, and that the purchase of supplies to be used or stockpiled vastly exceeded expenditures on wages for municipal officeholders.[3]

It will be apparent that the treasury carried over a healthy balance from the previous year, amounting to almost 50 percent of actual annual income. And because actual income in 1579 exceeded expenditures, the treasury was able to pass an even greater balance on to the next year's account. In addition—although this is not indicated on the Table—the city treasury in 1579 was recorded as being a creditor to the sum

[2] Totals of receipts and expenditures are not provided by the hospital accounts (Spitalrechnungen) until the late 1620's. Even after that date, moreover, the real value of the cash totals cannot be safely compared from one year to the next since hospital revenues and expenditures were in both cash and kind, and it is not clear whether the ratio between cash and kind income and outgo remained constant from one year to the next.

[3] KR 1579. The following clarifications are called for: *Receipts*: The bulk of the entry "taxes from citizens" consists of proceeds from the citizens' property tax which is described in detail in Chapter Four. However, I have also included under this heading the Nachsteuer levied on persons who left the citizenry, the fees for admission to the citizenry, and a very small amount from the so-called Paktbürger (see Chapter Two). *Expenditures*: The category labeled "purchase" includes both payments for commodities themselves and, to a lesser extent, payments of fees or wages to the persons engaged in producing, extracting or transporting these commodities. Imperial and Circle dues represent payments either to the Emperor, to a recipient designated by the Emperor, or to the treasury of the Swabian Circle.

of 35,300 fl.[4] Of this amount, some 14,800 fl. were "owed" to the treasury by other municipal agencies, especially the hospital and the infirmary for incurables. But there were also 20,500 fl. worth of "real" loans outstanding, including 3,000 fl. owed by Count Philip Ludwig of the Palatinate and 4,000 fl. owed by the Emperor himself. Clearly, the city treasury was in excellent health in 1579.

II

WHY did this financial health not persist? In attempting to answer this question, we must make two kinds of inquiry. First, we must determine how the demands made upon the treasury, and later also upon the Anlagskasse, changed over time, as reflected both in the volume and in the types of expenditure. Second, we must establish what sources of money the treasury and Anlagskasse relied upon to meet these changing levels of demand.

Figure 5.1 records the average annual expenditures of the city treasury and the Anlagskasse during each five-year period from 1576 to 1720 for which data are available. It must be stressed, however, that these findings are based on somewhat deficient records. The city treasury accounts are complete except for the years 1621 to 1633, when the books are either useless or missing altogether.[5] For the Anlagskasse, however, only about half of the account books between 1673 (the first year) and 1700 are extant; thus, the amounts recorded here represent the average expenditures for which-

[4] KR 1579, fols. 351-55. These figures are rounded off to the nearest 100 fl.

[5] During the hyperinflation of the early 1620's, the bookkeeping system of the city treasury broke down; although the inflation ended in 1624, the bookkeeping took longer to recover. From 1621 to 1629 the Kammerrechnungen are incomplete; from 1630 to 1633 they are missing altogether. Individual entries in the Kammerrechnungen were always made in fl. and krz., but until 1629 the totals were converted to and expressed in fl. münz. (One fl. münz was worth about 0.988 of a regular fl.) From 1634 onward, this clumsy process of conversion was abandoned, and all totals were given in fl. and krz.

ever years are available during any five-year period.[6] And there is one additional problem. Some amounts expended by the treasury were transferred to the Anlagskasse, where they were expended again. Thus, by adding Anlagskasse to treasury expenses, Figure 5.1 actually double-counts some funds. The tortuously complex bookkeeping methods of both agencies make it impossible to determine the exact amount of these funds; it is safe to say, however, that they rarely amounted to more than a few thousand gulden a year.[7] Thus, although from 1670 onward Figure 5.1 does not record the exact totals, it does correctly reflect the order of magnitude of expenditures made by the treasury and by its financial offspring, the Anlagskasse.

From Figure 5.1 it is apparent that civic expenditures rose during the Thirty Years War, declined after the war, and rose again after the second cycle of warfare began in the

[6] The Anlagsrechnungen are available for 1673-78, 1680, 1683, 1686-91, 1693, 1696, 1700, and 1702-19. (During the 1670's the accounts are for a fiscal year beginning in the spring and ending in the spring of the following year; from 1680 on the fiscal year coincides with the calendar year.) After 1719 the Anlagskasse was divided into two agencies: a Kriegskasse and an Anlagskasse.

[7] Although the revenues of the Anlagskasse often included amounts "from the city treasury," only some of these amounts appear in the treasury accounts as expenditures; in other cases the funds must have been provided by the treasury but not treated there as regular treasury revenues and expenditures. (For example, the Anlagskasse revenues for fiscal year 1675 include 43,925 fl. from the treasury, but this large amount does not appear under expenditures in the treasury accounts.) On the other hand, even when the treasury accounts do list expenditures of funds transferred to the Anlagskasse, the receipt of these funds is not necessarily recorded in the Anlagskasse accounts for the same year. Thus, even if all the account books were extant, it would be difficult to trace accurately all the transfers of funds from one agency to the other; and in fact, since some of the Anlagsrechnungen are missing, this is impossible. It should be emphasized, however, that except for its first three years the Anlagskasse never depended on the city treasury for the bulk of its revenues. The 32 extant Anlagskasse accounts from 1676 to 1719 show only six years in which as much as 10% of revenues came from the city treasury and no years in which more than 20% did so.

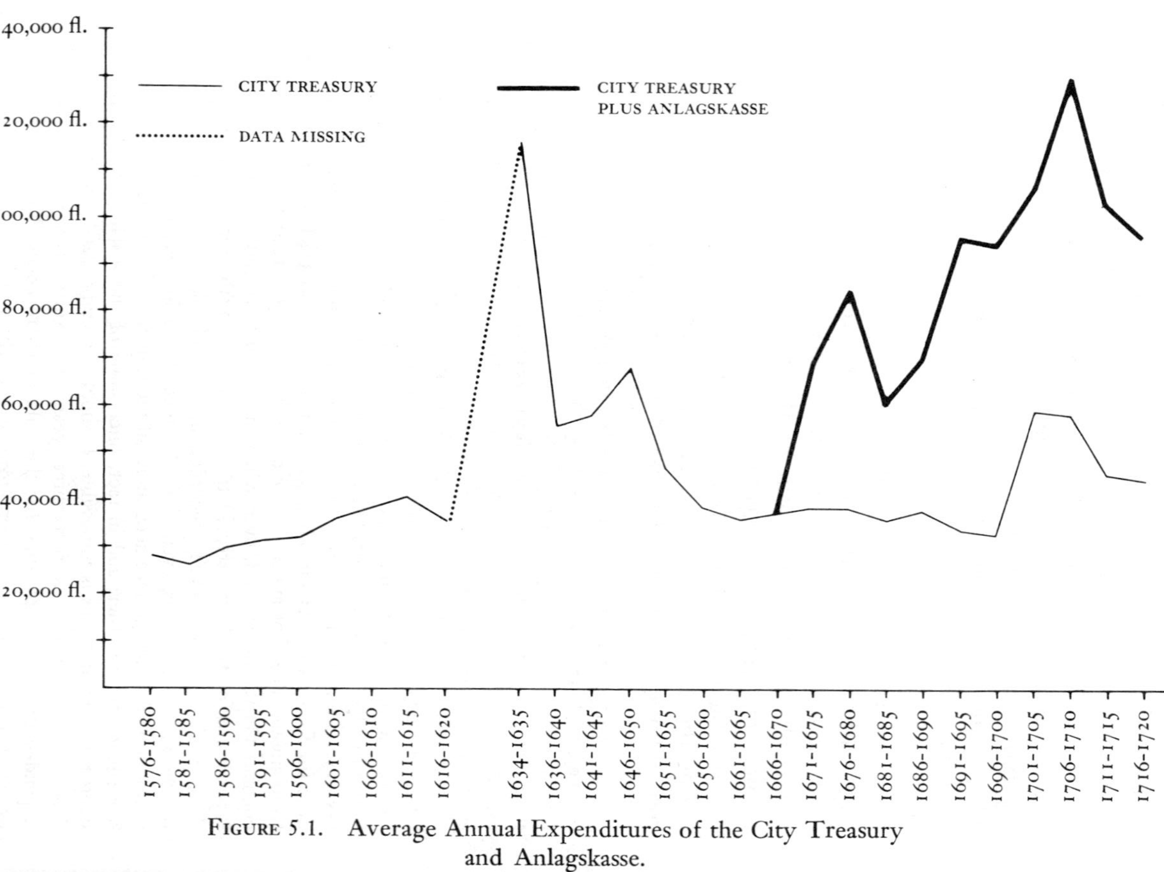

FIGURE 5.1. Average Annual Expenditures of the City Treasury and Anlagskasse.

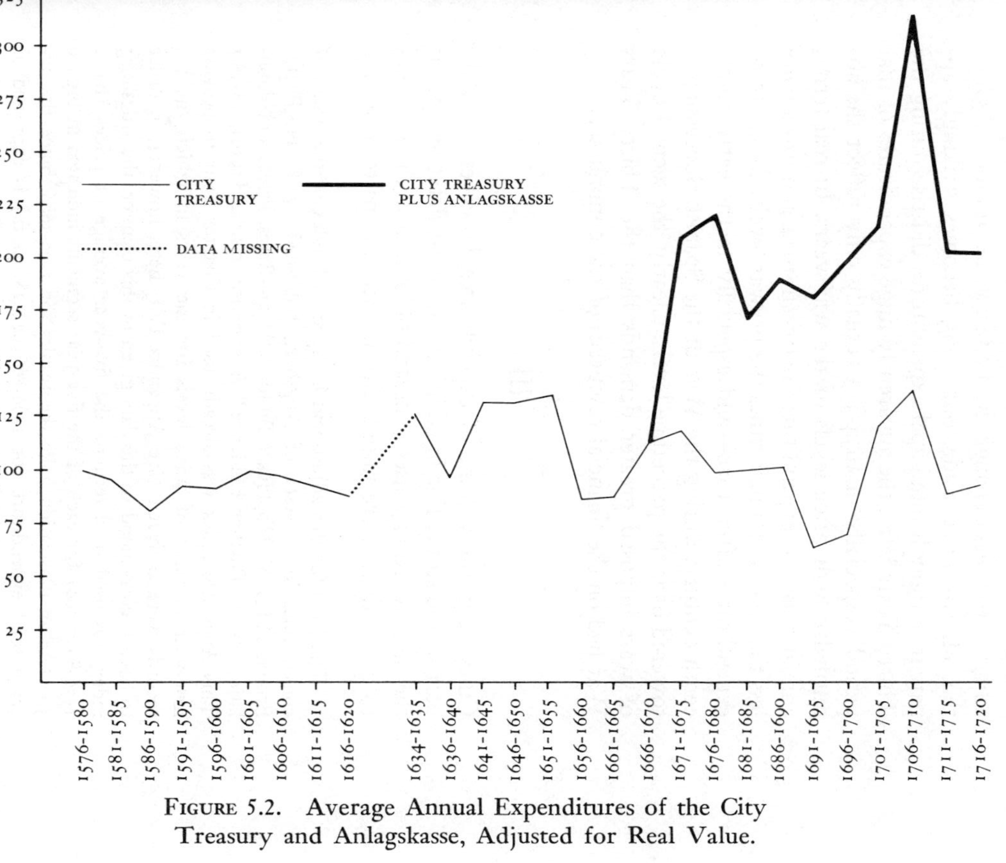

FIGURE 5.2. Average Annual Expenditures of the City Treasury and Anlagskasse, Adjusted for Real Value.

1670's. These figures, however, are given in nominal terms. In Figure 5.2 the same information is presented again, but adjusted to reflect changes in the real value of money.[8] Once this adjustment is made, one thing becomes strikingly apparent: although municipal expenditures did rise during the Thirty Years War, the apparently huge expenditures of that period (especially in 1634-35) actually only reflect the abnormally high price levels of the war years. In real terms, annual treasury expenditures between 1634 and 1655 were less than one and a half times the prewar levels. By contrast, expenditures after 1670—and especially in the early eighteenth century, during the War of the Spanish Succession—towered over the peacetime levels. Clearly, the second cycle of wars imposed greater demands than the Thirty Years War had on the financial resources of the community.

III

CHANGES in the volume of expenditures, however, are only part of the story. For in addition, one must determine what the heightened expenses consisted of, and how the revenues to cover them were raised. Up to 1620, the pattern of city

[8] The basis for this adjustment is the annual index of the prices of consumables in the city of Augsburg published by E. H. Phelps Brown and S. V. Hopkins ("Builders' Wage-Rates, Prices and Population: Some Further Evidence," *Economica*, n.s. 24 [1959], 18-38.) This Augsburg index was already used in Chapter Four to provide nine-year averages of price levels for the years in which the tax records were analyzed (see Appendix IV); here, however, in order to have it correspond to the data given in this chapter, the Augsburg index was used to determine the five-year average of prices (base: 1576-80 = 100) for each of the five-year segments indicated in Figure 5.1. (As an illustration, take the results for 1596-1600. Since the average total expenditure for 1576-80 [i.e., 28,200 fl.] is expressed as 100, the average total for 1596-1600 [i.e., 32,800 fl.] is expressed as 116. But the price index would show that the purchasing power of the gulden in 1596-1600 was only 79% of what it had been in 1576-80. Accordingly, the "real" level of expenditures in 1596-1600 was 79% of 116, or 92. This is the result that appears in Figure 5.2.)

treasury income and outgo remained essentially stable. Alcohol taxes and other indirect levies continued to account for close to half of the treasury revenues, with direct taxes and other sources making up the other half. The distribution of expenditures also remained roughly stable, although it is worth noting that there were two categories which often varied considerably from one period to the next, as a rule in roughly inverse proportion:

Expenditures (in fl.)[9]

	1591	1597	1603	1609	1615
Loans	400	11,300	5,600	300	8,100
Imperial and Circle dues	7,200	700	1,100	8,300	2,500

In the years when imperial and Circle dues were high, the city was evidently not in a position to offer extensive loans, but when imperial obligations were low, the city could do so.

Whatever changes occurred in the treasury budget before 1620, however, are insignificant when compared to the changes wrought by the Thirty Years War—not only in the level but also, and more importantly, in the types of expenditures. For the war imposed unprecedented financial demands upon the community—sometimes from imperial authorities, sometimes from Swedish officials, often directly from the troops who passed through the Ries or decided to establish themselves in the city. Much of what the soldiers wanted they took by simple plunder—especially in the unprotected villages—but to a large extent their financial demands were addressed to, and had to be met by, the city government.[10]

[9] KR, Ausgaben, for the years in question. The amounts have been rounded off to the nearest 100 gulden.

[10] According to an account prepared in the early eighteenth century, the community of Nördlingen had to pay over 2,000,000 fl. to the imperials, the Swedes, and other military recipients in the course

TABLE 5.2. Receipts and Expenditures of the City Treasury, 1634

Receipts	*fl.*	%	*Expenditures*	*fl.*	%
Taxes from Citizens	69,400	(64.8)	Salaries, Wages and Fees of		
Wine and Beer Taxes			Municipal Officeholders	11,800	(10.6)
(Umgelder von Wein & Bier)	12,400	(11.6)	Construction and Repairs (Wages)	4,300	(3.9)
Tolls and All Other Indirect Taxes	7,100	(6.6)	Purchase of Supplies and Commodities	7,200	(6.5)
Sale of Supplies and Commodities	3,700	(3.5)	Interest Payments and Annuities	2,200	(2.0)
Borrowed by the Treasury	3,400	(3.2)	Loans Repaid by the Treasury	1,400	(1.3)
Fines (e.g., for tax evasion)	7,900	(7.4)	Imperial and Circle Dues and		
All Other Sources	3,200	(3.0)	Other Military Payments	59,400	(53.4)
Total Receipts in 1634	107,100	(100.0)	"To the Soldiers"	11,700	(10.5)
			All Other Expenditures	13,200	(11.9)
			Total Real Expenditures	111,200	(100.0)
			Required to balance previous		
			year's budget	10,900	
			Total Expenditures	122,100	

Even from the incomplete account books of the 1620's, the extent of these demands becomes vividly clear. For instance, under the single heading "To the Soldiers," the treasury account books record payments of just under 28,000 fl. in 1628 and 16,500 fl. in 1629. Since, however, the total level of income and outgo in these years was not recorded, it is difficult to assess how great a share of the treasury expenditure such sums represented.

Beginning with 1634, however, complete account books are again available. In fact, the account book for that particular year deserves special scrutiny. It will be recalled that 1634 was an especially disastrous year for the city, and the records of the city treasury for that year accordingly display the sharpest possible contrast with a peacetime budget.

Table 5.2 summarizes the revenues and expenditures of the city treasury in 1634.[11] We have already seen from

of the Thirty Years War. These payments are broken down into six periods as follows (rounded off to the nearest 100 fl.):

1622-32	496,400 fl.
1632-34	264,700 fl.
1634-36	568,200 fl.
1636-40	170,600 fl.
1640-46	244,000 fl.
1646-50	349,900 fl.
Total	2,093,800 fl.

(*Unverwerffliche Causales, Warum . . . Nördlingen . . . eine nahmhaffte Moderation . . . zu suchen hat*, in: Acta der Nördlingische Matricular-beschwerden und die Untersuchung des Oekonomiestandes betreffend, B Num. VII, 1, pp. 7-8.) It is not clear how these totals were established. Since, however, these figures were presented as part of an attempt to describe the impoverishment of the community, we can assume that every effort was made to define military payments as broadly as possible, to include not only cash payments by the city treasury but also cash, plate, etc. which were handed over to soldiers directly. Thus, these amounts exceed by far the totals of all outlays to meet military demands recorded in the Kammerrechnungen.

[11] KR 1634. The clarifications made in note 3 apply also here.

Figure 5.2 that the total level of expenditures in real terms for 1634 stood above the peacetime norm. But the distribution of these expenditures in 1634 exhibits a much more drastic contrast to the peacetime budget of 1579. For almost two-thirds of the expenditures in 1634 were devoted to meeting direct military demands.

How were these heavy new financial obligations met? Indirect taxes, which had formed the backbone of the peacetime budget, clearly played a much less important role in 1634. Indeed, even if their rates were increased, tolls and other taxes which depended on a healthy volume of trade must have proved an inadequate source of revenue in the midst of war. Instead, the city had to turn to two other sources: direct taxation and borrowing.

In the year selected here, borrowing played a minimal role, and one can readily imagine why: in a disastrous year like 1634, the city's credit must have been very low. Instead, the magistrates in that year had to resort primarily to vastly increased direct taxation. Before the war, the only significant direct tax was the once-a-year property tax, amounting to one-half of 1 percent of each citizen's assessed worth. Under wartime stress, however, the city began to impose this half-percent tax over and over again within the course of a single year: in the case of 1634, for example, the ordinary tax was multiplied by a factor of eleven and a half.[12]

By 1636, however, the city fathers found this particular method of generating direct taxes unsatisfactory. Probably the chief weakness of this system lay in the fact that a man's property assessment might not always reflect accurately his real ability to hand over cash taxes at short notice, especially since the property taxes were reassessed only every third

[12] In addition to the ordinary property tax payment in November, citizens were required to pay extraordinary taxes as follows (expressed in terms of their ordinary tax amount): one full tax, one half-tax, and three triple taxes. (In addition, one half-tax was announced but not collected.) See the Extra-Ordinari Steuerbücher VIa, VIb (1634).

year. Accordingly, the magistrates introduced a new kind of tax, the Anlagen. Each citizen was assigned a specific amount which he would be required to pay every time an Anlage was announced.[13] Within months, the property tax had reverted back to its original, once-a-year status, and the Anlagen system became the principal method of direct taxation to meet wartime needs. In 1643, for example, treasury revenues totaled 64,100 fl.; of this amount, fully one-third was derived from 33 Anlagen levied at ten-day intervals.[14] Thus, although the methods had changed since 1634, direct taxation was still the single most important means of generating emergency income.

Anlagen continued to be imposed steadily until 1652; indeed, the amounts raised were particularly heavy in the years immediately following the Peace of Westphalia, when funds had to be raised throughout the Empire to pay off Swedish and other soldiers before they would end their occupation. Then, for the rest of the 1650's, the Anlagen apparently disappeared,[15] and municipal income and expenditures dropped back to their prewar level.

The early 1660's, however, brought renewed warfare to the Empire—this time against the Turks—and with it came renewed financial demands from the treasury of the Swabian Circle. Once again Anlagen were levied. It was only after 1672, however, when the first of the great wars against Louis XIV began, that these financial demands began to transform the fiscal structure of the community. The Circle authorities began to levy regular annual assessments on the municipality, and regular Anlagen once again became an

[13] For the introduction of this system, see OB 1612-40, fols. 319b-320a (12 Sept. 1636).

[14] See KR 1643: Einnehmen: Gemein Einnehmen.

[15] See KR for the years in question. It cannot be stated categorically that no Anlagen were levied between 1653 and 1660, but there appears no evidence from the Kammerrechnungen or the ordinance books to suggest that they were imposed, at least not as taxes on the entire citizenry. There were some Anlagen imposed on rural subjects of the city, but they were not financially significant.

important part of Nördlingen's financial life. It was in these years that the Anlagskasse emerged as an independent agency. By the last decades of the century, the proceeds from Anlagen in any given year routinely exceeded the proceeds from the tax on citizens' property.[16] In short, although before the Thirty Years War (and again in the 1650's), each citizen paid only half a percent of his total worth annually in direct taxes, by the last decades of the century he normally paid at least 1 percent and often much more in direct taxes each year. In fact, in the fiscal year 1676, during one of the wars against Louis XIV, the citizens of Nördlingen paid direct taxes which averaged out to over 3½ percent of their total property value.[17]

IV

An increased rate of direct taxation was not the only change which the seventeenth-century wars brought about in the financial structure of the community. There were new kinds of indirect taxes, too: in the 1690's, for example, new or additional excises on wine, beer, flour, meat and other com-

[16] For the renewed imposition of Anlagen in the 1660's, see OB 1641-88, fols. 198a-199a (9 Aug. 1661), 233b-234b (Apr. 1664), et al. For comparison of proceeds from the property tax and from the Anlagen, cf. KR (Einnahmen: Bürgersteuer) and AR (Einnahm von bürgerlichen/continuierenden Anlags-Terminen) for the years from 1676 onward.

[17] In 1676 the total assessed worth of the adult citizens of Nördlingen came to 866,700 fl. (see Appendix III). The total amount of direct taxes paid by citizens to the city treasury in 1676 and to the Anlagskasse in fiscal year 1676 was as follows:

4,718 fl.	(ordinary property tax)
4,665 fl.	(extraordinary property tax)
22,587 fl.	(Anlagen from citizens)
31,970 fl.	(Total)

This total represents 3.7% of the total assessed worth of the citizens in that year. (See KR 1676, Einnahmen; and AR 1676, Einnahmen.)

modities were introduced, and they soon became major sources of income for the treasury and the Anlagskasse.[18] But an even more important source of revenue consisted of loans, both from citizens and from foreigners. For beginning with the Thirty Years War, the city became increasingly dependent on borrowing in order to balance the budget of the treasury and, later, of the Anlagskasse. Let us look at each agency in turn.

For the period before and after the Thirty Years War—although not for the wartime era itself—it is possible to obtain some picture of the debts owed to and by the city treasury. These data are summarized in Table 5.3.[19] Before the war, the treasury does not appear to have owed any debts;[20] to the contrary, a substantial amount was normally

[18] For the introduction of these excises, see OB 1688-1706, pp. 69-75 (2 Sept. 1692) and pp. 193-99 (12 Jan. 1697).

[19] Source: KR for the years indicated; in each instance the debts are entered in a special section at the back of the volume. I have attempted throughout to eliminate "false" debts, i.e., amounts owed to the city treasury by one of the municipal foundations (e.g., the hospital), or else owed to one of these foundations by the treasury. *Amounts Owed to the Treasury*: For the 1579-1620 period, I have eliminated the debts owed by these foundations. Likewise, debts from foundations are not included for the years selected in the later period, except 1658 and 1670, when the total may include some funds owed by the Stipendiaten-Pflege. *Amounts Owed by the Treasury*: Under this heading I have combined the total amounts of Capitalien, Interesse, and "andere Schulden," except that I have eliminated 11,000 fl. owed during this period to the Stipendiaten-Pflege. If any other "false" debts are still included in the totals given, they are very minor.

[20] The city treasury certainly made annual interest payments throughout the period before 1620; it appears, however, that these did not involve interest on borrowed capital. Instead, this was evidently interest on certain kinds of annuities, in which a purchaser made a cash payment to the treasury (recorded under income) and was guaranteed an annual payment (recorded under expenditures). The impression that the city did not borrow capital during the prewar period is strengthened by observing the annual accounting procedure followed at the end of each year. In each volume of the

TABLE 5.3. Debts Owed to and Owed by the City Treasury (fl.)

Year	*Amount Owed to City Treasury*[a]	*Amount Owed by City Treasury*[a]
1579	20,500	—
1597	10,200	—
1609	19,800	—
1620	9,900	—
1657	3,600	151,200
1658	4,400	131,500
1670	6,900	88,300
1688	4,400	74,000
1695	3,800	79,800

[a] See note 19.

owed to the city, much of it by noble debtors. The Thirty Years War, however, changed all this. Throughout the war, and immediately after it, the city was required to borrow extensively from both outsiders and citizens. At times the city resorted to forced loans: in June 1649, for example, the council required loans not only from all citizens, but also from every Jew in the city "bei welchem noch etwas zu befinden," that is, who still had any money to lend.[21]

The first postwar accounting of the treasury's debts was made in 1657 and showed that the city owed its creditors

Kammerrechnungen, the actual assets of the treasury as of the year's end were determined in the following manner: (1) total income (including last year's cash balance) was determined; (2) total expenditures were subtracted, to determine this year's cash balance; (3) to this cash balance was added the total value of debts owed to the treasury, to determine total assets. Obviously, if the treasury owed any capital, the amount of this capital would have to have been subtracted to determine the total assets correctly.

21 OB 1641-88, fols. 80b-82a (17/18 June, 1649). Although Jews had been banished from Nördlingen at the start of the sixteenth century, during the Thirty Years War a number of them were permitted to live within the city for protection, and were subjected to tremendous financial exactions. (Müller, "Aus fünf Jahrhunderten [1. Teil]," pp. 115-18.)

over 151,000 fl., while itself being owed a mere 3,570 fl. From 1657 to 1658, the treasury was able to pay off at least 20,000 fl. of debts, and by 1670 it had liquidated another 43,000 fl. But the renewal of warfare around 1670 evidently made it impossible for the treasury to continue to discharge its obligations at the same rate; by 1695, treasury debts still amounted to almost 80,000 fl. Even though an exact accounting of debts is not available after that date, the continuing indebtedness of the treasury is evident from the account books of the following years. Consider, for example, the treasury budget for 1700 (Table 5.4).[22] In that year almost 25 percent of treasury expenditures were devoted to the payment of annuities and interest and the repayment of capital, and at the same time the treasury contracted 2,700 fl. in new debts.

Yet the debts of the city treasury were small compared to those of the Anlagskasse. This agency, as we have seen, had been established to administer the collection and disbursement of Anlagen, the special taxes levied to cover assessments imposed by the Swabian war treasury as well as financial demands made by soldiers quartered in or marching through the Ries. Right from the beginning, however, the Anlagen proved inadequate to meet these demands, and it was necessary to resort to other means—above all, borrowing. This meant that in addition to covering military expenses the Anlagskasse had to make interest payments and repay the loans when they expired. These expenditures, however, could only be met by further borrowing. The inevitable consequences are illustrated by Table 5.5: within 25 years of its establishment, the Anlagskasse had run up more than 400,000 fl. of debts.[23]

Loans to the Anlagskasse (as well as to the city treasury)

[22] KR 1700. The clarifications made in note 3 also apply here.

[23] These amounts are tabulated in the AR (Appendices) for 1677 to 1700/1702, after which this listing is discontinued. The amounts owed to the Anlagskasse were mostly hopelessly bad debts: unpaid Anlagen from ten or twenty years earlier.)

TABLE 5.4. Receipts and Expenditures of the City Treasury, 1700.

Receipts	*fl.*	%	*Expenditures*	*fl.*	%
Taxes from Citizens	6,500	(19.7)	Salaries, Wages and Fees of Municipal Officeholders	10,400	(31.2)
Wine and Beer Taxes (Umgelder von Wein & Bier)	12,900	(39.1)	Construction and Repairs (Wages)	2,700	(8.1)
Tolls and All Other Indirect Taxes	6,200	(18.8)	Purchase of Supplies and Commodities	4,300	(12.9)
Sale of Supplies and Commodities	2,700	(8.2)	Interest Payments and Annuities	4,500	(13.5)
Borrowed by the Treasury	2,700	(8.2)	Loans Repaid by the Treasury	3,300	(10.0)
All Other Sources	2,000	(6.1)	Imperial and Circle Dues	500	(1.5)
Total Receipts in 1700	33,000	(100.0)	All Other Expenditures	7,600	(22.8)
Balance from previous year	5,100				
Total receipts plus balance	38,100		Total Expenditures	33,300	(100.0)

TABLE 5.5. Amounts Owed to and Owed by the Anlagskasse (fl.)

Year	*Amount Owed to the Anlagskasse*	*Amount Owed by the Anlagskasse*
1678	2,700	n.a.
1679	3,200	135,800
1680	200	123,700
1686	300	128,400
1687	400	129,000
1688	500	134,300
1689	600	148,800
1690	2,200	163,900
1691	3,000	207,800
1693	5,000	284,700
1696	6,800	385,200
1700	11,200	428,700
1702	15,200	n.a.

were a reliable form of investment for those who advanced them, for the interest payments—normally 5 percent per annum—provided a form of regular annuity income. Among those who enjoyed such payments, often in small amounts, were scores of Nördlingen's own citizens. But the major beneficiaries were outsiders, for by far the greatest part of these loans were advanced by wealthy noncitizens, including many members of the Swabian nobility.

We can see this, for example, from the account book of the Anlagskasse for 1693. In that year the Anlagskasse made interest payments of 11,304 fl. on capital loans amounting to some 236,500 fl.[24] About 78 percent of this capital had been

[24] AR 1693, Ausgaben. Interest payments are listed under six headings: Ausgaab bezahlter . . . (1) Ausländischer, (2) Bürgerlicher Rabattischer, (3) Bürgerlicher Croattischer, (4) Palfischer Husaren, (5) Bürgerlicher Creiß-Mannschafft Anlehen, (6) Bürgerlicher Chur-Sächsischer Anlehen . . . Interesse und Zinß. (Despite its title, the first heading includes payments both to citizens and to noncitizens.) Each entry notes not only the amount of interest being paid but also the size of the original loan and the terms on which payment is being made (annually, semi-annually, etc.): this makes it possible to

TABLE 5.6. Receipts and Expenditures of the Anlagskasse for Selected Years (percent)

	1683	*1688*	*1693*	*1700*	*1710*	*1719*
RECEIPTS						
Surplus from Previous Year	3	3	4	8	2	0
From the City Treasury	7	6	1	2	6	4
Regular (Citizens') Anlagen	21	20	16	12	17	19
Borrowed Capital	58	45	53	33	34	28
Excise Taxes	—	—	10	21	18	17
Other Receipts	12	28	15	24	24	33
Total (fl.)	(28,200)	(34,000)	(64,900)	(63,300)	(57,000)	(54,800)
EXPENDITURES						
To the War Treasury of the Swabian Circle	11	26	8	18	38	2
To Soldiers Quartered or Recruited in the Region	15	6	43	11	17	8
Repayment of Borrowed Capital	40	29	7	34	8	42
Interest Payments	24	17	18	31	27	41
Other Expenditures	11	22	24	6	9	7
Total (fl.)	(25,100)	(37,900)	(64,500)	(58,900)	(55,500)	(54,400)

advanced by noncitizens. Some of these noncitizens did in fact live in the city—notably Baron Wilhelm Conrad von Goldstein, an official of the margraviate of Brandenburg who had settled down in Nördlingen in 1680 and who had lent the Anlagskasse a total of 12,000 fl. by 1693.[25] But most of the loans came from outside the community: from noble families of the region, from wealthy citizens of other towns, even from Catholic ecclesiastical institutions. Among the greatest creditors of the Anlagskasse in 1693—defined here as those who had lent it 6,000 fl. or more—we find two generals, six other nobles, two burghers (from Nuremberg and Vienna) and one ecclesiastical chapter.[26]

Some other sources of revenue were available, notably the excise taxes which were introduced in the 1690's. But, as Table 5.6 shows, loans were always a major source of revenue, while interest on or repayment of these loans always formed a major part of the Anlagskasse expenditures.[27] This became particularly apparent after the War of the Spanish Succession came to an end and the level of military expenses was reduced. One need only consider the Anlagskasse budget for 1719: in that year, a mere 10 percent of expenditures

give an accurate total of the amount of capital on which interest was being paid in one twelve-month period. The total amount given here (236,500 fl.) is somewhat lower than the amount recorded for 1693 in Table 5.5, for it includes neither interest-free loans made to the Anlagskasse nor loans taken up in 1693 on which the first payments were due only in 1694, e.g., 12,000 fl. from the count of Pappenheim (AR 1693, Einnahmen von aufgenommenen Capitalien).

25 Concerning Goldstein, see the entry in Daniel Eberhard Beyschlag and Johannes Müller, *Beyträge zur Nördlingischen Geschlechtshistorie, die Nördlingischen Epitaphien erhaltend*, 2 vols. (Nördlingen, 1801-?), vol. 2, pp. 143-46. In addition to his loans to the Anlagskasse, Goldstein also advanced considerable funds to the city treasury, which amounted to 6,000 fl. as of 1688 (KR 1688, Appendix).

26 The two greatest creditors of the Anlagskasse in 1693 were Goldstein and General Berner, each with loans totaling 12,000 fl. Next came Herr von Wollmershausen and the chapter of the princely prebend of Ellwangen, each with 11,000 fl.

27 Source: AR for the years in question.

went to cover military demands while over 80 percent was devoted to sustaining or repaying debts.[28] Founded as an institution for the raising and disbursement of military funds, the Anlagskasse had degenerated into an institution whose main purpose was to service its own debts.

The magistrates themselves recognized that this had taken place, and in 1720 they reorganized the Anlagskasse accordingly. Its original functions, such as raising money to meet the assessments of the Swabian war treasury, were now to be handled by a new agency, the Kriegskasse. The Anlagskasse itself would henceforth be concerned exclusively with raising funds to pay off its own debts.[29]

No amount of administrative reorganization, however, could solve the city's real financial problem: a perpetual shortage of revenues sufficient to cover both current expenses and interest payments on past loans. During the War of the Spanish Succession the magistrates began to resort to an unprecedented means of raising money: the alienation of city-owned land. In 1709, the hospital's holdings in the village of Reimlingen were sold; in 1712, its holdings in the village of Grosselfingen followed suit. Additional sales in subsequent years paved the way to the most drastic step of all: in 1739 Nördlingen's magistrates sold the entire village of Lierheim to the Order of Teutonic Knights.[30]

In the short run, such measures could provide the magis-

[28] By 1719 the total amounts lent by some creditors considerably exceeded those recorded for 1693. In 1719 the three greatest creditors of the Anlagskasse were: Herr von Fabricius with loans totaling 40,000 fl., Lothar Franz, Baron von Ostheim, with a total of 30,000 fl., and Maria Antonia Schenckin, Gräfin von Castell, with 20,000 fl. (AR 1719, Ausgaben auf Interesse und Zinsgellter).

[29] Lettenmeyer, *Finanzwirtschaft*, pp. 35-42.

[30] Ibid., pp. 55-56. According to Lettenmeyer, between 1701 and 1745, city-owned lands worth 170,000 fl. and hospital-owned lands worth 100,000 fl. were alienated. His source for these figures, however, is not clear. On the three villages, cf. Anton Steichele, *Bisthum Augsburg*, vol. 3, pp. 1077-78, 1192, 1255-56.

trates with ready cash. In the long run, however, they further weakened the city's fiscal position by diminishing the total amount of revenues from rural rents and taxes. Inevitably, the magistrates were thrown back onto further borrowing. By 1750, the combined debts of the city treasury and the two agencies derived from it—the Anlagskasse and the Kriegskasse—came to nearly 700,000 fl.[31] Even when inflation is taken into account, the city's indebtedness was by then almost three times what it had been after the Thirty Years War.[32]

To the magistrates of Nördlingen, a major cause of their city's financial problems was the excessive level of imperial and Circle assessments. A shower of petitions went forth in the early eighteenth century, in which the city fathers pleaded for reductions in the community's financial obligations. Finally, in 1748 the diet of the Swabian Circle granted Nördlingen a temporary exemption from its dues, but also sent an imperial commissioner to investigate the city's financial situation. He soon discovered that Nördlingen's problems were largely of its own making: an excessively large bureaucracy, grossly inflated salaries, and chaotic bookkeeping methods had all contributed to the city's per-

[31] Lettenmeyer, *Finanzwirtschaft*, pp. 53-54. The breakdown was as follows:

Borrowed capital	462,000 fl.
Unpaid interest payments	136,000 fl.
Imperial and Circle dues in arrears	98,000 fl.
Total	696,000 fl.

[32] The adjustment for inflation is made in accordance with the price index described in note 8. According to this index, taking as a base 1576-80 = 100, the price level for 1656-60 stood at 126 and for 1746-50 at 206. As Table 5.3 shows, the treasury's indebtedness in 1657 stood at 151,200 fl.; in 1576-80 terms this would have equaled 120,000 fl. As note 27 shows, indebtedness in 1750 stood at 696,000 fl.; in 1576-80 terms this would have equaled 337,864 fl., which is 2.8 times as much as 120,000 fl.

petual deficits. Between 1750 and 1780 imperial and Circle authorities forced the city to adopt a series of reforms, among them a reduction in the size of the bureaucracy—including the size of the council itself—and a strenuous program to repay capital loans and thus progressively reduce interest payments. By the 1780's Nördlingen's finances had been brought into order and the city once again showed an annual surplus.[33]

Along the way, however, something had been lost: a sense of civic pride and self-sufficiency. In the sixteenth century, Nördlingen had numbered among its debtors the Emperor himself; by the early eighteenth century, however, the city was turning desperately to the Emperor for financial relief. In doing so, the magistrates spared no efforts to paint their city's condition in the most humble possible colors. The petition they addressed to the imperial diet at Regensburg in 1721 described Nördlingen as "a poor and insignificant" city—language that would have been inconceivable 150 years earlier—and evoked its troubles thus:

> Because of the utterly ruinous Thirty Years War and the subsequent French wars, together with their consequent marches and counter-marches, camp-provisioning and winter-quartering, extortion from and plundering of the city's rural subjects, not to mention garrison costs, bombings, encampments and conquests, the city has gradually and unfortunately declined from its former sound position and has fallen into the uttermost ruin, so that not only has the citizenry—which formerly numbered 2,000 men and included various nobles and other prosperous families—now been reduced to less than half its original size, and those who are left are in such a state that the many houses which burnt down in the bombardment [of 1647] have still not been rebuilt, but also such an unspeakable amount of money has been extorted from

[33] Lettenmeyer, *Finanzwirtschaft*, pp. 127-214.

them over the years that one cannot read the financial records of these events without astonishment. . . .[34]

From the financial distress of the Thirty Years War the city might well have recovered on its own: as we have seen, the city treasury was rapidly reducing its debts until 1670. The beginning of a second round of warfare, however, made the recovery much more difficult—not only by introducing new and even heavier financial obligations, but also by spawning new agencies such as the Anlags- and Kriegskassen, which in turn added to the city's administrative expenses. By the time the second cycle of wars had ended in 1714, Nördlingen was helpless to solve its own financial problems. Only by intervention from above could the fiscal difficulties be resolved, and it took until the 1770's to do it. In the 1770's and 1780's the books were once again balanced. But then the wars of the French Revolution plunged the city deep into debt all over again.[35] Little wonder that the city fathers meekly accepted Nördlingen's loss of political independence in 1803, and with it their own relief from financial responsibility.

[34] *An eine hochlöblich Reichs-Versammlung zu Regensburg Unterthänig und geziemendes Memorial, . . . Puncto Moderationis Matriculae Cameralis,* in: Acta das Matricular-Moderations-Wesen betreffend, B Num. VI, 3, pp. 4-5.

[35] Lettenmeyer, *Finanzwirtschaft,* pp. 216-17.

Six

An Urban Elite: The City Council

THE highest status to which a citizen of Nördlingen could normally aspire was membership on the city council. No other rank or distinction set him so clearly apart from the mass of his fellow citizens. There were, of course, other positions of civic dignity, but they were empty honors. The large council was hardly ever summoned for consultation, and the city court, although it met regularly, had very restricted responsibilities.[1] In actual fact, all political authority in the community was embodied in the fifteen members of the *Innerer Rat*, or the city council.

The position of these fifteen men was enhanced by two circumstances which had prevailed since the constitutional change of 1552. In the first place, with only the rarest exceptions, once he was appointed, a councilman remained in office until the day of his death.[2] Second, the council was essentially a self-perpetuating body. Vacancies were filled by a committee of seven council members—the five top-ranking councillors, plus one each designated by the city court and by the large council.[3] But if the privilege of electing councillors was narrowly restricted, eligibility for membership on the council was very broad. Immigrants could not be appointed until they had lived in Nördlingen for at least five years, and it was forbidden for a father and son,

[1] See Chapter One, section II.

[2] Of the 123 councilmen listed in Appendix VII, one (Georg Berlin) was dropped from the council for unknown reasons, one (Michael Han) was dropped so that he could be appointed hospital-master, one (Johannes Lehlin) emigrated from Nördlingen, and five others (George Bin, Daniel Aislinger, Peter Lemp, Adam Frickhinger and Johann Lemp) retired, mostly shortly before their deaths. Two other men were dropped from the council but then reappointed (see note 5 below).

[3] See Chapter One, especially note 14.

or two brothers, to sit simultaneously on the council. Except for these limitations, however, every male citizen of Nördlingen was eligible.[4]

In reality, of course, only certain types of citizens were likely to be considered. In fact, the council appointments represent a particularly clear model of elite recruitment: from an unlimited pool of eligible citizens, the council selected those individuals who conformed to whatever qualifications it held necessary for political leadership. Between 1580 and 1720, a total of 108 citizens were selected to fill vacancies on the city council.[5] The deliberations of the committee which made these appointments were never recorded, and there is no way to establish precisely how or why it reached its decisions. Nor, in fact, do we know very much about the personal qualities of the men they selected —the intelligence, judgment, probity and other characteristics which, at least in principle, should have played a role in the appointments. But there is much that can be discovered about these men: their ages, occupations, wealth, family backgrounds and often much more. In examining the patterns of recruitment to the city council, we shall look at each one of these variables.

Before doing so, however, let us take a brief look at the composition of the council at the outset of this study. The

[4] Ratsordnung 1556, fol. 9a (folio numbering is not in the original); and Ratsordnung 1673, pp. 8-9. The prohibition extended to half-brothers and, as the 1673 ordinance makes clear, to stepfathers and stepsons.

[5] In two cases, a councilman was elected twice: (1) Hieronimus Welsch was elected in 1602, dropped the following year, and then reelected in 1606. (2) Wilhelm Friedrich Romul was elected in 1638, dropped in 1640 when he was appointed city recorder, and then restored to the council as a Bürgermeister, while still retaining supervision of the chancery, in 1656. In the tabulations which follow (e.g., the distribution of occupations), I have counted each of these men only once and listed him under his first year of appointment. For these and all other appointments to the city council, see the sources cited in Appendix VII; for Romul, see also Leichenpredigte: Wilhelm Friedrich Romul, 1682, pp. 95ff.

fifteen men who sat on the council in 1580 were collectively the product of appointments stretching back over nearly forty years: the senior member, Bürgermeister Johann Reuter, had joined the council in 1542, while the newest member, Johann Bosch, had served only since 1578. Although the data for these fifteen men (see Appendix VII) are somewhat sparser than for later generations, there is at least enough evidence to suggest that the council of Nördlingen in 1580 was a very heterogeneous group. Five members were craftsmen, two were engaged in food and drink trades, and at least three were active in retailing and commerce; in some other cases, the occupations are either uncertain or unknown. The richest member of the council, worth 12,000 fl. in 1579, was also a member of Nördlingen's most prominent family, the Frickhingers, who have been active in the municipal affairs of the community almost without interruption from the fourteenth century until the twentieth.[6] But the council also had room for much less wealthy men, such as Melchior Welsch, who was worth only 700 fl. And it had room for men with absolutely no family tradition of council service, such as Peter Seng: neither his father, nor his mother, nor any of his four successive wives came from a family which had been represented on the council of Nördlingen.[7]

But was the heterogeneous character of the council preserved? To answer that question we must trace the changing policies and standards of admission as they are displayed by council appointments over the next century and a half.[8]

[6] See Hermann Frickhinger, *Genealogie der Familie Frickhinger in Nördlingen: Ein Beitrag zu der Geschichte Nördlinger Geschlechter* (Nördlingen, 1907).

[7] A detailed and seemingly reliable genealogy of Peter Seng appears in Beyschlag and Müller, *Beyträge zur Nördlingischen Geschlechtshistorie*, vol. 1, pp. 293ff. Seng's mother and at least two of his wives were from out of town.

[8] A summary of the essential data for each councilman appointed during this period appears in Appendix VII.

I

In examining the patterns of appointment to any high political office, the first question logically concerns the appointees' formal background in government service. In the case of Nördlingen, this background normally took the form of membership on the city court, the permanent body of ten citizens appointed by the council to try minor civil cases.[9] Of the 108 men appointed to the council between 1580 and 1720, a total of 73 had been members of the court.[10] Another 21 appointees had not sat on the court but came to office with professional experience in government or training in the law. Thus, only 14 of the 108 councilmen assumed office without either of these two forms of experience, and of these 14 by far the majority were appointed during the troubled 1630's, when high mortality rates caused a particularly large turnover of council seats.

Membership on the city court was not only the most common avenue toward higher office, but to some extent a deliberate testing-ground. The councillors kept a close and critical watch on the behavior of their junior colleagues. In 1603, for example, the council confirmed the existing court in office, but then singled out one member, Caspar Appetzhofer, for a severe scolding: "his constant drinking was to be forbidden, with a reminder that he should behave according to his station, lest he become an object of derision."[11] It is perhaps not unrelated that two years later Appetzhofer, along with another man, was dropped from the court.[12]

[9] See Chapter One, section II.

[10] Members of the city court are listed under "Stattrichter Ayd" in Eidbuch II (1572-86) and Eidbuch IV (1587-1803).

[11] RP 3 Jan. 1603.

[12] RP 3 Jan. 1605: Appetzhofer and another member of the court "sollen uf dißmal feyren," and two other men are designated in their stead. From Eidbuch IV (1587-1803) it appears that neither of these men was ever reappointed to the court. While it cannot be assumed that these men were dropped from the court due to misconduct—it

Although the court was the main route for advancement, its importance in this regard underwent a slight decline during the seventeenth century. Before the Thirty Years War, over four-fifths of the councillors had some court experience. During the war this proportion dropped and it remained low after the war as well: of the 44 councillors appointed between 1651 and 1720, only two-thirds had sat on the court. The remaining third, however, all came to the council with bureaucratic or legal backgrounds. In fact, the council was becoming increasingly "professionalized"—a trend to which we shall return in greater detail below when we examine the changing occupational composition of the council.

In speaking of the councilmen's "experience," one must remember that this could be of very different lengths. Some men might spend only three or four years on the court or in government service before being promoted, while others might serve for decades before their election. The extent of these variations is suggested, in fact, if one examines the ages of the councillors upon their appointments. Beginning with the year 1590, in all but eight cases it is possible to establish this figure. Three of the councilmen were still in their mid-twenties when appointed: Johann Conrad Gundelfinger (1634), Johann Christoph Frickhinger (1661) and Johann Friedrich von Welsch (1719). All belonged to distinguished magisterial families and had been groomed for administrative careers.[13] The oldest appointee, aged 67, was Michael Streitter, an erstwhile immigrant who served for decades as a city official before his elevation to the council in 1683. The average age of appointment, however, was 44.5

---

could have been at their own request—it should be pointed out that departures from the court for reasons other than death or promotion to the council were not very common.

[13] All three had attended university (Kern, "Die Söhne der Reichsstadt Nördlingen," passim), and two—Gundelfinger and Frickhinger—were serving in the municipal administration at the time of their appointment.

years—a figure that remained remarkably stable throughout the period studied.[14] Thus, throughout this period old and young appointments were steadily—although surely unconsciously—balanced out at a steady rate.

II

WHEN, however, we turn from the ages at appointment to the occupation of each councilman upon his appointment; change over time becomes apparent. Appendix VII indicates the occupation of each councilman upon his appointment; in Table 6.1 these occupations are tabulated, with the men

TABLE 6.1. Occupations of Council Members upon Appointment, 1581-1700

	Years of Appointment			
	1581-1620	*1621-1650*	*1651-1690*	*1691-1720*
Tanners	6	1	2	0
All Other Crafts	6	4	1	0
Food and Drink Trades	6	6	3	1
Merchants and Retailers	5	8	5	2
Civic Administration	4	5	8	6
Other Legal/Bureaucratic	1	2	1	4
Medical Occupations	4	0	1	3
Misc. and Unknown	2	4	3	4
Total	34	30	24	20

grouped into four periods. Immediately evident from this Table is a drastic reduction in the number of craftsmen on the city council. In 1580, as we have seen, craftsmen made

[14] The ages at appointment for 89 men have been determined by calculating backward from their recorded ages at death. For the entire period 1590-1720, the average age at appointment was 44.5 years; broken down into periods the average age was as follows—1590-1610: 44.6; 1611-40: 44.9; 1641-70: 44.1; 1671-1700: 45.0; 1701-20: 43.5.

up one-third of the council, and Table 6.1 shows that this ratio was maintained during the years before the Thirty Years War. Thereafter, however, a sharp reduction in the number of craftsmen becomes evident. In fact, after the year 1652 only one artisan was appointed to the council. By 1700, not a single member of the council was a craftsman and, except for one borderline case, not a single councilman was even the son of a craftsman.[15] Clearly, in the course of the seventeenth century, the council had ceased entirely to represent the craft segment of the citizenry.

But who took the place of the craftsmen? During the Thirty Years War, as Table 6.1 shows, there was some increase in the number of merchants and retailers on the council; but this group declined in size again after the war. The sustained increase was experienced by a very different group: members of administrative and legal occupations. Most of them were officials in the city administration at the time of their appointments; a few others were employed by other governments, such as the house of Oettingen, or were trained lawyers without specific office. The members of these groups, taken together, accounted for only 15 percent of the councilmen appointed in the period before 1620 but fully 43 percent of those named after 1650.

We saw earlier that the legal and higher bureaucratic sector in Nördlingen underwent some increase in size during the seventeenth century. But this alone would not be sufficient to explain their increased representation on the council, for they still formed a very small fraction of the total population. In effect, the very nature of membership on the council underwent a significant change. In 1580, the council

[15] The borderline case was Johann Georg Lang, whose father was evidently a confectioner—an occupation that could easily be described as a craft, although I have classified the food and drink trades separately. The occupation of the father of Heinrich Martens is unknown, but it seems unlikely that a lawyer who emigrated from Hamburg was the son of a craftsman. (Information about the family backgrounds of council members is based on the sources described in note 23.)

represented the "community" as a whole: almost all the important occupational segments were represented, albeit by their more prosperous members. The chief omission, in fact, was the group of professional administrators, who functioned as impartial servants of the council and the community. By 1720, however, all this had changed: the "professionals" were no longer servants of the community; they were among the masters.

This entire development is closely related to two other fundamental changes in the nature of the city council. First, at the same time that it became increasingly possible for bureaucrats to become councilmen, it also became possible for at least some of them to retain their administrative offices while serving on the council. And second, membership on the council changed from an honorary position of civic responsibility into a source of considerable financial rewards. Both of these developments will become clear if we compare the income of council members in three selected years: 1579, 1652 and 1700.

In 1579, each member of the council received remuneration for attendance at council meetings amounting to about 2½ fl. per year. In addition, most councillors received a few gulden for exercising various judicial and inspectorial functions. For all but two council members, however, this was the total extent of income they received from any type of civic office. Only the two *Stadtkämmerer*—the councilmen responsible for the line-by-line supervision of the financial records—received considerable fees, totalling 32½ fl. each.

Taken all together, in 1579 members of the council received (in addition to payment for attending meetings) a collective total of 180 fl. for the exercise of their civic functions—an amount that represented only 3.1 percent of the total expenditure of the city treasury on salaries and fees for regular municipal officeholders.[16]

[16] KR 1579: Ausgaben. In that year the total expenditures of the city treasury on all salaries and fees for regular municipal officeholders (i.e., the total of all entries from "Belohnung der Reth" to

In 1652, attendance at meetings provided each councilman with about 8 fl., but this was the least of the increases. Each Bürgermeister now received a salary of 52 fl. for his term as mayor, plus 48 fl. for his services as a privy councillor. The two other privy councillors received 24 fl. apiece. Each Stadtkämmerer now enjoyed a salary and expense payments totaling 84 fl. a year, two councilmen collected 50 fl. each as inspectors of finished woolens, and four got 16 fl. each as alcohol-tax collectors. Furthermore, three members of the council held major positions within the city bureaucracy which provided salaries of 183 fl., 122 fl. and 79½ fl. respectively. These and a few incidental fees produced (in addition to attendance money) a total of 1,147½ fl.—an amount which represented some 13.5 percent of the treasury expenditures on salaries and fees.[17]

In 1700, the total salary intake for each Bürgermeister had doubled, to 200 fl. apiece, while the two additional members of the secret council now received 38 fl. apiece. Each Stadtkämmerer got 100 fl. Every one of the fifteen council members was now listed as an alcohol-tax collector, with a salary of 24 fl. to 30 fl., while the twelve nonmayoral councillors received 12 fl. each for judicial activity. Three council members were on the rolls with specific municipal offices worth 102 fl., 63 fl. and 52 fl. a year. These and other sources of income netted the council members a total of 1,886 fl. in salaries from civic office in addition to their attendance money—payments which now accounted for fully 18.1 percent of the total treasury expenditures on regular salaries

"Viertelgellt und Verehrung der Statboten," except for "Wochenbaw") came to 3,470 fl.

[17] KR 1652: Ausgaben. In that year the total expenditures of the city treasury on salaries and fees for regular municipal officeholders (i.e., the total of all entries under "Rathsgelder," "Amtsleuten" and "Bestallungen") came to 8,524 fl. The three regular municipal officeholders who were also councilmen were the Ammann, the clerk of the city court and the recorder of alcohol taxes.

and fees.[18] Thus, by the end of the seventeenth century, almost one-fifth of the city's outlay on ordinary salaries was funneled into the pockets of the fifteen men who sat on the council.

III

THIS is not to say, however, that membership on the council would make a poor man rich; it was more likely to have made a rich man richer. For in order to be appointed to the council in the first place, it was necessary to enjoy a certain level of wealth. Between 1579 and 1724, with one minor exception, membership on the council was limited to men who belonged to the richest 20 percent of the citizenry.[19]

In a sense, the fact that one-fifth of the entire citizenry was potentially eligible for membership suggests that the council was rather "open," especially since, as the preceding chapter has shown, there was considerable wealth mobility in Nördlingen, so that a citizen who began on a much lower level could often ascend to the upper fifth. One notable example of this phenomenon is provided by the career of Samuel Dehlinger, a tanner. In 1646, at the start of his career, Dehlinger was worth only 100 fl. By 1658, however, he had reached 1,400 fl.—no great fortune compared to the 15,000 fl. enjoyed by Nördlingen's wealthiest tanner in the same year, but enough to put Dehlinger within the top 20 percent. He was still within that group—though just barely—when he was appointed to the council in 1675.

[18] KR 1700: Ausgaben. In that year the total expenditures of the city treasury on salaries and fees for regular municipal officeholders (i.e., the total of all entries from "Rathsgelder" through "Bestallungsgelder") came to 10,407 fl. (The three municipal offices held by councilmen were inspector of construction, alcohol-tax recorder and city physician.)

[19] This statement is based on an analysis of the tax records at six-year intervals from 1579 to 1700, and for the years 1712 and 1724. Except for 1670, in each of these years all fifteen council members were among the richest 20% of the male citizens.

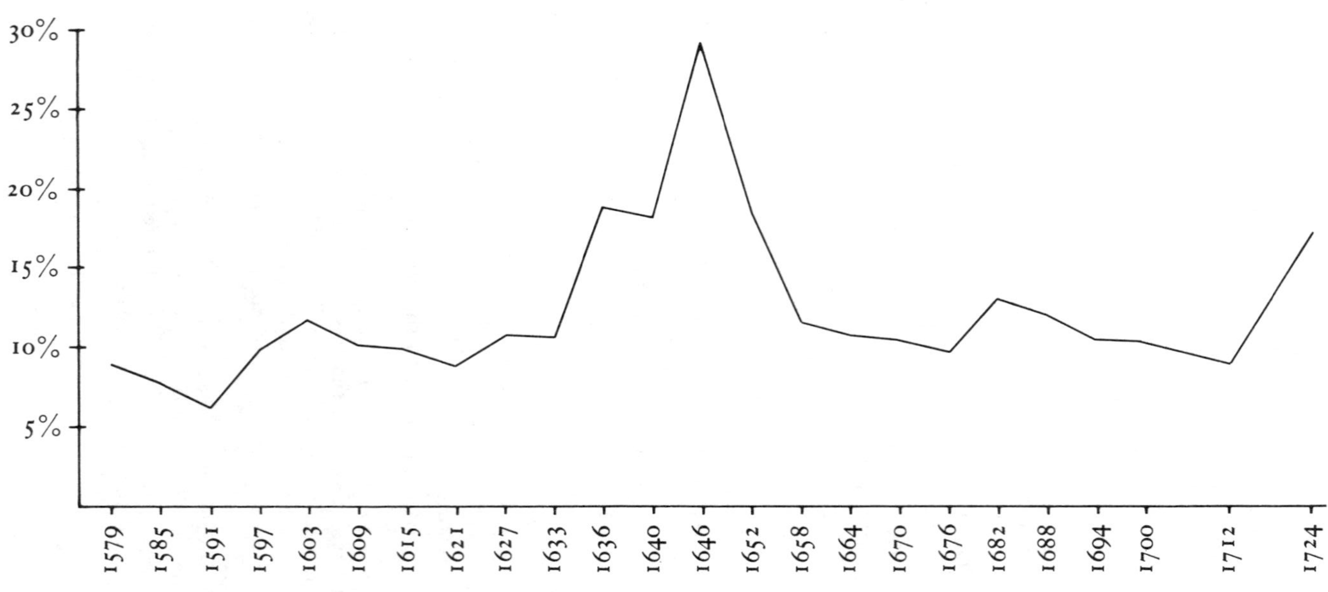

Figure 6.1. Proportion of the Total Wealth (of All Citizens)

But if membership on the council was available to men like Dehlinger, it was far more often enjoyed by men of much greater wealth. In certain years, two or three members might belong to the wealth level represented by a Samuel Dehlinger, but the rest would be clustered much higher up on the wealth hierarchy: throughout this period, ten to twelve members of the council would normally belong to the richest 5 percent of the citizenry. The very richest one or two citizens of Nördlingen would not necessarily be members but, taken collectively, the council was normally a very wealthy group.

The best way to establish just how wealthy the council was is by comparing its total collective wealth in any given year with that of the citizenry as a whole. For example, in 1579 the total assessed wealth of the 1541 male and female citizens of Nördlingen amounted to 699,922 fl.; of this amount, the fifteen councillors accounted for 62,500 fl., almost 9 percent of the total. The corresponding percentage has been calculated for 23 additional years between 1579 and 1724, and the results are plotted in Figure 6.1.[20]

From 1579 to 1633, despite some fluctuations, the councillors generally owned about 10 percent of the total wealth. Then, after 1633, there was a dramatic increase in this ratio: by 1646, the fifteen council members owned almost 30 percent of all the wealth in Nördlingen. Thereafter, however, there was an equally striking decline in this ratio, and between 1658 and 1712 the proportion of wealth held by the

[20] The total wealth of the entire citizenry is given in Appendix III. The wealth of each council member in any given year can be determined from the councillors' tax entries, listed on a special page of the Steuerregister. However, elections to the council were normally held only in January; thus, in some years there were vacancies on the council by the time the taxes were collected in November. Since the comparison of one year to another is only meaningful if a full complement of fifteen council members is always present, when there are vacancies I have included the council members who were still alive at the start of the year, using the last tax paid before their deaths as the basis for the calculations.

council members never exceeded 15 percent. Only in the 1720's did the percentage move significantly upward again.

The most dramatic increase in the relative wealth of the council coincided precisely with the second half of the Thirty Years War, beginning with the crucial period of siege, plague and military occupation in 1634. The stresses of war contributed to this development in a number of ways. First, Nördlingen suffered a dramatic loss of population during the 1630's. This meant that the fifteen council members accounted for a larger proportion of the total male citizenry than they had before the plague. And of course the plague may have served to consolidate the wealth of elite families into fewer hands. Above all, however, the increase in council wealth reflects the fact that during the war fewer craftsmen and more merchants were appointed to the council. The magistrates must have found it useful in this period to fill council vacancies with wealthy merchants, for, by having a share in the responsibilities of government, such men would feel particularly obliged to advance emergency loans when necessary. Yet enough wealth remained in their own hands to make the council of these years a very wealthy body. Only with the end of the war was the old balance restored—roughly 10 percent of the total wealth owned by council members, the rest by their fellow citizens.

If we attempt to summarize the patterns of both occupations and wealth between the late sixteenth and the early eighteenth century, we can see that the history of the council falls into three distinct phases. The first was the period before 1620, when the council represented a heterogeneous mixture of craftsmen, merchants and other citizens. In the second phase, which coincided with the Thirty Years War, craftsmen became less prominent and merchants more prominent among appointees to the council; for this reason the ratio of the total wealth enjoyed by council members moved sharply upward. In the third phase, craftsmen were completely eliminated from the council, but the number of merchants also declined. Their places were taken by lawyers and bureaucrats, who, by the end of the century, had come to form the largest group on the council. Many of these men were in city employ, but even those magistrates who were not so employed received considerable revenues from their offices. The council of 1700 was only slightly wealthier, in relative terms, than the council of 1580, but a much greater proportion of that wealth was derived from the city treasury itself.

Between 1712 and 1724, however, the relative wealth of the council suddenly doubled. The reasons for this are not hard to find. In 1716 the magistrates finally admitted to their ranks the scion of an extremely wealthy but highly unpopular merchant family: the Wörners. And the next year David Wörner was joined on the council by two other very wealthy men—his brother-in-law Johann Friedrich Stang and a confectioner named Johann Caspar Beyer. Although Stang died in 1721, the other two men still accounted for two-fifths of the council's total wealth in 1724, and their assessments explain most of the growth in the council's wealth relative to that of the citizenry as a whole.

Exactly why the magistrates appointed three such wealthy men all at once it is not clear. But subsequent appointments once again included men of much more modest wealth. In 1746, the last year for which tax records are available in any form, the wealth of council members ranged from a maximum of 20,200 fl. down to a minimum of only 1,500 fl.[21] In the mid-eighteenth century it was still possible for a man of relatively modest means to sit beside his wealthiest fellow citizens as a member of the council of Nördlingen.

IV

EXPERIENCE, age, occupation, wealth—all of these factors doubtless played a role as the seven electors deliberated on a citizen's fitness to join them on the city council. But one

[21] Steuerregister 1746: assessments for Bürgermeister Georg Friedrich Klein and Ratsherr Johann Daniel Hueber.

additional factor also played a crucial part in their decision making: each candidate's family background. Simply by scanning the list of councilmen who held office between 1580 and 1720, one begins to sense the frequency of interrelationships: of the 123 councillors, there are 5 each named Gundelfinger and Welsch, 4 each named Frickhinger and Jörg, and 3 each named Gering, Lemp, Niclas, Schöpperlin and Widenmann. Another 20 surnames appear twice. This leaves, of course, 50 family names which appear only once, but even among this group there were very many persons who were related to other councillors through their mothers or their wives. In short, a man's family background clearly played a crucial role in his appointment to the council.

Before we examine this role, however, it should be pointed out that the concept of family can be understood in two different ways. In the first place, there was what we might call the "patrilinear" family—the group of all males who shared a common surname and a common male ancestor.[22] This—the "family" in the narrow sense—is what the citizens of early modern Nördlingen had in mind when they talked about a man's *Geschlecht*. On the other hand, there was the entire network of a person's relatives by blood or marriage, which Nördlingers would probably have referred to as a person's *Freundschaft*. In a society in which multiple marriages and many children were the norm, the number of blood relatives or in-laws might assume vast proportions. In addition to his paternal and maternal grandparents, uncles, aunts and cousins, the average citizen might have half-brothers and half-sisters, step-parents and step-siblings, and, as his life went on, two or three separate sets of in-laws.

Some information about this broader family background for each council member is usually available, but it is almost impossible to reconstruct the entire network of maternal

22 The practice under which a male might assume a different surname from that of his father, while not completely eliminated in the sixteenth and seventeenth centuries, was extremely uncommon.

relatives, step-parents and in-laws in a complete and systematic fashion. And even if one could, it would be difficult to assess precisely which relationships should be regarded as significant: if we observe, for example, the appointment of a new councilman whose deceased wife's brother also sat on the council, should we attribute this appointment to the influence of family relationships? On the other hand, patrilinear relationships can almost always be established without difficulty, and can always be regarded as significant. Thus, in attempting to determine the extent to which membership on the council was "open" or "closed" in terms of family background, the first and most obvious step is to ask how often membership on the council was passed down from one generation to the next within a single Geschlecht. Let us begin, then, by looking at the patterns of patrilinear relationships among council members.[23]

Certainly, families in which the tradition of political leadership was handed down from one generation to the next did exist in Nördlingen. The most prominent such family was the Frickhingers, who were already represented on the city council in the fourteenth century and who, as Figure 6.2 shows, continued to be civic leaders throughout the period of our study. Between 1546 and 1778, seven members of the family sat on the council, including three—Hieronimus, Adam and Johann Christoph—who served as Bürger-

[23] The indispensable starting-point for all genealogical research on the prominent families of Nördlingen is Beyschlag and Müller, *Geschlechtshistorie.* While this work contains errors and must be used with great caution, it does provide an indispensable framework of information. Cases of confusion or doubt have been clarified wherever possible by using the parish registers, which have also been checked for any information about those few councilmen whose families are not described by Beyschlag and Müller. The use of the parish registers for this purpose has been facilitated by the existence of the excellent set of alphabetical indexes prepared by Dr. Gustav Wulz and available in the Stadtarchiv Nördlingen. For a few families, special genealogical studies (which are listed in the Bibliography) were also helpful.

FIGURE 6.2. The Frickhinger Family (A Selective Genealogy).

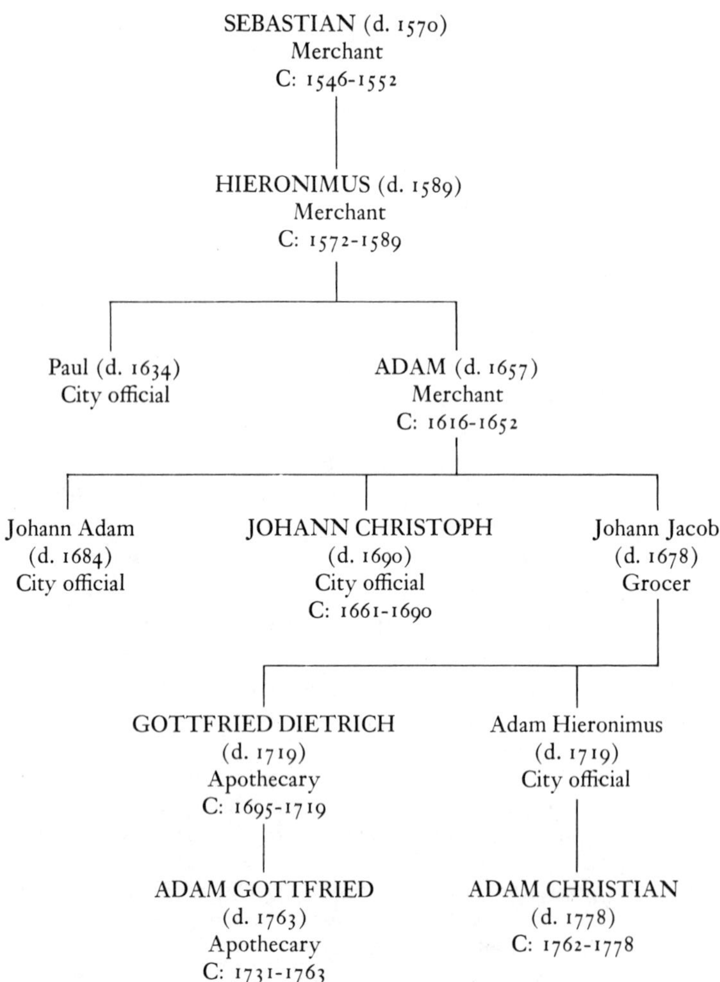

Names of men who sat on the city council are capitalized.
C = the years during which they sat on the council.

meister. Orignally active in the cloth trade, in the middle of the seventeenth century the family changed its occupational orientation. Some became civil servants, while one branch turned to retailing: Johann Jacob became a grocer, and his son in turn founded a pharmacy which was still being maintained by a member of the Frickhinger family in the 1970's.[24]

Many other families were also richly represented in the city's political elite. Two branches of the Gundelfingers, for example, accounted for five council members between 1570 and 1670, while a sixth member of the family held the influential post of city counsel.[25] Johann Jörg was succeeded on the council first by his brother and then, in later years, by his nephew and great-nephew.[26] A particularly versatile line was the Welsch family: in addition to producing five councilmen between the late sixteenth and the early eighteenth century, including one who was a soldier, the family also included three clergymen and two medical doctors.[27]

Of course, patrilinear families of this particular type, which were represented for generation after generation at the highest level of government, were relatively rare. In fact, only nine families were represented by 3 or more council members between 1580 and 1720, accounting for 33 men, or scarcely a quarter of the 123 councillors who sat during this period. But if we broaden our range to include all patrilinear families which produced at least 2 councillors during these years, the number of men involved rises to 73, or about three-fifths of the total.[28] And patrilinear relationships, of

24 See Frickhinger, *Familie Frickhinger.*

25 See Beyschlag and Müller, *Geschlechtshistorie*, vol. 1, pp. 110-13, 268-75; vol. 2, pp. 153-61.

26 See ibid., vol. 1, pp. 264-68, 289-90; vol. 2, pp. 243-49.

27 See ibid., vol. 2, pp. 535-41.

28 In the case of the Welsch family, the relationship between some of the earlier members is uncertain (Beyschlag and Müller are unreliable on this matter, and the parish registers are not available for the period before 1579), but there is no doubt that all four councilmen named Welsch did belong to the same family. The same applies to

course, only represent one possible type of family connection.

Exactly how many men, at the moment of their appointments, belonged to families which had already been repre-

TABLE 6.2. Family Backgrounds of Council Members, 1580-1720

	Members Appointed				
	1581-1620	*1621-1650*	*1651-1690*	*1691-1720*	*Total*
At least one patrilinear relative had been a council member:					
Definitely	15[a]	15	11	8	49[a]
Possibly	6[b]	—	1	—	7[b]
No patrilinear relative had been a council member	13	15	12	12	52
Total	34	30	24	20	108

[a] Includes four men whose relatives had sat on the council as guild-masters before 1552.

[b] Includes one man whose relative had possibly sat on the council as a guild-master before 1552.

sented on the council? Table 6.2 indicates the number of cases in which one or more patrilinear relative had sat on the council within the previous three generations.[29] Eleven cases are difficult to classify; in seven instances a relationship is possible but not certain; in four other cases the only patri-

the two councilmen named Reuter, and the two named Weckherlin.

[29] I have endeavored to trace each patrilinear family back three generations (i.e., back to great-grandfathers). In some cases, however, the information or linkage for the earlier period was unclear or uncertain. Thus, there may be a slight undercounting of distant patrilinear ancestors, especially for the group of men who were appointed soon after 1580. I have counted as "definites" only those persons for whom a specific patrilinear relationship to an earlier councilman can be established; thus, I have included among the "possibles" all cases in which an exact relationship cannot be pinned down, even though it is reasonably certain that some family connection existed.

linear relative who had sat on the council had done so before the constitutional change of 1552, not as a member of the "old council" but only as an elected representative of his guild.[30] But no matter how we choose to classify these two groups, about half of the council members who were appointed between 1580 and 1720 came from families which had already been represented on the council, and this proportion remained roughly constant throughout the era under study.

This still leaves, of course, at least 52 men who had no patrilinear connection at the time of their appointment. A few, in fact, had no family connections of any kind to current or past members of the council. This was particularly true of immigrants who did not happen to marry into local elite families, but it also applied occasionally to natives. A striking example is the tanner Samuel Dehlinger, who was appointed in 1675: not only can it be shown with almost complete certainty that Dehlinger had no council relatives, but he was a man of little wealth by council standards and he was the only craftsman to be appointed after the year 1652.[31] Dehlinger must have had formidable personal qualities to compensate for his lack of wealth and family connections.

But cases like these were extremely rare. It was far more common for appointees to have at least some family connection to the council. In some cases the link was through the man's mother, who might have been the daughter or sister of a council member. Occasionally it was through a step-parent. And often the link was through the man's wife, who may have been the daughter, sister, niece or widow of someone who belonged, or had belonged, to the council.

Take, for example, the case of Wilhelm Friedrich Romul. Neither his father's nor his mother's family had enjoyed

[30] See Chapter One, section II.

[31] For Dehlinger's wealth, see discussion earlier in this chapter. The parish registers indicate that Dehlinger's mother was the daughter of one Jacob Schneider and that his only wife was the daughter of Baltassar Knorz; neither are council names.

membership on the council, but his marriage in 1632 linked him simultaneously to two council families: his bride was the niece of the deceased councilman Hieronimus Welsch and the widow of Daniel Gering, the son of another deceased councilman. Soon after this marriage, Romul was appointed to a civic office in Nördlingen, and in 1638—although his first wife had already died—he was elevated to the council.[32]

A similar story is that of Johann Georg Aurenhammer, the son of a wagon builder. His ancestry shows no links to the council, but in 1659 he became city clerk, and married the daughter of Bürgermeister Seefried. A few years later he, too, was elevated to the council.[33]

In short, conjugal linkages could sometimes prove more important than the basic kinship connection in gaining a man access to the council. It is important to stress this point, for it illustrates the degree to which the council was still open to "outsiders," even in the late seventeenth century. Certainly, such a man was almost never selected unless by the time of his appointment he had acquired some family connection to the council. But this is very different from being born into the elite. After all, to marry the mayor's daughter, as Aurenhammer did, was part of the very process by which a born outsider might be accepted into the ruling elite.

Thus, by gradual absorption, one family after another might be drawn into the inner circle. A particularly striking example of this process at work over the generations is pro-

[32] Romul was descended on his father's side from a family of clerics, who almost certainly were not related to the Rummel family, one member of which had sat on the council in the early sixteenth century. Romul's mother was born Margareta Eckart—a family name with no council connections in the sixteenth or seventeenth centuries. See Beyschlag and Müller, *Geschlechtshistorie*, vol. 2, pp. 413-17; and Leichenpredigte: Wilhelm Friedrich Romul, 1682.

[33] Aurenhammer was born in 1630, and was thus the product of his father's third marriage, which, as the parish registers show, took place in 1629 to the widow of a citizen of Oettingen. See also Beyschlag and Müller, *Geschlechtshistorie*, vol. 2, p. 18.

vided by the careers of two contemporaneous council members: Georg Widenmann, who served from 1629 to 1637, and Georg Bommeister, who sat from 1630 to 1661.[34] The backgrounds of these two men were not very similar: Widenmann's father had been one of Nördlingen's wealthiest citizens and a member of the city court, while Bommeister's father had been an undistinguished hatter. But in both cases, neither the father's nor the mother's family had been represented on the council. And both men became linked to the council by marriage.

Georg Widenmann's first marriage was to the daughter of Bürgermeister Caspar Haider, and this connection patently assisted his entry into the council. In 1629, Haider died, and in a special mid-year election Widenmann was elected to the council "because," as the oath-book of Nördlingen records, "his father-in-law Caspar Haider, Bürgermeister, has died."[35] After the death of his first wife, Widenmann was married two more times, in both cases to women from outside Nördlingen, before he died in 1637. His third wife survived him, and a year later she married Georg Bommeister.

As to Bommeister, in 1624 he had married the daughter of Georg Haas, a deceased councilman, and shortly thereafter ascended first to the city court and then to the city council. After this wife and a second one had died, he married again in 1638; his bride, as we have just seen, was the widow of Georg Widenmann. Bommeister apparently had no children of his own, but by this marriage he acquired a stepdaughter, Elisabeth Widenmann, whom he raised. In 1654, Elisabeth married the widower Johann Lorenz Rehm, a bureaucrat in the service of the house of Oettingen. Late in his life, Rehm moved to his wife's home town; and their son Georg Philip—the grandson of one councilman and the stepgrandson of another—was appointed to the council in 1700.

[34] See the entries under the names Widenmann, Bommaister and Rehm in ibid. For detail on Georg Philip Rehm's wife, see also the parish registers.

[35] Eidbuch IV, under Ratsherrn for 1629.

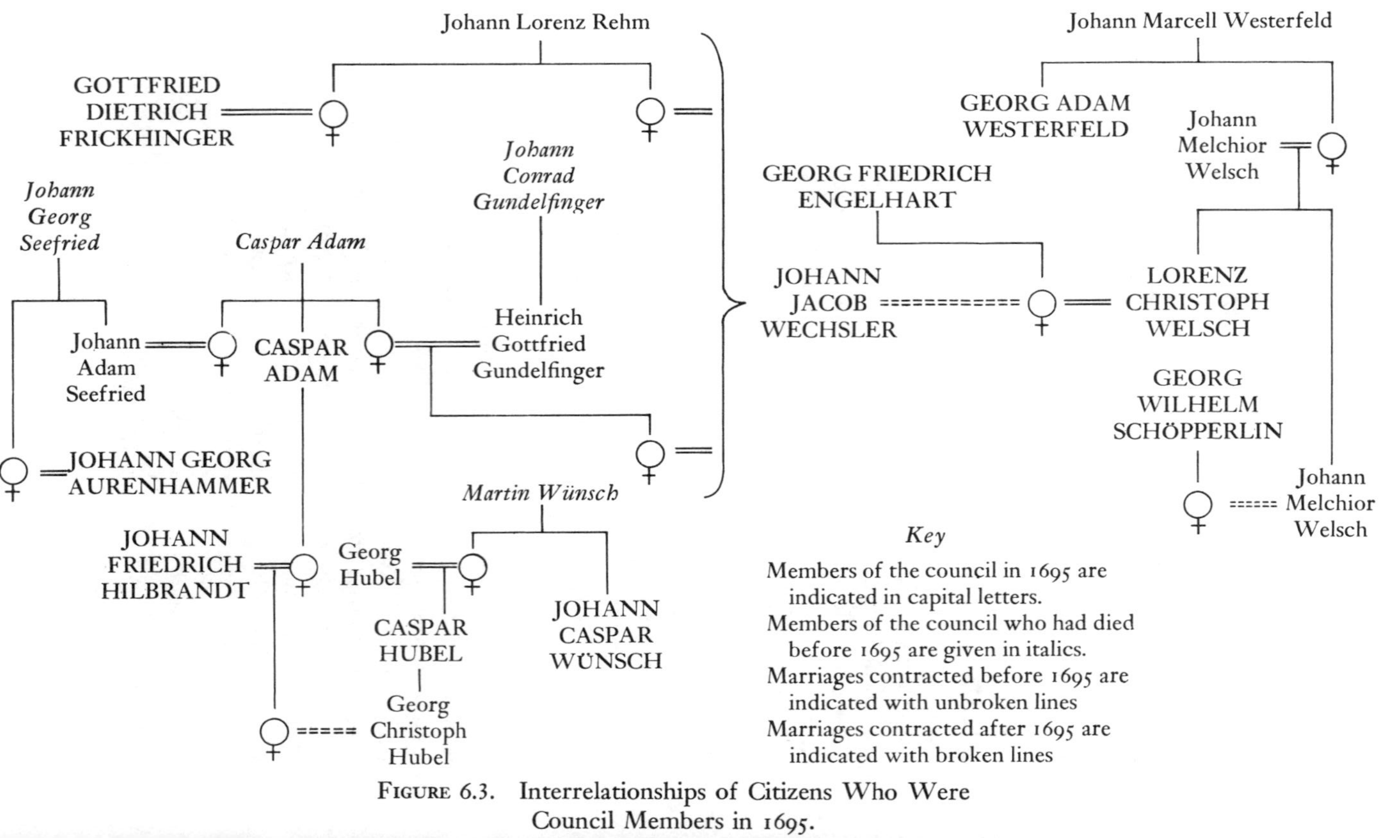

FIGURE 6.3. Interrelationships of Citizens Who Were Council Members in 1695.

Georg Philip's first wife, be it added, was the daughter of Bürgermeister Wilhelm Friedrich Romul.

In fact, not only were most appointees related to some previous council member, but many councillors at any given moment were related to each other. To illustrate this point, we might take a detailed look at the composition of the city council in 1695. Five of the men who sat on the council in that year were the sons of earlier council members; a sixth was a grandson; and a seventh—a Frickhinger—was the great-grandson, grandson and nephew of councilmen.[36] But even more striking is the degree to which the families of these fifteen men were either related to each other as of 1695 or were destined to become so as a consequence of later marriages.[37]

These interrelationships, which are illustrated in Figure 6.3, can most easily be summarized by tracing the connections established by Johann Jacob Wechsler as a result of his three marriages. Wechsler's first wife had been Katherina Rehm, daughter of the Johann Lorenz Rehm described above; her sister was married to Gottfried Dietrich Frickhinger. Wechsler's second marriage, in 1686, was to Regina Katherina Gundelfinger, both of whose grandfathers had been councillors, and whose uncle Caspar Adam belonged to the council in 1695. Adam's sister was married to the brother-in-law of Johann Georg Aurenhammer, while

[36] Ranked in order of seniority, the members of the council in 1695 were: (1) Johann Georg Aurenhammer; (2) Caspar Adam; (3) Georg Wilhelm Schöpperlin; (4) Johann Caspar Wünsch; (5) Heinrich Martens; (6) Johann Sophonias Eckh; (7) Georg Friedrich Engelhart; (8) Georg Adam Westerfeld; (9) Caspar Hubel; (10) Johann Jacob Wechsler; (11) Johann Ernst Jörg; (12) Johann Friedrich Hilbrandt; (13) Lorenz Christoph Welsch; (14) Johann Philipp Stang; (15) Gottfried Dietrich Frickhinger. Of these, nos. 2, 4, 10, 11, and 12 were the sons of councilmen; no. 13 was a grandson. For no. 15, see Figure 6.2.

[37] The principal source for this reconstruction is Beyschlag and Müller, *Geschlectshistorie*, supplemented in cases of doubt or confusion by the parish registers.

Adam's daughter was married to Johann Friedrich Hilbrandt. Some years later, Hilbrandt's daughter acquired as a father-in-law Caspar Hubel, who in turn was the brother-in-law of Johann Caspar Wünsch.

In 1705, Wechsler married for a third time. His newest bride was the daughter of one man who had belonged to the council in 1695—Georg Friedrich Engelhart—and the widow of another—Lorenz Christoph Welsch. Welsch, in turn, had been the nephew of Georg Adam Westerfeld, and his brother had married a daughter of Georg Wilhelm Schöpperlin. Only four of the fifteen councillors of 1695 are not included in this network, and with additional information at least some of them could doubtless also be linked.

This breadth of interrelationship certainly could not be illustrated for a period before the late seventeenth century. But this does not necessarily demonstrate a "closing of the ranks," a consolidation into a ring of close-knit and exclusive elite families. In the first place, the genealogical information is simply much more complete for the late seventeenth century than for earlier periods. Secondly, the citizenry of Nördlingen was smaller in the second half of the seventeenth century than it had been before the Thirty Years War, and the proportion of natives who married outsiders was considerably lower than it had been a century earlier.[38] Under these circumstances, the likelihood of interrelationships between any fifteen people in Nördlingen would inevitably have increased.

Finally, and most importantly, the fact that councilmen were closely interrelated does not of itself prove that they were genealogically isolated from the rest of the citizenry. That would only have been the case if elite families had married exclusively among themselves or into families of comparable status from other cities. Certainly, such marriages were frequent, but it is also true that many of the siblings or children of council members were connected by

[38] Cf. Chapter Two, section IV.

marriage to less prominent families, which, in turn, were linked to even less distinguished ones. Nor was a patrilinear family necessarily of uniform status; in fact, as we shall see in Chapter Nine, it was possible in the late seventeenth century for the richest man in Nördlingen to have a second cousin who was one of the city's poorest.

If the family tree presented in Figure 6.3 were taken as the starting-point for a model of Nördlingen's society in 1695, we would find the branches at the center of the tree—near Johann Jacob Wechsler—heavily intertwined. Further away from the center, the network of branches would become thinner and thinner, with the persons at the edge of the tree connected by only one or two twigs to the inner section. But in a community of 1,100 households, almost every citizen would have at least some connection, however distant, to a member of the council. We can see this, for example, in the case of the Geisslers, that very ordinary Nördlingen family whose genealogy was charted at the beginning of Chapter Three. Caspar Geissler's oldest son Johann, a weaver, was married in 1625 to Maria Blatzer; Maria's sister Barbara was married to the wealthy weaver Georg Haas, the grandson of a councilman, and their son Johann sat on the council from 1675 to 1684. A second, but less direct link, between the Geisslers and the city council was through David, the innkeeper. David's third wife, Apollonia, had been married twice before; her first husband had been Ferdinand Gering, whose brother Jacob sat on the council from 1650 to 1678.[39]

On the individual level, such remote links gave the citizen no special advantage in his dealings with the council. But on a more general level, in the way it shaped the councillors' own attitudes about their function in the community, this

[39] Genealogical information about the Geisslers and their marriage partners was obtained as part of the letter-G reconstitution described in Chapter Two. For additional information about the Blatzers, Gustav Wulz, *Die Ahnen der Johanna Luise Heidenreich, verehelichten Beck* (Nördlingen, 1959), was useful.

network of relationships must have played some role: the magistrates could never completely forget that the citizenry over which they ruled was not an alien group of strangers but instead included many of their own near or distant kin.

There is no doubt that between 1580 and 1720 the council became isolated from the mass of citizens in some respects—above all, by the exclusion of craftsmen from membership. Yet the growth of this isolation must not be exaggerated, especially since the community was smaller at the end of this period than at the beginning. Indeed, if we define families in the patrilinear sense, mobility from nonelite families into council membership was as high in the late seventeenth century as it had been a century earlier. Nördlingen was governed by an elite, but membership in this elite was not restricted to those who could claim it by inheritance—it could still be acquired by ability, marriage or a combination of the two.

There were cities in seventeenth-century Germany in which the councillors had developed into a closed, aloof patriciate, sometimes with pretensions to noble status.[40] There were cities in which the magistrates had come to regard their fellow citizens as "subjects."[41] But such developments were generally limited to larger communities than Nördlingen. The magistrates of Nördlingen were certain of their exalted position and intolerant of any popular partici-

[40] See, for example, Gerhard Hirschmann, "Das Nürnberger Patriziat," in Hellmuth Rössler, ed., *Deutsches Patriziat 1430-1740* (Limburg/Lahn, 1968), esp. pp. 267-69.

[41] The development of a tendency among the magistrates of larger cities, e.g., Hamburg and Frankfurt am Main, to regard citizens as subjects is discussed by Otto Brunner, "Souveränitätsproblem und Sozialstruktur in den deutschen Reichsstädten der früheren Neuzeit," *Vierteljahrschrift für Sozial- und Wirtschaftsgeschichte*, 50 (1963), 329-60. It is true that in 1659 the council of Nördlingen angrily reproached persons who sowed discord "zwischen Obrigkeit und Unterthanen" (OB 1641-88, fol. 180b), but even in this very generalized form the use of the term "Untertanen" in referring to citizens was extremely uncharacteristic in Nördlingen.

pation in political life. But—at least in the seventeenth century—they had not yet come to believe that their own interests were fundamentally different from those of the citizenry as a whole. This will become evident in the following chapters, as we examine both the general relationship between the council and the citizenry and the council's response to a specific crisis at the end of the seventeenth century.

Seven

In Search of Order: The Politics of Paternalism

EVERY Monday, Wednesday and Friday morning, the council of Nördlingen met in regular session. Punctuality was demanded: when a meeting was about to begin, the "mayor's bell" was sounded from the tower of the city hall and at the same moment an hourglass was turned in the council chamber; councilmen who arrived after the sand had run out. were required to pay a fine. The meetings proceeded according to an agenda drawn up by the mayor. Council debates were not recorded, but there must have been vigorous discussions: the council bylaws stipulated that members were not to interrupt each other or create disturbances, and specified that if an argument turned to animosity the mayor could eject both parties from the council chamber. But the bylaws also stressed that once a vote was taken, "those who did not agree with it must give the majority decision as much help and support . . . as if they themselves had agreed with it."[1] The content of the meetings was never to be discussed in public; the oath that each member swore upon assuming office bound him to "keep the council's secrets to the end of his days."[2] The magistrates were determined to present a united front to their fellow citizens and to posterity.

In this they succeeded, for we know nothing today about

[1] Ratsordnung 1556, fols. 3b-8b (my pagination). The same clauses reappear in the revised council bylaws of 1673 (Ratsordnung 1673). The bylaws were read aloud to the council members about once a year between 1558 and 1652, and once a year again in the early 1670's (Ratsordnung 1556, fols. 13b ff.); they were read aloud every second or third year between 1678 and 1801 (Ratsordnung 1673, p. 17).

[2] Ratsordnung 1556, fol. 13a.

the discussions that took place among the council members. But we know much about the decisions they made. The disposition of each item on the agenda was fully recorded in the council minutes, and decisions which were announced to the general public are recorded in the city's ordinance books. Together, these volumes yield a rich picture of the council's concerns and actions during the early modern era.

I

NOTHING is more striking about the council of Nördlingen than the breadth of its concerns. Everything came within its purview, from the weightiest issues of state to the smallest cases of individual misbehavior. For all significant decision making in the community was vested in these fifteen men alone, and they enjoyed a broad conception of their mandate. On one level, the council of Nördlingen, like virtually all governments, was concerned with the maintenance of order, the protection of property, and the preservation of its own authority and resources. Yet at the same time, the councillors attributed to themselves a God-given duty to supervise in close detail the moral conduct of the thousands of souls under their charge.

This multiplicity of responsibilities was often encompassed within a single decision or decree; nowhere is this more evident than in the council's legislation concerning the social and moral behavior of the citizenry. An ordinance of 1585, for example, cracked down on citizens who drank to excess, a vice which was blamed not only for inducing a vast array of sins on the part of the individuals concerned—blasphemy, adultery and manslaughter were among those mentioned—but also for damaging the material interests of the community: wives and children were being driven to beggary, and the hospital and other municipal charities were thus being greatly overburdened.[3]

[3] OB 1567-87, fols. 191b-194a (3 May 1585).

Edicts of this sort, in various guises, were issued throughout the century and a half under study. In the 1670's, for example, the council became particularly concerned with the immodest behavior of the city's young people. One ordinance forbade the daughters of humble artisans and day-laborers, as well as servant girls of "bad and low origin," to squander their meager dowries on provocative clothing, which not only led to misbehavior with young men but also rendered the girls so poor that no men would want to marry them.[4] A later decree chastised parents for handing house keys over to their children and letting them stay out all night dancing, "under the godless pretext that otherwise they will lose every opportunity to get married . . . which, however, they cannot hope to answer for before Almighty God."[5]

A recent dissertation on the punishment of sexual crimes in Nördlingen has detected two waves of heightened severity in legislation dealing with various forms of social and moral misconduct. The first wave occurred in the middle decades of the sixteenth century, when—partly under the impact of the Reformation and partly as a result of the guilds' loss of political power—the city council developed a broader concept of its moral responsibilities. The second wave began in the mid-seventeenth century, when, under the influence of nascent Pietism, the city's wartime sufferings came to be seen as divine retribution for its sins—sins which could only be atoned for by harsher forms of punishment.[6]

But the council's concern with the conduct of Nördlingen's inhabitants was by no means confined to these two periods. For in fact the city fathers were engaged in a never-ending effort to hold virtually every form of spontaneous social behavior in check. Formal events were subject to de-

[4] OB 1641-88, fols. 315a-316b (5 July 1672).

[5] Ibid., fols. 326b-327a (23 Feb. 1674).

[6] Alfons Felber, *Unzucht und Kindsmord in der Rechtsprechung der freien Reichsstadt Nördlingen vom 15. bis 19. Jahrhundert* (Dissertation, Bonn, 1961), pp. 109-32 and passim.

tailed regulation: not only did the council specify the number of guests permitted at a wedding and the number of courses permitted at the wedding feast, but the numbers were changed from time to time as the magistrates decided to sanction a greater or lesser degree of frivolity.[7] Furthermore, the council assigned itself the unenviable task of attempting to forbid almost every activity that threatened the serenity of life in and around the city—from nighttime revelry to nude swimming, "tobacco-drinking," excessive consumption of food and drink and even the throwing of snowballs.[8]

All governments, of course, are concerned with maintaining order in their communities, and most governments identify the maintenance of order with the maintenance of their own authority. But it is important to emphasize the complete hostility with which the rulers of Nördlingen regarded any form of popular participation—or even interest—in the decision-making process. Before 1552, as we have seen, formal channels had existed for a large portion of the citizenry to participate in the municipal government, through the guild representatives on the council.[9] But after the guilds' political role was eliminated in 1552, only two legitimate channels remained for the citizenry to make its wishes known: either by expressing its views when asked to do so, usually through the rarely summoned "large council," or else by presenting petitions and requests for redress of grievances. Any other spontaneous initiative on the part of the citizenry—even the mere discussion of public affairs—was regarded as dangerously subversive.

[7] E.g., OB 1567-87, fols. 168a-177a (23 April 1582); OB 1612-40, fols. 92b-96a (7 Feb. 1621), 113b-114b (6 May 1622), 137b-142a (16 March 1624), etc.

[8] E.g., OB 1612-40, fols. 5b-6a (24 Oct. 1613), 26b-28a (3 June 1614), 212b-213a (25 Oct. 1630), 235a-b (14 Dec. 1631), etc. OB 1640-88, fols. 116b-117a (26 Apr. 1652), 185b-186a (26 Sept. 1659), etc. See also L. Mußgnug, "Alte Wintergesetze," *Rieser Heimatbote*, no. 49 (Dec. 1928), p. 3.

[9] See Chapter One, section II.

In fact, throughout the period of this study, there appears to have been only one episode that might be described as open protest: a spate of bread riots in the famine year 1693-94. And even these riots were directed not so much against the magistrates as against the grain dealers, who were blamed for the high price of foodstuffs.[10] Normally, popular discontent remained underground, or, when it surfaced, it generally appeared in a form more likely to render the protester safe from retribution. Throughout the seventeenth century, the most customary form of popular protest in Nördlingen was the posting of "Pasquills"—anonymous flyers, often in verse, containing attacks on the authorities and posted at one or more strategic locations in the town.

In 1614, one of the counts of Oettingen was killed by soldiers from Nördlingen in a hunting dispute.[11] Not long thereafter, an attack on Nördlingen's government, presumably penned by an Oettingen partisan, was posted in the town; this in turn was answered by a "counter-poem" in defense of the magistrates. From the council's point of view, both flyers were equally objectionable, and citizens were notified that they would be punished if they failed to destroy copies of either Pasquill in their possession.[12] Another attack upon authority occurred two years later, when a fox-tail was hung from the church bells and an insulting letter was thrown at the door of the city pastor—actions which led the council to offer a 25 fl. reward for information about the perpetrator.[13]

A much more alarming episode—and a more alarmed response—occurred in 1624, when a series of letters were posted which attacked the entire council in a highly scur-

[10] See OB 1688-1706, pp. 97-99 (4 Oct. 1693) and 113-17 (22 June 1694). One of these disturbances is also described in "Mötzel," *Rieser Heimatbote*, no. 43 (1928), p. 4, but Mötzel erroneously gives the date as 1692.

[11] See Chapter One, section III.

[12] OB 1612-40, fol. 33b (20 Feb. 1615).

[13] Ibid., fols. 63b-64a (26 Nov. 1617).

rilous manner. This time the magistrates offered a tempting reward of 100 fl., with obvious success, since a week later a 33-year-old weaver named David Gruber was arrested and confessed.[14] Exactly why Gruber posted these letters is unclear, but he was obviously a boisterous sort: while his wife was pregnant with their ninth child he was carrying on an affair with one Ursula Hardtmann.[15] Gruber enjoyed considerable public sympathy—a few weeks after his arrest the council had to order citizens to stop harrassing the informants.[16] But murmurings of public support could only have compounded the gravity with which the magistrates viewed Gruber's offense. The council initially sentenced him to a whipping followed by perpetual banishment—a sentence which was later "moderated" to imprisonment for an unspecified number of years.[17] The conditions of imprisonment were doubtless very grim, although the council did allow one shutter to be opened so that Gruber could read and (five months after his arrest) permitted him to take a bath.[18]

Remarkably, David Gruber managed to escape from prison.[19] But the way in which he was treated makes clear why Pasquills were posted so rarely. Every such placard, no matter how innocuous, was regarded as a grave attack on the authority of the council and the peace of the community. The magistrates did, however, take careful note of the exact degree to which their own authority was impugned. In 1659 a reward of 50 Reichsthaler (75 fl.) was offered for information about a Pasquill which attacked the mayor and council,

[14] OB 1612-40, fols. 144b-145b (6 Aug. 1624); RP 17 Aug. 1624. (Two concurrent volumes of Ratsprotokolle cover the period 1623-25; unless otherwise indicated the version in full folio size is cited.)

[15] Gruber's family circumstances have been established as part of the letter-G reconstitutions described in Chapter Two. For his affair with Ursula Hardtmann, see RP 8 Oct. 1624 and RP (small folio) 11 Oct. 1624.

[16] OB 1612-40, fols. 146b-148a (22 Sept. 1624).

[17] RP 20 and 30 Sept., 1 Oct. 1624.

[18] RP 8 Oct. 1624; RP (small folio) 27 Dec. 1624.

[19] RP 18 Jan. 1625.

while in 1667 a Pasquill which merely attacked certain "innocent decent people" rated a reward of only 12 Reichsthaler.[20] In 1691, seven Pasquills were posted which specifically attacked Bürgermeister Weng by name; the reward was escalated to 200 fl.[21]

In the absence of more systematic information about the Pasquills, episodes like these can tell us little about the nature and extent of social discontent in Nördlingen. They do, however, reinforce our picture of a magistracy that was intolerant of even the most trivial expressions of protest or discontent—or in fact, as we have seen, of any excessive display of spontaneous behavior on the part of the public. The social order was a delicate mechanism, in the magistrates' eyes, and any form of disorder might threaten to rend it asunder. They, and they alone, were responsible for making sure that this would never happen.

To say this, however, is not to suggest that the mayor and councilmen of Nördlingen were necessarily arbitrary or abusive in the exercise of their exclusive powers. In the first place, the magistrates could scarcely dare to remain indifferent to the needs or wishes of their fellow citizens. For if the social order was really as delicate as they believed it to be, then in large measure they, too, had a role to play in maintaining the equilibrium. Their own powers of enforcement were strictly limited, and the obedience of the inhabitants had to be obtained in large measure by providing them with a just and sympathetic administration. And even beyond this, it is clear that—at least in the sixteenth and seventeenth centuries—the councillors took their obligations to uphold the public welfare seriously and felt a real sense of paternal obligations toward their fellow citizens.

Perhaps nothing illustrates this so clearly as the way in which the magistrates reacted to changes in the organization of economic life. Throughout the seventeenth century, the

[20] OB 1640-88, fols. 180b-181a (9 Feb. 1659), 251a-b (15 Nov. 1667).

[21] OB 1688-1706, pp. 57-58 (23 Sept. 1691).

artisans of Nördlingen felt themselves to be threatened in three different ways. In the first place, they were constantly concerned that too many outsiders might be admitted to their crafts, and thus too many masters might end up competing for a share of the local market. Second, they were troubled by an increase in the number of village craftsmen, who presented them with unfamiliar and unwelcome competition. Third, and perhaps most significantly, they were confronted within the city itself by the gradual introduction of the putting-out system, which threatened ultimately to destroy their economic independence.

In all of these concerns, the craftsmen found the city council to be sympathetic. To limit the number of outsiders admitted, the magistrates were normally quite willing to enact the craftsmen's own wishes regarding the number and qualifications of persons to be accepted as apprentices, journeymen and masters.[22] And although they were powerless to act against village artisans outside their political control, the magistrates were certainly sympathetic to the city craftsmen's point of view. An ordinance of 1667 vividly illustrates this point. Having discovered that various citizens of Nördlingen were giving out work to cabinetmakers in the nearby village of Baldingen, the council angrily pointed out that such commissions ran "against the usage and customs of the crafts, . . . since these [village] cabinetmakers are neither guilded nor have they produced a masterpiece." And even beyond this, the council went on, it was wrong in principle to employ the village artisans: "[The citizens], who should stand by one another through thick and thin, and must partake of each other's joys and sorrows, [should not] cause any further diminution of each other's livelihoods, which are already far too difficult to obtain, by grant-

[22] For a particularly clear example, involving linen-weavers, see OB 1640-88, fols. 359b-361a (12 March 1679). See also Heinz Dannenbauer, "Das Leinenweberhandwerk in der Reichsstadt Nördlingen," *Zeitschrift für bayerische Landesgeschichte*, 3 (1930), 275-76 and passim; and Ebert, *Lodweberei*, p. 19 and passim.

ing a foreigner their money. . . ." In the future, the council decreed, a citizen who wanted any work done was to apply to the city's own masters.[23]

It was easy enough, of course, for the council to sympathize with the artisans' hostility toward outsiders. But it is noteworthy that the magistrates also attempted to defend the craftsmen against economic threats that arose within the city itself. By the end of the seventeenth century, the lines of economic conflict were clearly drawn, at least in the city's major industry, between artisans struggling to maintain their independence and entrepreneurial capitalists whose practices were gradually turning craftsmen into contract laborers. Before the end of the *ancien régime*, it is true, the magistrates would come to share the views and interests of Nördlingen's leading capitalists, but this had not yet happened at the end of the seventeenth century, when the councillors still felt bonds of association and obligation to the artisans who made up so much of the city's population.

All this, however, is a story that must be told in greater detail. In Chapter Nine we shall trace the development of one capitalist fortune in Nördlingen, and examine how the community and the council responded to the emergence of entrepreneurial capitalism in this city. But this was a gradual process, to which the magistrates could work out a measured response. The real test of their effectiveness in ruling the city inevitably came during times of crisis. How successfully did the magistrates combine paternalistic concern with rigid control under conditions of political or social stress? To answer this question, we shall examine the magistrates' behavior during two periods of acute disequilibrium: the Nördlingen witch-craze of the 1590's and the Thirty Years War.

II

It is always tempting to interpret a witch-craze as the re-

[23] OB 1641-88, fol. 252a-b (16 Dec. 1667).

flection of some social conflict, either between two social groups within the same community or between fundamentally antagonistic social or cultural groups within the larger society.[24] If members of the upper classes were among the victims, one might interpret a witch-craze as the consequence of a power struggle within the confines of a single elite group. None of these approaches, however, seems to help us understand the Nördlingen witch-craze of 1589-94. For the social origins of the victims were so widespread—and the apparent motivations behind the accusations so varied—that an interpretation based on social conflict would hardly fit the facts.

The Nördlingen witch-craze has already been carefully researched and described by a local historian, Dr. Gustav Wulz.[25] His findings form the basis for all the information presented here about the basic history of this episode, and about the identity and backgrounds of the victims. But the interpretation toward which Wulz leaned—that of an oppressive and irresponsible magistracy—deserves some reconsideration. For it can be argued that the city council was motivated, at least to some extent, by a sincere intention to protect the community from what it believed to be malevolent and dangerous forces.

Southern Germany, like much of Europe, experienced a

[24] For examples of the first approach, see Keith Thomas, *Religion and the Decline of Magic* (New York, 1971), esp. pp. 435-583, and Alan Macfarlane, *Witchcraft in Tudor and Stuart England: A Regional and Comparative Study* (London, 1970). (This approach, incidentally, is most productive for a country like England, where accusations were not obtained by torture but instead normally arose spontaneously from within the community.) A celebrated example of the second approach is that of H. R. Trevor-Roper, "The European Witch-Craze of the Sixteenth and Seventeenth Centuries," in *Religion, the Reformation and Social Change* (New York, 1968), pp. 90-192.

[25] "Nördlinger Hexenprozesse," *JHVN*, 20 (1937), 42-72; 21 (1938-39), 95-120; and "Die Nördlinger Hexen und ihre Richter," *Rieser Heimatbote*, nos. 142-45, 147 (1939).

dramatic increase in witch hunting during the second half of the sixteenth century. The reasons for this increase are still a matter of controversy.[26] The case of Nördlingen, however, illustrates the importance of one frequently cited factor: the growing acceptance of the principles of Roman law, which emphasized the need for confessions, even if they had to be obtained by torture. Since the victim was often required to name accomplices as well, an isolated arrest for witchcraft could rapidly initiate a chain reaction of further accusations and arrests.

The first woman arrested in Nördlingen, Ursula Haider, was a mentally deficient spinster who may actually have considered herself a witch, and it is thus understandable that accusations were made against her. But once this first arrest had given official sanction to the idea that witchcraft existed in Nördlingen, latent suspicions and hostilities that had long lain dormant suddenly bubbled to the surface, and many unquestionably innocent women were caught in the web of accusations.

In the course of five years, a total of 33 persons were executed for witchcraft in Nördlingen.[27] Of these victims, all but one were women; to this extent, the accusations—whether made voluntarily or not—conformed to the contemporary stereotype of the witch as a female. But from the very start of the witch-craze, the accusations involved persons whose backgrounds covered the entire social spectrum

[26] Some of the suggested reasons are enumerated in H. C. Erik Midelfort, *Witch Hunting in Southwestern Germany, 1562-1684: The Social and Intellectual Foundations* (Stanford, Calif., 1972), pp. 68-71, which emphasizes the changes in legal practices and the "new fascination with and fear of the devil."

[27] Between 1589 and 1594, 29 women and 1 man were executed as witches; in addition, three accused women died in prison and their bodies were burnt, indicating that the council was convinced of their guilt. Wulz also lists 10 women who were arrested but released; most of them came from nearby villages, and the council may have been unsure of its legal rights or unwilling to get into a jurisdictional dispute with the counts of Oettingen. A few other women were accused but not arrested.

of the community. At one end of the scale were women who lived on the margins of destitution—one was a rag picker—while at the other end were distinguished members of the civic elite, including the widows of four council members.

Of the 33 persons executed, about a third had been spontaneously accused by their fellow inhabitants. In some cases, women long suspected of witchcraft were now openly named; in other cases, family or neighborhood hostilities were clearly the motivating factor: one husband, for example, accused his wife of using witchcraft to make him sick. The other two-thirds of the victims were named by earlier suspects themselves: forced under torture to identify their accomplices, almost all of the arrested women broke down and implicated others. But the accusations which, in their desperation, these women made suggest a wide range of motives. In some cases, the tortured woman simply came up with the names of her neighbors, which explains why a particularly high proportion of victims lived on or near the Weinmarkt in the southwestern part of the city. In other cases, the motivation was clearly revenge for distant or recent slights: understandably, one woman implicated the wife of the man who had been the presiding mayor at the time of her arrest. In still other cases, family tensions came into play: in at least one instance a victim caused the arrest of her own mother.

The city council, of course, had the exclusive power to order the arrests and tortures which led the victims to their confessions and executions. Indeed, the magistrates placed great emphasis on their sole responsibility: when the city's chief pastor expressed doubts from the pulpit about the council's method of procedure, he was enjoined to silence. Nevertheless, it is scarcely possible to interpret the witchcraze of Nördlingen as the product of the magistrates' hostility toward any particular inhabitants or group of inhabitants of the city. For, after all, the roster of victims was almost entirely selected by the citizens themselves or by the accused women. The council's real responsibility, then, lies not in having selected victims but in having blindly obeyed the dictates of the Roman law, under which an accused person was almost invariably tortured until she both confessed and named "accomplices." While the magistrates proceeded cautiously, often pausing before any new step to await detailed advice from their legal counsel, there is no evidence that they ever questioned the legal premises under which they acted, or that they ever doubted that a severe menace to the city's well-being had suddenly been exposed and required relentless persecution. From their own point of view, the magistrates were not fighting any particular segment of the citizenry—they were fighting Satan.

The witch-craze ended in 1594, but not because the council suddenly realized the injustice of its actions. Instead, the chain of accusations was simply broken when one suspect, Maria Holl, managed to withstand 62 applications of torture without confessing or naming "accomplices." Under pressure from her relatives, the council finally released this woman, without, however, formally exonerating her.

Certainly, the magistrates did not cease to believe in witchcraft; in fact, two additional women were executed as witches in 1598. But it is equally apparent that the councillors now proceeded with greater caution, for they were content to burn these women without trying to ferret out the names of accomplices. The executions of 1598 were the last witch burnings in Nördlingen, and it appears that the magistrates subsequently took a dim view of groundless or careless accusations of witchcraft when they arose among the citizens.[28]

In fact, the end of the witch-craze in Nördlingen con-

[28] For example, in August 1613 one woman was punished for calling another "a conscious witch, who would soon certainly be burnt." A few days later, six tanners were punished for spreading the rumor that Georg Wörner's wife was training her maid in witchcraft. Both incidents are recorded on fol. 41 of the Urfehdebuch 1609-14; for the second incident, see also Chapter Nine.

forms almost precisely to the model presented in H. C. Erik Midelfort's recent study of witch-hunting in the German southwest, which argues that after a long spate of witch trials the magistrates would often face a sudden "crisis of confidence." Frequently, as Midelfort describes it, this crisis would be triggered by some unexpected hitch or obstruction in the proceedings, which would cause the magistrates to doubt the efficacy or reliability of their own judicial techniques: "Witch hunters in many regions stopped hunting and executing witches not because they no longer believed in them, but because they no longer knew how to find them."[29]

But the witch-craze of Nördlingen is also instructive from a very different point of view. For it illustrates vividly that a witch-craze could take place without any undertones of social conflict. We have already seen that the victims in Nördlingen came from an extensive variety of backgrounds; clearly the witch hunt did not reflect the hostility of one social group toward another. Nor, in fact, did it reflect tensions within the elite, or hostility toward particular families.

This becomes abundantly clear when we look at the widowers or children of the women executed for witchcraft. If, after all, the execution of women from the town's leading families had actually reflected tensions within the civic elite, then we would expect to find that the families of these women also suffered disgrace. But in fact nothing of the sort happened. Take, for example, the Gundelfinger family.[30] In 1592, Bürgermeister Karl Gundelfinger died, and in January of the following year his nephew Johann Wilhelm Gundelfinger was elected to fill the council vacancy that Karl's death had created. In November 1593, Karl's widow Dorothea was arrested for witchcraft; after considerable torture she died in prison and her body was burned in disgrace. Yet

[29] Midelfort, *Witch Hunting*, chapter 6; the quotation, however, is from p. 6.

[30] For additional information about the councilmen mentioned in this and the next paragraph, see Appendix VII.

her nephew continued to sit on the council and later became mayor, while her son Johann Conrad Gundelfinger spent his whole career in the city's service and eventually also was elected mayor. Clearly, the Gundelfinger family had suffered no disgrace: the stigma of having submitted to Satan's will was an entirely personal one.

Or consider the case of Katherina Kessler, a tanner's wife. Katherina was arrested in June 1590 and—after being briefly released in December to give birth to a child—she was burnt as a witch the following May. Yet her son Daniel later became the first member of his family to be appointed to the city council.

The most unusual case, however, was that of Peter and Rebekka Lemp. Peter Lemp was an eminent civic personage who held the responsible position of Zahlmeister, or collector of indirect revenues. In June 1590 his wife, the mother of six children, was arrested on accusation of witchcraft. The Lemps were a devoted couple, and the nature of their relationship—and their beliefs—is suggested by the letters which Rebekka wrote to her husband from prison.[31] The first was sent shortly after her arrest:

> My beloved treasure, have no fear. If a thousand people accuse me, I am still innocent—or let all the devils come and tear me apart. And if they interrogate

[31] These letters came into the hands of the council and were included in its files on the Lemp case; until recently most of them were on display in the Nördlingen city museum. The texts were published by Wulz in *JHVN*, 20 (1937), pp. 61-68 passim. In addition to the letters quoted below, the collection includes a letter written to Rebekka Lemp by her children two days after her imprisonment: "Our affectionate and filial greetings, dearly beloved mother. We want you to know that we are well. . . . May almighty God grant you his grace and Holy Spirit, so that you, God willing, may come back to us in peace and good health, Amen. Dearest mother, buy some beer . . . and have them get you some fish and have them get you a chicken from us. . . . You must not worry about the household until you come back to us. . . ." The letter was written by her oldest daughter and signed by most of the younger children.

> me under torture, I could confess nothing, even if they tear me into a thousand pieces. . . . Father, if I am guilty, then may God never let me appear before his face for all eternity. If they don't believe me, God Almighty will watch over me and send them a sign. For if I am abandoned in my need, then there is no God in heaven. . . .

Lemp submitted an impassioned testimonial to the council, asserting his wife's innocence, piety and devotion as a wife and mother. But it was to no avail: shortly thereafter the council proceeded to order interrogation under torture. Rebekka broke down and made a series of confessions, which, however, she repudiated in a second letter to her husband:

> O my chosen treasure, must I thus be torn in all innocence from you? That will cry out to God for all time. They force one, they make one talk; they have tortured me. I am as innocent as God in heaven. If I knew as much as one iota of these things, then I would deserve that God should deny me paradise. . . . Father, send me something so that I die, otherwise I will break down under torture. . . .

By now Rebekka had lost all hope. To her husband she sent her remaining jewelry with detailed instructions: "Wear the ring in memory of me. Divide the necklace into six pieces and have our children wear them on their hands for the rest of their lives. . . ."

Rebekka still managed to have one conference with her husband and her brother. But whatever it was she said to them she was forced to retract in a final, unconvincing note to her husband:

> Father, may God protect you. I have been unjust to my lords in what I said to you and my brother. I have confessed everything again and so it is true that I am what I said I was in my statement.

In September 1590 Rebekka Lemp was burnt at the stake. There is no doubt that Peter Lemp mourned her deeply as an innocent victim of the magistrates. Yet his life went on as it would have for any widowed member of the civic elite. Four months after the execution Peter Lemp married the widow of city clerk Paul Mair and received a handsome wedding present from the council. In 1594, again a widower, Lemp married the daughter of Ratsherr Peter Mayinger, who had served on the council throughout Rebekka Lemp's trial. In 1596 Lemp himself was elevated to membership on the council, and later that year he contracted his fourth and last marriage—to a daughter of the deceased councilman Georg Mair and his wife Rosina, who had also died at the stake as a witch. A career like Lemp's would be hard to understand if the women executed as witches had been regarded as social reprobates who had brought disgrace upon their families. But clearly they were seen in other terms: as individual agents, or even victims, of a satanic force that had attempted to invade the community.

III

A GENERATION later the community was confronted with a more obvious—and more prolonged—kind of invasion. For thirty years, almost without interruption, soldiers of every stripe either marched through the town or stayed to establish quarters there. As these troops swarmed in and out of the city, and as material conditions grew worse and worse, any disturbance began to carry the potential for setting off a violent social explosion. From the very start of the Thirty Years War we can sense the council's urgent concern with this problem.

The most obvious source of friction lay in contacts between the citizenry and the soldiers. As early as 1619 and 1620, the council warned citizens not to get involved in the soldiers' activities and arguments and to avoid inciting the troops to any kind of violence; similar decrees were issued recurrently throughout the war.[32] But even the most innocuous kind of commotion posed threats to the social order, especially during the tense wartime situation. Over and over, the council demanded that the inhabitants stop rushing to the walls or out of the city gates every time something seemed to be happening before the town: sooner or later, the council warned in 1634, a disaster might befall the deserted city, or in any case those who rushed into the fields "might be sent back in without their heads."[33] A later decree warned that such excited excursions could result in citizens' being "returned with bloody heads, or even shot down, or else captured and dragged off for ransom."[34]

Throughout the Thirty Years War, the city council was engaged in a continuing effort to protect the citizenry from the invading troops. The best way to do so was by appeasing the soldiers' insatiable demands for money. Sometimes the army or political league in control of the region would levy specific "contributions" on the town, at other times demands arose spontaneously from soldiers on the spot, but either way the council was desperately afraid of what might happen if such demands were not at least substantially satisfied.

Above all, the magistrates feared that the soldiers might take matters into their own hands. Indeed, a mere apprehension that the soldiers might do so could have dangerous social consequences. In a decree of August 1627, for example, the council pointed out that if military demands were not satisfied, then peasants would abandon their land in fear of retribution and "leave the fruits of the fields unharvested, and thereby all the payments, tithes and other dues owed to the authorities would certainly be lost. . . ."[35]

[32] OB 1612-40, fols. 74b (29 Dec. 1619), 82a-b (20 Apr. 1620); e.g., also fols. 180b-182a (26 July 1627), 265b-266a (6 Nov. 1633); OB 1641-88, fols. 59b-60a (5 June 1647).

[33] OB 1612-40, fol. 275a-b (5 June 1634).

[34] OB 1641-88, fols. 64b-65a (2 Nov. 1647).

[35] OB 1612-40, fols. 182a-183a (6 Aug. 1627).

So unsettling was the presence of soldiers, in fact, that the council regarded almost any cash payment as preferable to having to quarter troops in the town. In December 1636, for example, the magistrates triumphantly reported that they had secured for the city a release from all quartering during the winter in return for pledging a flat fee of 10,000 fl. The citizens, they insisted, should "gratefully acknowledge" God's "wonderful mercy and goodness" in making this arrangement possible, and thus should gladly make their payments.[36]

Most of the time, of course, the community was not so "fortunate"—it had to put up with both soldiers and contributions at the same time. Earlier chapters have already indicated the extent to which wartime requisitions drained the community of its wealth; here, however, we must comment on the council's role in effecting the transfer of funds. For, throughout the war, the council was cast in the delicate role of middleman between soldiery and citizenry. Obviously if military appetites were not appeased, the soldiers might resort to force. But on the other hand, if the citizens were pressed too hard, or could not be persuaded of the gravity of the situation, their frustrations might erupt into open disorder or even revolt.

Throughout the war, then, the council made a continuing effort to convince the citizens that the special military taxes were necessary, or at least unavoidable. In the course of the conflict, however, the magistrates' methods underwent some significant changes. At first, the council frequently appealed to the citizens' patriotism or religious loyalties. When they imposed the first special tax of the war, in 1619, the magistrates explained that the community had to admit and support a Protestant company in order to preserve the town's political liberties and religious faith.[37] A typical decree of

[36] Ibid., fols. 322b-323a (23 Dec. 1636). Cf. also fols. 157b-158a (30 Aug. 1625).

[37] Ibid., fols. 70b-72a (8 July 1619).

the 1620's emphasized that the magistrates alone could not bear the cost of securing "our fatherland's liberty and its conservation for our dear posterity"—and therefore the citizens had to share in providing the necessary funds.[38] In July 1631, when the Emperor's forces were dominant in the area, the council explained that a failure to meet imperial demands would threaten both the city's Protestant faith and its "liberty and freedom, hard-earned by our honored ancestors"; every "well-intentioned patriot," they were sure, would understand the need for further taxation.[39] When Protestant troops were in the ascendancy, the council could play even more directly on the citizens' religious sympathies, as in 1633, when the magistrates reminded the community of earlier Catholic atrocities while warning that the enemy was intent on destroying the Evangelical cause—clear reasons for prompt payment of the special assessments.[40]

By the 1630's, however, such appeals were wearing thin, and they had to be underlined—or replaced—by the threat of force. At times, the magistrates simply relayed to the citizenry the threats they themselves had received from the regional military command: that if the community were remiss in its payments, it would be punished with an "execution" in which the army would satisfy its demands by military means.[41] Another approach, however—and one that was within the council's own power to enforce—was the threat to single out households that had failed to pay their assessments and to quarter soldiers there until the back taxes were produced, or simply to permit the soldiers to satisfy their wants directly out of the household's own supplies, in lieu of cash. What could happen under such circumstances

[38] Ibid., fols. 193a-b (30 July 1628).

[39] Ibid., fols. 225b-226b (13 July 1631).

[40] Ibid., fols. 255b-258a (10 Apr. 1633).

[41] For example, ibid., fols. 287b-289a (20 Jan.-5 Feb. 1635), 314b-315a (1 July 1636); see also fol. 257a (10 Apr. 1633).

is easy to imagine—and the council made clear that it would have no pity for those who had brought this situation upon themselves.[42]

But while force, or the threat of force, may have been more effective than patriotic appeals in securing prompt payments, it was also bound to raise the temperature of popular discontent. Thus, the council also had to convince the community that its actions were indispensable to the common good. In moments of supreme crisis, the council might summon the city court and large council to review the situation, so that the citizenry could be informed that all three bodies had agreed on the imposition of some new tax.[43] But sharing power never came easily to the magistrates of Nördlingen. Much of the time they simply tried to persuade the citizenry that they were, in fact, doing their best. In 1635, for example, they expressed their wonder that citizens could be so ungrateful to a council that worked "night and day" for the good of the city.[44] In an even more maudlin mood, they assured the populace in 1643 that "it grieves the honorable council and breaks our hearts that once again our own loyal, beloved citizenry . . . must and will unavoidably be troubled and burdened with heavy contributions," before they proceeded to announce a new round of taxes to be paid at ten-day intervals.[45]

The council was not just concerned to dampen sources of discontent; to whatever extent possible it attempted to stifle all public discussion. In 1639, the magistrates discovered that the latest military occupation of the city had given rise to all sorts of "wicked, restless and irresponsible talk," and they decreed that if any further incidents of such talk were reported "by the persons specially designated to that

[42] E.g., ibid., 243b-244b (12 July 1632), 294b-295b (27 May 1635), 304a-305a (14 Sept. 1635).

[43] Ibid., fols. 306a-307a (7 Nov. 1635). A less clear-cut case of consultation is indicated in fol. 281a-b (8 Sept. 1634).

[44] Ibid., fols. 296b-297b (1 July 1635).

[45] OB 1641-88, fols. 27b-28b (26 Dec. 1643).

end," harsh punishments would ensue.[46] In 1646, the council again warned citizens not to discuss the war or to spread any rumors about it; instead, the magistrates suggested, concerned citizens should pray for a change in the situation.[47] A year later, they theatened to punish anyone who talked about things "which it is not fitting for ordinary people and private persons to discuss, in particular all discussions which could lead now or later to any difficulties, whether [such talk] be directed against ordinary persons or high ones. . . ."[48]

The magistrates were convinced, of course, not only that they alone were capable of making decisions for the community, but that they alone were entitled to do so. An elaborate manifestation of this attitude was provided in December 1647, after the city had suffered from a highly destructive bombardment by a Bavarian detachment—an event whose effects were evidently aggravated by a widespread failure to observe fire-prevention regulations. The ensuing message gave the council an opportunity both to offer its explanation for the disaster and to define clearly the proper relationship between the governed and their governors. After taking note of the fact that citizens had not only ignored earlier directives, but also openly disparaged their rulers, the council proceeded to point out that

> no authority or communal life can exist or last if the orderly commands and prohibitions laid down by God are ignored; and the righteous God (without whom no government is established) always punishes terribly those who violate his ordinances . . . a sorrowful display of his righteous anger has already been witnessed in this our city, and it could easily happen that the whole city . . . could go up in fire and smoke as a result of inadequate rescue arrangements. . . .

[46] OB 1612-40, fols. 337b-338b (14 Jan. 1639).
[47] OB 1641-88, fol. 55a (17 Aug. 1646).
[48] Ibid., fol. 62a-b (15 Sept. 1647).

In short, the magistrates interpreted the recent disaster as divine retribution for the citizens' failure to obey secular authority. Having made this point, the council proceeded to list anew the fire-prevention regulations, which citizens were expected to obey not only to mitigate the effects of any future bombardments but also, it is clear, to demonstrate their obedience to authority.[49]

Taken as a whole, the council's tactics can be said to have succeeded. By the end of the war, despite murmurs of discontent among the populace, the magistrates had never really lost control of the situation—either to the soldiers or to the citizens. In nearby Rothenburg ob der Tauber, the wartime financial policies of the city council had come to evoke widespread popular distrust: in 1645 a member of the large council of Rothenburg physically assaulted the mayor, accusing him and his colleagues on the inner council of stealing the citizens' money, and after the war the citizenry appealed to the Emperor for the right of inspection over municipal finances.[50] But relations between the council and citizenry of Nördlingen never deteriorated to such an extent. Clearly, one factor in this must have been the magistrates' success in persuading the citizens that no matter what financial burdens it imposed upon them, its actions were intended to protect the community from even greater harm.

The later years of the seventeenth century brought renewed warfare to the Empire, and with it came renewed occupations and financial demands. Once again we find the council anxiously attempting to minimize the friction between soldiers and citizens.[51] Even more importantly, the

[49] Ibid., fols. 66b-68a (17 Dec. 1647).

[50] Karl Rank, *Die Finanzwirtschaft der Reichsstadt Rothenburg ob der Tauber während des Dreissigjährigen Krieges: Ein Beitrag zur Geschichte des Kontributionswesens* (Erlanger Abhandlungen zur mittleren und neueren Geschichte, N.F. 5; Erlangen, 1940), pp. 126-27.

[51] E.g., OB 1640-88, fols. 335a-336a (1674).

council was again obliged to cajole supplementary taxes or special loans of increasing magnitude out of an ever more reluctant citizenry. In one decree of the 1690's, for example, we can see how the old appeal to civic patriotism was revived, when the council argued that every citizen in whom "even a glimmer of natural love and affection for the fatherland still persists" would surely make the payments necessary to save the community from total confusion and ruin.[52] More frequently, the magistrates threatened those in arrears with punishment—and above all, the magistrates emphasized that the community would be visited with military execution by the Swabian Circle if it failed to meet its obligations.[53] Once again the council was attempting to make clear that in demanding money from the citizenry, it was only trying to protect the community from even greater disasters. The economic consequences of these later wars were, as we have seen, in many ways even greater than those of the Thirty Years War. But the means which the magistrates had summoned to hold together the social fabric during the earlier period of warfare still proved effective, and the council survived the epoch of French and Turkish wars with no challenge to its authority over the community.

Yet in the last analysis social control, especially in times of crisis, could not be guaranteed by even the shrewdest combinations of persuasion and punishment. To be effective, such measures also depended on the existence of deep-seated patterns of deference and obedience to authority among the inhabitants. Many institutions contributed to instilling such attitudes in seventeenth-century Nördlingen, but two were uniquely important: church and school. To them we now turn.

[52] OB 1688-1706, pp. 65-69 (17 Feb. 1692).

[53] E.g., ibid., pp. 53-56 (12 Jan. 1691), 111-113 (31 Jan. 1694), 117-120 (1 Aug. 1694).

Eight

To Make Them Fear the Lord: Church and School in a Lutheran Community

RELIGION and education were part of one enterprise in seventeenth-century Nördlingen, and both came under the close supervision of the city council. Having once accepted the Reformation, the magistrates never wavered in their adherence to Lutheran orthodoxy, and their perception of their own duties was deeply shaped by Lutheran teachings. It was their responsibility to make sure the people of Nördlingen behaved as good Christians and as good citizens, which, in fact, they perceived as much the same thing. And to this end it was necessary that "Christian order and discipline be maintained in church and school."[1]

Compared to the late middle ages, when some eighty priests, monks and nuns lived in the city,[2] the clerical establishment in post-Reformation Nördlingen was small indeed. At its head stood the superintendent, generally a distinguished theologian summoned by the council to serve both as pastor of St. Georg's and as supervisor of church and schools. Other members of the Nördlingen ministry included the three deacons at St. Georg's, the preacher at the former Carmelite church, the hospital chaplain, and the pastors of villages whose clerical appointments were controlled by the city: Goldburgshausen, Nähermemmingen and Schweindorf.[3]

[1] From the Nördlingen Kirchenordnung of 1579, in Emil Sehling, ed., *Die evangelischen Kirchenordnungen des sechzehnten Jahrhunderts*, vol. 12 (Tübingen, 1963), p. 336.

[2] This figure is based on the census of 1459. Cf. Chapter Two, note 1.

[3] See Sehling, *Kirchenordnungen*, vol. 12, p. 340. This can be com-

The duties of the superintendent and his colleagues were laid down in a series of ordinances issued by the council, most importantly the comprehensive church ordinance of 1579. Drawn up in consultation with Tübingen theologians and with the city's own ministers, the 1579 ordinance governed such matters as ordination of ministers, rules of marriage, the liturgy and inspection of schools. A consistory made up of three ministers and three members of the council was established in 1578 to function as a clerical court, under constant supervision by the council itself.[4]

Ministers were appointed (and dismissed) by the council: an attempt by the superintendent in 1564 to gain control of clerical appointments had been swiftly blocked by the magistrates.[5] But this does not mean that the clergymen were in every respect creatures of the magistrates. Some, especially the superintendents, were not native to Nördlingen. All had attended university and belonged to a mobile professional group with widespread contacts throughout Lutheran Germany. There were, in fact, cases of tension between clerics and council—notably in 1589, when Superintendent Lutz criticized the proceedings of the council during an early phase of the witch-craze.[6] But for the most part the ministers and magistrates acted in harmony, and over the long run there was hardly any disagreement over political or theological matters.

I

ONE area of mutual concern was education. As orthodox Lutherans, ministers and magistrates alike were persuaded

---

pared to the description of the ministry in 1700 provided by "Mötzel," *Heimatbote*, no. 46 (1928).

4 The background of the 1579 ordinance is discussed in Sehling, *Kirchenordnungen*, vol. 12, pp. 282-83. The text itself is published on pp. 335-93.

5 Ibid., p. 282.

6 Wulz, "Nördlinger Hexenprozesse," *JHVN*, 20 (1937), 58.

of the need to inculcate habits of obedience and piety at an early age. Their reasoning is clearly exemplified by the preamble of the revised school ordinance of 1652:

> . . . the honorable council of this holy imperial city of Nördlingen, as a Christian authority, has had occasion to consider how remarkably much the common weal depends on well-conducted schools, and how one of the duties of rulers is to insure that young people be diligently educated, with great circumspection and appropriate severity, and that they be restrained from evil and be habituated, aroused and encouraged to do what is good . . . it is well known that whatever is planted into the hearts and minds of the young at an early stage can never be rooted our during the adult years, but instead all citizens of this republic, be they of clerical or secular station, will inevitably have those qualities, be they good or evil, which became established in their youth or first education. . . .[7]

A few paragraphs later the ordinance continues:

> Inasmuch as the fear of the Lord is the beginning of all wisdom, so therefore we earnestly order that every youth who wishes to be admitted to and instructed in this school, be he foreign or native, should fear the just and almighty God as the punisher of all evil, and in all his actions at all times and in all places should have the Lord in mind.[8]

These passages come from an ordinance regulating the Latin school of Nördlingen, which provided a rigorous education for a few score boys. But the objectives expressed here also

[7] *Ernewerte Schul-Ordnung E.E. Rahts des H. Römischen Reichs Statt Nördlingen . . . M.DC.LII.* (Nördlingen, 1652).

[8] Ibid., paragraph II(i). The 1652 ordinance was a revised version of earlier ordinances, which in turn had been strongly influenced by the Württemberg Schulordnung of 1559: Hans Ockel, "Die lateinische Schule der Reichsstadt Nördlingen," *Zeitschrift des historischen Vereins für Schwaben und Neuburg*, 34 (1908), 136-37.

applied to the six (later five) German schools, where hundreds of children—boys and girls alike—received an elementary education in reading, writing and Christian fundamentals.

The Latin school was, of course, the jewel of the Nördlingen educational system. By the late middle ages it had already become a municipal institution; indeed, in the late fifteenth century the schoolmaster and his assistants were sometimes laymen.[9] But since the Reformation the magistrates had appointed only university-trained theologians as instructors; many of them, in fact, eventually moved on to ministerial positions in Nördlingen or elsewhere.[10]

In the seventeenth century the Latin school of Nördlingen was organized into five classes. This does not mean, however, that a pupil normally completed his education in five years; in fact, it might take two or three years before he could pass the Easter examination which would qualify him to move up to the next level. In the lowest class much of the instruction was still in German, but by the fifth class pupils were reading the Latin of Cicero, Vergil and Terence and the Greek of Erasmus' New Testament. Logic, rhetoric and arithmetic were also taught; history and geography, however, were only added in 1708.[11]

Many hours, of course, were also devoted to religion. The pupils were repeatedly drilled in Luther's catechism, both German and Latin. Equally important was the musical instruction provided by a teacher with the title of cantor. For centuries it had been the duty of pupils to serve as choristers during church services, vespers, funerals and the like. Each school ordinance laid down in detail the pupils' singing obligations.[12]

Finally, the school was to serve as an institution for incul-

[9] Ibid., pp. 133-34.

[10] Gustav Wulz, "Die Rektoren und Präzeptoren der Lateinschule Nördlingen vom 13. bis 18. Jahrhundert," in *Jahresbericht des Theodor-Heuss-Gymnasiums Nördlingen 1965/66*, pp. 47-64.

[11] Ockel, "Lateinische Schule," pp. 134-40 passim.

[12] Ibid., p. 138. See also the *Ernewerte Schul-Ordnung*, esp. section I.

cating the values of a strict and deferential social order. "All instructors," according to the 1652 ordinance, "should serve as models of piety, sobriety, temperance and honesty for their pupils," while in turn "every pupil should show respect, in school and out, for honorable persons such as mayors, council members, pastors, teachers, worthy matrons, the elderly and the aged, and should never pass them by without a sign of reverence." The ordinance included a long list of prohibitions—touching everything from "long, messy, military-style hair" to speaking German in the upper classes—and students were enjoined to adhere to these rules "more out of a love of virtue and honor than from a fear of punishment."[13]

In actual fact fear of punishment must have played a much greater role in educational practice than the magistrates hoped. Beatings were frequent, and sometimes ferocious, as suggested by the charges leveled at the school's rector in 1586. Bürgermeister Haider's son Gottfried had died, and the rector, Theophilus Regner, was accused of having caused his death by an excessive application of punishment. The delicate issues raised by this accusation were referred for consideration to the faculty of law at Tübingen and to two eminent theologians, who evidently decided in Regner's favor, since he was allowed to remain at his post.[14]

The boys who attended the Latin school were a far from homogeneous group. Many came from the city's best families, but about forty places were reserved for charity pupils whose tuition was provided by various stipends, and who were expected in return to provide extra choir services. Pupils were admitted to the school at various ages, often after having attended a German school, since after 1621 a reading knowledge of German was required for entry.[15]

[13] Ibid., paragraph I(3) and section II, passim.

[14] Wulz, "Rektoren und Präzeptoren," p. 58. Müller *Merkwürdigkeiten der Stadt Nördlingen*, p. 68, also alludes to an instance of Regner's brutality toward a pupil.

[15] Ockel, "Lateinische Schule," p. 134; *Ernewerte Schul-Ordnung*, sections I and III.

For the seventeenth century, we have no information about the names of individual pupils. But in 1708 a new rector, Georg Friedrich Dolp, began to keep a matriculation book which provides an instructive glimpse into the makeup of the student body in his day.[16] Each pupil is listed with his age and some indication of his proficiency. For 1709, the first complete year, Dolp recorded the admission of fifteen pupils. The oldest was Johann Andreas Haas, aged 11 ("reads German, spells in Latin"); the youngest was Dolp's own son, aged 6, who could already read both German and Latin. One pupil, 10-year-old Johann Caspar Stamm, was listed as illegitimate, but "reads both German and Latin, writes a beautiful hand, etc."

The following year Dolp began to record the fathers' occupations, and for 1711 he provided precise information about the parentage of all but one of the fourteen pupils admitted. Four were the sons of clergymen, and the other fathers included the city counsel, a surgeon, a miller, a blacksmith, a goldsmith, a tailor and an innkeeper, as well as one Oettingen functionary. Of those parents who can be identified from the tax registers, all were of above-average wealth, which suggests that charitable stipends may have been diverted to pupils who were not particularly needy.[17] But some poor students were still being accepted: in 1710 Dolp registered the sons of a linen weaver and of a wool weaver, both from very modest families.[18] One of these boys, moreover, could only read German, and that poorly.

[16] Matrikel der Lateinschule Nördlingen 1708-1817.

[17] Except for three of the clergymen and the Oettingen official, all the fathers whose names are given can be traced in the 1700 or 1712 tax register. Their wealth ranges from 600 fl. to 5,800 fl., which places them all well above the median wealth for 1700 (220 fl.) or 1712 (200 fl.): StR 1700, 1712.

[18] The boys in question were Johannes Knorzinger, linen weaver's son, and Caspar Braun, wool weaver's son. Six linen weavers with the surname Knorzinger are listed in the tax register for 1712; three were worth 100 fl. each and the other three ranged from 150 fl. to 400 fl. There were two wool weavers named Braun, worth 100 fl. and 300 fl. respectively. StR 1712.

No doubt there was substantial attrition in the student body between the first and fifth classes. (Figures from the late eighteenth century are instructive here: in 1795 the Latin school had 113 pupils, of whom the first to fifth classes had 49, 23, 14, 19, and 8 respectively.)[19] But those who completed the final round of examinations were fully equipped to go on to university, and many did so, especially before the Thirty Years War. In the late sixteenth century an average of at least five Nördlingers a year began university studies; in the late seventeenth century the figure was somewhat lower, largely, of course, due to the decrease in the city's population.[20] Many of these students never returned to Nördlingen—some died, others settled down in different communities. But those who did return could be found in a broad spectrum of occupations: clergymen, schoolteachers, municipal officials, professional men, merchants.[21]

For the sons of wealthy men, study at the Latin school and university was a way of being groomed for the careers to which their birth directed them, and they were free to

[19] Daniel Eberhardt Beyschlag, *Versuch einer Schulgeschichte der Reichsstadt Nördlingen* (Nördlingen, 1793-97), 3. Stück, p. 12.

[20] This calculation is based on Karl Kern's extensive, though not exhaustive, list of Nördlingers who appear in the matriculation lists of German universities: "Söhne der Reichsstadt Nördlingen auf hohen Schulen," pp. 17-48. For the years 1590-99 Kern lists 50 Nördlingen students who matriculated for the first time, or an average of 5 a year (students who matriculated at more than one university are counted only once). For the years 1680-99 Kern found only 42 students, or an average of 2.1 a year. This reduced figure may be due partly to less complete information—for example, the Wittenberg matriculation lists used by Kern only went up to 1602—but they must also reflect a real decline in attendances.

[21] Of the 50 students listed by Kern for the 1590's, 20 can be unambiguously identified in later Nördlingen tax registers. They included 7 clergymen (mostly citizens resident elsewhere), 6 municipal or foreign bureaucrats, 3 Latin school teachers, 2 merchants, 1 doctor and 1 apothecary. Of the 42 students listed for the 1680's and 1690's, 16 appear in later tax records, 7 as lawyers or bureaucrats, 3 as clergymen, 3 as Latin schoolteachers, and 1 each as an organist, medical doctor and bookbinder.

choose the field of study that would serve them best: arts, law, medicine, theology. But the sons of poorer men, supported at school and university by civic stipends, were almost always steered into theological study. Nevertheless, university education offered these youths rich opportunities —not to amass wealth but to acquire the prestige and relative security offered by a clerical career. Throughout the seventeenth century one finds youths of humble background for whom university education made possible distinguished careers in Nördlingen—men like Tobias Scheublin (1590-1644), son of a modest tailor, who studied at Wittenberg and Jena before returning home to serve as Latin schoolteacher, pastor in Schweindorf and finally deacon at St. Georg's, or Melchior Schneidt (1633-90), son of a poor wool weaver, who took a degree at Tübingen and returned to become a teacher at the Latin school and then preacher at the Carmelite church.[22]

II

Opportunities like these were, of course, confined to a very small number of men. But at the heart of the Lutheran conception of education lay the principle that the entire community must be exposed both to the word of God and to the habits of thought that would render it effective.[23] This objective was to be served in Nördlingen by the institution of German schools to which most of the city's children—boys and girls alike—would have access.

[22] Wulz, "Rektoren und Präzeptoren," pp. 59-60. From the tax records it can be seen that Scheublin's father never had more than 200 fl. (1591-1603), and Schneidt's father was even poorer (50 fl. in 1633).

[23] For an illuminating discussion of early Lutheran attitudes toward education, see Gerald Strauss, "Reformation and Pedagogy: Educational Thought and Practice in the Lutheran Reformation," in Charles Trinkaus and Heiko A. Oberman, eds., *The Pursuit of Holiness in Late Medieval and Renaissance Religion* (Studies in Medieval and Reformation Thought, 10; Leiden, 1974), pp. 272-93.

The German schools of Nördlingen were conducted as private enterprises by schoolmasters dependent for their income on fees paid by the parents. The teachers were not necessarily highly educated, but none could open a school before being certified by the council, and lessons had to conform to precise and uniform stipulations. In 1555 the council drew up a weekly lesson plan to guide the schoolmasters in organizing their instruction; in 1584 they issued a general ordinance for the German schools which was frequently renewed in later years. From these edicts is possible to establish what was expected both of teachers and of pupils in the German schools.[24]

School was to be held five days a week, from 7 a.m. to 10 a.m. and from noon to 3 p.m., except on Wednesday, when the afternoon was free. Each school was to be divided into two classes—one for beginners and one for children who had already mastered the rudiments of reading and writing. Boys and girls were to be seated separately, with the best pupils placed toward the front of the room to assist the slower ones in their recitations and spur them on to further progress.[25]

According to the lesson plan of 1555, pupils in the lower class were to spend the morning learning to recite passages from the catechism. During the first two hours each afternoon they were to repeat their lessons and learn spelling. But the last hour of each day was devoted to a different task: the pupils were to learn "a short proverb from the holy scriptures in Latin, which they are to repeat before their parents at home." (No doubt many parents would only believe their children were learning something if they heard them reciting in Latin.) Pupils in the higher class were to

[24] Akten Deutsche Schulen, Schulordnungen: Ordnung der deutschen Schulen für die Knaben und Junckfrewlin zu Nördlingen, anno 1555 . . . ; Schulordnungen 1584, 1603, 1644 (printed), 1715 (printed): the latter four are the same except for minor changes in spelling or phrasing.

[25] Ibid., Schulordnung 1644.

spend the first hour each day learning to recite a passage from the catechism. The second hour was devoted to reading—probably of the same passage—and the third hour to writing. Two hours in the afternoon were to be spent reading and writing, while the third hour, once again, was to be spent learning a Latin proverb to recite at home. Wednesday mornings could be used to repeat their lessons or learn a psalm by heart. Each school day was to begin and end with the singing of a hymn.[26]

A regimen such as this must have caused many children to lose interest, and some children to start misbehaving. Firm discipline was considered indispensable. But the magistrates ordered that "in disciplining, schoolmasters shall use the rod with restraint, and not pull the children's hair, hit them on the head, or whip them on the back with switches, but instead they shall make use of punishment in such a way as to improve the children rather than to make them terrified of school. . . ."[27]

Such were the intentions of the magistrates. How effectively were they carried out? From time to time the council ordered the superintendent and his colleagues to undertake a visitation of schools, and from the ensuing reports we can gain some impression of actual conditions in the classrooms of Nördlingen.

In 1597, for example, the visitation committee inspected all six German schools. The first two were the largest:

> First, we found 150 children in the school of Johann Beck, notary, and observed that they were being rather diligently instructed in the catechism as well as in writing and reading. There is no lack of good discipline here. However, we have been told by others that he is sometimes too hard on the tender children, and is too harsh and punitive in disciplining. Carries out legal work on the side.

[26] Ibid., Ordnung der deutschen Schulen, 1555.

[27] Ibid., Schulordnung 1644.

> Modista Weiber has 200 children, and does the best in teaching the catechism and other things. But sometimes does medical work on the side when he is needed.[28]

The next three schools—with 70, 100 and 30 pupils respectively—were all found to be satisfactory. The committee was particularly sympathetic to the master at the smallest school, Johann Philipp Forster, who "teaches only twenty, but would spare no effort, if only he had more schoolchildren."[29]

Exactly why the 570 schoolchildren were so unevenly distributed among the six schools in unclear. But it is apparent that teachers competed vigorously for pupils: the visitation report for the following year remarks on hostility among the teachers due to the practice of raiding pupils from each other by offering reduced fees.[30]

Altogether, in fact, the 1598 report painted a grim picture of conditions in the German schools. Teachers complained that parents were not paying the fees—a perennial problem—and that "children are no longer willing to let themselves be disciplined," a circumstance which was blamed on parents "who are no longer willing to tolerate that appropriate discipline and punishment be applied to their children." The visitation committee was concerned that some schools taught the catechism only once a week instead of daily, and complained of a general lack of diligence in teaching the basics of spelling, "syllabifying," reading and writing.[31]

Two generations later, in 1644, the visitation committee found 400 pupils attending six German schools, including one conducted in the foundling-house. The largest school

[28] Akten Deutsche Schulen, Führung des Unterrichts/Visitationen: Unterthänige Relation wegen der besuchtenn Deutschen Scuelenn, 1597.

[29] Ibid.

[30] Ibid., Unterthänige Relation, . . . der Deutschen Schul Visitation halben, 1598.

[31] Ibid.

had 134 children; the smallest one 28. The committee was satisfied with the performance of the schoolmasters but found most of them complaining about the master of the foundling-house, for in addition to educating his own charges he was teaching (and collecting fees from) other children of the city or nearby villages.[32]

After the mid-seventeenth century, the practice of school visitations virtually died out. But a visitation was undertaken in 1712, and the ensuing report contrasts sharply with those of earlier years. For now individual pupils suddenly come into focus.

The largest school, conducted by Herr Johann Martin Stahringer, had 62 boys and 92 girls. Of these pupils, 65 were able to read and write, 40 could only read, 41 could spell and 8 had begun their ABC's. Three pupils were singled out for their accomplishments in learning texts by heart: Felicitas Barbara Schröppel, aged 12 (with 50 psalms and 100 songs), Regina Salome Schöpperlin, 11 (55 psalms and 100 songs), and Lorenz Weng, 9 (50 psalms and 50 songs). As for the teacher, "He complains about the incorrect payments, and requests on behalf of the children that they may be taken to the 'Staben' [the annual children's festival]; and though the bigger ones are embarrassed about going, they are needed there because of the singing."[33]

Altogether there were five German schools in 1712, with a total of 585 pupils. Girls outnumbered boys 325 to 260.[34] But it must be remembered that the Latin school, with per-

[32] Ibid., Memorial wegen Visitation der Teutschen Schulen, 1644.

[33] Ibid., Relation von der in denen Deutschen Schulen beschehen Visitation, 1712. The annual children's festival, the so-called *Stabenfest*, held in a meadow outside the city, was a tradition dating at least to the late sixteenth century. Permission to take the children there was by no means granted routinely by the magistrates, who were generally worried about the possibility of disorder. See Ludwig Mußgnug, "Zur Geschichte des Stabenfestes," *Rieser Heimatbote*, no. 66 (1930).

[34] Akten Deutsche Schulen, Führung des Unterrichts/Visitationen: Relation von der . . . Visitation, 1712.

haps 75 pupils, was confined to males alone, so that in fact boys and girls were attending school in roughly equal numbers.

It was certainly the intention of Nördlingen's rulers that every child should get some education. We do not know for sure what proportion of children in Nördlingen ever entered school, or how long a child was likely to stay there. But it is indicative that over 600 children were enrolled in Latin or German schools in 1712, at a time when the city could not have had many more than 600 children aged 7 to 12.[35] By the eighteenth century, if not sooner, the overwhelming majority of children in Nördlingen certainly received at least some primary education. But parents sometimes withdrew their children from school before they had fully mastered the catechism. To compensate for this, in 1683 the council ordered special catechism lessons, to be attended by every youngster between the age of 8 and the age of marriage, whether enrolled in school or not.[36]

The products of this whole system of instruction were expected to become literate, obedient and, above all, pious. Most of them did so, although the obedience, as we saw in the last chapter, was sometimes strained. And the piety induced by such instruction was inevitably of a narrow and intolerant kind. Antisemitism was practiced as a matter of

[35] There is no direct information about the number or age distribution of children in early eighteenth-century Nördlingen. But from the parish registers, as described in Chapter Two, it is possible to arrive at a reasonable approximation. During the years 1701-10 there was an average of 271 baptisms a year. During the same years, an average of 146 infants (up to 1 year old) and 25 children (aged 1 to 12) died each year. This would leave a total of between 125 and 100 children in each age cohort between 1 and 12 years, with the number getting increasingly lower in the older age groups. Thus, we can assume that there were not many more than 100 children in each age cohort from 7 to 12 years old. (These calculations are based on the data given in Appendix I.)

[36] OB 1640-88, fols. 394b-396b (4 Apr. 1683).

course: on the few occasions when Jews were allowed to reside temporarily in the city they were subject to extensive restrictions and humiliations.[37] The conversion and baptism of a Jewish youth from Oettingen in 1660—no doubt a shattering blow to the Jews of the Ries—was celebrated as a major triumph for Nördlingen.[38] Relations with Catholics were equally strained. Some Catholics did, in fact, live in Nördlingen, as occupants of the collection houses of ecclesiastical institutions with tenants in the Ries. Monks resident in the collection house of Kaisheim abbey were even allowed to celebrate the mass, although the city posted guards outside to make sure that no other Catholics, even travelers, would slip in to participate. There was also a collection house of the Teutonic Order in Nördlingen. In 1716 its custodian attempted, over the council's objections, to install a large new picture of the Virgin over the portal—only to be confronted by an angry mob of protesting citizens. The council ordered the picture removed and two years of litigation took place before it was finally installed.[39]

III

THERE is no question that church and school were the main instruments for the transmission of cultural values to the inhabitants of Nördlingen. Nevertheless, there were other cultural influences as well. In the first place, many of Nördlingen's inhabitants had traveled extensively—as students or, more often, as journeymen—and had seen something of the world before they settled down. And a stream of travelers passed through the city, ranging from eminent royal personages to itinerant merchants and retailers. Troupes of touring actors regularly stopped in Nördlingen to perform high-

[37] L. Müller, "Aus fünf Jahrhunderten (1. Teil)," pp. 115-23.

[38] TR 18 March 1660.

[39] Steichele, *Bisthum Augsburg*, vol. 3, pp. 1051-55.

minded dramas or popular comedies—always, of course, after getting the magistrates' approval for the proposed offerings.[40]

From the 1630's onward, Nördlingen was also the seat of a vigorous printing establishment.[41] The first printing enterprise there, founded in 1538, appears to have failed after about ten years.[42] But in 1632 a printer named Lucas Schultes transferred his operation from Oettingen to Nördlingen, where he proceeded to print one of Germany's earliest periodic newspapers. This "Zeitung" was published twice a week, containing in alternate issues dispatches from Augsburg and from Nuremberg. Schultes died in 1634, but the shop was taken over by his widow's next husband, Heinrich Chorhammer, who continued to publish regular "Zeitungen" throughout the 1640's. Their circulation throughout the region must have been extensive, for Chorhammer complained in 1639 that a rival in Schwäbisch Hall was threatening his business.[43]

Chorhammer's successor—his stepson, Friedrich Schultes—evidently continued to publish newspapers, as did Johann Christoph Hilbrandt, who took over the shop in 1685. By then, in fact, the newspaper was considered a major public service, and the magistrates insisted on regular and accurate publication. In 1695 the council warned Hilbrandt to "display more diligence in publishing the weekly newspapers here, and to submit them for correction to Herr Geyer, rector of the school." The next year Hilbrandt was twice

[40] See, for example, Bärbel Rudin, "Der 'Hochfürstlich Eggenbergische Comoediant' Johann Carl Samenhammer: Ein Beitrag zur Theatergeschichte Nördlingens," *Nordschwaben*, 2 (1974), 161-64.

[41] On this entire subject, see Gustav Wulz, "Das Nördlinger Buchgewerbe vom 15. bis 18. Jahrhundert," *JHVN*, 22 (1940/41), 90-118.

[42] Gustav Wulz, "Die Anfänge des Buchdrucks in Nördlingen," in *Aus der Frühzeit des Nördlinger Buchdrucks* (Nördlingen, 1963), pp. 9-14.

[43] Heinrich Goschenhofer, *Von Nördlinger Buchdruckern vor 1763* (Nördlingen, 1938), pp. 8-11; Helmut Fischer, *Die ältesten Zeitungen und ihre Verleger* (Augsburg, 1936), pp. 58-64, 105-09.

reprimanded for failing to publish issues on time. And in 1702 he was briefly arrested for a misprint: he had gravely embarrassed the city by printing "electorate of Bavaria" instead of "electorate of Cologne."[44]

The printers of Nördlingen were not confined to publishing newspapers, of course. They routinely printed council decrees, funeral orations and religious tracts, particularly those penned by the local ministers. In 1718, however, Hilbrandt unwisely accepted a commission from the Catholic count of Oettingen-Wallerstein to publish a tract on "The Consolation of Souls in Purgatory," for which he was severely reprimanded and fined by the council.[45]

Throughout the period of this study, Nördlingen harbored a tiny elite of citizens with literary or intellectual interests—men like Peter Lemp, who maintained one of the city's most impressive chronicles, or Georg Brentel, the painter, mathematician and astronomer, who emigrated to Nördlingen from Lauingen in 1621.[46] But the intellectual life of Nördlingen in this period cannot compare in significance to that of the pre-Reformation era, when residents of the city played a notable role in the humanist culture of southern Germany.[47] A more dynamic atmosphere was maintained, at least until the Thirty Years War, among men whose backgrounds lay in the world of the crafts. The prosperous decades before 1618 witnessed a rash of building projects in Nördlingen and a flowering of artistic activity, especially painting. To this era, for example, can be dated the present appearance of the city's fortifications and of the

[44] Goschenhofer, *Nördlinger Buchdruckern*, pp. 11-15.

[45] Ibid., p. 17.

[46] The Chronik of Peter Lemp, which goes up to 1610 and contains extensive information about local and international events as well as astronomical and astrological notations, is contained within the Kaiserempfangsbuch. For brief summaries of the careers of Brentel and other painters, see Gustav Wulz, "Die Nördlinger Maler vom 15. bis 18. Jahrhundert," *JHVN*, 18 (1934/35), 69-79.

[47] On this whole subject, see Wulz, "Historische Einleitung," pp. 21-27.

Nördlingen city hall. Even after the Thirty Years War a number of artists were active in Nördlingen—in 1700, for example, the city still had the services of a portrait painter who had studied in Rome and Venice. But he only lived in the city part-time, and he never took out citizenship.[48] For by then a small Protestant city with growing financial difficulties no longer offered many opportunities for artists. There was much more to lure them to noble and princely courts, even in nearby Oettingen.

In short, there was a diminished demand for artistic products in late seventeenth-century Nördlingen. But artists, like clerics and teachers, enjoyed a certain amount of mobility in south German society. Not so the average craftsmen—least of all those in an overpopulated craft with declining markets. And such was the case in Nördlingen's largest industry, wool weaving, toward the end of the seventeenth century. In the following chapter we shall explore the history of one successful wool-weaving family in Nördlingen, and see how its members came into increasingly bitter conflict with the members of their own craft.

[48] Concerning this man, Georg Marcell Haack, see the notation in Wulz, "Nördlinger Maler," p. 75. On sculptors in the city, see Gustav Wulz, "Die Nördlinger Bildhauer vom 15. bis 18. Jahrhundert," *JHVN*, 20 (1937), 30-36.

Nine

Capitalism and Its Enemies: The Wörner Family and the Weaving Industry of Nördlingen

IN February 1560, Andreas Wernher, a wool weaver from Lauingen on the Danube, was enrolled as a citizen of Nördlingen. In the course of fifty years he gradually accumulated property, increased his wealth, and fathered at least nine children. Two of his sons established families which survived in the male line down to the eighteenth century or beyond.

These two lines of the Wernher, or Wörner, family experienced very different histories in the course of the seventeenth century. One branch produced the wealthiest citizens of Nördlingen, while the other branch gradually lost its property and sank to a level of barely respectable poverty. Thus, extreme upward mobility and gradual downward mobility can be observed simultaneously in the history of a single family.

The story of this family between the late sixteenth and early eighteenth centuries is presented here partly as a case study, to complement the predominantly statistical picture of Nördlingen's society which was offered earlier in this book. But in the political and economic history of Nördlingen, the Wörners—at least those of the wealthy branch—proved highly important in their own right. For more than anyone else, they were responsible for the emergence of large-scale monopoly capitalism in Nördlingen's largest industry, the production of heavy woolen cloth—a development which boldly challenged the traditional system of production centered on the independent master.

This development led, moreover, to one of the most explosive episodes in Nördlingen's economic history. It is scarcely surprising that the Wörners' activities encountered resentment among the threatened weaving masters. But in 1698 these masters were able to mount a major legal challenge to the activities of the Wörners, and—with the sympathy and support of the city council—they succeeded in obtaining important concessions from the city's wealthiest family. How this conflict emerged and how it was resolved will be examined in the course of our history of the Wörners.

No private records concerning this family are known to exist in Nördlingen, but the city and church records include more than enough material for a study of the Wörners, as indeed they do for the study of almost any citizen family in Nördlingen. This in itself is an illuminating fact, for it illustrates the tremendous amount of information which was available to municipal and religious officials about the personal and economic lives of their fellow citizens. It is precisely the nature of Nördlingen's early modern government that makes possible the intensive study of a family whose private documents are no longer available.[1]

The basic genealogy of the Wörner family is presented in Figure 9.1.[2] This chart is not complete, for the fourteen

[1] There is no published literature on the history of the Wörner family, except for the entry in the standard genealogical work: Beyschlag and Müller, *Geschlechtshistorie*, vol. 2, pp. 582-87. While this entry is reasonably accurate for the later period, it is sketchy and contains severe errors on the early part of the family's history. (For example, the founder, Andreas Wernher, is treated as two individuals instead of one.) The conflict between the weavers of Nördlingen and the Wörners in 1698 received brief treatments in two earlier works: Ebert, *Lodweberei*, p. 40, and Wolfgang Zorn, *Handels- und Industriegeschichte Bayerisch-Schwabens, 1648-1870: Wirtschafts-, Sozial- und Kulturgeschichte des schwäbischen Unternehmertums* (Veröffentlichungen der schwäbischen Forschungsgemeinschaft bei der Kommission für bayerische Landesgeschichte, Reihe 1, Bd. 6; Augsburg, 1961), pp. 100-03.

[2] This table is based on my complete genealogical reconstitution of

male descendants of Andreas Wörner who married before 1700 had a total of at least 108 offspring; the most prolific of them (Daniel, 1652-1733) fathered 21 children by four different wives. But the chart does include those males of the family who survived to adulthood in the city. These are the men whose lives and careers provide a framework for the history of the Wörner family in seventeenth-century Nördlingen.

I

WE begin with Andreas Wernher, the wool weaver from Lauingen who arrived in Nördlingen in 1560.[3] Andreas probably came to Nördlingen as a journeyman and possibly worked for the wool weaver Gabriel Blatzer, whose daughter he married upon becoming a citizen in 1560. Andreas' first tax payment as a citizen in 1560 was 3 fl., representing property assessed at 600 fl.[4] Most of this assessment covered

---

the Wörner family in Nördlingen from 1560 to the early eighteenth century, a copy of which has been deposited in the Stadtarchiv Nördlingen. This reconstitution is based primarily on the parish registers: Tauf- und Eheregister I-X (1579-1745) and Sterberegister I-IV (1618-1775), of the evangelische Gemeinde, Nördlingen, and the Trau- und Sterberegister I-IV of the Spitalpfarrei Nördlingen, now held by the parish of Nähermemmingen. Since the burial registers provide ages at death for many persons born before 1579, at least the approximate year of birth could be calculated. Since marriage entries give names of parents, parentage of persons born before 1579 could also be established. Some additional genealogical information has been gleaned from the Steuerregister, Pfandbücher and other sources.

[3] His admission as a citizen is recorded in KR 1560, fol. 46b, and Bürgerbuch, fol. 125a. (The spelling of the family's name appears mostly as Wernher or Wernherr in the sixteenth century, to be superseded by the spelling Wörner or Werner in the seventeenth. For uniformity, I have spelled Andreas' name as Wernher and his descendants' name as Wörner.)

[4] This and all subsequent information concerning tax payments by members of this family or other citizens come from the Steuerregister for the years concerned.

Figure 9.1. The Wörner Family (A Selective Genealogy).

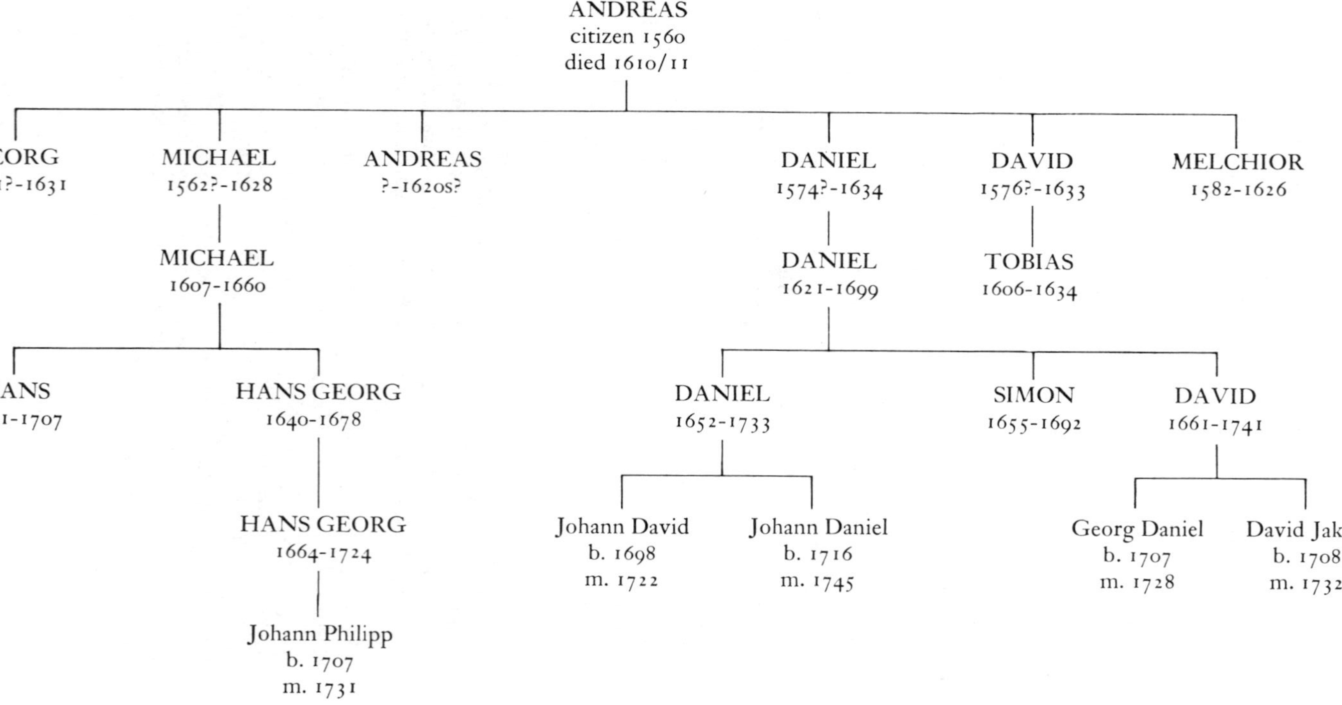

the value of the house he had bought in February of that year, two weeks after his admission as a citizen. The purchase price of the house was 385 Rhenish gulden, of which 200 fl. were to be paid in cash and the remainder was to be paid in annual installments.[5] It was located near the Löpsinger gate, an area where many wool weavers lived, and from the purchase price we can surmise that it was a house of medium size.

Andreas was, and throughout his life remained, identified as a wool weaver, but this assessment of 600 fl. distinguished him at the outset from the great mass of wool weavers who formed the most impoverished section of the citizenry. He was still far from a wealthy man. But over the next fifty years he gradually amassed property, and in the tax registers one can trace his growing prosperity. By 1600, if not sooner, he numbered among the fifty wealthiest men in the city;[6] in 1603 he attained his peak assessment of 5,000 fl.

Exactly how Andreas Wernher augmented his wealth cannot be documented. But certain features are clear. Unlike the majority of wool weavers, he began his career with enough capital so that he could buy wool with cash and could thus avoid slipping into debt to the middlemen who provided raw materials.[7] Only with this initial security from indebtedness could a wool weaver begin to increase his wealth, for example, by investment in real property. Marriage into a prosperous family was also an advantage to Andreas: the tax records indicate that he and his wife inherited 600 fl. when his mother-in-law died in 1579.[8]

5 Pfb. 17, fol. 388.

6 Gustav Wulz, "Die reichsten Nördlinger, ausgezogen aus den Steuerbüchern des Stadtarchivs Nördlingen," typewritten ms. in Stadtarchiv Nördlingen.

7 A similar point is made concerning Wernher's own father-in-law Gabriel Blatzer in the genealogical pamphlet by Wulz, *Ahnen der Johanna Luise Heidenreich*.

8 His mother-in-law's death is indicated by the cross which appears next to her name in the 1579 Steuerbuch.

But the chief factor in Andreas Wernher's increasing prosperity was undoubtedly his own aggressive temperament. Nothing illustrates this aggressiveness better than the bitter quarrel which he initiated in 1583 with Hans Husel, a textile merchant who was the wealthiest man in Nördlingen, and Husel's son Georg. Andreas publicly accused the younger Husel of "trying to take the very bread out of his, his wife's and his children's mouths" by the ruthless practice of *Fürkauf*—referring to the technique by which a trader would buy and hoard wool until it became scarce and he could sell it to weavers at a higher price. Intending to be "his own avenger," as he put it, Wernher assaulted the younger Husel, leading to a quarrel in which the elder Husel also got involved. Ultimately both sides were heavily fined, although Wernher's fine was later modified.[9]

What is curious about this incident is that Wernher himself was by no means a poor man at the time. The entire episode suggests something closer to economic rivalry, however unbalanced, than a case of bald exploitation by a very rich man of a very poor one—the kind of exploitation which, as it happens, Wernher's own descendants were to practice a century later.

The forms of property which Andreas Wernher accumulated during his lifetime were diverse. The municipal *Pfandbücher*, or mortgage books,[10] demonstrate that he was a vigorous investor, frequently engaged in buying or selling houses and other forms of real property.[11] At the time of

[9] RP 16 and 23 Oct. 1583.

[10] The Pfandbücher recorded debts contracted in the city and the security offered. In was normal, when a house or other property was purchased, to make a down payment and pay the rest in installments, with the property in question offered as security. In cases of default of payment, the property could be sold by the city and the proceeds used to satisfy the creditor, under conditions described by Kurt Gebhardt in *Das Pfandrecht und Vollstreckungsrecht der Reichsstadt Nördlingen* (Diss., Tübingen, 1953), esp. pp. 113-44.

[11] For example, in 1569 he sold the house he had purchased nine years earlier: Pfb. 20, fol. 193. In 1582 he sold another house: Pfb. 22, fol. 498.

his death, as we know from an inventory taken in 1611,[12] he was in possession of five houses. Andreas himself occupied only one of these; the other four houses were either rented out or occupied by his sons, to whom title to some of them passed after his death.

At the time of his death, Andreas Wernher's property was assessed at 4,400 fl. In addition to the five buildings, the inventory shows that his property included 521 fl. in cash, 398 fl. in debts owed to him, 60 Loden (finished woolen cloths), a few acres of cultivated land, and the family's holdings in silver, furniture and household belongings. Among these belongings were a Bible, ten books in folio and a number of smaller volumes.

In the half century of their marriage, Andreas and Elizabetha Wernher produced at least nine children.[13] Only one daughter is known to have reached the age of marriage,[14] but six sons survived to adulthood. Of these six, five followed their father into the trade of wool weaving and one became a clergyman. Let us consider these sons one by one.

[12] Inventare, 1609-11, fols. 269b-277a. This inventory, dated 6 May 1611, is in the name of Andreas' widow Elizabetha. It is not clear whether she was still alive at the time the inventory was taken or whether she, too, had died by then, but either way it is clear that the inventory represents the full extent of Andreas' property before its division among the heirs. Of these five houses, one had been inherited from Andreas' father-in-law (cf. Wulz, *Ahnen*, p. 23), and the purchase of two others by Andreas is recorded in the Pfandbücher: Pfb. 27, fol. 330b; 30, fol. 583.

[13] We know for certain of the existence of only nine children: three whose births were recorded after 1579, and six whose marriages were recorded after 1579 or who are known from some other documentary source. There may, however, have been others: since the parish registers only began in 1579, any child born before that year who either died in childhood or moved away from Nördlingen without getting married would remain unknown.

[14] Anna, who married the widower Michael Widenmann, a ropemaker, in 1589.

GEORG WÖRNER was the oldest and most successful son. Born in 1560 or 1561, he married in 1583 and began to pay taxes the following year. From the tax registers we can see that his assessment rose from 400 fl. at the start to 11,000 fl. in 1624. At his death in 1631 the assessment had declined to 7,600 fl.: clearly, the financial demands made upon citizens during the Thirty Years War had started to cut into his fortune.

Like four of his brothers, Georg began life as a wool weaver, but he alone succeeded in rising above this station. In 1613 he was named by the council as *Vorgeher*, or master, of the entire craft of wool weavers.[15] But two years later he resigned the position,[16] and soon after he appears in the records as a *Handelsmann* or *Factor*—a textile merchant. His father had aided his progress by arranging an advantageous first marriage, and Georg succeeded in reinforcing his status at least in his third marriage.[17]

Like his father, Georg augmented his income from the production and distribution of woolen cloths by investments in property. But where his father had picked quarrels with the wealthiest men of his time, Georg instead worked together with them. In 1599 we see him borrowing 900 fl. in partnership with Georg Widenmann, his relative by marriage and a prosperous merchant who was to become enormously wealthy by the start of the Thirty Years War.[18]

[15] RP 25 May 1613.

[16] RP 25 Oct. 1615.

[17] Georg's first father-in-law, as listed in the parish registers, was Martin Maier, Zoller. This was certainly one of the two wealthy men of this name listed in the tax books as a Bierbräuer and as Gerichtsschreiber respectively. It was more probably the former, who died in 1590-91, since immediately after his death Georg's assessment increased sixfold. Georg's second wife was the widow of Georg Heidenreich, a man much poorer than himself. But the third wife, whom he married in 1618, was the daughter of the ropemaker Balthas Zaiser, who was assessed at 4,000 fl. in 1615.

[18] Widenmann's first wife was Afra Blatzer, the daughter of Georg Wörner's maternal uncle Gabriel. Widenmann's assessment in 1621 was 80,000 fl., which vastly exceeded that of any other citizen.

The records of this transaction[19] show that Georg Wörner already owned extensive cultivated fields outside the city. Ten years later he and Georg Widenmann jointly paid 5,100 fl. to purchase additional large tracts of land near the city.[20]

But certainly the main source of Georg's wealth was his activity as a cloth merchant. Normally such merchants attempted to control cloth production by dealing in both raw and finished products, and certainly Georg was no exception. There is specific proof, in fact, that he was engaged in selling wool to weavers in addition to dealing with finished cloths.[21] He is also occasionally recorded as having advanced loans to wool weavers.[22]

Not surprisingly, Georg's economic activities made enemies. In 1605 a weaver was fined for having roundly insulted him in public with a pointed allusion to "ill-gotten gains."[23] And the criminal records of 1613 record the hostile conduct of six young tanners. The six men appeared before Wörner's door and "some of them climbed up, looked through the lattice, and then gave out that Wörner's wife was turning the maid into a witch." This was more than idle gossip in a town which had experienced a major witch-craze twenty years before, and the six men were imprisoned briefly, fined, and enjoined to "eternal silence" about the rumor.[24] Although the specific background of this incident

19 Pfb. 29, fol. 121. Pfb. 28, fol. 10 (1596) records one of Georg's earlier land purchases.

20 Pfb. 33, fols. 20-21.

21 Pfb. 39, fol. 141 (1628): debt of 43 fl. by Christoph Dreibler, Loder, to Georg Wörner, "umb, und für aberkauffte Wollen."

22 Pfb. 37, fol. 44 (1624); Pfb. 38, fol. 235 (1626).

23 Urfehdebuch 1601-08, fol. 177: Wörner had politely asked Caspar Beck ("guetlich angesprochen") about trading conditions in Nürnberg, and received the hostile reply: "Wörner soll das 5 Capitel im Syrach lesen, da werde er finden, was er für ein gesell seye." The allusion was undoubtedly to the passage in Sirach (Ecclesiasticus) 5 which begins, "Do not rely on ill-gotten gains, for they will not avail in times of calamity. . . ."

24 Urfehdebuch 1609-14, fol. 41; and RP 30 Aug. 1613.

is unknown, it is worth noting that tanners were frequently engaged in competition with cloth merchants because both tried to deal in wool.

In his first and third marriages, Georg Wörner fathered a total of seventeen children. No sons survived to maturity, but six daughters did. For the three from his first marriage, Georg himself was able to arrange excellent marriages. But for the three by his third marriage, who came to maturity long after their father's death, the guardians were unable to do nearly so well.[25] The huge financial demands imposed during the Thirty Years War had clearly drained much of the estate their father had left them and made them less attractive to potential suitors: a posthumous fortune was even more vulnerable than the wealth of a living man to the vicissitudes of war.

MICHAEL WÖRNER, the second son of Andreas Wernher, represented a sharp contrast to his older brother Georg. As a youth he may have been something of a troublemaker: in 1587, when he was 25 or 26, he and one other "junger geselle" were arrested by the authorities for loud and immodest behavior late at night and for refusing to go home when ordered.[26] Michael remained in his father's household astonishingly long—not until he was over 40 did he get married, set himself up as a wool weaver and begin to pay taxes. Like those of all his brothers, his assessment jumped considerably upon his father's death (from 200 fl. to 1,000 fl.), but he was the only brother who never succeeded in boosting his wealth above the inherited amount. In fact, he even

[25] The year of each daughter's first marriage, the man she married, and her husband's assessment in that or a nearby year is as follows—1603: Hans Settelmaier (innkeeper, 1,200 fl.); Melchior Münzinger (weaver, 1,800 fl. in 1609); Sebastian Gering (2,400 fl. in 1618); *but*, 1640: Hans Moll (innkeeper, 200 fl.); 1646: Michael Holzinger (coppersmith, 200 fl.); 1652: Baptist Jörg (blacksmith, 400 fl.)

[26] Urfehdebuch 1587-92, fol. 28.

lost most of this, and at his death his wealth had fallen to 400 fl. It is scarcely surprising that Michael's second wife sorely distrusted her husband's ability to manage his—or her —financial affairs.[27]

In 1628, not long after another brush with the law,[28] Michael Wörner died. Of his four children, one son evidently died in the plague of 1634 and the only daughter also died young. Another son, as we can see from much later records, disappeared at the age of 20 in the crisis year 1634 and was never heard from again.[29] Only one child, Michael's eldest son and namesake, survived to adulthood in Nördlingen.

ANDREAS WÖRNER, who was probably the third son of Andreas Wernher,[30] had a career which differed sharply from those of his five brothers. Having undoubtedly attended the Latin school in Nördlingen, he was enrolled in April 1591 as a student in Tübingen. Six months later he received his B.A., and in February 1593, his M.A.[31] Andreas

27 The contract for Michael's second marriage contained the normal guarantees for the children of his first marriage (Heiratsbriefe, 23 April 1623), which were backed up by the arrangements evident in Pfb. 37, fol. 246. For the subsequent complaints by Michael's second wife and their resolution, see RP 14 Sept., 7, 16, 21 Nov. and 2 Dec. 1625; Pfb. 38, fol. 66.

28 RP 19 Oct. 1627: Michael and his brother David were briefly imprisoned for singing insulting songs at the landlady and other misconduct—"as is usual with them"—at a wedding.

29 Pfb. 37, fol. 246b. An entry for April 1668 notes that Hieronymus Wörner has been "ausser landts erschollen" for 34 years. In May, 1672, the city council was told concerning Hieronymus: "wo er sich befinde und ob er am Leben oder nit? in 38 jahren nichts gehört wurden [ist]." RP 20 May 1672.

30 Since Andreas did not die in Nördlingen, there is no parish register entry from which to calculate his year of birth. If he began studying in 1591, it seems likely that he was older than Daniel, who was born 1573/4, although he may have been slightly younger.

31 Heinrich Hermelink, *Die Matrikeln der Universität Tübingen*, vol. 1 (Stuttgart, 1900), p. 683.

returned to Nördlingen and evidently married in 1596;[32] the following year he was entered into the tax books. But Nördlingen always produced many more clergymen than could be employed in the city itself, and from 1600 on Andreas is listed as being pastor of a village in the duchy of Pfalz-Neuburg. Later he must have moved to Baden, possibly when the Counter-Reformation was introduced in Pfalz-Neuburg after 1614.[33] Throughout most of his life, Andreas retained his links with his native city,[34] but from 1621 on he failed to make his tax payments and in 1630 his name was dropped from the tax lists. Two of his children, however, subsequently died in the hospital in Nördlingen—one as a youth in 1633, the other as a spinster of 70 in 1678.[35]

THE next two sons of Andreas Wernher were men whose careers might have appeared more impressive if they were not overshadowed by the achievements of their oldest brother Georg. Born about two years apart, Daniel and David had almost identical careers. Both married only once—Daniel in 1601, David three years later—and both died in the most hectic phase of the Thirty Years War—David early in 1633, Daniel in the plague of 1634. Both brothers began their careers with an identical assessment of 300 fl.; both enjoyed a substantial inheritance upon their father's

[32] RP 1 and 19 Nov. 1596 mention his engagement, to someone who did not belong to a Nördlingen citizen family. But there is no parish register entry.

[33] Evidently he moved to Baden-Durlach in 1618 or before. His brother Georg's marriage contract, which he witnessed (Heiratsbriefe 18 March 1618) identifies him as "Fr. Marggr. Bad. [=?Fürstlich-Markgräflicher Badischer] Pfarrherr zu Ohringen." His daughter's death notice, cited below, listed her deceased father as a Pfarrer im "Durlachischen."

[34] In 1617, he petitioned for extension of his citizenship and asked that his son be considered for future vacancies in the city's stipends for students: RP 3 Sept. 1617. The son is not named, but was probably the Johann Wörner who did, in fact, receive a stipend from the city from 1618 to 1623: RP 16 March 1618; 11 Aug. 1620; 8 Jan. 1623.

[35] Spitalpfarrei Sterberegister, 2 June 1633, 15 Jan. 1678.

death and continued to build on this amount. David attained a maximum of 3,200 fl. in 1621, while Daniel increased his assessment to a total of 3,600 fl. by the time of his death.

Such prosperity placed them vastly over the normal wealth level of their fellow wool weavers. And possibly, as men of property, the two brothers did not ply their craft very actively.[36] But on the other hand, there is no evidence to suggest that they escalated their activities to become cloth merchants. And, unlike their brother Georg, they never appear with the honorific "Herr" before their names in municipal documents.

Daniel and David appear in city records only rarely, and when they do, it is chiefly in connection with the type of bitter squabbles which are such a common subject of the council minutes. David, for example, is seen lodging a complaint when his wife was publicly insulted by her stepfather.[37] And Daniel brought charges in 1630 against a man who not only owed him 88 fl. but publicly insulted him as well.[38]

In 1632 David's son Tobias married a spinster fourteen years his senior,[39] and the next year he began to pay taxes as a wool weaver. But Tobias and his bride both perished, a a few days apart, in the plague of 1634. The same fate evidently claimed the lives of David's other two children, who were still unmarried.[40]

Daniel's family was more fortunate. In addition to at

[36] From 1609 to 1629 both are listed in the tax records without occupational designation. But certainly neither gave up the craft entirely, for they are listed as wool weavers in other sources from this period. And in the tax books they reappear as wool weavers from 1630 on: perhaps the financial demands of the war obliged them to carry out their occupation more actively.

[37] RP 17 and 24 Dec. 1623.

[38] RP 15 and 18 Oct. 1630.

[39] Margareta Dreibler, whose father Hans had been by no means a wealthy man. (Constant assessment: 200 fl.)

[40] Although the parish records are slightly unclear, the Heiratsbrief (6 Jan. 1635) of David's widow, who was planning to remarry, states explicitly that she had no living children at that time.

least two daughters who reached the age of marriage,[41] Daniel left a son. This son, also named Daniel, grew to play an important role in the city's history and will be discussed at length below.

MELCHIOR WÖRNER was the youngest son of Andreas Wernher. Like his brother Michael, he was rather unsuccessful in life, at least when compared to the four other brothers. Melchior was scarcely able to augment the level of wealth obtained by inheritance from his father, and it appears that his lackluster fortunes forced him eventually to give up the substantial house he had inherited, a building once owned by his maternal grandfather.[42] In 1624 he sold this house to his prosperous brother David and on the same day purchased a simpler house for less than half as much.[43] Two years later he died at the age of 43; his only child had died in infancy.

SINCE Andreas Wernher had six adult sons, one might have expected a multitude of descendants, but the disastrous plague of 1634 decimated this family as it did so many others. By the end of the year, only two of his descendants in the male line were alive in Nördlingen: his grandson Michael, a man of 27, and his grandson Daniel, a youth of 13. And from here on, the Wörner family became sharply divided. The older grandson, Michael, fathered a line which was to become progressively poorer and more inconspic-

[41] In Pfb. 40, fol. 356, of 31 Dec. 1634, Daniel's widow, who was about to remarry, guaranteed to her son, to her married daughter Catherina and to her grandchildren by her deceased daughter Margareta inheritances from Daniel's property.

[42] In 1611, when Michael borrowed 200 fl., he had put up this house as security. Dr. Gustav Wulz identifies this house as C221 (in the later municipal numbering system), the same house cited by Wulz in *Ahnen*, p. 23.

[43] Pfb. 37, fol. 464, involving house C221; and Pfb. 29, fol. 662.

uous. The younger grandson, Daniel, founded the richest, most powerful, and for years the most hated family in the city. We shall look at these two branches of the Wörner family one at a time, beginning with the senior branch founded by Michael and then returning in the following section to the junior but more prominent branch headed by Daniel.

II

As is the case for most of the world's poor, the circumstances of the younger Michael Wörner's life (1607-60) were dictated by his birth. As we have seen, his father Michael had been the least successful of the six Wörner brothers, the only one who died poorer than his father had left him; this meant, of course, that he had little to pass on to his son. Thus, when the younger Michael married a poor widow and began adult life as a wool weaver in 1630, two years after his father's death, his property assessment was a mere 50 fl.[44] Michael did have three very wealthy uncles, but this fact in no way benefited him—a striking illustration of the patterns of inheritance in seventeenth-century Nördlingen. His uncles Georg and Daniel each left heirs who divided the property among themselves. As for his uncle David, although all descendants were dead by 1634, the inheritance passed to the widow, who succeeded in retaining a substantial part of it until her own death in 1665. And this widow specified her own siblings and their children—not David Wörner's nephews—as her heirs.[45]

[44] The poverty of his wife is suggested by the fact that she could promise to her two sons by her previous marriage only 10 fl. each as inheritance from their father: Heiratsbriefe 23 Aug. 1630. (By contrast, when Georg Wörner's third wife remarried in 1632, her intention was to guarantee her three daughters 400 fl. each as inheritance from their father: Heiratsbriefe 9 May 1632.)

[45] In the contract for her prospective remarriage in 1635 (Heiratsbriefe 6 Jan. 1635), David's widow Margaretha, whose children had all died and who is described as being beyond child-bearing age, lists

On top of all this, Michael may have suffered from some personal shortcomings. It appears from a reference in the council minutes of 1625, when he would have been 18, that he was thought to be dim-witted.[46] Clearly, this was not the case, as he was later appointed to a minor city office, but perhaps he was not too intelligent.

Michael continued to occupy his father's house, and in 1634 he arranged to buy out the other heirs' interest in the building in order to become its sole owner.[47] In the same year he requested and received appointment as a *Weinlader*, a minor functionary concerned with unloading, measuring and collecting tolls on wine stored in the city warehouse.[48] From the date of his appointment it is obvious that he was named to replace someone who had died in the plague.

As a combined wool weaver and Weinlader,[49] Michael succeeded in increasing his wealth somewhat; his assessment stood at 400 fl. in 1655. In the same year his first wife died, but nine months later Michael got married again, to a wool weaver's widow. The fact that each spouse already owned a house had evidently proved a thorny problem in the marriage negotiations, but the final settlement provided that

---

her siblings and their children as her only heirs aside from her prospective husband, although it is true that an additional sum was set aside over the disposition of which she could later decide. (This betrothal to Hans Beck, genannt Löpsinger, fell through; until her death, Margaretha continued to be listed in the tax registers, Pfandbücher and other records as David's widow.)

[46] RP 6 May 1625: "Michael Wörner hat am Sambstag ein Seckhel ufm Markht abgeschnitten, Sol blöd im Haupt sein, Sol also zugesehen werden." Of course, the reference could have been to his father, but it seems unlikely that such an entry would have referred to a 60-year-old man.

[47] Pfb. 37, fol. 246; Pfb. 38, fol. 66.

[48] To cover the cost of any damages or deceit he might inflict during his service, Michael had to put up a 50 fl. "Caution," using his house as security. Pfb. 40, fol. 330.

[49] Michael remained a Weinlader until 1656 or slightly before; see ibid.

each was to retain ownership of his or her own house and pass it on to his or her own children.[50]

The second marriage produced no offspring, so when Michael died in 1660 he left only the children of his first marriage: a daughter, who married a wool weaver in 1665, and two sons. The older son, Hans, had already married in 1653; not surprisingly, his wife was a weaver's daughter. (Although the richer members of the Wörner family chose spouses for themselves or their children from a wide circle of occupational groups, the poorer members of the family selected spouses almost exclusively from within the wool-weaving craft.) In 51 years of marriage, Hans Wörner and his wife produced no children; perhaps for this reason Hans had some success in holding on to a respectable amount of property, at least until his middle age. By 1685 his wealth had risen to 500 fl. Thereafter, however, Hans' assessments began to decline, and by the later years of the seventeenth century he was appearing before the city council year after year to plead for reductions in his Anlagen assessments.[51] In the last few years of his life Hans was listed as paying no property taxes at all, possibly because he had been admitted to live in the city hospital.[52] Hans' most noteworthy appearance in the city records, however, came in 1698, when, as we shall see, he was reluctantly drawn into the quarrel between his wealthy cousins and the wool-weaving craft.

[50] Heiratsbriefe 26 June 1656. There are two drafts of this marriage contract, which differ only in regard to the question of the houses. That separate ownership was the final settlement is confirmed by the fact that tax payments for his new wife's house were listed separately from Michael's in the tax registers—an unusual, though not unique arrangement.

[51] For example, RP 2 July 1688; 31 July and 23 Dec. 1689; 21 July and 22 Sept. 1690; 9 Feb. 1691; 7 March and 2 Sept. 1692; etc.

[52] From 1702 on there are no entries in the tax books; indeed, the word "obiit" appears from then on, although Hans actually died only in 1707. But as early as 1700 Hans had applied for admission to the hospital (RP 5 Nov. 1700); at that time he was instructed to first sell his house, which he seems to have done only in 1705 (RP 6 Apr. 1705).

Michael Wörner had left both his sons with a modest inheritance. Hans was able to increase his property, at least for a number of decades, but not so the younger son, Hans Georg. After his marriage in 1663 Hans Georg proceeded to father ten children, at least five of whom survived infancy. Not surprisingly, his assessment declined, from 75 fl. at the outset to 50 fl. from 1670 on. He was the first member of his family to have fallen unequivocally into poverty.

Undoubtedly it was to house his growing family more securely that Hans Georg had arranged in 1668 to buy out his brother's and sister's shares in the house they had inherited jointly from their father.[53] But this expense, added to the cost of maintaining his family, was clearly too much for Hans Georg to handle on his income as a wool weaver. He soon fell deeply into debt. By 1673 he had sold the house and had evidently moved in with his mother-in-law; in any case he offered her house as security for a loan. By 1676 this house had passed to him, and he used it as security for two more loans. When he died in 1678, aged 37, Hans Georg left a widow, at least four children, a heavily mortgaged house and personal debts of 213 fl.[54]

Less than two months after Hans Georg's death, his widow Sibylla was forced to borrow again;[55] the following year she sold the house.[56] This may have made it possible to clear up the debts, but there was evidently little left over. The council minutes show that within two years of her husband's death Sibylla had become one of those destitute

[53] Pfb. 46, fol. 185.

[54] Pfb. 47, fols. 55, 193, 488 and 515. In addition to covering debts that Hans Georg himself had incurred, at the time of his death the house was being offered as security for 140 fl. in debts for which the family of Hans Georg's wife was responsible. As to the number of children, four were definitely alive in 1678 and a fifth, Michael, born 1672, probably was: there is no marriage or death entry for him in the parish registers, meaning that he probably survived through childhood and emigrated from Nördlingen during his adolescence.

[55] Pfb. 48, fol. 135.

[56] Pfb. 48, fol. 222.

citizens who had to turn to the city council to support their basic needs. In August 1679, she was granted "half a loaf of bread," presumably on a periodic basis.[57] In 1687 she asked for a grant of money, and was given a pittance of 6 kreuzers.[58] Frequently, during her 35 years of widowhood—she died in 1713—Sibylla appealed to the council to grant her an outlay of wood for the winter.[59]

Three children of Hans Georg and Sibylla survived to adulthood: two daughters, who died as middle-aged spinsters in the city hospital, and a son, also named Hans Georg, who married three times. Like all his Wörner ancestors in Nördlingen, Hans Georg was a wool weaver, and like his more immediate ancestors, he was a poor one. Throughout his life he paid the minimum allowable tax, until during the last few years before his death in 1724 he ceased to pay any taxes at all. In the contract for his second marriage in 1698, he could guarantee his two living children only 4 gulden apiece as inheritances from their mother.[60] Like his uncle Hans, Hans Georg appeared repeatedly before the council to petition for remission of his Anlagen.[61]

Of Hans Georg's eleven children, only two grew to adulthood in Nördlingen.[62] One was a daughter who died single at the age of 45; the other a son who established himself as a wool weaver in 1731 and apparently lived, like his father, in considerable poverty.[63]

57 RP 18 Aug. 1679.

58 RP 26 Jan. 1687.

59 For example, RP 4 Dec. 1685; 16 Jan. 1688; 27 Nov. 1689; 24 Nov. 1690, etc. Often 30 krz. was granted in lieu of wood.

60 Heiratsbriefe 25 Oct. 1698.

61 RP 21 Feb. 1696; 18 Jan. 1697 (when he received the bureaucratic reply, "man könne in das neulich revidirte Register nicht Bruch machen"); also 1697, fol. 549.

62 Seven children died in childhood and for two more, both sons, there is no information in the parish registers. Very possibly they both emigrated before marriage to towns where there was more hope of economic success.

63 The tax records show that Johann Philipp paid 1 fl. in 1732,

Throughout this period, however, the other branch of the Wörner family was accumulating enormous riches. But the city records give virtually no hint of contact between the two wings of the family, and the circumstances of the poorer branch suggest that they received no assistance from their wealthy relatives: in seventeenth-century Nördlingen the responsibilities of the extended family obviously did not extend to second cousins. The descendants of Michael Wörner, wool weavers all, stood passively by as their cousins became the city's richest inhabitants—and did so by transforming the structure of the local wool-weaving industry. When we move from one branch of the Wörner family to the other, we also move from the short (though never simple) annals of the poor to one of the great dramas of Nördlingen's economic history.

III

Toward the end of the seventeenth century, perhaps the most important and certainly the most controversial citizens of Nördlingen were Daniel Wörner (1621-99) and his sons. During the half-century following the Thirty Years War, Daniel Wörner had established himself as Nördlingen's first great entrepreneur—a textile magnate with scores of wool-weaving masters directly dependent on him or his family for their livelihoods. The story of the Wörners, in fact, provides us with a vivid case study in the development of entrepreneurial capitalism in a German community of the early modern era.

But Daniel Wörner's career is also of interest because of the difficulties against which he contended. For in the course of his career, Wörner generated ever-increasing hostility, not only from the wool weavers themselves, but also from the members of the communal elite who controlled the city

absolutely nothing in 1733-39, 1 fl. again in 1740-41, and then 15 kr. from 1742 until the tax-book series ends in 1746.

government. To some extent, the hostility that Wörner and his sons engendered among the civic elite may have reflected personal antagonisms or jealousy of the family's economic success. But beneath this lay another factor, for the kind of energetic entrepreneurial capitalism in which the Wörners engaged violated the traditional economic mores of the city in which they lived: the ideology of *bürgerliche Nahrung*—economic self-sufficiency for every citizen—continued to motivate the magistrates of Nördlingen until the opening of the eighteenth century. Thus, in 1698, when the wool weavers of Nördlingen launched an unprecedented collective attack on the monopolistic practices of the Wörner family, the city council proved to be a sympatheic ally. A century later, when a similar conflict erupted in Nördlingen, the civic magistrates were to demonstrate a completely different attitude, but at the end of the seventeenth century, entrepreneurial capitalism in its most aggressive form was still highly suspect in a community like Nördlingen.

The type of woolen cloth produced in Nördlingen was a local specialty. Most textile-producing cities in seventeenth-century Swabia manufactured linen, fustian or lightweight woolens; Nördlingen was certainly the leading producer of Loden—heavy woolen cloths, each about one yard wide and forty yards long.[64] The manufacture of these woolens in Nördlingen after the Thirty Years War was still carried out on the basis of production by independent and theoretically equal masters of the craft. Each master was entitled to buy

[64] Hermann Kellenbenz, "Die Wirtschaft der schwäbischen Reichsstädte zwischen 1648 und 1740," *Jahrbuch für Geschichte der oberdeutschen Reichsstädte (Esslinger Studien)*, 11 (1965), 128-65; Wolfgang Zorn, "Zur Geschichte der schwäbischen Wirtschaft, 1368-1869," in Wolfgang Zorn and Leonhard Hillenbrand, *Sechs Jahrhunderte Schwäbische Wirtschaft: Beiträge zur Geschichte der Wirtschaft im bayerischen Regierungsbezirk Schwaben* (Augsburg, 1969), p. 44. Ebert, *Lodweberei*, p. 27, gives the dimensions of a Loden in seventeenth-century Nördlingen as 1¼ Ellen wide and 52 Ellen long. (The Elle varied from city to city but was typically about three-quarters of a meter.)

wool, manufacture cloth and sell his product independently on the open market. In 1657, for example, the city council reaffirmed earlier rules designed to protect access by individual masters to raw materials: merchants would normally be forbidden to purchase wool within five miles of the city (the area most accessible to the artisans), while the weavers were barred from buying more wool than they themselves could work and attempting to sell the surplus. Altogether, the council decreed,

> the woolen trade is to remain, as it has been, a free trade, such that any master of the wool-weaving craft be allowed to accumulate his woolens, and also, to the extent that his powers permit, to buy what is needed, and in turn to send [woolens] or to sell them wherever he wants, bearing in mind, however, that moderation is to be preserved and others are not to be pushed aside.[65]

Yet at the same time, the success of this industry was heavily dependent on merchants and middlemen. For without the fluidity of capital which these men could provide, a poor weaving master—and most wool weavers were, after all, among the poorest citizens of Nördlingen—could scarcely survive seasonal changes in the supply of raw products or the demand for finished goods. Such dependency was a normal feature of economic life in preindustrial times, but under certain circumstances, as is well known, it could give way to the permanent, contractual dependency embodied in the *Verlagssystem*—the putting-out system.[66] Precisely this happened in Nördlingen toward the end of the seventeenth century.

The Verlagssystem as such had already penetrated the

[65] OB 1641-88, fols. 175a-176a. See also Ebert, *Lodweberei*, pp. 8-11.

[66] For a general introduction to this subject, see Fridolin Furger, *Zum Verlagssystem als Organisationsform des Frükapitalismus im Textilgewerbe* (Beihefte zur Vierteljahrschrift für Sozial- und Wirtschaftsgeschichte, 11, 1927).

surrounding region before the end of the sixteenth century, for in 1585 this form of production had been introduced in the town of Harburg, some twelve miles south of Nördlingen. Under the patronage of the count of Oettingen-Oettingen, the Augsburg capitalist Carl Imhoff had contracted with the weavers of Harburg to provide them with the wool they required and to purchase all the cloth they produced.[67] In Nördlingen itself, however, no such developments took place as early as the sixteenth century. On the one hand, the city and its textile-producing industry were too large to be subjected to economic domination from outside, while on the other hand, there were evidently no merchants in Nördlingen who could mobilize the financial capital required for a full-fledged putting-out system. And beyond this, the social traditions of Nördlingen were hostile to the introduction of such a sharp economic distinction among citizens. Characteristically, the city council felt obliged to protect the interests of smaller masters against any monopolization of the wool supply which would permit middlemen to manipulate wool prices to the masters' disadvantage. Such regulations, already evident in the fifteenth century, continued to be renewed from time to time until the eighteenth[68]—an illustration of the responsibility that the council continued to feel for the small independent craftsmen long after they had ceased to be represented in the government.

Nevertheless, as we have noted, the merchants played a crucial role in the city's textile industry. These merchants, as a rule, fell into one of three groups: men whose inherited wealth was sufficiently large that they could identify themselves as merchants from the beginning; wealthy tanners, whose dealing in sheep hides frequently led to involvement in the sale of wool; and, finally, men who identified them-

[67] Rudolf Endres, "Kapitalistische Organisationsformen im Ries in der zweiten Hälfte des 15. Jahrhunderts," *Jahrbuch für fränkische Landesforschung*, 22 (1962), 89-99.

[68] Ebert, *Lodweberei*, pp. 8-11.

selves as weavers but who owned enough financial capital to make cash advances to other, poorer weavers and to receive finished woolens as payment, an activity which almost inevitably led to a full career as a textile merchant. It was to this last category that the most enterprising members of the Wörner family in Nördlingen belonged—Andreas in the late sixteenth century, his son Georg in the first generation of the seventeenth, and now Georg's nephew Daniel.

Initially, Daniel Wörner's career did not differ sharply in terms of business techniques from the careers of others who had preceded him. But the times themselves had changed, so that the economic consequences of these techniques were now very different. For the late seventeenth century was an age of economic and demographic recession in Nördlingen. Although the city had enjoyed a period of economic recovery following the Thirty Years War, this recovery had tended to benefit craftsmen of middling wealth more than those in the bottom stratum, to which so many of the wool weavers belonged. And when, as we have seen, this trend was reversed and a new cycle of warfare after 1670 began to inflict a crushing financial burden on the community, the wool weavers were among those who suffered the most. Structural changes in the economy were equally detrimental to their position. One consequence of Nördlingen's reduced population and growing communal indebtedness was a steady decline in the city's economic domination of the surrounding district. This gave rise to increasing competition from village weavers, who could carry out their trade unencumbered by the dues, regulations and careful inspections to which city weavers were subject. Inevitably the demand for Nördlingen's own woolens diminished in the surrounding countryside, and the city's weavers thus became increasingly dependent on more distant markets. Indeed, the principal market for Nördlingen woolens after the Thirty Years War was in remote Switzerland, especially in Zürich and at the Zurzach trade fair from which most of the cloth moved on to Italy.

But how were Nördlingen's weavers to gain access to such distant markets? A few weavers managed from time to time to make the journey to Switzerland and sell their wares on the spot,[69] but for most of them such a long and time-consuming trip was out of the question. Inevitably, then, as local demand for their wares diminished, the weavers of Nördlingen became more dependent than ever on the services of a middleman—not only as a source of loans and cash advances but also as the agent to carry their products to the distant markets which they themselves could not reach.

Increased reliance on a middleman need not, as such, have proved harmful to the artisans. But this development coincided with another trend in seventeenth-century Nördlingen: the growing tendency for the members of wealthy families to enter professional or administrative careers rather than mercantile ones. By the late seventeenth century, as we have seen, merchants made up a considerably smaller part of Nördlingen's wealthy elite than they had three generations earlier.[70] The implications of this are obvious: as competition from other merchants decreased, it became increasingly easy for any one merchant to obtain a monopoly over an industry dependent on the services of a middleman. This was particularly so if the merchant in question was a ruthless operator willing to violate the paternalistic mores of the traditional small-town economy. Such a man, as we shall see, was Daniel Wörner.

Wörner's business techniques contributed to a sharpening of the social distinction between capitalist and laborers within the citizenry of Nördlingen. But for precisely this reason, his conduct offended and alienated the more traditional-minded members of his own social class. This fact was

[69] For a specific example, see Lodweberakten, Loder c. Wörner: Supplicationes, Verhören, Berichte und Rhats-Bescheide (hereafter: Supplicationes), Nr. 1: "Bitt und Klag Schreiben . . . wegen der 2 Werner . . . ," p. 4. Cf. Gustav Wulz, "Zurzacher Messe," *Der Daniel*, 6 (1970), no. 2, pp. 23-25.

[70] See Chapter Four.

to make it possible for weavers and magistrates to join before Wörner's death in a common effort to humble, at least temporarily, the city's most powerful merchant family.

DANIEL WÖRNER was 13 when his father of the same name died in the plague of 1634. He probably spent his adolescence in the home of his stepfather, Tobias Haider, until he married Magdalena Wünsch in January 1647. His wife, the daughter of a prosperous hatmaker, was to provide her husband with twelve children, observe with him a fiftieth wedding anniversary, and survive him to die in 1720 at the venerable age of 94.

Daniel's father had been a moderately prosperous man, and the young man's guardians succeeded in preserving for him a reasonable portion of the father's wealth, despite the incessant financial demands imposed on the citizens of Nördlingen during the later phases of the Thirty Years War. The tax register for 1652 shows an assessment of real and personal property worth 1,300 fl. Thus, at the start of his adult life, Daniel was a man of middling means—equally distant from the impoverished citizens assessed at 50 fl. or less and from the city's wealthy elite whose assessments totaled fifteen or twenty times his own.

Like all of his Wörner ancestors in Nördlingen, Daniel initially identified himself as a wool weaver, but the degree of his wealth clearly separated him from the great majority of wool weavers who were among the poorest citizens. It is impossible to tell whether at the start of his career Daniel sometimes sat at his loom or left this chore entirely to journeymen, but it is clear that, like his father before him, he had inherited sufficient wealth to free him from the need to perform manual labor. Unlike his father, however, Daniel was not willing to sit quietly and nurse an inherited fortune. His initial career resembles far more that of his grandfather Andreas, whose energetic trading and property investments had laid the basis for the family's prosperity.

In the course of the 1650's, Daniel Wörner's assessment rose steadily—from 1,300 fl. in 1652 to 3,100 fl. by 1660. Occasional entries in the council minutes indicate that he was building his fortune by investing in real property and by making cash advances to poor weavers who had to commit themselves to repay in money or in woolens not yet produced.[71] There are numerous indications of what were regarded as unscrupulous methods on his part. In 1662, when he demanded payment of an overdue debt of woolens, the accused weaver countered by reporting that Wörner had already collected one finished cloth as "interest" on the unfulfilled obligation—an unorthodox procedure that aroused the council's deep concern.[72] A few years later, the magistrates were investigating another suspicious practice: it was charged that Wörner was selling finished cloths without paying the appropriate toll charges.[73]

By 1668, Wörner's assessment had climbed to 4,800 fl., and in the same year he resigned from the wool-weaving craft and began to be designated as a textile merchant.[74] But in actual fact, his economic activities had long since become those of a merchant. A few years later the council's suspicions were once again aroused when it was observed that Wörner had paid toll on only one woolen cloth during all of 1672.[75] In the following years Wörner occasionally appealed to the magistrates again for assistance in collecting debts; not only citizen weavers but also a number of Jews were by now substantially in his debt.[76]

71 See RP 1660, fol. 185a/b and 1661, fol. 165b.

72 RP 26 March 1662.

73 RP 14 March 1666.

74 RP 30 March 1668. The council denied Daniel permission to be identified as a weaver and a merchant simultaneously, but it was sympathetic to his cautious request that if he failed as a merchant he might be restored immediately to his full status as a weaver without the normal probationary period of five years.

75 RP 24 Dec. 1672.

76 RP 1676, fol. 19a; 1677, fols. 36b, 42b, 48a, 49a, 59b. The Jews had been banished from Nördlingen in 1507, but in the seventeenth cen-

Throughout this period, Daniel Wörner and his son of the same name, who began to function as his father's partner around 1680, were undoubtedly engendering the hostility of the impoverished weavers whose feelings were to come to the surface so clearly in 1698. But at the same time, the Wörners were also coming into conflict with members of their own social class—the governing elite and the leading merchant families. Already in 1663 the elder Daniel had scandalized the magistrates by complaining about the special taxes levied to support the anti-Turkish war and stating that "the Turkish danger is not as great as it is made out to be."[77] But by 1680, economic rivalry also entered the picture. The Wörners—by now the leading exporters of Loden from the city—were accused of underselling other Nördlingen cloth merchants on the Swiss market, forcing their rivals to reduce their prices, which in turn forced them to lower the amount they could offer the city's weavers for finished cloth. The Wörners, however, denied the charge and in fact turned their reply into an attack on the growing involvement of tanners in the cloth trade, which, they evidently felt, should remain the exclusive province of cloth merchants.[78]

Meanwhile, the council received complaints from Swiss merchants, who formed the chief market for Nördlingen's woolens, about the poor quality of the city's products. The masters were using poorer and thinner threads, which, the council recognized, was due to the low prices they received for their goods. In 1681, an ordinance was passed to regulate the entire situation in the local industry. Masters were ordered to uphold the traditional standards of quality. Tanners were barred from all trading in raw wool and finished cloth. And the cloth merchants were enjoined "to agree with

---

tury a few Jews were granted special permission to live in the city or to commute to the city from nearby villages. Most of the Jews were petty traders or retailers. L. Müller, "Auf fünf Jahrhunderten (1. Teil)," pp. 75-77, 115-20.

[77] RP 3 Aug. 1663.

[78] RP 26 Nov. 1680.

one another on a certain price, both in purchasing here and in selling in Switzerland, . . . and none to offer goods more cheaply to the others' injury, or otherwise place others at a disadvantage, but instead to conduct this trade in such a way that both sectors, the masters and the merchants, can have an honest living from it."[79] Thus, the council not only attempted to protect the weaving masters from depressed prices, but also to protect the merchants from the tanners, and from one another. The traditional urban ideology which favored communal and group needs over individual success still dominated the thinking of Nördlingen's magistrates.

The council also attempted to limit the number of finished cloths that any one merchant might export from Nördlingen each year; the surplus was to be submitted for sale within the city. A major factor in this policy was undoubtedly the desire to attract foreign merchants to the community, and in particular to stimulate activity at the city's annual Pentecost fair. Yet these attempts to regulate market conditions met with little success. Already in 1682 the council had to reprimand Wörner for exporting more cloths than allowed. In his reply, Wörner first offered the lame excuse that he "had not correctly understood the promulgated ordinance when he heard it, and thought it was only to take effect the following year." But the next part of his reply warned that "if his hands were thus tied, and he was prevented from sending woolens away, he would not be able to buy any more woolens from the weavers nor to give them any money."[80] This was a potent threat, for dozens of weavers had already become dependent for their livelihoods on Wörner's purchases of their output. The council was forced to recognize this and did not attempt to punish Wörner for past transgressions—but they still tried to lay down rules for the future: Wörner "was not to let the poor masters suffer want but instead was to take their woolens from them and collect them together until he is allowed to send them

[79] OB 1641-88, fols. 383a-384a (10 Aug. 1681).
[80] RP 6 Nov. 1682.

away." The council also attempted to establish a fixed price for both raw wool and finished cloth.[81]

The council's actions at this juncture illustrate vividly the dominant position that Wörner had already attained in the Nördlingen wool industry. The magistrates tried to protect the right of other merchants to compete with the Wörners. In 1687, for example, one rival, the widow of the merchant Theodor Seefried, asked the council to make sure that Wörner would not export beyond the permitted limit; the magistrates obligingly ordered Wörner to cease all exporting until Frau Seefried had caught up with him by sending out an equal number.[82] But in fact true competition among the wool merchants was no longer possible, as illustrated by the council's reaction when Wörner threatened to stop buying woolens altogether. For there were simply no other merchants with sufficient capital to finance the dozens of weavers who had become dependent on Daniel Wörner. By the end of the decade Wörner was certainly financing many more weavers than any other merchant; in fact he was beginning to develop what was to become a near-monopoly over the woolen industry of Nördlingen.

By 1690 Wörner was 69 years old and all his surviving children were adults. His eldest son, Daniel, was in partnership with the father; by 1690 he was already into the second of his four marriages and worth 3,800 fl. But the second son, Simon, was a bachelor, and by all evidence a habitual troublemaker. In 1688 he was hauled before the council and forced to apologize for insulting remarks he had made about members of the wool-weaving craft.[83] The following year it was established that he had tampered with the boundary stones that separated his father's fields south of the city from

[81] Ibid.

[82] RP 2 Sept. 1687. Wörner was also instructed not to evade the rule by shipping out woolens in his son's name.

[83] RP 1 Feb. 1688.

the neighboring ones. When one of the neighbors objected to his removing grain from her side of the real boundary, Simon had compounded his misconduct by calling her a "whore and a witch."[84] He was briefly imprisoned and then fined 112 Reichstaler. Whether he was deliberately kept home as his father's henchman is not clear, but when he died in 1692 at the age of 36 he was still an unmarried member of his father's household.

The third surviving son was David. It was recalled after his death that David had hoped to study for a religious career but, at his father's insistence, had come around to the view that "he could also serve God and his fellow-man in the universally obliging and useful status of a merchant."[85] After some training in a mercantile house of Nuremberg and eight years as his father's assistant, David married the widow of a well-to-do ironmonger in 1689. Evidently David took over his predecessor's business, for he broke with his family's traditional interest in cloth production to become an ironmonger.

Two of Daniel's daughters were also married by 1690. The third and youngest daughter, however, remained unmarried until 1698. Apparently she succeeded David as her father's assistant or bookkeeper, for in 1698 she was summoned along with her father and older brother Daniel to give testimony concerning the family business.

In 1690, Daniel Wörner was assessed at 12,800 fl., making him the richest merchant and the fourth richest citizen of Nördlingen.[86] Adding his sons' assessments to the total, the Wörner family was worth 18,800 fl., or about one-fiftieth of the total wealth of the citizenry. While this proportion was

[84] RP 1689, pp. 268-69, 274-75, 280, 288.

[85] Leichenpredigte: David Wörner, 1741, pp. 8-10.

[86] The three richer citizens were nonmerchants: the widow of Hans Christoph Frickhinger, a municipal bureaucrat who had become Bürgermeister; Georg Friedrich Weng, the city counsel; and the widow of Adam Rehlin, a brewer. Cf. Gustav Wulz, "Die reichsten Nördlinger."

still to increase considerably in the years to come, the Wörners had already become firmly established as one of the richest—and one of the most disliked—families in the city. Perhaps nothing illustrates the latter point more clearly than the persistent rumor that the older Wörner had attempted to commit suicide, presumably out of remorse for his conduct—a far from trivial accusation in a society which disposed of its suicides in the burying ground for carrion.[87] In 1688 Wörner insisted on an investigation to stamp out the rumor, but five years later the story surfaced again and a weaver's wife was imprisoned for disseminating it.[88]

While Wörner was also by no means popular with the magistrates, his substantial wealth obliged the council to appoint him at last to an office of civic dignity. In 1693 he was named a member of the city court, while his younger son David was granted a seat on the powerless large council.[89] For the Wörners were by now an indispensable part of the city's economic and financial life. Not only did they provide scores of weavers with a market for their products, but they were also called upon to make substantial loans to the ever-desperate city treasury. In 1697, for example, the elder Wörner granted a short-term loan of 1,000 fl. while his son Daniel either provided or arranged for a loan of 1,000 Reichstaler to the city.[90]

Meanwhile, the Wörners were again having trouble with the Swiss merchants to whom they normally sold cloth produced in Nördlingen. In 1694, some Zürich merchants started to complain that the cloth they received was falling short of the standard length.[91] In 1696, one Zürich merchant even returned six unsatisfactory cloths to Nördlingen, where for years they remained in a city warehouse while officials evi-

[87] Such treatment of suicides in Nördlingen is recorded in "Mötzel," *Heimatbote*, nos. 25-67 (1926-1930), passim.

[88] RP 1 Feb. 1688; 8, 10 and 29 March 1693.

[89] RP 3 Jan. 1693.

[90] RP 30 Apr. and 18 Aug. 1697.

[91] RP 14 Dec. 1694; 4 and 18 March, 26 Apr. 1695.

dently debated whether the Wörners were entitled to get them back.[92]

Seeing their Swiss customers grow restive, and spurred by competition from other German cities, the Wörners undertook considerable efforts in the 1690's to undersell other purveyors of cloth on the Swiss market. But a reduction in the sale price of Nördlingen cloth also meant a reduction in the amount that Nördlingen weavers would receive for their finished goods. Indeed, the Wörners made sure that the weavers rather than they themselves would bear the brunt of depressed prices: often they would decline to pay the weavers outright for the cloths but instead only accepted cloths to be sold on a commission basis. In other words, they might provide a weaver with some wool or cash when he delivered his finished cloth, but the accounts would only be drawn up and settled after the cloth had been sold on the Swiss market.[93]

Inevitably many weavers, unable to control or even know in advance the price of their goods, became dependent on and hopelessly indebted to the Wörner family. In response to this situation, the weavers had only two forms of recourse. First, they might try to play the Wörners off against the other cloth merchants in the city. But these other merchants tended to have much less capital and thus were unable to purchase woolens from nearly as many weavers as the Wörners controlled. Second, the weavers might appeal to the city council. It was the latter form of recourse to which they turned early in 1698.

WHEN the weavers submitted their petition to the council in February 1698, the magistrates already had the Wörner family very much on their minds. For they were currently

[92] RP 22 and 31 Jan. 1696; 22 Feb. and 21 Apr. 1697; 12 May and 30 July 1700.

[93] Both Ebert, *Lodweberei*, p. 39, and Zorn, *Industriegeschichte*, p. 100, draw attention to this technique.

investigating a criminal incident which, although completely unrelated to the economic conflict, inevitably added to the general hostility toward the Wörner family. In January of 1698 a woman named Margareta Möschlin was brutally beaten by the recruiting clerk of a regiment then quartered in the city. The reasons for this beating remain unknown, but three of Daniel Wörner's children were present and evidently participated: David, the ironmonger; Barbara, a married daughter; and Catherina, the unmarried daughter who served as her father's assistant. The three siblings were briefly placed under arrest and then subjected to prolonged investigation. Although punishment was not meted out until much later, from the beginning the Wörners had been tainted with participation in a sordid and scandalous episode.[94]

Thus, the family's reputation was freshly besmirched at the time the weavers opened their offensive against the Wörners in February 1698. What actually triggered the weavers' action, however, was a dramatic downward spiral in the price of finished cloths at a time when consumer prices in general were apparently rising.[95] A Loden which would have received 16½ fl. in 1696 was worth only 11½ fl. by the beginning of 1698.[96] Since the price of a hundredweight of raw wool—sufficient to make, at most, three Loden—had increased to 40 fl. by 1698,[97] there was no longer any chance of making a profit. In fact, the weavers did not even have the option of ceasing to weave: indebted as they were to the Wörners for advances of cash or wool,

[94] RP 24, 27, 28 and 31 Jan.; 1 and 11 Feb. 1698; 14 Feb., 3, 7 and 20 March 1699.

[95] The annual price index for Augsburg worked out by E. H. Phelps Brown and Sheila V. Hopkins, "Builders' Wage-rates, Prices and Population: Some Further Evidence," *Economica*, n.s. 24 (1959), 18-38, shows a short-term increase in prices of 23% between 1696 and 1698.

[96] Lodweberakten, Loder c. Daniel Wörner 1698 (Loder c. Wörner): Confrontations-Protocoll, pp. 9-10 and passim.

[97] Ibid., p. 5 and passim; Ebert, *Lodweberei*, pp. 33, 36, 38.

they had to continue to produce and provide cloth simply to maintain their credit. Before the dispute was settled later in the year, 44 masters owed a total of about 2,000 fl. to the Wörners.[98] Obviously, this contributed to their bitterness, especially since, as we shall see, the Wörners were held responsible for manipulating the prices of wool and cloth to the weavers' disadvantage.

The petition submitted to the council on February 9, appealing for relief from the "unmerciful, unchristian, and with bloody tears to be lamented conduct" of Daniel Wörner and his son, was drafted by the weaver Hans Caspar Deffner and signed by himself and 39 others of his craft.[99] Of these 40 weavers, all but 2 can be identified in the tax records, which show that 25 of them had assessments of 100 fl. or less, with most of the remainder scarcely above that level.[100] In other words, the petitioners were among the very poorest of Nördlingen's citizens, at the very opposite end of the economic spectrum from the elder and younger Wörner, whose combined assessments in 1697 totaled 28,200 fl. Within a few weeks, the original 40 petitioners were joined by about 20 more weavers who added their names to the protest document.[101]

From this petition, and from a corroborating one which accompanied it,[102] a clear picture emerges of the weavers' grievances against the Wörners. For the petitions trace in passionate but precise detail the record of events since Oc-

98 Loder c. Wörner: Austeilung der Wernerischen 4,000 fl. an die Loder wie auch dern Abzug von Schulden betreff.: Debts to the elder Daniel Wörner totaled, in his reckoning, 1,435 fl. 14 kr., and debts to his son Daniel came to over 500 fl.

99 Loder c. Wörner: Supplicationes, Nr. 1: "Bitt und Klag Schreiben . . . wegen der 2 Werner. . . ."

100 StR 1694 and 1700. Only Schtoffel Blanck and H. Brach (?) cannot be traced.

101 RP 21 Feb. 1698.

102 Loder c. Wörner: Supplicationes, Nr. 2: "Underthänig und Fuessfälligstes Clag Memoriale," submitted by Hans Herpfer Mittel and Hans Jörg Hochstetter Jung, both Lodweber.

tober 24, 1696, when the Wörners had instituted the practice of *Einsetzen* of cloth. This meant that while a weaver would continue to deliver finished cloths, the Wörners would no longer pay him or credit to his account a fixed amount right away. Instead, they would wait till they had sold the cloth and then credit his account accordingly. This practice added uncertainty to the weavers' other woes. But their major grievance was that the price at which the Wörners settled accounts under this system was constantly dropping. The Wörners' justification for this was simple: that the Swiss demand for finished cloth—and thus its market price—was falling. Eventually, however, in order to appease the weavers, the Wörners promised that if ever any other Nördlingen merchant offered a fixed price for woolens, they would settle their accounts at the same price.

In February 1697, two local merchants began to settle accounts with "their" weavers at 14½ fl. per Loden, and the Wörners were asked to follow suit. But they reneged on their promise. The other merchants were dealing with only a few weavers each, the Wörners pointed out; they themselves could not afford to settle on the same terms with the far greater number of weavers whose Loden they had accepted. Feeling betrayed, the weavers assembled, marched to the younger Wörner's house, and Deffner forced his way in. A bitter confrontation ensued:

> I, Deffner, said, now I could fully see that you want to forcibly ruin me with my wife and child and fellow masters; so he [Wörner] burst out with harsh and unfriendly words, I should shut up, or he would throw me down the stairs; so I, Deffner, lost my patience and said, Just step outside the room and we shall see who throws the other down. . . .[103]

As a consequence of this confrontation, the Wörners finally agreed to settle accounts at 14½ fl. per Loden, a price

[103] Loder c. Wörner, Supplicationes, Nr. 1.

which was maintained until the summer. But the weavers' difficulties were far from over. In the first place, the Wörners now introduced an unprecedented service charge of ⅛ fl. for each Loden which they accepted and resold. Some weavers agreed to the new charge, but others resisted. In fact, some weavers evidently considered selling their Loden to other local merchants, some of whom had already established contact with the Swiss market. But the Wörners, as usual, succeeded in thwarting such attempts to bypass their near-monopoly. With their greater capital resources, they were in a position to undersell their rivals, and according to the weavers' petition, they now offered Loden to Swiss merchants at such drastically reduced prices "that the Swiss themselves were amazed." The other Nördlingen merchants could not match these price reductions and so, the weavers charged, the Wörners drove their rivals off the Swiss market. Having done so, however, they were no longer willing to settle accounts with the weavers at 14½ fl. In the course of a few months the price dropped first to 13 fl. and then to 11½ fl.

This, then, was the burden of the weavers' complaint: that the Wörners had deliberately manipulated the Swiss market for Loden in such a way as to depress the price of finished output back home in Nördlingen. By having obtained a virtual monopoly in selling Nördlingen cloth in Switzerland, the Wörners had made sure that almost all woolen cloth produced for export from the city would be sold to them at whatever price they offered. At the same time, the Wörners controlled the supply of raw wool, and the weavers complained that they had to pay 39 fl. for a hundredweight of wool of indifferent quality.

"O help, O help, for the sake of God's mercy, yes, for the sake of so many hundreds of children, yes, for the sake of the poor craft of wool weavers, help us whoever can and will—and should. . . ." Thus the weavers pleaded in their petition, and the plea was not ignored. The council immediately appointed five of its members as a special committee to examine the entire situation.[104] The committee undertook its work carefully but very slowly, and by March the weavers were again growing restless. Alarmed by their heated public discussions and nighttime meetings, the council issued a proclamation to explain the delay: until now it had still not been able to examine the matter "fully and in each and every respect." The weavers were enjoined to be patient and nighttime gatherings were forbidden.[105]

Despite its bureaucratic slowness, however, the council was sincerely interested in the weavers' plight. By the middle of May, the committee was at last ready to hold "confrontation hearings." A list of 27 points, incorporating all the charges made in the original petition and some additional ones, had been drawn up. Now, for a month, the antagonists were to appear face-to-face before the committee to comment on the points and to confront each other with their charges and counter-charges. On the one side were the Wörners: father, son Daniel and daughter Catherina. On the other side there appeared on various days a succession of different weavers.[106]

The minutes of the hearings reveal numerous grievances against the Wörners. They were accused of dishonest bookkeeping, of charging unreasonable interest on loans, of providing low-grade wool to the weavers, of favoring rich weavers over poor ones, and the like.[107] Repeatedly, bitterness was expressed about the *Einsetzen* system, which, in the words of the weaver Matthias Schweyer, was "the ruin of the craft."[108] But above all, the Wörners were accused over and over again of manipulating the market in Switzerland and of deliberately driving the price of finished Loden downward to the weavers' disadvantage. As Schweyer com-

[104] RP 9 Feb. 1698.

[105] OB 1688-1706, pp. 241-45 (23 March 1698).

[106] Loder c. Wörner: Confrontations Puncten, so den 17. Mai 1698 vorgenommen worden; and Confrontations-Protocoll.

[107] Loder c. Wörner: Confrontations-Protocoll, pp. 5, 11, 85ff., 139ff. and passim.

[108] Ibid., p. 7.

plained: "It is indeed an unchristian thing to have brought the Loden down 5 fl. per piece in a year and a quarter, and to have extorted [acceptance of] this from the poor masters, inasmuch as the wool still remained at the high price of 40 fl."[109] If such practices continued, it was charged, the weavers would become the "slaves and serfs of the Wörners."[110]

In making these complaints, the weavers did not stand alone. For the small-scale cloth merchants of Nördlingen had also suffered from the Wörners' practices and power to undersell them in Switzerland. One such minor rival of the Wörners, the merchant Johann Friedrich Epplin, told the committee: "He held it likely that they, the Wörners, had brought the [price of] Loden in Switzerland down; if, however, they do not admit to having done so, they must prove that others did and name these. It can, however, be assumed that the Wörners had done so, for after all, whenever they came back from Switzerland, they had invariably settled accounts with Loden reduced to a lower price."[111]

Over and over again the Wörners rejected the charges that they had dealt unfairly with the weavers. The elder Wörner, for example, insisted from the start that "he had traded like an honest man, and had forced or obliged nobody to come to him to sell Loden," and his son echoed him.[112] As to the basic accusation, that they had deliberately depressed the price of Loden, the Wörners attempted to shift the blame onto other shoulders. Catherina, for example, blamed the drop in prices on the Strasbourg merchant Johann Brandhofer, who was engaged in buying Nördlingen cloth through intermediaries.[113] Later the Wörners put the blame on competitors from other German cities and sug-

[109] Ibid., p. 5.

[110] Ibid., p. 157.

[111] Ibid., pp. 160-61.

[112] Ibid., p. 6; for the younger Daniel: pp. 13ff.

[113] Ibid., p. 12. Brandhofer was also a councillor of the duchy of Württemberg and administrator of mines in Königsbronn, about 25 km. southwest of Nördlingen: Zorn, *Industriegeschichte*, p. 100.

gested that an oversupply of woolens to Switzerland was responsible for the entire episode.[114] But the committee was evidently not impressed by the Wörners' testimony, as the subsequent actions of the council suggest. Altogether, the hearings had put the Wörners in a bad light. At one point a weaver accused them of keeping his debt on their books after he had paid it—"which," the minutes record, "neither father nor daughter is able to deny."[115] At another point, desperate to show that at least some weavers viewed them favorably, the Wörners called upon their own cousin Hans Wörner to testify on their behalf. Hans, however, did not appear and replied that "he would not come, the entire affair had nothing to do with him. . . ."[116]

A few weeks later the Wörners did succeed in inducing their cousin Hans and five other weavers to submit a statement to the council supporting them. This document attacked Deffner and a handful of other "malcontents" for having stirred up irresponsible expectations among the weavers. Most blame for the crisis, however, was again attributed to the outsider Brandhofer, who was accused of encouraging widespread production and then not buying the cloth produced. "Herr Brandhofer," the statement said, "bought many Loden by commission and gave local masters cause to carry out their craft so energetically that thereby the [price of] wool went up to 40 fl., but thereafter, since Herr Brandhofer's Loden (which before that had been going for 16½ fl.) remained standing in considerable numbers, the Loden fell in price. . . ."[117]

Doubtless the depression in Loden prices was at least

[114] Loder c. Wörner: Confrontations-Protocoll, pp. 157-58.

[115] Ibid., p. 11.

[116] Ibid., pp. 18, 20.

[117] Lodweberakten, Lodenhandel 1696-1715 (-1759): "Unterth. Anzeig . . . die fortführung der Wörn. Lodenhandel betrf.," 15 July 1698, pp. 3-5. The names of four other weavers were subsequently added to this statement, but they insisted to the council that this had been done without their permission and demanded that their names be deleted. RP 5 Aug. 1698.

partly due to circumstances outside the Wörners' direct control, for in selling woolens to the Swiss they did face competition—and probably increased competition—from producers in some other German cities, notably Ulm. But this made little impression on the Wörners' contemporaries in Nördlingen. In the first place, Nördlingen was still the major source of Loden for the Zürich and Zurzach markets, and thus it was easy to assume that the Wörners had played the decisive role in price determination. Altogether, in fact, the countless ways in which the Wörners had taken advantage of local masters dependent upon them had prejudiced large parts of the community against them, and gave substance to the suspicion that the 5 fl. drop in prices was entirely their work. By July, if not sooner, the council was sufficiently convinced of their misconduct to order the Wörners to suspend all exports of Loden until the dispute was settled, and the magistrates stuck to this prohibition despite the Wörners' assiduous efforts to have it lifted.[118]

The council's deliberations dragged on, and again in October the magistrates had to order the weavers to cease their disturbances, in which murderous threats had been uttered.[119] But finally, at the end of the month, the council worked out a settlement. The 63 complaining weavers had previously articulated their grievances into individual claims for compensation totaling 5,133 fl. 20 kr.[120] The council's settlement upheld in principle this demand for compensation, although the precise amount was reduced and rounded off to a total of 4,000 fl., which the Wörners were to pay in two installments. At the same time, the Wörners were permitted to resume their economic activities, "freely and as befits honest merchants." Insults and injuries attributed to both sides were laid aside permanently, and the antagonists were enjoined to avoid any further exchange of charges.[121]

[118] RP 15 July and 3 Aug. 1698.

[119] OB 1688-1706, fols. 249a-250b (21 Oct. 1698).

[120] Loder c. Wörner: Austeilung der Wernerischen 4,000 fl.

[121] RP 1 Nov. 1698.

The settlement fully satisfied the weavers, who immediately submitted their effusive thanks to the council[122] and then proceeded to the painstaking task of dividing up the 4,000 fl. among themselves in accordance with their respective claims. Of the total amount, about two-thirds fell to the 44 masters then in debt to the Wörners and the remainder went to the 19 plaintiffs who were at the time debt-free.[123] Even when divided, the compensation was a handsome windfall for the weavers.

The crisis of 1698 emphasized the extent to which a new economic relationship had emerged within the textile industry of Nördlingen. For whatever their status in theory, in actual fact the weaving masters were no longer free agents as their forefathers had been. Most of them were completely dependent on a capitalist business enterprise which enjoyed a virtual monopoly in the community and could regulate both the supply of raw products and the demand for finished ones. But what they had lost in independence, the weavers could make up for by an increased recognition of their own mutual interest against the power of capital. One cannot speak of a true class consciousness as having emerged in Nördlingen by the 1690's, but some of its preconditions were clearly taking shape.[124]

Yet it is equally significant that to protect their basic interests the weavers turned to the city council. The councils of the larger south German cities—Augsburg and Ulm, for example—persistently favored the interests of commerce and capital in this period.[125] But in the smaller and more backward city of Nördlingen, where an older concept of

[122] Lodweberakten, Lodenhandel 1696-1715 (-1759): "Unterthänig gehorsamste dancksagung . . . ," 31 Oct. 1698; and RP 31 Oct. 1698.

[123] Loder c. Wörner: Austeilung der Wernerischen 4,000 fl.

[124] Cf. Christopher R. Friedrichs, "Capitalism, Mobility and Class Formation in the Early Modern German City," *Past and Present*, no. 69 (Nov. 1975), 24-49.

[125] Zorn, *Industriegeschichte*, p. 258, draws attention to the distinction between council policy in the larger cities and in Nördlingen.

community still prevailed, the council acted to protect the interests of a more humble stratum of the citizenry, the craftsmen. It must be remembered that in 1698, unlike a century before, not a single member of the council was himself a craftsman—all fifteen magistrates belonged to legal, professional or commercial occupations.[126] But none were quite as wealthy as the Wörners, and as a group they were hostile to the kind of single-minded, ruthless capitalistic enterprise which the Wörners represented. The council in 1698 still embodied the traditional spirit of paternalistic responsibility.

In February 1699, a few months after the settlement had been imposed, Daniel Wörner senior died at the age of 78. But his widow and son carried on the family's business. The weavers were still in a very weak economic position, for the settlement had only reproved and punished the Wörners without providing the weavers with an alternative means of gaining access to the market. And in fact, by imposing the 4,000 fl. fine, the council had robbed the Wörners of the ready capital with which they could continue to purchase Loden. The effects of this became dramatically clear within weeks after the settlement. In order to make his compensation payment, Daniel junior had obtained a short-term loan of 1,000 fl. from the richly endowed city hospital. But already in January a number of weavers asked the council to convert this loan into a long-term one, so that Wörner would have enough cash on hand to continue buying Loden from them.[127]

Obviously, the settlement had not provided a permanent solution to the weavers' difficulties and their dependence on the Wörners. Throughout 1699 and 1700, we can see the community groping, hesitantly and experimentally, toward a more basic redefinition of relationships within the textile industry. Despite the settlement, a whole new series of

126 See Appendix VII, as well as the discussion in Chapter Six.
127 RP 5 Jan. 1699.

disputes, charges and counter-charges arose between the weavers and the Wörners.[128] Meanwhile, the council was supervising the Wörners' activities closely, for example by regulating the price of certain Loden to be sold in Switzerland.[129] In October 1699, evidently frustrated by such controls, the Wörners petitioned for permission to suspend trading in Loden altogether.[130] The request opened a whole series of grave questions for the council. On October 27 it debated whether free trade in woolens should be allowed, "without any limitation or restrictions," or whether, on the contrary, a flat, universal price for Loden should be decreed. The magistrates decided to permit free trading; "a fixed price for Loden," they concluded, "could not currently be stabilized," although they reserved the right to impose one later on.[131] The Wörners were permitted to suspend trading "ad interim."[132] But the suspension was evidently only a short or incomplete one. By the following autumn, there were new complaints against the Wörners that they had arbitrarily stopped buying cloth from the weavers. At the same time, three weavers who had been particularly active in the agitation of 1698 complained of discrimination: since the settlement, the Wörners had bought nothing, or almost nothing, from them.[133] Clearly, the Wörners still maintained their central position as the clearinghouse for Loden produced in the city.

Only a radical reorganization of the economic structure of the textile industry could really free the weavers from dependence on the Wörners. And it was exactly this step that the council was ready to take by the end of 1700. In

[128] E.g., RP 1699, pp. 218, 259, 493; RP 1700, pp. 375, 521.

[129] As shown by RP 18 Oct. 1699.

[130] RP 23 Oct. 1699.

[131] RP 27 Oct. 1699.

[132] Ibid., and RP 17, 20 and 29 Nov. 1699.

[133] 27 Aug., 6 and 13 Oct. 1700. The three men who charged the Wörners with discrimination were Matthias Schweyer, Hans Adelgoss and David Lemp, whose names appear particularly frequently among the accusers in the Confrontations-Protocoll.

the course of 1701, the council established a civic cooperative, the Lodenkasse, to conduct business, mostly with Switzerland, on behalf of any interested weavers. In order to assure a starting capital of some thousands, the city made a substantial initial investment in the venture, but all weavers were also invited to invest. The cooperative would accept Loden for resale at a commission, and the profits of the cooperative, instead of coming into private hands, would be redistributed to member investors in the form of dividends.[134]

For some years, this attempt by the city fathers to free their poorer fellow citizens from economic servitude seemed destined to success. Until 1709, the cooperative turned a profit each year. But then it began to fail. As the sole market for most weavers' products, it became glutted with finished goods and by 1708 it had to restrict the number of cloths that each master could submit. Meanwhile the weavers themselves began to lose their enthusiasm for the project, for under this system—as under the Wörners—their goods were sold by commission. Payments were delayed and they were as dependent as ever on credit. From 1710 on, the venture showed a deficit, and in 1712, unpopular both with the merchants and with the weavers it was supposed to benefit, the cooperative was abandoned and free trading reinstituted.[135]

When this happened, the Wörners were prepared to resume their dominant position in the city's economy. We cannot here trace in detail the careers of Daniel Wörner's sons following his death in 1699, but it must be emphasized that the family's setback had been more of a social and political one than a financial one. Daniel, the elder son, continued to augment his wealth: undoubtedly inheritances from his father, from his second wife (who died in 1704) and from his third wife (who died before 1711) must all have contributed to the increase in his wealth. By 1712, when the field was again open for extensive trading in tex-

[134] Ebert, *Lodweberei*, p. 41.

[135] Ibid., pp. 42-44.

tiles, his assessment stood at 26,600 fl., and it continued to grow somewhat until his death in 1733.

Even more successful, however, was the younger son, David. As an ironmonger, he was less affected than his brother by setbacks in the family's textile business. Around 1703 his designation in the tax registers changed from ironmonger to "merchant," and it is clear that he became increasingly involved in purely financial activities. Municipal records of the early eighteenth century show him making extensive loans (mostly at the customary rate of 6 percent per annum) to his fellow citizens.[136] By 1725, when he reached his peak assessment of 56,000 fl., he was securely established as the wealthiest man in the city, a position he retained until his death in 1741.

David was also the first member of his family to play a major role in the government of Nördlingen. To be sure, the beginning was not easy. After his father's death in 1699, David wanted to fill the vacancy thus created in the city court, but his family's reputation was then at its nadir. Only by virtually bribing the council—in the form of a 600 fl. gift to the hospital—did David obtain the coveted appointment.[137] Thereafter, however, his public career proceeded smoothly. In 1716, he was appointed to the city council and in 1733 to the privy council. By the time of his death, David had filled almost every position of dignity available to council members short of Bürgermeister.[138]

[136] Up to 1717 the loans normally involved amounts up to a few hundred gulden but from 1718 to 1723 he sometimes lent sums of 1,000 fl. or more. E.g., Pfb. 53, fols. 99, 112, 147, 272, 323; Pfb. 54, fols. 118, 182, 184, 248, 423, 471, 476b; Pfb. 55, fols. 105, 186, 198. The last-cited entry involves a loan of 3,000 fl.

[137] RP 5 Feb. 1700. This gift was the only recorded charitable grant by a member of the Wörner family in Nördlingen prior to the nineteenth century, according to the extensive, if not absolutely complete, list of such grants prepared by Hermann Frickhinger: "Die Stiftungen der Stadt Nördlingen (Schluss)," *JHVN*, 13 (1929), 43.

[138] Leichenpredigte: David Wörner, 1741, p. 16. During his membership on the council, he was elected at various stages to the posts

The Wörner family remained prominent in the public life of Nördlingen for the remainder of the eighteenth century. In the 1770's two Wörners—Daniel's son Johann Daniel and David's grandson Wilhelm Heinrich—became members of the city council.[139] By the middle of the century, the Wörners were related by marriage to many of the leading families of Nördlingen who dominated membership on the council.

But meanwhile the Wörners began to lose their position of economic dominance in Nördlingen. This role was taken over by Georg Christian von Troeltsch, a medical doctor of immense political and economic ambitions. By the middle of the eighteenth century, linen production had become one of Nördlingen's major industries, and it was in this field that Troeltsch developed a capitalist monopoly in many ways reminiscent of the Wörners'. But there was one crucial difference. The Wörners had built up their monopolistic position in the face of persistent hostility from the city government; Troeltsch worked from the inside. With imperial favor, he obtained appointment to the council in 1762 and soon after became Bürgermeister.[140] Only after he had established strong personal control over the council and the city government did he proceed to establish his commercial domination. Troeltsch first obtained control of the city's bleaching facilities; in addition, he began to secure a monopoly on yarn by systematically buying up all current and future crops of flax produced in the region. Eventually he succeeded in placing local weavers entirely at his mercy.[141]

Once again a ruthless entrepreneur aroused the hatred of weavers in Nördlingen, but this time the weavers had no recourse to a sympathetic council, for the council was headed by the very source of their grievances. Years of

---

of Oberrichter, Kriegsamtsverwalter, Hospitalpfleger and Consistorial-Rat.

139 Eidbuch IV (Jurament Buch), Rhatgeben Ayd.

140 Ibid., Bürgermeister Ayd and Rhatgeben Ayd.

141 Heinz Dannenbauer, "Leinenweberhandwerk," pp. 305-08.

struggle, including an appeal to the Reichshofrat in Vienna, proved futile for the weavers. Finally, in 1796, the weavers besieged the city hall and refused to let the council members leave until Troeltsch had promised to stop dealing in yarn "for ever and eternity." But the victory was short-lived. No sooner had he escaped the weavers' control than Troeltsch arranged for an imperial investigation of the incident: some of the leaders were imprisoned, and his signed promise was retracted as having been extorted by force.[142] This counter-attack severely crippled the weavers' movement, which finally died out during the Napoleonic era.

In 1803, the free city of Nördlingen was incorporated into the Kingdom of Bavaria, and Troeltsch lost his uniquely powerful political position. But the impact of his years of dominance persisted. For it was largely as a consequence of his activities that, in the words of a modern historian, the linen weavers of Nördlingen began "to sink from their old status as independent practitioners of a craft to wage-laborers in the service of excessively powerful capital."[143] This was, in fact, the same threat that had faced the wool weavers of Nördlingen a century earlier. But the city council of that era, though it no longer included craftsmen among its members, had still been dominated by a more traditional attitude toward the structure of the community: it was not prepared to let anyone drive an irrevocable wedge between laborers and capitalists within the same body of citizens. During the eighteenth century, however, the composition and attitudes of the council underwent considerable change. Its direct links to the craftsmen were totally lost; its membership became increasingly inbred and close-knit;[144] and after 1770 the council included, in the person of Troeltsch, the fusion of supreme political and economic power. The magistrates were by now far more inclined to serve as the agents of capitalist entrepreneurs than as the

142 Ibid., pp. 309-12.

143 Ibid., p. 314.

144 Lettenmeyer, *Finanzwirtschaft*, pp. 114-15.

protectors of a stratum of independent craftsmen. Seen in the context of these later events, Daniel Wörner and his sons appear more clearly as the precursors of a modern era and their opponents emerge as the last defenders of the medieval tradition in Nördlingen.

Ten

Conclusion

THE German language makes no distinction between "city" and "town"—the word *Stadt* covers both. In early modern Germany this term was applied to a great variety of urban settlements, ranging from cosmopolitan centers of 40,000 or 50,000 inhabitants down to market towns of 500 souls who tenaciously clung to the medieval privilege of calling their community a Stadt.

Our image of urban society in early modern Germany is largely formed by what we know of the first kind of community: cities of international importance like Hamburg, Frankfurt, Nuremberg or Cologne. Ruled by aristocratic patriciates; economically dominated by active and ambitious merchants; inhabited not only by industrious artisans but also by floating populations of laborers, beggars and vagrants; characterized by a hierarchical and highly stratified social structure—such was the Augsburg of the Fuggers or the Frankfurt of young Goethe's time.[1]

There was also, however, a very different type of urban society in early modern Germany. In his provocative study of German "home towns" after 1648, Mack Walker has

[1] On Augsburg, see Friedrich Blendinger, "Versuch einer Bestimmung der Mittelschicht in der Reichsstadt Augsburg vom Ende des 14. bis zum Anfang des 18. Jahrhunderts," in Erich Maschke and Jürgen Sydow, *Städtische Mittelschichten* (Veröffentlichungen der Kommission für geschichtliche Landeskunde in Baden-Württemberg, Reihe B, Bd. 69; Stuttgart, 1972), pp. 32-78; on Frankfurt, see Gerald Lyman Soliday, *A Community in Conflict: Frankfurt Society in the Seventeenth and Early Eighteenth Centuries* (Hanover, N.H., 1974). The standard comparative study of larger German cities remains Hans Mauersberg, *Wirtschafts- und Sozialgeschichte zentraleuropäischer Städte in neuerer Zeit, dargestellt an den Beispielen von Basel, Frankfurt a.M., Hamburg, Hannover und München* (Göttingen, 1960).

focused attention on the smaller cities of the Holy Roman Empire, backwater communities which rarely amounted to more than 10,000 inhabitants. Such communities, he argues, were economically self-sufficient, hostile to outsiders, and demographically almost self-contained. "Both city and countryside," Walker tells us, "experienced greater mobility of population than the small town."[2] Above all, the "home town" tended to be socially homogeneous:

> Of course the community knew clear gradations of wealth, influence and social standing. . . . But it did not tolerate too wide a spread or too rapid a shift, nor did the gradations make differences among home-townsmen even comparable to the differences between themselves and other castes. The home town maintained a steady pressure on all members toward the median. . . . Guilds were conscious and recognized institutions for maintaining a satisfactory degree of equality. . . .[3]

What we have learned about Nördlingen does not conform closely to either of these images of urban society in early modern Germany. Nördlingen was much too small to rank as one of Germany's cosmopolitan cities. Yet at the same time it fits only partly Walker's description of the classic "home town." In fact Nördlingen combined features of both types of community, and it is just this which makes Nördlingen interesting as a case study of urban society in early modern times.

To start with, Nördlingen was highly stratified in terms of wealth. Indeed, tremendous variations were evident not only in the community as a whole but also within individual occupational groups. Far from maintaining equality among

[2] Mack Walker, *German Home Towns: Community, State and General Estate, 1648-1871* (Ithaca, N.Y., 1971), pp. 26-33 and passim. (The quotation is from p. 31.)

[3] Ibid., pp. 133-34. It may be noted that Walker specifically cites Nördlingen in his analysis of "hometown" political mores, pp. 42-43.

its members, each craft organization was likely to harbor a vast range of different wealth levels.

Extensive mobility also characterized Nördlingen's society during the sixteenth and seventeenth centuries. Occupational mobility was limited—only two out of every five men chose careers different from their fathers', and only one of six changed occupations during his lifetime. But mobility of wealth was the norm in Nördlingen, resulting from a ceaseless interplay of inheritances, marriages and economic success or failure. Equally striking was the extent of geographical mobility: emigration and immigration. Indeed, geographical mobility was built right into the fabric of urban life in early modern Germany: the system of *Wanderjahre*, for example, sent young men hundreds of miles away from home in search of training and—in many cases—in search of women to marry and places to settle in. The society of Nördlingen was profoundly affected by such movement. No records exist for the systematic study of emigration from the city, but marriage and citizenship records do make clear the enormous importance of immigration to seventeenth-century Nördlingen. Before the Thirty Years War, nearly half of the children born in Nördlingen must have had at least one foreign-born parent; a much greater proportion would have had at least one foreign-born grandparent.[4]

But various types of mobility, no matter how extensive, must not be equated with instability, and in a community like Nördlingen the situation was often quite the opposite. In the first place, all forms of mobility were carefully watched and closely regulated. For an outsider to take up residence in the city or for a citizen to move elsewhere (let

[4] Table 2.1 (Chapter Two) shows that between 1581 and 1610, 41% to 47% of the spouses in Nördlingen marriages were immigrants to the city. The children of these marriages had at least one foreign-born parent; to these must be added the children of immigrant couples who were already married before they settled down in Nördlingen.

alone for the former to acquire citizenship or for the latter to terminate it), permission from the city council was always necessary. Similarly, changes in occupation required the magistrates' approval. Wealth mobility did not as such require the council's permission, of course, but changes in wealth took place within a framework of specific inheritance laws and marriage customs, not to mention the close supervision of all property transactions and trading activities.

In the second place, mobility did not necessarily involve a significant change in social status. Balancing out geographical mobility, for example, were a number of integrative mechanisms which functioned to reduce the cleavage between natives and newly admitted aliens. Each craft organization, as we have seen, was part of a network of guilds that stretched from one city to the next, and this made it easier for the newcomer to adjust to a fresh milieu. In addition, since most immigrants married into local families, their children would have grandparents, uncles and aunts who were natives. Occupational mobility did not always involve a change in consciousness: a citizen would frequently retain his sense of identification with the craft for which he had been trained. Much the same is true of wealth mobility. In fact, precisely because wealth mobility was so normal a feature of a citizen's career, it would not necessarily bring about a change in the way either he or others viewed his social status.

Far from being an instrument of social change, mobility often served to stabilize the social order. The huge increase in immigration which followed the plague of 1634 is a vivid example of the restorative function of geographical mobility. An equally stabilizing effect can be attributed to wealth mobility, for as long as upward wealth mobility could form part of his normal expectations—or at least his aspirations—even the poorest citizen of Nördlingen was likely to accept his lot in life.

Seen in this light, it would appear that the greatest threat to social harmony lay not in an increase but in a decrease of wealth mobility: only when poorer citizens sensed that the avenue to advancement was blocked were they likely to rise in protest. Precisely this happened in the late seventeenth century. In the 1690's there were two episodes of explosive protest in Nördlingen—bread riots in 1693-94 and agitation among the weavers in 1698. It is no accident that these outbursts coincided with a period of particularly limited wealth mobility in Nördlingen.

The targets of these protests were not the magistrates of Nördlingen; indeed, Nördlingen remained remarkably free of the kind of structured conflict between council and citizenry which animated the political life of so many German cities in the early modern era.[5] In the late seventeenth century the magistrates of Nördlingen were still dedicated to paternalistic principles of government, and the citizens recognized this fact. Their animus was directed instead against unscrupulous merchants—whether corn traders or textile magnates—who were seen to be violating the traditional norms of community life.

Yet protests of this sort could hardly stem the tide of change in Nördlingen. Even the magistrates found it impossible in the long run to prevent new economic attitudes and practices from taking root in Nördlingen. For these new practices were only part of a broad pattern of economic and social changes—changes whose origins were closely bound up with the fact that the seventeenth century was an age of war in Nördlingen.

ANY discussion of the impact of warfare on seventeenth-

[5] On this subject, see Reinhard Hildebrandt, "Rat contra Bürgerschaft: Die Verfassungskonflikte in den Reichsstädten des 17. und 18. Jahrhunderts," *Zeitschrift für Stadtgeschichte, Stadtsoziologie und Denkmalpflege*, 1 (1974), 221-41, and Christopher R. Friedrichs, "Citizens or Subjects? Urban Conflict in Early Modern Germany," in Miriam Usher Chrisman and Otto Gründler, eds., *Social Groups and Religious Ideas in the Sixteenth Century* (Studies in Medieval Culture, 13; Kalamazoo, Mich., 1978), pp. 46-58, 164-69.

century Nördlingen must, of course, begin with the Thirty Years War. For the war of 1618-48 did have a devastating impact on the community—on the solvency of the municipal treasury, on the size of the community and on the collective and per capita wealth of its citizens. Yet our results have also suggested how misleading it is to single out this war as the one crucially destructive event in German history of the seventeenth century. For in fact, as we have seen, the citizenry of Nördlingen enjoyed a significant economic recovery in the peaceful years following the Peace of Westphalia. It was a new series of wars—the imperial conflicts against the Turks and the French—that arrested this recovery and once again drained the community of its resources.

Certainly, the later wars of the seventeenth century did not exact the same toll in human lives in Nördlingen as had the Thirty Years War. But these wars did arrest the demographic recovery which Nördlingen had experienced ever since the catastrophe of the 1630's. And the economic effects of the French and Turkish wars equaled or even exceeded those of the Thirty Years War. Civic expenditures in real terms soared far above the level of the 1630's, imposing a massive debt burden on the community. The effects of these financial demands were clearly mirrored in the declining wealth of Nördlingen's inhabitants. By the early eighteenth century the gains which Nördlingen's citizens had made between 1650 and 1670 had been completely wiped out.

An analogous pattern can be observed if we look at the changing distribution of wealth in Nördlingen. In 1579, the richest tenth of the citizenry had possessed some 60 percent of the community's total wealth, and by the end of the Thirty Years War this group had increased its share to 74 percent: wartime taxation evidently took a relatively smaller amount from the rich than from the poor. But the economic recovery of the 1650's and 1660's coincided with a significant redistribution of wealth: by 1670, the proportion of wealth owned by the richest tenth had dropped down to

54 percent, and the share owned by the bottom nine-tenths obviously rose correspondingly—a clear gain for the middling and (to some extent) the poorer citizens. The year 1670, however, was the high watermark in the redistribution of wealth. The renewed arrival of war—and of wartime taxation—saw the arrest and reversal of this trend, and by 1724 the distribution of wealth was approaching the highly skewed pattern of 1646. In short, the second round of imperial wars had two basic effects on Nördlingen: it both terminated a general economic recovery and restored an older, more unequal pattern of wealth distribution.

Facts like these can serve to remind us powerfully of the conservative potential of warfare—a potential, moreover, which can become evident not only in terms of social or economic structures, but also in terms of political behavior. We are accustomed to thinking of wars as having a profoundly disturbing effect on society, dissolving old social routines and creating new patterns of allegiance. But wars can also have a conservative effect, for in times of stress people may rally behind accustomed leaders or take comfort in traditional ways of doing things. Certainly, none of the seventeenth-century wars caused any dramatic changes in the patterns of political authority or behavior in this community. The continuity of political leadership—both in terms of personnel and in terms of institutions—was never broken.

To be sure, during the course of the seventeenth century there was a change in the composition of the community's major political organ, for craftsmen came to be completely excluded from membership on the city council. But in fact this trend was symptomatic of a much more fundamental social transition—one which the brief redistributory tendency of the interwar years was unable to stem: a slow but pronounced loss of status on the part of the community's craftsmen.

In the course of the seventeenth century the status of the craft masters was increasingly threatened. In the first place, the traditional urban monopoly on production broke down as city craftsmen were faced with serious competition from village artisans. Often the development of rural industry was encouraged by capitalist entrepreneurs who put the villagers on the domestic system, supplying them with raw materials and buying back the finished products. It was easy for entrepreneurs to do this in the countryside, where there were no guild traditions and where less humiliation was attached to a status of economic dependency. But eventually, as we have seen, many urban masters also began to fall into this relationship with the entrepreneurs. In the case of Nördlingen's principal industry, wool weaving, this development appears to have begun in the last decades of the seventeenth century —precisely the period when, after the years of recovery, the economic position of the city's poorer citizens was again being eroded by the renewed imposition of huge wartime taxes.

Thus, by the end of the seventeenth century, a number of interrelated developments can be detected in Nördlingen: the breakdown of an urban monopoly on industrial production, the growth of entrepreneurial capitalism, the decline of the traditional craft system based on independent masters, and a loss of political and social status by the artisanry. None of these developments, of course, was unique to Nördlingen: sooner or later virtually every European city experienced these things as part of the transition from a medieval to a modern outlook and social structure. But this transition did not occur in each place at the same time, or at the same tempo, or in the same way. It is for precisely this reason that it is important for historians to examine the history of individual communities—not just to find out what happened but also to establish when it happened and how it came about. For the more we learn about when and how this fundamental transition occurred in specific local regions and communities, the better we will understand how the process of change took place in general.

From this point of view, it is particularly important to

emphasize that the developments summarized above were only starting to appear in Nördlingen by the end of the seventeenth century. Many craftsmen, as we have seen, were beginning to sink into economic dependency, but this pattern had not yet extended to all artisans—nor even to all wool weavers—by 1700. Furthermore, the community as a whole was still completely unwilling to accept the implications of this incipient change in its economic structure. The ruling elite of commercial and professional groups in the late seventeenth and early eighteenth centuries was still prepared to defend the interests of the craftsmen against the intrusions of entrepreneurial capitalism. To some extent, the magistrates were influenced by personal hostility toward the leading entrepreneurial family. But beneath this lay a more fundamental aversion toward any threat to the traditional economic independence of the citizen-master. This attitude, we can be sure, was not based on a mere nostalgia for an older way of life; after all, the artisan who had become economically dependent on another man was also more likely, in times of stress, to become dependent on the community itself. For under the traditional ethos which still prevailed in 1700, when a man became a citizen he assumed certain obligations toward the community, but the community also assumed certain obligations toward him.

In the course of the eighteenth century, however, all this changed. By the late 1700's, the magistracy had become identified—in both policy and personnel—with the interests of entrepreneurial capitalism. The linen weavers of the late eighteenth century, like the wool weavers of the late seventeenth, attempted to fight against their transformation into contract laborers, but now they found the oligarchy of Nördlingen ranged solidly against them. It seems likely, moreover, that this change in the attitude of the elite both reflected and contributed to a continuing loss of economic status on the part of the industrial craftsmen. The attitude of the late eighteenth-century magistracy makes clear that the craftsmen, while still citizens, had continued to lose standing and importance in the eyes of the elite; in fact, the city's rulers no longer felt an obligation to protect them from the consequences of a freely-operating capitalist system. The transition from a traditional, protective, guild-oriented economy and society to a capitalist economy and class society was everywhere a very gradual one. Yet the crucial breakthrough in Nördlingen clearly took place in the eighteenth century.

If this is so, however, then the Thirty Years War can hardly stand out as a crucial determinant in this transition. Indeed, deleterious as its effects were, the war was followed by a period of economic recovery, in which the poorer strata, including the craftsmen, fully participated. It was only the renewal of warfare and military taxation in the later seventeenth century that seems to have had a permanently crippling effect on the artisans: and it is certainly during this period that we can observe the first major episode in their decline into economic dependence.

It would be injudicious, of course, to minimize the impact of the Thirty Years War on Nördlingen. But in attempting to understand the structural changes in the city's society, it would be even more misleading to neglect the importance of the second round of warfare, which began in the 1660's, intensified in the 1670's and continued with few interruptions until 1714. Nor was the impact of these wars limited to Nördlingen alone. As the study of German urban and social history continues, the old debate about the effects of the Thirty Years War must give way to a new and more comprehensive discussion about the impact of the whole cycle of wars which affected Germany during the century between the Defenestration of Prague and the Peace of Utrecht.

APPENDIX I

Population Statistics for Nördlingen, 1579-1720: Baptisms, Marriages, Burials

THE tables in this appendix provide aggregate demographic statistics for the city of Nördlingen from 1579 to 1720. The main sources for the demographic history of Nördlingen are the marriage and baptismal registers of the parish church of St. Georg (available from 1579 onward) and the burial register of St. Georg (available from April 1618 onward). All baptisms and most marriages and burials which took place in the city were recorded in these registers. Some additional marriages and burials were recorded in the registers of the Nördlingen hospital parish (available from 1602 onward; now deposited in Nähermemmingen). The following statistics combine data from both series.

It should be stressed that in addition to recording vital events for all the inhabitants of Nördlingen, the St. Georg and hospital registers also include data for a number of nonresidents. All children from the village of Baldingen were baptized at St. Georg's, and Baldingen marriages and burials were entered in the hospital register. In addition, baptisms, marriages and burials of numerous other villagers, soldiers, travelers, religious refugees and other nonresidents were recorded in both series of registers. In order to provide a meaningful analysis of demographic trends for the city of Nördlingen itself, it is necessary to distinguish between residents and nonresidents, as has been done in the following tables.

For baptisms, the data are complete from 1579 onward. Since parents who were nonresidents of Nördlingen are always indicated as such, it is easy to divide the children into the two categories.

For burials, the data given here commence with 1619, the first full year for which both the St. Georg's and the hospital parish registers are available. It is normally easy to distinguish between residents and nonresidents. It should be stressed, however, that the distinction is made not on the basis of place of origin but on the basis of place of residence at the time of death. For example, a person denoted as "Hans Schmidt from Bopfingen, for many years servant in the hospital" would be recorded as a resident. By contrast, soldiers quartered in Nördlingen, journeymen temporarily in the city, and of course travelers and villagers are recorded as nonresidents.

Virtually every burial entry in the Nördlingen registers includes an indication of the deceased's age at death. The reconstitution study described in Chapter Two has made clear that these entries are generally very accurate; even in the case of adults they are rarely off by more than one year. The tables below divide all burials into three categories: infants (up to one year), children (ages 1-12) and youths and adults (over 12 years); the entries are also, of course, divided by sex. Even in the occasional cases in which age at death was not given, it was easy to determine to which of the three broad age categories the deceased belonged.

The St. Georg's marriage register recorded each marriage for which the banns were read. The register is available from 1579 onward, with the exception of 1640, for which no entries are extant. From 1602 onward, a few additional marriage entries are also available from the hospital parish registers and these marriages have been added to the total figures recorded below. Thus, the figures for 1579-1601 may slightly undercount the total number of marriages performed in Nördlingen; but there is no danger of significant distortion. (For example, for the period 1602-20 there are on the average 83 marriages per year in the St. Georg's register but only 6 per year in the hospital register, of which almost all involve villagers only.)

Though the St. Georg's register actually records banns read, the few instances in which the marriage did not subsequently take place—for example, due to the death of one partner—were carefully recorded and have not been counted in the tables below. There were also some cases in which the banns were read in Nördlingen but the marriage was performed elsewhere. These cases have been included, since it can be shown that such couples often returned to settle down in Nördlingen right after the wedding. Marriages for which the banns were read in late December, but which were only solemnized in January, are counted under the later year.

The distinction between residents and nonresidents is less self-evident in the case of marriages than in the case of baptisms or burials, since it frequently happened that one partner was a native and one partner was not. In this tabulation, the column marked "residents" denotes all those marriages for which it can be ascertained or assumed that the marriage partners settled down in Nördlingen after the wedding, no matter whether one or both spouses had come from out of town. Under "nonresidents" are recorded marriages among Baldingen residents or other villagers, marriages of travelers and soldiers, and marriages in which there is some other indication that the couple concerned did not live in Nördlingen.

For the period before about 1650 there are a few cases in which the distinction between resident and nonresident couples is not completely obvious; as a rule, couples have been classified as residents unless there is specific information to suggest otherwise. From about 1650 on there are no ambiguous cases, because the groom's place of residence is always listed in addition to that of his father.

For more detailed information about the origins of spouses among the resident couples, see Table 2.1 in the text.

TABLE A.I.1. Marriages and Baptisms

	Marriages		*Baptisms*					
			Residents			*Nonresidents*		
Year	*Residents*	*Nonresidents*	*M*	*F*	*Total*	*M*	*F*	*Total*
1579	101	3	202	189	391	21	25	46
1580	81	2	217	194	411	19	23	42
1581	79	3	187	186	373	27	24	51
1582	66	2	213	194	407	21	23	44
1583	108	1	176	201	377	24	23	47
1584	97	—	215	182	397	25	25	50
1585	78	7	211	217	428	26	21	47
1586	76	5	196	179	375	20	20	40
1587	69	4	179	168	347	23	23	46
1588	77	8	167	201	368	22	23	45
1589	61	2	195	165	360	29	21	50
1590	68	2	197	176	373	24	19	43
1591	73	12	180	158	338	22	12	34
1592	80	1	184	171	355	24	25	49
1593	63	—	185	173	358	22	24	46
1594	85	2	159	167	326	23	21	44
1595	74	7	176	181	357	32	28	60
1596	90	7	183	176	359	22	19	41
1597	78	10	175	168	343	27	17	44
1598	89	5	172	153	325	22	25	47
1599	84	6	175	170	345	24	8	32
1600	68	6	167	179	346	28	22	50
1601	58	3	186	139	325	18	18	36
1602	76	9	157	165	322	20	14	34
1603	100	6	158	157	315	20	19	39
1604	83	9	166	165	331	18	21	39
1605	92	12	159	149	308	15	23	38
1606	102	14	177	187	364	19	24	43
1607	86	7	177	190	367	14	14	28
1608	63	10	190	185	375	15	19	34
1609	70	11	174	146	320	18	19	37
1610	85	12	173	189	362	23	22	45

TABLE A.I.1. Marriages and Baptisms—(Cont.)

	Marriages		*Baptisms*					
			Residents			*Nonresidents*		
Year	*Residents*	*Nonresidents*	*M*	*F*	*Total*	*M*	*F*	*Total*
1611	80	19	163	164	327	15	14	29
1612	69	15	163	160	323	22	24	46
1613	65	8	163	173	336	15	16	31
1614	56	13	172	161	333	21	18	39
1615	53	9	152	144	296	15	20	35
1616	64	17	138	178	316	14	21	35
1617	63	13	150	130	280	16	15	31
1618	90	13	145	141	286	27	24	51
1619	91	11	154	147	301	15	21	36
1620	75	14	156	161	317	29	19	48
1621	76	17	143	144	287	25	21	46
1622	75	11	150	165	315	27	26	53
1623	85	9	155	137	292	21	18	39
1624	82	16	161	138	299	25	28	53
1625	65	14	172	154	326	12	25	37
1626	65	10	140	135	275	28	18	46
1627	63	12	144	124	268	8	27	35
1628	37	7	159	147	306	10	15	25
1629	48	9	152	142	294	30	19	49
1630	81	24	129	137	266	33	18	51
1631	45	9	141	161	302	44	42	86
1632	60	17	131	131	262	39	46	85
1633	114	43	127	126	253	59	56	115
1634	47	28	135	123	258	80	74	154
1635	200	55	68	63	131	22	23	45
1636	55	30	110	116	226	39	30	69
1637	33	21	107	115	222	45	53	98
1638	38	22	108	102	210	70	57	127
1639	41	14	91	110	201	83	76	159
1640	—	—	104	96	200	64	57	121

TABLE A.I.1. Marriages and Baptisms—(Cont.)

Year	Marriages: Residents	Marriages: Nonresidents	Baptisms: Residents M	Baptisms: Residents F	Baptisms: Residents Total	Baptisms: Nonresidents M	Baptisms: Nonresidents F	Baptisms: Nonresidents Total
1641	31	16	106	122	228	72	80	152
1642	42	16	95	116	211	59	60	119
1643	35	11	105	115	220	64	66	130
1644	44	22	103	105	208	60	35	95
1645	32	25	109	111	220	98	104	202
1646	39	20	105	95	200	108	79	187
1647	38	37	100	103	203	109	101	210
1648	36	29	105	106	211	134	113	247
1649	39	23	111	82	193	48	61	109
1650	45	23	89	99	188	38	34	72
1651	40	16	99	94	193	26	22	48
1652	33	16	106	98	204	27	24	51
1653	40	13	97	117	214	21	18	39
1654	50	17	103	94	197	18	25	43
1655	39	14	126	109	235	22	18	40
1656	41	16	111	99	210	18	10	28
1657	32	9	119	110	229	16	6	22
1658	30	11	92	112	204	16	12	28
1659	58	15	104	95	199	13	16	29
1660	32	14	119	110	229	12	8	20
1661	43	10	96	102	198	12	13	25
1662	52	7	111	94	205	10	7	17
1663	43	18	118	109	227	13	11	24
1664	50	11	109	117	226	13	9	22
1665	54	13	116	117	233	9	13	22
1666	62	12	104	110	214	16	13	29
1667	36	16	100	136	236	9	13	22
1668	55	6	104	128	232	17	15	32
1669	53	9	116	110	226	14	15	29
1670	54	15	126	119	245	19	8	27

TABLE A.I.1. Marriages and Baptisms—(Cont.)

	Marriages		Baptisms					
			Residents			Nonresidents		
Year	Residents	Nonresidents	M	F	Total	M	F	Total
1671	51	7	139	109	248	10	14	24
1672	48	10	143	117	260	12	9	21
1673	63	11	128	146	274	12	10	22
1674	60	15	153	148	301	19	15	34
1675	45	13	143	129	272	6	8	14
1676	47	16	150	131	281	10	16	26
1677	43	13	150	146	296	15	12	27
1678	49	18	131	139	270	12	11	23
1679	64	14	140	164	304	11	10	21
1680	50	15	175	117	292	20	11	31
1681	58	13	160	140	300	12	14	26
1682	51	11	136	172	308	10	14	24
1683	45	14	158	141	299	11	15	26
1684	37	8	139	148	287	15	13	28
1685	63	16	135	135	270	7	14	21
1686	56	12	157	140	297	13	8	21
1687	45	6	162	153	315	11	18	29
1688	57	12	156	129	285	12	19	31
1689	56	18	132	135	267	17	10	27
1690	44	8	140	149	289	13	14	27
1691	41	12	130	130	260	13	14	27
1692	33	11	128	132	260	14	9	23
1693	48	10	108	123	231	12	16	28
1694	56	18	103	106	209	17	12	29
1695	46	12	109	108	217	19	17	36
1696	54	24	122	128	250	15	22	37
1697	43	19	123	116	239	19	12	31
1698	48	15	117	119	236	16	18	34
1699	54	15	122	107	229	18	14	32
1700	51	9	125	106	231	7	14	21

TABLE A.I.1. Marriages and Baptisms—(Cont.)

	Marriages		*Baptisms*					
			Residents			*Nonresidents*		
Year	*Residents*	*Nonresidents*	*M*	*F*	*Total*	*M*	*F*	*Total*
1701	52	11	116	153	269	14	13	27
1702	41	7	112	120	232	11	15	26
1703	40	16	117	136	253	41	32	73
1704	68	11	130	117	247	32	29	61
1705	102	30	123	123	246	19	12	31
1706	54	12	140	147	287	17	14	31
1707	41	16	147	156	303	11	16	27
1708	52	10	148	136	284	17	12	29
1709	50	16	140	160	300	8	14	22
1710	51	11	142	146	288	14	11	25
1711	47	10	133	125	258	15	20	35
1712	44	11	121	129	250	17	13	30
1713	56	12	124	107	231	8	10	18
1714	33	11	124	124	248	15	14	29
1715	68	17	146	111	257	20	17	37
1716	59	13	149	132	281	23	20	43
1717	46	13	151	125	276	22	17	39
1718	54	9	147	153	300	21	10	31
1719	53	9	145	142	287	21	10	31
1720	63	16	151	150	301	15	13	28

TABLE A.I.2. Burials: (A) Residents

Year	Adults and Youths M	Adults and Youths F	Children (ages 1-12) M	Children (ages 1-12) F	Infants (under 1) M	Infants (under 1) F	Total
1619	48	58	13	8	35	30	192
1620	42	58	31	39	57	45	272
1621	54	88	12	26	46	45	271
1622	51	85	10	13	43	41	243
1623	72	94	22	24	81	39	332
1624	31	61	11	37	65	42	247
1625	40	50	6	13	50	56	215
1626	38	76	10	12	64	41	241
1627	63	114	22	16	39	31	285
1628	48	83	13	12	44	47	247
1629	107	171	53	67	82	61	541
1630	78	107	18	34	50	29	316
1631	42	65	11	9	63	51	241
1632	139	144	21	22	71	66	463
1633	114	150	16	22	79	74	455
1634	493	667	127	154	58	50	1,549
1635	48	50	11	16	22	17	164
1636	28	30	6	7	41	34	146
1637	21	40	11	3	54	45	174
1638	30	35	11	4	47	32	159
1639	17	42	6	14	47	45	171
1640	23	22	7	14	47	42	155
1641	11	23	11	4	40	29	118
1642	15	26	5	7	42	31	126
1643	28	26	13	17	42	34	160
1644	23	25	23	20	37	41	169
1645	39	48	20	35	67	76	285
1646	29	27	15	12	45	32	160
1647	23	38	10	15	50	44	180
1648	36	32	9	8	53	49	187
1649	25	29	6	6	35	31	132
1650	24	21	7	11	36	34	133

TABLE A.I.2. Burials: (A) Residents—(cont.)

Year	Adults and Youths		Children (ages 1-12)		Infants (under 1)		Total
	M	F	M	F	M	F	
1651	21	32	12	14	33	34	146
1652	20	22	11	7	39	31	130
1653	19	24	8	2	39	41	133
1654	14	34	9	8	38	24	127
1655	14	32	11	13	40	35	145
1656	26	24	12	5	41	25	133
1657	22	28	13	10	53	36	162
1658	16	34	7	2	39	34	132
1659	20	25	16	17	41	34	153
1660	20	33	6	11	42	52	164
1661	24	40	6	4	46	27	147
1662	22	37	6	6	50	35	156
1663	17	38	8	13	50	28	154
1664	53	39	12	16	48	37	205
1665	33	46	8	6	58	27	178
1666	30	41	9	11	31	37	159
1667	30	38	5	8	39	38	158
1668	31	48	6	4	38	33	160
1669	27	52	39	54	65	66	303
1670	39	45	2	6	48	37	177
1671	20	43	4	7	54	40	168
1672	33	52	8	10	66	39	208
1673	33	47	9	6	51	52	198
1674	22	50	12	12	73	57	226
1675	36	69	37	39	64	53	298
1676	45	55	15	19	78	65	277
1677	23	37	6	11	65	52	194
1678	53	67	10	19	68	80	297
1679	38	50	27	20	67	79	281
1680	34	38	7	5	93	64	241
1681	28	49	11	12	71	51	222
1682	36	37	14	10	55	58	210
1683	30	42	24	27	95	68	286
1684	39	46	7	11	71	77	251
1685	35	42	6	14	68	56	221

TABLE A.I.2. Burials: (A) Residents—(cont.)

Year	Adults and Youths M	Adults and Youths F	Children (ages 1-12) M	Children (ages 1-12) F	Infants (under 1) M	Infants (under 1) F	Total
1686	33	49	18	20	86	70	276
1687	37	42	17	16	76	74	262
1688	38	51	12	13	90	71	275
1689	43	44	11	16	60	47	221
1690	44	53	14	20	62	67	260
1691	30	53	22	15	76	81	277
1692	39	53	12	6	70	55	235
1693	55	84	29	35	61	68	332
1694	57	67	11	14	65	52	266
1695	34	52	17	12	53	46	214
1696	24	36	11	10	57	52	190
1697	35	34	8	21	55	56	209
1698	33	39	17	20	67	55	231
1699	25	38	6	13	69	42	193
1700	38	56	6	13	76	50	239
1701	27	49	13	13	55	72	229
1702	24	44	5	5	48	63	189
1703	59	81	15	15	73	72	315
1704	75	77	28	21	99	98	398
1705	31	40	20	10	54	59	214
1706	23	32	10	17	74	64	220
1707	32	41	7	7	75	64	226
1708	27	41	17	9	88	73	255
1709	38	34	14	12	76	91	265
1710	29	38	4	7	80	79	237
1711	23	41	6	14	67	57	208
1712	39	48	7	14	67	53	228
1713	32	49	11	16	50	50	208
1714	40	55	13	17	66	40	231
1715	42	51	12	12	79	63	259
1716	31	44	6	16	74	56	227
1717	41	49	25	43	100	82	340
1718	39	28	10	7	78	70	232
1719	41	61	16	11	82	63	274
1720	31	53	17	16	73	54	244

TABLE A.I.3. Burials: (B) Nonresidents

	Adults and Youths		*Children (ages 1-12)*		*Infants (under 1)*		
Year	*M*	*F*	*M*	*F*	*M*	*F*	*Total*
1619	13	7	—	3	1	—	24
1620	10	5	1	2	1	1	20
1621	12	10	—	2	—	1	25
1622	9	8	—	1	3	—	21
1623	3	6	—	2	5	1	17
1624	9	6	2	2	1	1	21
1625	9	12	2	—	2	—	25
1626	7	9	2	3	1	—	22
1627	9	9	—	—	1	2	21
1628	6	8	—	1	1	1	17
1629	11	26	6	7	1	—	51
1630	9	11	—	—	2	1	23
1631	5	5	—	—	2	3	15
1632	52	40	5	7	12	10	126
1633	53	51	10	9	11	12	146
1634	137	135	26	23	14	8	343
1635	22	12	1	1	—	—	36
1636	14	11	—	—	3	3	31
1637	9	12	4	4	7	9	45
1638	12	9	4	—	17	14	56
1639	22	18	8	5	18	19	90
1640	6	9	1	3	23	19	61
1641	11	14	2	4	13	22	66
1642	1	8	2	3	14	12	40
1643	10	9	2	4	15	21	61
1644	7	11	9	9	25	14	75
1645	26	32	29	25	51	50	213
1646	18	13	6	12	37	21	107
1647	10	21	6	9	41	32	119
1648	31	17	7	13	36	30	134
1649	7	13	5	4	18	6	53
1650	1	12	6	3	9	5	36

TABLE A.I.3. Burials: (B) Nonresidents—(cont.)

	Adults and Youths		*Children (ages 1-12)*		*Infants (under 1)*		
Year	*M*	*F*	*M*	*F*	*M*	*F*	*Total*
1651	6	10	2	3	8	6	35
1652	3	11	3	1	5	7	30
1653	5	5	—	1	7	5	23
1654	3	11	1	—	5	7	27
1655	6	8	—	2	6	4	26
1656	5	10	3	—	4	6	28
1657	5	4	2	3	8	2	24
1658	2	7	2	1	4	1	17
1659	6	5	2	2	6	4	25
1660	6	8	—	2	4	5	25
1661	4	11	—	1	2	5	23
1662	8	8	2	1	5	5	29
1663	10	11	—	—	4	5	30
1664	8	4	1	1	7	6	27
1665	2	1	1	2	6	2	14
1666	4	12	—	3	3	4	26
1667	2	6	1	—	2	2	13
1668	7	9	—	—	6	1	23
1669	6	10	2	4	3	4	29
1670	4	12	1	—	5	4	26
1671	4	9	1	3	3	3	23
1672	5	4	1	1	4	2	17
1673	12	6	1	—	3	3	25
1674	2	9	1	—	7	4	23
1675	15	19	3	2	2	1	42
1676	7	11	1	1	4	5	29
1677	7	7	2	2	4	4	26
1678	5	6	2	2	9	5	29
1679	4	12	1	1	5	7	30
1680	3	13	1	—	6	4	27
1681	5	4	—	—	3	6	18
1682	7	5	—	2	3	5	22
1683	4	8	—	—	4	7	23
1684	8	10	3	2	6	8	37
1685	—	8	—	2	3	4	17

TABLE A.I.3. Burials: (B) Nonresidents—(cont.)

Year	Adults and Youths		Children (ages 1-12)		Infants (under 1)		Total
	M	F	M	F	M	F	
1686	1	8	—	1	5	7	22
1687	8	9	—	2	7	5	31
1688	4	3	2	1	7	6	23
1689	7	9	1	—	8	—	25
1690	7	13	—	2	6	8	36
1691	5	3	—	2	6	5	21
1692	4	10	—	1	4	6	25
1693	10	10	4	3	8	7	42
1694	8	7	1	7	4	5	32
1695	9	5	1	2	7	7	31
1696	2	8	3	—	6	10	29
1697	2	5	2	—	13	6	28
1698	3	1	—	1	8	8	21
1699	3	13	—	2	9	8	35
1700	4	7	1	1	9	6	28
1701	3	7	1	1	13	7	32
1702	6	6	2	3	7	9	33
1703	29	16	4	4	11	16	80
1704	134	7	9	8	24	19	201
1705	5	3	—	2	5	1	16
1706	4	10	1	2	9	7	33
1707	2	6	—	—	8	2	18
1708	7	9	1	5	11	9	42
1709	3	4	1	—	7	4	19
1710	3	4	2	1	4	2	16
1711	3	8	2	3	4	11	31
1712	3	5	2	—	7	5	22
1713	6	4	2	3	4	5	24
1714	2	10	1	—	5	3	21
1715	1	8	2	1	8	3	23
1716	1	6	1	—	9	1	18
1717	2	5	1	—	6	5	19
1718	3	4	2	2	8	6	25
1719	5	7	4	2	11	9	38
1720	4	7	1	—	3	4	19

APPENDIX II

Distribution of Occupations Among Male Citizens In Five Selected Years

In order to illustrate the whole range of occupations in Nördlingen, this appendix records all male occupations listed in the tax records for 1579-1724, even if no representative of a given occupation happens to be recorded in one of the five years selected here.[a] Spelling of most German designations has been modernized.

Occupation	*Most Common German Designation(s)*	*1579*	*1615*	*1652*	*1700*	*1724*
	TEXTILE AND CLOTHING CRAFTS					
Weaving						
Wool weaver	Loder	269	344	113	138	134
Fine-cloth weaver	Geschlachtwander/ Tuchmacher	64	32	1	15	14
Cloth weaver	Zeugmacher	—	—	1	11	26
Linen weaver	Leinenweber/Weber	15	24	13	38	65
Silk weaver	(Engel)seitenmacher	1	1	—	—	—
Other Textile Crafts						
Cloth shearer	Tuchscherer	11	6	6	4	3
Dyer	Färber/Schönfärber	3	4	2	5	7
Bleacher	Bleicher	1	1	—	—	1
Carder	Kämmer	2	—	—	—	—
Cloth stitcher	Tuchhefter	3	—	—	—	—
Knitter	Stricker	—	4	4	4	6
Felt maker	Filzmacher	—	—	—	—	—
Clothing						
Tailor	Schneider	24	30	18	21	36
Hatter	Hüter	11	13	4	9	12
	LEATHER AND FUR CRAFTS					
Leather						
Tanner	Gerber/Lederer	108	137	59	75	61
Shoemaker	Schuhmacher/Schuster	60	61	34	35	41
Purse maker	Säckler	23	11	3	9	8
Belt maker	Gürtler	12	9	1	1	2
Saddler	Sattler	9	9	6	4	7
Thong maker	Nestler	7	6	4	3	3
Strapmaker	Riemer	1	1	—	—	—
Pocket maker	Taschner	—	3	—	—	—

Occupation	Most Common German Designation(s)	1579	1615	1652	1700	1724
Fur						
Furrier	Kürschner	29	44	21	14	24
	OTHER CRAFTS					
Construction						
Mason	Maurer	22	20	6	9	8
Brickmaker	Ziegler/Ziegelknecht	11	5	4	7	6
Chimneysmith	Kaminschmidt,-setzer	2	—	—	—	1
Carpenter	Zimmermann	8	10	9	6	13
Master builder	Baumeister	2	1	1	2	—
Building foreman	Werkmeister	1	1	1	1	1
Street paver	Pflasterer	2	5	6	7	6
Stonecutter	Steinmetz	1	—	—	—	—
Mortarmixer	Mörtelrührer	—	—	—	—	—
Woodworking						
Cabinetmaker	Schreiner	19	17	5	9	9
Cooper	Binder/Büttner	16	27	11	9	10
Wagonwright	Wagner	13	6	4	8	8
Tubmaker	Wannenmacher	1	3	—	—	—
Turner	Drechsler/Beindreher	3	9	4	10	11
Woodcarver	(Docken)schnitzer	2	2	—	—	—
Other woodworkers	Sonstige Holzarbeiter	—	—	—	1	—
Metalware						
Cutler	Messerschmidt	8	10	3	3	2
Coppersmith	Kupferschmidt	8	8	4	5	6
Tinsmith	Zinnschmidt	—	—	1	4	4
Tankard maker	Kantengiesser	3	4	1	—	—
Sieve maker	Sieber/Siebmacher	2	4	2	3	7
Locksmith	Schlosser	6	7	4	6	8
Padlocksmith	Lethschlosser	—	1	—	—	—
Axe smith	Beihelschmidt	3	1	2	3	2
File smith	Feilhauer	—	—	—	—	1
Chain smith	Rinkenschmidt	—	—	—	—	—
Sickle/scythe smith	Sichelschmidt/ Segenschmidt	1	—	—	—	—
Nail smith	Nagler/Nagelschmidt	—	5	2	9	8
Needle maker	Nadler	3	2	2	3	2
Tinker	Spengler/Blechler	1	2	1	1	1
Grinder	Schleifer	1	—	1	—	—
Metal founder	Gschmiedgiesser	—	1	—	—	—
Bell founder	Glockengiesser	—	—	—	—	—

Occupation	Most Common German Designation(s)	1579	1615	1652	1700	1724
Horse Gear						
Blacksmith	(Huf)schmidt	17	14	9	8	6
Spurrier	Sporer	6	2	—	2	4
Weaponry						
Weapon smith	Waffenschmidt	—	—	—	—	—
Sword smith	Schwerdtfeger	3	3	—	—	—
Sword-handle maker	Kreuzschmidt	—	—	1	—	—
Helmet smith	Haubenschmidt	—	1	—	—	—
Armorer	Harnischbauer	—	—	—	—	—
Armor-plater	Platner	7	6	1	—	—
Armor worker	Banzenmacher	3	2	—	—	—
Armor polisher	Ballierer	—	1	—	—	—
Rifle maker	Büchsenschmidt/ Büchsenschufter	7	11	4	5	2
Gunpowder maker	Pulvermacher	—	—	1	1	—
Precious Metals						
Goldsmith	Goldschmidt	8	14	3	1	—
Gold-leaf maker	Goldschlager	2	—	1	3	8
Ropemaking						
Ropemaker	Seiler	20	29	15	21	21
Pottery and Glass						
Potter	Hafner	9	7	5	5	5
Glazier	Glaser	4	5	4	3	3
Accessories						
Brush binder	Bürstenbinder	1	1	—	2	2
Braid maker	Bortenmacher	—	—	1	4	5
Comb maker	Kammacher	—	—	1	5	5
Basket maker	Kretzenmacher	—	—	2	1	2
Button maker	Knopfmacher	—	—	—	—	6
Soap boiler	Seifensieder	—	—	—	2	1
Complex Instruments						
Clock maker	Uhrmacher	2	2	—	2	2
Organ builder	Orgelmacher	—	—	—	1	2
Winch maker	Windenmacher	1	1	1	2	2
Books and Paper						
Printer	Buchdrucker	—	—	—	1	4
Bookbinder	Buchbinder	2	2	3	3	4
Parchment maker	Per(ga)menter	—	1	1	1	1
Card maker	Kartenmacher	1	1	1	1	2

Occupation	Most Common German Designation(s)	1579	1615	1652	1700	1724
Artists						
Painter	Maler	5	4	1	—	1
Sculptor	Bildhauer	—	1	—	1	—
	FOOD AND DRINK TRADES					
Meat and Fish						
Butcher	Metzger	54	68	51	75	101
Fishmonger	Fischer	9	6	—	1	1
Bread and Flour						
Baker	Bäcker	48	61	48	50	55
Gingerbread baker	Lebküchler/Leezelter	2	2	1	4	5
Sweet baker	Zuckerbäcker	—	—	—	1	4
Flour dealer	Melber	2	3	1	—	2
Miller	Müller	6	8	5	8	6
Brewing and Distilling						
Beer brewer	Bierbreu/Biersieder	7	15	7	9	9
Beer brewer's assistant	Breuknecht	—	2	1	—	—
Brandy distiller	Brantweinbrenner	—	1	—	—	—
Mead brewer	Methsieder	—	—	—	—	—
Taverners						
Innkeeper, Taverner	Gastgeber/Wirt/ Bierwirt	33	51	33	41	46
Wine taverner	Weinschenk	3	—	—	—	—
	COMMERCE AND RETAILING					
Merchants						
Textile Merchant	Tuchhändler/ Gwandhändler/ Gwandschneider	5	9	4	2	—
Merchant	Handelsmann	1	15	3	6	11
Retailers						
Shopkeeper	Krämer	11	14	16	13	14
Small retailer	Huck(l)er	3	6	2	4	14
Grocer	Materialist	—	—	—	1	1
Ironmonger	Eisenhändler/ Eisenkrämer	3	3	1	3	1
Feather dealer	Federhändler/ Federkäufer	—	3	1	5	8
Bookseller	Buchführer	1	—	—	—	—

Occupation	Most Common German Designation(s)	1579	1615	1652	1700	1724
	LEARNED OCCUPATIONS					
Clergy						
Clergyman in Nördlingen	Geistlicher in Nördlingen	4	7	6	6	4
Law						
Attorney	Procurator	—	—	—	3	2
Licentiate	Licentiat	1	1	—	3	—
Medicine						
Medical doctor	Doctor med./Physicus	—	2	2	3	2
Apothecary	Apotheker	3	5	3	2	3
Teaching						
Rector of Latin school	Lateinischer Schulmeister/Rektor	—	—	—	—	1
Latin school teacher	Collaborator/ Praeceptor/ Supremus/Infimus/ Schuldiener	1	2	2	5	3
Latin school cantor	Vorsinger/Cantor	1	—	1	1	2
German schoolmaster	Deutscher Schulmeister	9	6	3	4	6
Other Learned Occupations						
Administrator of a nonmunicipal foundation in Nördlingen	Stiftshauspfleger, Kästner in Nördlingen	1	1	1	—	—
Notary	Notar	—	—	1	1	2
Former professional bureaucrat	Ehemaliger Verwalter	—	3	5	4	4
Other learned occupation	Sonstiger Studierte	1	2	1	2	2
Citizens in Foreign Service						
Clergyman outside Nördlingen	Geistlicher ausserhalb Nördlingen	17	27	13	4	9
Teacher outside Nördlingen	Schulmeister, Schuldiener ausserhalb Nördlingen	—	4	—	1	1

Occupation	Most Common German Designation(s)	1579	1615	1652	1700	1724
Administrator for another government	Schreiber, Kastner, Vogt, Rat usw. im fremden Dienst	4	7	—	2	—
MUNICIPAL AND HOSPITAL ADMINISTRATION						
High City Administrators						
City counsel	Advocat/Consulent	1	—	—	2	—
Imperial Ammann	Stadtammann	1	1	—	1	1
Hospital master	Spitalmeister	2	1	1	2	1
Armaments superintendent	Zeugverwalter/ Zeugverkäuffer	—	—	1	1	1
School overseer	Scholarcha	—	—	1	—	—
Administrator of a dependent village	Vogt	2	2	1	1	—
Buildings inspector	Bau-Inspektor	—	—	—	1	—
City Clerks						
City recorder	Stadtschreiber	—	1	1	1	1
Hospital recorder	Spitalschreiber	1	1	2	1	1
City treasury recorder	Kammerschreiber	1	1	1	1	1
Other city or hospital clerk	Sonstiger Schreiber im Stadt- oder Spitaldienst	3	7	4	7	7
City Collectors and Inspectors						
Wine-toll master	Zahlmeister	1	1	1	1	1
Tithe master	Zehentmeister	—	—	—	1	1
City toll collector	Stadtzoller	1	1	1	1	1
Market master	Marktmeister	—	—	—	—	—
Wine agent	(Wein-) Underkeuffel	2	2	—	—	—
Barrels supervisor	Visierer	—	1	—	1	1
Grain official	Kornstreicher, -richter, -messer	2	2	2	2	3
Bread official	Brothüter	—	1	—	—	1
Loading official	Schmirber	1	1	1	—	—
Wine loader	Weinlader	3	3	—	1	—
Weighing master	Waagmeister	—	1	1	1	1
Measuring master	Eichmeister	1	1	—	1	1
Coal measurer	Kohlmesser	1	—	—	—	—

Occupation	*Most Common German Designation(s)*	*1579*	*1615*	*1652*	*1700*	*1724*
Wood measurer	Holzmesser	—	1	1	1	1
Other collectors or inspectors	Sonstige Einnehmer oder Aufseher	1	1	1	1	2
City watchmen						
Captain or co-captain of the watch	Wachtmeister/Unterwachtmeister	—	4	1	1	2
Gatekeeper	Torwart	5	5	5	6	5
Tower guard	Turmhüter/Turmer	1	2	—	—	5
Watchman	Wächter/Scharwächter	—	—	1	2	3
Tower trumpeter	Turmblaser	—	—	1	—	1
City-hall custodian	Rathaus Bewohner	—	—	1	—	1
Master of keys	Schliessmeister	1	—	—	—	—
Other watchmen	Sonstige Wächter	—	—	1	—	—
Mounted and Forest Officials						
Chief forester	Forstmeister	—	1	1	1	1
Forester	(Ober)holzwart	—	—	—	—	—
Mounted hospital official	(Spital)überreuter	—	2	1	1	1
Lower City Servants						
Council, treasury or court servant	Rats-, Kammer-, Gerichtsknecht	2	1	2	3	3
Sexton	Kirchenhüter/Mesner	2	1	2	3	3
Tithe servant	Zehentknecht	1	—	—	2	1
Prison guard	Gefangenhüter	—	—	—	—	—
Beadle	Bettel-, Gassenvogt	—	—	—	—	2
Hospital servingman	Spitalkeller	—	—	—	1	1
Hospital servant	Spitalknecht/Lazarettknecht	3	5	—	1	—
OTHER NONCRAFT OCCUPATIONS						
Carters						
Driver	Fuhrmann/Gut-, Weinführer	12	3	4	6	6
Carter	Karremann/Karrenzieher	8	6	—	2	1
Driver's or carter's assistant	Fuhrknecht/Karrenknecht	4	3	—	1	1
Wagon loader	Wagenspänner/Spenknecht	—	1	—	1	2

Occupation	*Most Common German Designation(s)*	*1579*	*1615*	*1652*	*1700*	*1724*
Messengers and Riders						
Messenger	Bote/Stadtbote/ Postknecht	3	6	4	1	3
Mounted messenger	Ainspänniger/ Reisiger Knecht	2	1	—	—	1
Rider	Reuter	—	1	—	2	—
Music						
Organist	Organist	—	1	—	1	1
Musician	Spielmann/Musicant	—	4	2	6	6
City piper	Stadtpfeiffer	—	1	—	—	—
Fiddler	Geiger	—	—	—	—	—
Lower Medical Occupations						
Surgeon	Wundtarzt	—	2	3	1	1
Barber	Barbierer	5	1	—	3	2
Bath attendant	Bader/Badknecht	7	11	6	7	4
Agriculture						
Gardener	Gärtner	2	2	1	7	7
Farmer	Baursmann	1	—	—	—	—
Shepherd, Swineherd	Hirt/Stadthirt/ Schweinhirt	2	2	—	3	3
Field watchman	Fluorhay/Feldknecht	2	2	1	3	2
Woodcutter	Holzhauer/Holzhacker	—	—	—	—	—
Menial Occupations						
Day laborer	Taglöhner	18	4	—	3	1
Carrier	(Sack)träger	—	—	—	—	2
Sweeper	Kehrer/Kehrmeister	—	—	—	1	1
Stone breaker	Steinbrecher	—	—	—	—	—
Chalk cutter	Kalkschneider	—	—	—	—	—
Gravedigger	Totengräber	1	1	1	1	2
General servant	Knecht/Stubenknecht/ Aufwärter/Diener	3	1	—	1	2
Miscellaneous Service Occupations						
Cloth-press operator	Mangmeister	1	2	—	—	—
Stablemaster	Stallmeister/ Marstaller	1	—	—	—	—
Guild servant	Zunftknecht	—	—	2	2	2
Military						
Soldier	Soldat	1	4	2	11	17

Occupation	Most Common German Designation(s)	1579	1615	1652	1700	1724
	NO OCCUPATION[b]					
No occupation: maximum wealth over 200 fl.	Kein Beruf: höchstes Vermögen über 200 fl.	23	9	19	6	11
No occupation: wealth never exceeds 200 fl.	Kein Beruf: höchstes Vermögen nie über 200 fl.	11	4	3	2	11
TOTAL		1,266	1,456	715	952	1,113

[a] The only specifically female occupations ever listed in the tax registers are sewer (Näherin), midwife (Hebamme/Kindbettkellnerin) and hospital mistress or attendant (Spitalziechenmeisterin/Spitalkellerin). No representatives of these occupations, however, appear in the five years recorded here.

[b] The designation "no occupation" pertains only to a citizen for whom no occupation is indicated at any time during his career. A citizen for whom no occupation is given in one of the years selected here but whose occupation can be determined from an earlier or later tax register is entered under that heading.

Source: StR.

APPENDIX III

Citizens of Nördlingen, 1579-1724: Mean, Median and Total Wealth (fl.)

	ALL CITIZENS				MALE CITIZENS			
Year	*No.*	*Mean Wealth*	*Med. Wealth*	*Total Wealth*	*No.*	*Mean Wealth*	*Med. Wealth*	*Total Wealth*
1579	1,541	454	100	699,922	1,266	485	140	613,504
1585	1,661	486	100	806,582	1,396	500	100	698,000
1591	1,626	495	100	804,220	1,361	507	140	690,027
1597	1,659	589	160	976,487	1,412	628	200	886,454
1603	1,644	728	180	1,196,503	1,374	792	200	1,087,933
1609	1,741	813	200	1,415,433	1,449	805	200	1,166,155
1615	1,713	870	200	1,489,625	1,456	863	200	1,256,237
1621	1,697	1,184	260	2,009,587	1,447	1,193	300	1,726,850
1627	1,658	989	200	1,639,430	1,435	993	220	1,425,242
1633	1,441	890	180	1,282,778	1,176	910	200	1,070,395
1636	934	709	120	661,832	777	737	120	572,804
1640	839	752	140	630,592	682	793	200	541,099
1646	844	690	100	582,022	693	744	160	515,315
1652	887	769	200	682,103	715	793	220	567,281
1658	952	888	320	845,186	789	913	380	720,673
1664	1,027	831	320	853,848	852	841	340	716,702
1670	1,069	852	340	910,788	901	905	380	815,765
1676	1,116	777	300	866,686	939	801	320	752,139
1682	1,145	714	240	817,530	965	718	260	692,870
1688	1,170	768	260	898,560	970	797	280	772,896
1694	1,115	778	220	867,247	914	789	260	721,329
1700	1,147	822	220	942,834	952	866	260	824,051
1712	1,242	768	200	953,440	1,054	808	200	852,100
1724	1,323	800	200	1,058,020	1,113	808	200	898,800

Source: StR.

APPENDIX IV

Price Index for 1579-1724

THE following index of prices in Swabia is based on data for the city of Augsburg published by E. H. Phelps Brown and S. V. Hopkins in "Builders' Wage-Rates, Prices and Population: Some Further Evidence," *Economica*, n. s. 24 (1959), 18-38. Drawing on the standard source for German price data (M. J. Elsas, *Umriss einer Geschichte der Preise und Löhne in Deutschland*, 2 vols. [Leiden, 1936-49], vol. 1), Phelps Brown and Hopkins calculated an index of the price of a composite unit of consumables in Augsburg for each year between 1499 and 1753. I have used these data to determine a nine-year average of the index price for each year between 1579 and 1724, taking the nine-year average for 1579 as a base of 100. The table below records the nine-year average for each year.

1579[a]	100	1601	136	1623	277
1580	101	1602	137	1624	286
1581	104	1603[a]	137	1625	289
1582	109	1604	139	1626	275
1583	112	1605	139	1627[a]	220
1584	114	1606	140	1628	215
1585[a]	118	1607	142	1629	232
1586	123	1608	145	1630	261
1587	126	1609[a]	148	1631	279
1588	128	1610	153	1632	285
1589	130	1611	156	1633[a]	285
1590	131	1612	158	1634	286
1591[a]	128	1613	158	1635	287
1592	126	1614	156	1636[a]	290
1593	126	1615[a]	155	1637	286
1594	125	1616	154	1638	263
1595	123	1617	167	1639	222
1596	126	1618	224	1640[a]	194
1597[a]	130	1619	235	1641	179
1598	132	1620	242	1642	171
1599	132	1621[a]	254	1643	169

1600	133	1622	266	1644	173
1645	179	1672	122	1699	176
1646[a]	175	1673	123	1700[a]	179
1647	171	1674	125	1701	180
1648	169	1675	129	1702	180
1649	168	1676[a]	134	1703	176
1650	164	1677	137	1704	169
1651	158	1678	138	1705	167
1652[a]	151	1679	138	1706	165
1653	146	1680	138	1707	169
1654	133	1681	136	1708	170
1655	128	1682[a]	135	1709	169
1656	127	1683	133	1710	170
1657	129	1684	132	1711	174
1658[a]	132	1685	132	1712[a]	179
1659	137	1686	132	1713	180
1660	141	1687	140	1714	180
1661	143	1688[a]	147	1715	180
1662	140	1689	158	1716	180
1663	141	1690	166	1717	174
1664[a]	141	1691	171	1718	172
1665	140	1692	174	1719	170
1666	135	1693	175	1720	169
1667	130	1694[a]	178	1721	166
1668	125	1695	186	1722	166
1669	121	1696	186	1723	165
1670[a]	120	1697	184	1724[a]	164
1671	121	1698	177		

[a] Years for which data from Nördlingen tax registers were analyzed in Chapter Four.

APPENDIX V

Calculation of Wealth Distribution for 1579

Table 4.2 in Chapter Four records the estimated proportion of the total wealth of adult citizens held by members of twelve different wealth categories in 1579. The method used for calculating these figures requires careful explanation, particularly since the findings concerning wealth distribution in various years offered later in the chapter (e.g., in Figure 4.5) rely on data calculated by this method.

Theoretically it would have been possible to compute the exact percentage of the total wealth held by the members of each wealth bracket in 1579 with total precision. This would have been a very complicated procedure, however, and an unnecessary one, since it is possible to obtain very satisfactory approximations on the basis of grouped data, such as appear in the first column of Table 4.2. With certain exceptions, the basic technique for estimating the total wealth of all persons in any one wealth category consists of multiplying the number of persons in that category by a figure representing the midpoint of the interval covered by that category. The exceptions are as follows:

1. In category I almost all the assessments are recorded as 25 fl. and in category II almost all of them are recorded as 50 fl. Therefore, these amounts have been used instead of the midpoints.
2. Since the top category is open-ended, no midpoint can be established. Instead, the original information concerning all taxpayers in the top category (in 1579, there was only one) has been retrieved and thus the exact amounts are used.

The table in this appendix not only lists the categories and their midpoints, but also makes clear how the results for 1579 were obtained. The percentages given in the second column of Table 4.2 are based on the last column of the above calculations (e.g., Category V: 55,800 fl. is 7.9 percent of the total of 707,125 fl.). Incidentally, the fundamental reliability of this technique is suggested by the fact that the total wealth as yielded by this method comes out to 707,125 fl.—which exceeds by only 1 percent the actual recorded wealth in 1579, which was 699,922 fl.

Cat.	*Wealth Range (fl.)*	*Midpoint (fl.) × Number*				*Est. Total (fl.)*	*Percent*
0	0	0	×	19	=	0	(0.0)
I	1-25	25	×	415	=	10,375	(1.5)
II	26-50	50	×	212	=	10,600	(1.5)
III	51-100	75	×	164	=	12,300	(1.7)
IV	101-200	150	×	179	=	26,850	(3.7)
V	201-400	300	×	186	=	55,800	(7.9)
VI	401-800	600	×	150	=	90,000	(12.7)
VII	801-1,600	1,200	×	118	=	141,600	(20.2)
VIII	1,601-3,200	2,400	×	65	=	156,000	(22.1)
IX	3,201-6,400	4,800	×	26	=	124,800	(17.6)
X	6,401-12,800	9,600	×	6	=	57,600	(8.1)
XI	12,800 and over	Exact Amount		1	=	21,200	(3.0)
		Total		1,541		707,125	(100.0)

APPENDIX VI

Wealth Mobility Tables

THE tables in this appendix record the wealth mobility of six different cohorts of Nördlingen citizens. For each group, the wealth of every man shortly after his admission to adult citizenship has been compared with his wealth twenty-four years later, if he was still living. In determining changes in the real level of any citizen's wealth over twenty-four years, account was taken of changes in the value of the gulden during the same period, as indicated by the price index presented in Appendix IV. The figures in parentheses, however, indicate changes in nominal wealth, when changes in the value of the gulden are not taken into account.

The category "Same" refers to all those whose wealth in the later year equaled 1.0.-1.99 of their wealth in the earlier year: the category "2×-4×" includes those whose wealth in the later year was 2.0-4.99 of their wealth in the earlier year, and so on.

TABLE A.VI.1. Wealth Mobility, 1585-1609

Wealth Level in 1585 (fl.)	*Total No. of Cases*	*Number of Men Whose Wealth in 1609 Was:*				
		Lower	*Same*	*2×-4×*	*5×-9×*	*10× or more*
Up to 100	128	39 (14)	10 (31)	39 (29)	18 (21)	22 (33)
101-400	41	13 (13)	8 (6)	11 (11)	6 (7)	3 (4)
Over 400	18	6 (5)	5 (5)	6 (4)	1 (3)	0 (1)
Totals	187	58 (32)	23 (42)	56 (44)	25 (31)	25 (38)
Totals in %		31 (17)	12 (22)	30 (24)	13 (17)	13 (20)

353 men became adult citizens in 1580-85; 187 of them (53%) were still alive in 1609. This table compares the real wealth of these 187 men in 1585 and 1609, taking into account a decline of 20% in the real value of the gulden. (Data in parentheses compare the nominal wealth of these men in 1585 and 1609.)

TABLE A.VI.2. Wealth Mobility, 1603-1627

Wealth Level in 1603 (fl.)	*Total No. of Cases*	*Number of Men Whose Wealth in 1627 Was:*				
		Lower	*Same*	*2×-4×*	*5×-9×*	*10× or more*
Up to 100	73	26 (16)	15 (13)	18 (11)	8 (20)	6 (13)
101-400	49	23 (14)	10 (14)	10 (8)	6 (8)	0 (5)
Over 400	34	15 (10)	8 (8)	8 (7)	3 (6)	0 (3)
Totals	156	64 (40)	33 (35)	36 (26)	17 (34)	6 (21)
Totals in %		41 (26)	21 (22)	23 (17)	11 (22)	4 (14)

253 men became adult citizens in 1598-1603; 156 of them (62%) were still alive in 1627. This table compares the real wealth of these 156 men in 1603 and 1627, taking into account a decline of 38% in the real value of the gulden. (Data in parentheses compare the nominal wealth of these men in 1603 and 1627.)

TABLE A.VI.3. Wealth Mobility, 1627-1652

Wealth Level in 1627 (fl.)	*Total No. of Cases*	*Number of Men Whose Wealth in 1652 Was:*				
		Lower	*Same*	*2×-4×*	*5×-9×*	*10× or more*
Up to 100	26	4 (4)	3 (9)	12 (7)	4 (4)	3 (2)
101-400	29	10 (10)	4 (7)	6 (4)	5 (6)	4 (2)
Over 400	14	5 (6)	2 (3)	3 (3)	3 (1)	1 (1)
Totals	69	19 (20)	9 (19)	21 (14)	12 (11)	8 (5)
Totals in %		28 (29)	13 (28)	30 (20)	17 (16)	12 (7)

280 men became adult citizens in 1622-27; 69 of them (25%) were still alive in 1652. This table compares the real wealth of these 69 men in 1627 and 1652, taking into account an increase of 46% in the real value of the gulden. (Data in parentheses compare the nominal wealth of these men in 1627 and 1652.)

TABLE A.VI.4. Wealth Mobility, 1652-1676

Wealth Level in 1652 (fl.)	*Total No. of Cases*	*Number of Men Whose Wealth in 1676 Was:*				
		Lower	*Same*	*2×-4×*	*5×-9×*	*10× or more*
Up to 100	43	0 (0)	19 (19)	15 (15)	5 (5)	4 (4)
101-400	39	2 (2)	14 (14)	12 (13)	9 (8)	2 (2)
Over 400	20	9 (9)	4 (6)	5 (4)	2 (1)	0 (0)
Totals	102	11 (11)	37 (39)	32 (32)	16 (14)	6 (6)
Totals in %		11 (11)	36 (38)	31 (31)	16 (14)	6 (6)

174 men became adult citizens in 1647-52; 102 of them (59%) were still alive in 1676. This table compares the real wealth of these 102 men in 1652 and 1676, taking into account an increase of 13% in the real value of the gulden. (Data in parentheses compare the nominal wealth of these men in 1652 and 1676.)

TABLE A.VI.5. Wealth Mobility, 1670-1694

Wealth Level in 1670 (fl.)	*Total No. of Cases*	*Number of Men Whose Wealth in 1694 Was:*				
		Lower	*Same*	*2×-4×*	*5×-9×*	*10× or more*
Up to 100	26	13 (8)	8 (11)	4 (6)	1 (0)	0 (1)
101-400	42	25 (17)	9 (11)	8 (12)	0 (2)	0 (0)
Over 400	32	15 (9)	7 (10)	9 (8)	1 (4)	0 (1)
Totals	100	53 (34)	24 (32)	21 (26)	2 (6)	0 (2)
Totals in %		53 (34)	24 (32)	21 (26)	2 (6)	0 (2)

174 men became adult citizens in 1647-52; 102 of them (59%) were still alive in 1676. This table compares the real wealth of these 102 men in 1652 and 1676, taking into account an increase of 13% in the real value of the gulden. (Data in parentheses compare the nominal wealth of these men in 1652 and 1676)

TABLE A.VI.6. Wealth Mobility, 1700-1724

Wealth Level in 1700 (fl)	*Total No. of Cases*	*Number of Men Whose Wealth in 1724 Was:* Lower	Same	2×-4×	5×-9×	10× or more
Up to 100	49	7 (7)	6 (6)	28 (28)	4 (4)	4 (4)
101-400	36	4 (4)	19 (19)	11 (11)	2 (2)	0 (0)
Over 400	18	5 (6)	6 (5)	6 (6)	1 (1)	0 (0)
Totals	103	16 (17)	31 (30)	45 (45)	7 (7)	4 (4)
Totals in %		16 (17)	30 (29)	44 (44)	7 (7)	4 (4)

185 men became adult citizens in 1695-1700; 103 of them (56%) were still alive in 1724. This table compares the real wealth of these 103 men in 1700 and 1724, taking into account an increase of 9% in the real value of the gulden. (Data in parentheses compare the nominal wealth of these men in 1670 and 1694.)

APPENDIX VII

Members of the City Council of Nördlingen, 1580-1720

THE tables in this appendix give basic biographical information about each member of the Nördlingen city council between 1580 and 1720.

TABLE A.VII.1. Council Members in 1580 (listed in order of seniority)

Term[a]	*Name*	*Age*[b]	*Bgmsr*[c]	*Occupation*[d]	*Wealth*[e]
c.1542-1587	Reuter, Johann	?	c.1549	Cloth merchant	6,000
c.1550-1589	Seng, Peter	?	c.1567	Ironmonger?	10,600
c.1552-1587	Flanser, Joachim	?	—	*n.k.*	2,500
c.1555-1588	Haider ("Schmid"), Georg	?	c.1570	Cloth merchant?	5,000
c.1563-1609	Welsch, Melchior	?	—	Fine-cloth weaver	1,600
c.1565-1587	Niclas, Georg	?	—	Butcher	3,600
c.1567-1581	Vogelmann, Georg Victor	?	—	*n.k.*	4,100
c.1570-1599	Ostertag, Georg	?	1593	Wool weaver	2,100
c.1572-1583	Mair, Georg	?	—	Taverner	4,600
c.1572-1589	Frickhinger, Hieronimus	?	1587	Cloth merchant	14,500
1573-1586	Degenhart, Johann	?	—	Ironmonger	4,000
1576-1592	Gundelfinger, Karl	?	1589	Goldsmith	1,200
1576-1582	Schöpperlin, Caspar	?	—	Tanner	4,000
1576-1588 (d. ?)	Berlin, Georg	?	—	Apothecary	2,200
1578-1595	Bosch, Johann	?	1588	Fine-cloth weaver	2,000

TABLE A.VII.2. Council Members Appointed Between 1581 and 1720

Term[a]	*Name*	*Age*[b]	*Bgmsr*[c]	*Occupation*[d]	*Wealth*[e]
1582-1610 (d. ?)	Bin, Georg	?	—	Tanner	6,000
1583-1586	Spangenberger, Leonhard	?	—	Tanner	1,800
1584-1604	Pferinger, Johann	51	1589	Cabinetmaker	1,700
1586-1598	Haas, Georg	?	—	Purse maker	3,800
1587-1591	Holl, David	?	—	Apothecary	2,400

Term[a]	Name	Age[b]	Bgmsr[c]	Occupation[d]	Wealth[e]
1587-1595	Diethay, Thomas	?	—	*n.k.*	2,300
1588-1596	Beyschlag, Gangwolf	?	—	Tanner	1,600
1588-1612	Baur, Johann	?	—	Furrier	2,600
1589-1601	Mayinger, Peter	?	—	Cloth-press operator	8,000
1589-1599	Herlin, Caspar	?	—	Taverner	4,400
1589-1605	Jörg, Johann	?	1596	Cloth merchant	26,000
1590-1605	Niclas, Georg	39	—	Taverner	11,600
1591-1615	Rehlin, Paul	51	—	Butcher	8,000
1593-1630	Gundelfinger, Johann Wilhelm	32	1600	Cloth merchant	12,000
1596-1605	Weckherlin, Sebastian	?	—	Gold-leaf maker	4,800
1596-1629 (d. 1630)	Lemp, Peter	44	1605	City official	8,000
1597-1617	Gering, David	?	—	Brewer	30,000
1598-1629	Haider, Caspar	44	1606	Apothecary	33,500
1600-1604	Kleyer, Paul	?	—	Tanner	3,800
1600-1617	Ernst, Georg	50	—	Wool weaver	2,400
1602 and 1606-1630	Welsch, Hieronimus	47	—	City official	6,600
1603-1606	Degenfelder, Wolfgang	?	—	City official	9,200
1604-1624 (d. 1624)	Aislinger, Daniel	56	—	Tanner	4,200
1605-1631	Reichart, Sebastian	44	1629	City official	25,000
1606-1615 (d. ?)	Han, Michael	?	—	Bureaucrat in foreign employ	2,000
1606-1639	Jörg, Johann Baptist	46	1630	Taverner	19,600
1607-1633	Reuter, Hans Ludwig	?	—	Taverner	4,000
1610-1639	Kobelt, Ludwig	39	—	Coppersmith	4,800
1610-1634	Wuest, Ulrich	43	—	Apothecary	7,000
1613-1623	Weckherlin, Johann	56	—	Ironmonger	5,200
1616-1631	Strobel, Andreas	48	—	Retailer	9,600
1616-1652 (d. 1657)	Frickhinger, Adam	39	1631	Cloth merchant	15,000
1618-1621	Gering, Melchior	53	—	Apothecary	10,000
1618-1634	Nuefer, Sigmund	42	—	Tanner	22,000
1622-1646 (d. 1653)	Lemp, Johann	52	1640	Taverner	7,000
1624-1634	Mayinger, Georg	56	—	Cloth-press operator	10,000

Term[a]	*Name*	*Age*[b]	*Bgmsr*[c]	*Occupation*[d]	*Wealth*[e]
1624-1634	Walderman, Johann	50	—	Wool weaver	2,000
1629-1637	Widenmann, Georg	39	—	Merchant	21,000
1630-1661	Bommeister, Georg	45	1633	Bureaucrat in foreign employ	14,600
1631-1633	Gundelfinger, Johann Conrad	58	1631	City official	3,600
1631-1634	Schisler, Georg	59	—	Belt maker	3,000
1631-1633	Fetzer, Sebastian	51	—	Cloth merchant	1,600
1631-1637 (d. ?)	Lehlin, Johann	?	—	Taverner	8,000
1633-1636	Seng, Matthias	50	—	Ironmonger	3,000
1633-1646	Niclas, Eucharius	42	—	Ropemaker	12,000
1633-1672	Seefried, Johann Georg	34	1648	Merchant	9,000
1634-1638	Gundelfinger, Daniel	33	—	*n.k.*	10,000
1634-1648	Welsch, Johann Melchior	35	1646	Soldier	18,000
1634-1668	Jörg, Michael	44	—	Taverner	8,400
1634-1670	Gundelfinger, Johann Conrad	25	1661	City official	8,200
1634-1652	Kessler, Daniel	50	—	Tanner	3,600
1637-1650	Ostertag, Georg	57	—	Wool weaver	3,200
1638-1655	Adam, Caspar	40	1653	Merchant	56,000
1638-1640; 1656-1682	Romul, Wilhelm Friedrich	37	1656	City official	10,400
1638	Widenmann, Daniel	43	—	Merchant	18,000
1638-1664	Arnold, Caspar	44	—	Retailer	4,500
1640-1645	Kobelt, Niclaus	29	—	Taverner	1,200
1640-1674	Wünsch, Martin	45	—	City official	5,000
1641-1675	Herlin, Joachim	50	—	Taverner	8,000
1645-1652	Aschenhofer, Gabriel	52	—	City official	20,000
1646-1652	Lemp, Gottfried	46	—	Taverner	6,800
1646-1683	Kleyer, Paul	36	—	*n.k.*	9,000
1648-1695	Weng, Georg Friedrich	32	1673	Bureaucrat in foreign employ	15,400
1650-1678	Gering, Jacob	52	—	Cloth merchant	7,400
1652-1667	Rueger, Philipp	42	—	Apothecary	6,900
1652-1669	Beyschlag, Joachim	46	—	Tanner	3,500
1652-1690	Hilbrandt, Johann Friedrich	40	1683	City official	10,400
1652-1687	Heuber, Johann Christoph	50	—	Ropemaker	4,400

Term[a]	Name	Age[b]	Bgmsr[c]	Occupation[d]	Wealth[e]
1661-1690	Frickhinger, Johann Christoph	26	1670	City official	28,400
1666-1709	Aurenhammer, Johann Georg	36	—	City official	3,000
1667-1704	Adam, Caspar	37	1695	Merchant	4,000
1668-1692	Widenmann, Georg Wilhelm	40	—	*n.k.*	3,200
1670-1683	Kessler, Daniel	59	—	Taverner	6,000
1670-1675	Heidenreich, Johann	61	—	Brewer	12,000
1673-1703	Schöpperlin, Georg Wilhelm	37	1690	Organist	14,000
1675-1689	Wechsler, Johann Sigmund	61	—	Grocer (?)	3,200
1675-1684	Haas, Johann	47	—	City official	4,000
1675-1692	Dehlinger, Samuel	59	—	Tanner	2,600
1679-1699	Wünsch, Johann Caspar	42	—	Merchant	11,000
1683-1686	Streitter, Michael	67	—	City official	2,400
1684-1717	Martens, Heinrich	41	1703	Lawyer	8,400
1684-1697	Eckh, Johann Sophonias	63	—	Ironmonger	2,200
1685-1700	Engelhart, Georg Friedrich	37	1690	City official	4,200
1687-1728	Westerfeld, Georg Adam	34	1705	*n.k.*	15,000
1688-1701	Hubel, Caspar	60	—	Merchant	3,400
1690-1727	Wechsler, Johann Jacob	28	1700	City official	21,800
1690-1704	Jörg, Johann Ernst	43	—	Taverner	8,400
1690-1718	Hilbrandt, Johann Friedrich	36	—	City official	5,800
1693-1705	Welsch, Lorenz Christoph	27	1704	Lawyer	11,000
1693-1716	Stang, Johann Philipp	44	—	City official	3,000
1695-1719	Frickhinger, Gottfried Dietrich	31	—	Apothecary	8,000
1698-1715	Weng, Daniel	43	—	City official	3,000
1700-1712	Lang, Johann Georg	58	—	Barber-surgeon	1,400
1700-1726	Rehm, Georg Philipp	41	—	Bureaucrat in foreign employ	5,000
1702-1731	Klein, Daniel	33	1717	City official	13,400
1703-1733	Scheid, Philipp Jacob	44	1727	*n.k.*	17,300

Term[a]	*Name*	*Age*[b]	*Bgmsr*[c]	*Occupation*[d]	*Wealth*[e]
1704-1724	Claus, Hans Ulrich	44	—	"Registrator"	1,000
1704-1709	Romul, Wilhelm Friedrich	?	—	City official	600
1705-1740	Schöpperlin, Esaias	37	—	Organist	5,000
1710-1717	Wucherer, Johann Jacob	59	—	City official	3,300
1710-1743	Hetsch, Johann Friedrich	30	1731	Musician	3,000
1713-1756	Engelhart, Wilhelm Christoph	38	1733	Lawyer	19,600 [1746]
1716-1741	Wörner, David	54	—	Merchant	42,000
1716-1748	Wolff, Christian Friedrich	51	—	City official	2,800
1717-1730	Beyer, Johann Caspar	57	—	Confectioner	19,800
1717-1721	Stang, Johann Friedrich	46	—	Merchant	35,000
1718-1740	Köhler, Johann Friedrich	48	—	Apothecary	5,000
1719-1743	Welsch, Johann Friedrich von	24	1728	*n.k.*	16,000

[a] Year of appointment and the year when the councilman's term of office ended, usually at his death. In the rare cases when the term ended by resignation or retirement, the year of death, if known, is indicated in parentheses.

[b] Councilman's age at the time of his appointment to the council, determined by counting backwards from his age at death, if known.

[c] Indicates whether the councilman was elevated to the position of Bürgermeister (mayor) during his term of office, and if so when.

[d] Councilman's occupation at the time of his appointment to the council; *n.k.* signifies occupation not known.

[e] Councilman's wealth (in fl.) at the end of his term of office, i.e., in most cases at the time of his death.

Source:

For dates of appointment: Ayd Buch der Statt Nördlingen Anno 1572 [Eidbuch II, 1572-86] and Jurament Buch [Eidbuch IV, 1587-1803]. For appointments before 1573, approximate dates were determined from the Steuerregister.

For dates of death (and ages at death): Sterberegister I-III [1618-1738] and Daniel Eberhard Beyschlag and Johannes Müller, *Beyträge zur Nördlingischen Geschlechtshistoirie, die Nördlingischen Epitaphien erhaltend*, 2 vols. (Nördlingen, 1801-?).

For occupations: In most cases, from the Steuerregister. In a few cases, where the tax registers lacked this information, from Beyschlag and Müller.

For wealth: Steuerregister. The figure given is based on the most recent assessment before the councilman's death or departure from the council.

SELECT BIBLIOGRAPHY

This bibliography lists all primary sources consulted, as well as secondary sources which deal (in whole or significant part) with Nördlingen or the immediately surrounding region during the period studied. Secondary sources used for comparative or methodological purposes are not listed here, but a full citation for each such work will be found at the first reference in any chapter.

I. Primary Sources

A. Stadtarchiv Nördlingen

(i) Bound Volumes

(The dates cited indicate the years covered by the volumes actually used in this study. In many cases, these volumes form part of a longer series.)

Anlagsrechnungen: 1676-1719.

Bürgerbuch 1513-1672.

Chronik Peter Lemp, in: Kaiserempfangsbuch.

Eidbücher: Eidbuch II, 1572-86 (Ayd Buch der Statt Nördlingen, Anno 1572).
Eidbuch IV, 1587-1803 (Jurament Buch).

Extra-Ordinari Steuerbücher VIa, VIb (1634).

Inventare: 1609-11, 1682-88.

Kammerrechnungen (Stadtrechnungen): 1560, 1579-1720.

Matrikel der Lateinschule Nördlingen 1708-1817.

Ordnungsbücher: OB 1553-67.
OB 1567-87 (Allerhand Handwerck Ordnungen).
OB 1612-40.
OB 1641-88.
OB 1688-1706.
OB 1706-31.

Pfandbücher Nr. 17-56: 1557-1726.

Ratsordnungen: Ainss Ersamen Raths der Stat Nördlingen Raths Ordnung, 1556.
Eines Ersamen Raths der Heyl. Reichs Statt Nördlingen Rathsordnung, Ao. 1673.

Ratsprotokolle: 1568-1700.

Spitalrechnungen: 1583-1701.

Steuerregister (Steuerbücher): 1495-1746.
Urfehdebücher: 1587-92, 1601-14.

(ii) Unbound Material

Acta das Matricular-Moderations-Wesens betreffend, B Num. VI, 3.
Acta der Nördlingische Matricular-beschwerden und die Untersuchung des Oekonomiestandes betreffend, B Num. VII, 1.
Akten Deutsche Schulen: Führung des Unterrichts/Visitationen.
Schulordnungen.
Heiratsbriefe: 1618-98.
Leichenpredigte.
Lodweberakten: Loder contra Daniel Wörner, 1698 (Prozess der Loder gegen den Lodenhändler Daniel Wörner, 1698).
Lodenhandel, 1696-1715 (-1759).
Zeidler, Andreas. Delinatio Vera Imperialis Civitatis ad Aras Flavias Sive Nördlingen (map), 1651.

B. Evangelische Gemeinde, Nördlingen

Sterberegister I-IV (1618-1775).
Tauf- und Eheregister I-X (1579-1745).

C. Pfarrei Nähermemmingen

Trau- und Sterberegister der Spitalpfarrei Nördlingen und Pfarrei Baldingen I-IV (1602-1802).

D. Published Primary Sources

Erneuwerte Schul-Ordnung E.E. Rahts des H. Römischen Reichs Statt Nördlingen . . . M.DC.LII. Nördlingen, 1652.
Mayer, Johannes. *M. Johannis Mayeri Historia Caesareae Obsidionis et Expugnationis Liberae S.R.I. Civitatis Nördlingensis in Bello Tricennali Ao. MDCXXXIV*, ed. Christian Friedrich Georg Meister. Göttingen, 1756. (This work also appears in a German translation by Ludwig Mußgnug as *Die Belagerung von Nördlingen 1634, Erinnerungsrede des Magisters Johannes Mayer.* Nördlingen, 1927.)
Mötzel, Johann Christoph. "Johann Christoph Mötzels Chronik von Nördlingen" [written 1733-34], *Rieser Heimatbote*, nos. 25 (Dec. 1926)-67 (Oct. 1930).

Romul, Friedrich Wilhelm, ed. "Der Stadt Nördlingen Statuta und Satzungen . . . übersehen, confirmirt, verbessert, erleutert und erklärt den 16 Decembr. An. 1650," in D. August Friedrich Schott, *Sammlungen zu den Deutschen Land- und Stadtrechten*, vol. 1 (Leipzig, 1772), pp. 201-40.

Sehling, Emil, ed. *Die evangelischen Kirchenordnungen des sechzehnten Jahrhunderts*, vol. 12 (Tübingen, 1963), pp. 271-393.

II. Secondary Sources

A. Local Periodicals

Der Rieser Geschichtsfreund, 1922-24.

Der Rieser Heimatbote, 1924-43 (appeared as supplement to local newspapers).

Der Daniel: Heimatkundlich-kulturelle Vierteljahr-/Zweimonatschrift für das Ries und Umgebung, 1965-72.

Jahrbuch des historischen Vereins für Nördlingen und das Ries [cited: *JHVN*], published 1912- . Appeared 1912-36 under the title *Jahrbuch des historischen Vereins für Nördlingen und Umgebung*, and 1937-41 under the title *Jahrbuch des Rieser Heimatvereins e.V., Sitz Nördlingen.*

Nordschwaben: Zeitschrift für Landschaft, Geschichte, Kultur und Zeitgeschehen (Der Daniel), 1973- .

B. Books and Articles

Albrecht, Dieter. "Die freie Reichsstadt Nördlingen und der Spanische Erbfolgekrieg bis zum Ausgang des Jahres 1704," *JHVN*, 2 (1913), 32-185.

Berger, Heinz. *Nördlingen: Die Entwicklung einer Stadt von den Anfängen bis zum Beginn der sechziger Jahre des 20. Jahrhunderts.* Dissertation, Erlangen, 1969.

Beyschlag, C. *Geschichte der Stadt Nördlingen bis auf die neueste Zeit.* Nördlingen, 1851.

Beyschlag, Daniel Eberhardt. *Versuch einer Schulgeschichte der Reichsstadt Nördlingen*, 5 parts. Nördlingen, 1793-97.

——— and Johannes Müller. *Beyträge zur Nördlingischen Geschlechtshistorie, die Nördlingischen Epitaphien erhaltend, gesammelt und mit historischen Anmerkungen erläutert*, 2 vols. Nördlingen, 1801-?.

Dannenbauer, Heinz. "Das Leinenweberhandwerk in der Reichsstadt Nördlingen," *Zeitschrift für bayerische Landesgeschichte*, 3 (1930), 267-316.

Dorner, Friedrich. *Die Steuern Nördlingens zu Ausgang des Mittelalters*. Dissertation, Munich, 1905.

Ebert, W. H. Konrad. *Die Lodweberei in der Reichsstadt Nördlingen*. Nördlingen, 1919.

Endres, Rudolf. "Kapitalistische Organisationsformen im Ries in der zweiten Hälfte des 16. Jahrhunderts," *Jahrbuch für fränkische Landesforschung*, 22 (1962), 89-99.

———. *Die Nürnberg-Nördlinger Wirtschaftsbeziehungen im Mittelalter bis zur Schlacht von Nördlingen, Ihre rechtlich-politischen Voraussetzungen und ihre tatsächlichen Auswirkungen*. Schriften des Instituts für fränkische Landesforschung an der Universität Erlangen-Nürnberg, 11. Neustadt/Aisch, 1962.

Felber, Alfons. *Unzucht und Kindsmord in der Rechtsprechung der freien Reichsstadt Nördlingen vom 15. bis. 19. Jahrhundert*. Dissertation, Bonn, 1961.

Fischer, Helmut. *Die ältesten Zeitungen und ihre Verleger*. Augsburg, 1936.

Frickhinger Hermann. *Genealogie der Familie Frickhinger in Nördlingen: Ein Beitrag zu der Geschichte Nördlinger Geschlechter*. Nördlingen, 1907.

———. "Die Stiftungen der Stadt Nördlingen," 5 parts, *JHVN*, 9 (1922/24), 28-112; 10 (1925/26), 33-128; 11 (1927), 45-118; 12 (1928), 90-152; 13 (1929), 7-54.

Friedrichs, Christopher R. "Capitalism, Mobility and Class Formation in the Early Modern German City," *Past and Present*, no. 69 (Nov. 1975), 24-49.

———. "Marriage, Family and Social Structure in an Early Modern German Town," *Canadian Historical Papers 1975*, pp. 17-40.

———. "Nördlingen, 1580-1700: Society, Government and the Impact of War." Ph.D. dissertation, Princeton University, 1973.

Gebhardt, Kurt. *Das Pfandrecht und Vollstreckungsrecht der Reichsstadt Nördlingen*. Dissertation (typescript), Tübingen, 1953.

Goschenhofer, Heinrich. *Von Nördlinger Buchdruckern vor 1763*. Nördlingen, 1938.

Grupp, Georg. "Aus der Geschichte der Grafschaft Oettingen," in *Rieser Heimatbuch*, published by the Gesellschaft für Volksbildung, Nördlingen (Munich, 1922), pp. 154-77.

Häffner, Arnulf, "Forst- und Jagdgeschichte der fürstlichen Standesherrschaft Oettingen-Wallerstein," *JHVN*, 16 (1932), 1-112; 17 (1933), 1-120.

Kammerer, J. "Die Nördlinger Verfassungsveränderung vom Jahre 1552," *JHVN*, 14 (1930), 44-64.

Kellenbenz, Hermann, "Die Wirtschaft der schwäbischen Reichsstädte zwischen 1648 und 1740," *Jahrbuch für Geschichte der oberdeutschen Reichsstädte*, 11 (1965), 128-65.

Kern, Karl. "Die Söhne der Reichsstadt Nördlingen auf hohen Schulen," *JHVN*, 5 (1916), 17-48.

Kobelt, Gustav. *Geschichte der Familie Kobelt*. Darmstadt, 1912.

Kudorfer, Dieter, *Nördlingen*. Historischer Atlas von Bayern, Teil Schwaben, Heft 8. Munich, 1974.

Lenz, Rudolf, and Gundolf Keil. "Johann Christoph Donauer (1669-1718): Untersuchungen zur Soziographie und Pathographie eines Nördlinger Ratskonsulenten aufgrund der Leichenpredigt," *Zeitschrift für bayerische Landesgeschichte*, 38 (1975), 317-55.

Leo, Erich. *Die Schlacht bei Nördlingen im Jahre 1634*. Hallesche Abhandlungen zur neueren Geschichte, 39. Halle, 1900.

Lettenmeyer. Wilhelm Friedrich. *Der Niedergang der reichsstädtischen Finanzwirtschaft Nördlingens und die Tätigkeit der kaiserlichen Subdelegationskommission (XVIII. Jahrhundert)*. Dissertation, Munich, 1937.

Mayer, Christian. *Die Stadt Nördlingen: ihr Leben und ihre Kunst im Lichte der Vorzeit*. Nördlingen, 1876.

Meier, Andreas. "Der Reichsdeputationshauptschluss und das Ende der freien Reichsstadt Nördlingen," *JHVN*, 3 (1914), 50-151.

Müller, Johannes. *Merkwürdigkeiten der Stadt Nördlingen, nebst einer Chronik*. Nördlingen, 1824.

Müller, L. "Aus fünf Jahrhunderten. Beiträge zur Geschichte der jüdischen Gemeinden im Riess," *Zeitschrift des historischen Vereins für Schwaben und Neuburg*, 25 (1898), 1-124; 26 (1899), 81-182.

Mußgnug, Ludwig. "Alte Wintergesetze," *Rieser Heimatbote*, no. 49 (1928).

———. "Gustav Adolf in Nördlingen," *Rieser Heimatbote*, nos. 83-84 (1932).

———. "Nördlingen unter Oberst von Bülow (1646-1650)," *Rieser Heimatbote*, no. 78 (1931).

———. "Ein 'peinlicher Rechtstag' in Altnördlingen," *Der Rieser Geschichtsfreund*, 1 (1922), nos. 2 and 3.

———. "Die Rieser Siedlungen," *Rieser Heimatbote*, nos. 11 (Oct. 1925) -90 (Apr. 1933).

———. "Zur Geschichte des Stabenfestes," *Rieser Heimatbote*, no. 66 (1930).

Nördlingen: Porträt einer Stadt. Oettingen/Bayern, 1965.

Ockel, Hans. "Die lateinische Schule der Reichsstadt Nördlingen," *Zeitschrift des historischen Vereins für Schwaben und Neuburg*, 34 (1908), 133-45.

O.S. [O. Seefried?]. *Die Bürgerliche Familie Seefried (Seefrid) aus Schwaben.* Görlitz, 1908.

Riezler, Sigmund. "Die Schlacht bei Alerheim, 3. August 1645," *Sitzungsberichte der philosophischen-philologischen und der historischen Classe der königlichen bayerischen Akademie der Wissenschaften*, 1901, pp. 477-548.

Röhrig, E. W. *Zur Geschichte der Familie Klein aus Nördlingen.* Essen, 1941.

Rudin, Bärbel. "Der 'Hochfürstlich Eggenbergische Comoediant' Johann Carl Samenhammer: Ein Beitrag zur Theatergeschichte Nördlingens," *Nördschwaben*, 2 (1974), 161-64.

Steichele, Anton, *Das Bisthum Augsburg, historisch und statistisch beschrieben*, vol. 3. Augsburg, 1872.

Steinmeyer, Heinrich. *Die Entstehung und Entwicklung der Nördlinger Pfingstmesse im Spätmittelalter, mit einem Ausblick bis ins 19. Jahrhundert.* Dissertation, Munich, 1960.

Storm, Peter-Christoph. *Der Schwäbische Kreis als Feldherr: Untersuchungen zur Wehrverfassung des schwäbischen Reichskreises in der Zeit von 1648 bis 1732.* Schriften zur Verfassungsgeschichte, 21. Berlin, 1974.

Vann, James Allen. *The Swabian Kreis: Institutional Growth in the Holy Roman Empire, 1648-1715.* Studies Presented to the International Commission for the History of Representative and Parliamentary Institutions, 53. Brussels, 1975.

Weng, Johann Friedrich. *Die Schlacht bei Nördlingen und Belagerung dieser Stadt in den Monaten August und September 1634.* Nördlingen, 1834.

Wulz, Gustav. *Die Ahnen der Johanna Luise Heidenreich, verehelichten Beck.* Nördlingen, 1959.

———. "Die Anfänge des Buchdrucks in Nördlingen," in *Aus der Frühzeit des Nördlinger Buchdrucks.* Nördlingen, 1963, pp. 1-14.

———. "Bader und Barbiere in Nördlingen. Ein anrüchiges und ein angesehenes Gewerbe," *JHVN*, 24 (1969), 74-85.

———. "Bauchronik der Nördlinger Stadtbefestigung," *JHVN*, 21 (1938/39), 50-95.

———. "Chronik der Kriegsereignisse des Sommers 1634," *Rieser Heimatbote*, nos. 101-02 (1934).

———. "Historische Einleitung," in Karl Grober and Adam Horn, eds., *Die Kunstdenkmäler von Schwaben und Neuburg, II: Stadt Nördlingen.* Die Kunstdenkmäler von Bayern. Munich, 1940, pp. 1-45.

———. "Italienische Kaminkehrer und Südfrüchtehändler in Nördlingen," *Schwäbische Blätter für Heimatpflege und Volksbildung*, 10 (1959), 122-28.

———. "Die Niklas, 500 Jahre Metzger," *Rieser Heimatbote*, no. 149 (1940).

———. "Nördlingen von A bis Z: Beckenschule," *Der Daniel*, 1967, no. 4, p. 9.

———. "Nördlingen von A bis Z: Zurzacher Messe," *Der Daniel*, 1970, no. 2, pp. 23-25.

———. "Die Nördlinger Bildhauer vom 15. bis 18. Jahrhundert," *JHVN*, 20 (1937), 30-36.

———. "Das Nördlinger Buchgewerbe vom 15. bis 18. Jahrhundert," *JHVN*, 22 (1940/41), 90-118.

———. "Die Nördlinger Glockengiesser und Zinngiesser," *JHVN*, 19 (1936), 82-92.

———. "Die Nördlinger Goldschmiede vom 15. bis 18. Jahrhundert," *JHVN*, 16 (1932), 126-38.

———. "Nördlinger Hexenprozesse," *JHVN*, 20 (1937), 42-72; 21 (1938/39), 95-120.

———. "Die Nördlinger Hexen und ihre Richter," *Rieser Heimatbote*, nos. 142-45, 147 (1939).

———. "Die Nördlinger Maler vom 15. bis 18. Jahrhundert," *JHVN*, 18 (1934/35), 69-79.

———. "Die reichsten Nördlinger, ausgezogen aus den Steuerbüchern des Stadtarchivs Nördlingen." Typewritten manuscript in the Stadtarchiv Nördlingen, 1971.

———. "Die Rektoren und Präzeptoren der Lateinschule Nördlingen vom 13. bis 18. Jahrhundert," in *Jahresbericht des Theodor-Heuss-Gymnasiums Nördlingen 1965/66*, pp. 47-64.

Württemberg, königliches statistisch-topographisches Bureau. *Beschreibung des Oberamts Neresheim.* Stuttgart, 1872.

Zorn, Wolfgang. *Handels- und Industriegeschichte Bayerisch-Schwabens, 1648-1870: Wirtschafts-, Sozial- und Kulturgeschichte des schwäbischen Unternehmertums.* Veröffentlichungen der schwäbischen Forschungsgemeinschaft bei der Kommission für bayerische Landesgeschichte, Reihe 1, Bd. 6. Augsburg, 1961.

——— and Leonhard Hillenbrand, *Sechs Jahrhunderte Schwäbische Wirtschaft: Beiträge zur Geschichte der Wirtschaft im bayerischen Regierungsbezirk Schwaben* (Augsburg, 1969).

INDEX

Actors, 235-36
Adam, Balthas (merchant), 101, 141n
Adam, Caspar (Bürgermeister), 193, 333
Aislinger, Daniel (council member), 170n, 331
Alerheim: battle of, 30-31
Aliens, *see* Immigrants, Immigration
Ammann, 13
Anlagen, 145, 156-58
Anlagskasse, 144-45, 158-59, 169; debts of, 161-67; expenditures of, 148-52, 163-66
Annuities, 159n, 161-63
Appetzhofer, Caspar, 173
Apprentices, 41
Apprenticeship: age of, 87-88
Art and artists, 237-38
Artisans, *see* Craftsmen
Augsburg, 280, 288; Peace of, 23; prices in, 103, 322-23
Aurenhammer, Johann Georg (council member), 190, 193, 333

Bakers, 63, 107-108, 134, 135
Baldingen, 22n, 205, 298
Baptisms, *see* Births, number of
Bavaria, 13, 29-31, 33-34, 286
Beck, Johann (teacher), 231
Berlin, Georg (council member), 170n, 330
Betrothals, *see* Marriages
Beyer, Johann Caspar (council member), 183, 334
Bin, Georg (council member) 170n, 330
Birth rate, 37-38
Births: number of, 37-38, 46, 47-51, 59, 71, 301-311
Blatzer (family), 195, 241, 243n, 246n
Blenheim: battle of, 33-34
Bombardment of 1647, 9n, 31, 219-20
Bommeister, Georg (Bürgermeister), 191, 332
Bopfingen, 20
Borrowing: by city, 156, 159-66
Bosch, Johann (Bürgermeister), 172, 330
Brandhofer, Johann (merchant), 277-78
Bread riots, 202, 292
Brentel, Georg (painter), 237
Bürger, *see* Citizenship
Bürgerbuch, 53-54
Bürgermeister (mayor), 13, 178, 198
Burials, *see* Deaths, number of
Butchers, 81, 107-108, 134, 135

Cabinetmakers, 205-206
Capitalism, 206, 239, 258-64, 280-81, 286, 295-97
Catechism, 225, 230-32, 234
Catholics, 10n, 235
Census of 1459, 35
Charitable stipends, 226-27, 229
Charles V (Emperor), 12, 15
Chimney sweeps, 62
Chorhammer, Heinrich (printer), 236
Church, 17, 222-23. *See also* Clergy
Citizenry: size of, 36, 38, 42, 43-44, 51
Citizenship, 39; admission to, 39-40, 53-62, 69-70

City council, *see* Council
City court, *see* Court
City officials, 14, 90, 92-93, 142; on council, 176-79, 182-83
City treasury, *see* Treasury
Clergy, 17, 35, 222-23, 229, 250
Cloth production, 6, 55, 78-79, 82. *See also* Fine-cloth weavers; Linen weavers; Wool weavers
Coinage and currency, xvi, 26-28
Consistory, 223
Constitution: changes in, 11-12, 13n, 170, 189, 201
Council: composition of, 11-13, 168, 170-97, 281, 286, 294; election to, 12, 170-71, 182-83; eligibility for, 170-71; functions of, 13-15, 199-201; organization of, 13; procedures of, 198-99; attitudes toward citizenry of, 195-97; 201-204; 219-21, 292; and citizenship, 55-56, 59-62; educational and cultural policy of, 223-26, 229-31, 234-37; economic policies of, 204-206, 258-61, 280-81, 285-86, 296-97; immigration policies of, 55-56, 59-62, 69-71; marriage policy of, 64; and popular disorder and discontent, 201-204, 214-21; religious policy of, 222-23, 234-35, 237; social policy of, 199-201; taxation policies of, 100-101; and the witch-craze, 207-14; and the wool-weaving industry, 240, 258-61, 265-68, 271-83
Council members: age of, 174-75, 330-34; family background of, 183-96; income of, 177-79; interrelationships among, 189-94; list of, 330-34; occupations of, 172, 175-77, 330-34; wealth of, 172, 179-83, 330-34
Court, 13-14, 170, 173-74, 218
"cow war," 31
Crafts: organization of, 17-18
Craftsmen, 55, 62-64, 78-79, 91-93, 204-206, 237-38, 291 294-97; on city council, 175-76, 182, 196, 294; wealth of, 106-110, 124, 131-37

Danube (river), 4, 33-34
Deaths: number of, 45-49, 50, 71, 301-311
Debts: municipal, 159-67; private, 27-28
Deffner, Hans Caspar (weaver), 273-74, 278
Dehlinger, Samuel (council member), 179-81, 189, 333
Demography, 35-72. *See also* Births, number of; Citizenry, size of; Deaths, number of; Households; Immigration; Marriages; Population
Dolp, Georg Friedrich (school rector), 227

Education, 222, 223-35
Eger (river), 4, 131
Elsas, M. J. (historian), 103
Emigration, 53
Emperor, 148. *See also* Charles V; Imperial government
Engelhart, Georg Friedrich (Bürgermeister), 194, 333
Epplin, Johann Friedrich (merchant), 277
Excise taxes, 158-59, 165
Executioner, 14n

Family: concepts of, 184, 258; reconstitution, 66-69, 73n, 85-87
Fine-cloth weavers, 78, 80, 81, 83, 107-109, 132, 133

Fire prevention, 219-20
Food and drink trades, 79, 82-83, 133-35, 136. *See also* Bakers; Butchers; Taverners
Forster, Johann Philipp (teacher), 232
Foundling-house, 232-33
Frankfurt am Main, 288
French Revolution, 169
French wars, 32-34, 116, 157, 168, 220-21, 293-94
Frickhinger (family), 142, 172, 184, 185-87; Adam (Bürgermeister), 141n, 170n, 185, 331; Hieronimus (Bürgermeister), 185, 330; Johann Christoph (Bürgermeister), 174, 185, 333; Gottfried Dietrich (council member), 193, 333; Johann Jacob (grocer), 187
Furriers, 132, 133

Geider (family), 87
Geissler (family), 73-76, 85, 87, 195
Genzler (family), 87
Geographical mobility, 62-63, 290-91
Gering (family), 184, 190, 195; Jacob (council member), 195, 332
German schools, 225, 229-34
Geyer, Johann Caspar (school rector), 236
Goldburgshausen, 21, 222
Goldstein, Baron Wilhelm Conrad von, 165
Goschenhofer (family), 87
Government of Nördlingen, 11-16; finances of, 144-69. *See also* Council; Court; Justice, administration of
Gregorian calendar, xvi
Grosselfingen, 166
Gruber, David (weaver), 203
Grundherrschaft, 19
Guilds, 11-12, 18, 200, 201. *See also* Crafts, organization of
Gundelfinger (family), 184, 187, 193, 211; Dorothea (witch suspect), 211; Johann Conrad (Bürgermeister, d. 1633), 212, 332; Johann Conrad (Bürgermeister, d. 1670), 174, 332; Johann Wilhelm (council member), 211, 331; Karl (Bürgermeister), 211, 330
Gustavus Adolphus (king of Sweden), 29

Haack, Georg Marcell (painter), 238n
Haaf, Peter, 101
Haas (family), 195; Georg (council member), 191, 330; Johann (council member), 195, 333
Haider, Caspar (Bürgermeister), 191, 331; Georg (Bürgermeister), 226, 330; Ursala (witch suspect), 209
Han, Michael (council member), 170n, 331
Handwerke, *see* Crafts, organization of
Harburg, 261
hatmakers, 19n, 63
Heilsbronn abbey, 22n
Hilbrandt: Johann Christoph (printer), 236-37; Johann Friedrich (council member), 194, 333
Höchstädt: battle of, 33-34
Holl, Maria (witch suspect), 210
Holy Roman Empire, 3, 289. *See also* Imperial government
"home towns," 288-89

Hospital, 17, 19, 36n, 199; revenues and expenditures of, 145-46
Households: number of, 38, 42, 43-44, 51; size of, 36, 38
Houses: ownership of, 103-104, 243-45, 254-56
Hubel, Caspar (council member), 194, 333
Husel, Hans (merchant), 105, 245

Illegitimacy, 37
Imhoff, Carl (merchant), 261
Immigrants: marital status of, 54; number of, 54-59, 65; occupations of, 54-55, 61-62; origins of, 60-62
Immigration, 40, 52, 53-64, 290-91; of women, 69-70
Imperial government, 15-16, 24, 167-68, 285-86
Inflation, *see* Kipper- und Wipperzeit
Inheritance patterns, 253
Interest: paid by city, 159n, 161-68; rate, 284
Inventories, 101-102
Italy: trade with, 7, 84, 262

Jews, 10n, 35, 36, 160, 234-35, 265n
Jörg (family), 184, 187; Johann (Bürgermeister), 187, 331
Journeymen, 36n, 41, 63
Justice: administration of, 14-15, 207-211

Kaisheim abbey, 20, 235
Kessler: Daniel (council member), 212, 332; Katherina (witch suspect), 212
Kipper- und Wipperzeit, 25-28, 131, 148n
Knights of Malta, 6
Kriegskasse, 166-67, 169. *See also* Anlagskasse

Landeshoheit, 20-22
Lang, Johann Georg (council member), 176n, 333
Large council, 13, 170, 201, 218
"lark war," 23
Latin school, 224-29
Lawyers, *see* Professionals
Leather industry, 6, 79, 82. *See also* Shoemakers, Tanners
Lehlin, Johann (council member), 170n, 332
Lemp (family), 184, 212-14; Johann (Bürgermeister), 170n, 331; Peter (Bürgermeister), 170n, 212-14, 237, 331; Rebekka (witch suspect), 212-14
Lierheim, 166
Linen weavers, 78, 83-84, 132, 133, 285-86, 296
Loans: by city, 147-48, 153
Loden, *see* Wool weavers
Lodenkasse, 283
Louis XIV (king of France), 157-58
Lutheranism, 10, 22-23, 222-23, 229
Lutz, Wilhelm Friederich (clergyman), 223

Magistrates, *see* Council; Council members
Mair: Georg (council member), 214, 330; Paul (city clerk), 215; Rosina (witch suspect), 214
Marriage: age at, 64, 68-69, 72, 89; regulation of, 64
Marriages: endogamous and exogamous, 47, 53, 65; marital status of partners in, 66-68;

number of, 37, 47-49, 50, 57, 301-311; occupational background of partners in, 85-87
Martens, Heinrich (Bürgermeister), 176n, 333
Mayinger, Peter (council member), 214, 331
Mayors, *see* Bürgermeister
Merchants, 79-80, 247, 260-64, 271, 274-78; on city council, 182-83; wealth of, 124, 137-42
Midelfort, H. C. Erik (historian), 211
Ministers, *see* Clergy
Mobility, 239, 289-92. *See also* Geographical mobility; Occupational mobility; Wealth mobility
Morality: regulation of, 200-201
Mortality, *see* Deaths, number of
Music, 225

Nähermemmingen, 20-21, 222
Netherlands: trade with, 7, 83
Niclas (family), 184
Noncitizens, 40-43, 111n
Nördlingen: battle of, xvi, 29-30; second battle of, 30-31
Nördlingen contingent, 32-34
Nuremberg, 16; trade with, 4, 7

Occupation: changes of, 77, 88-93
Occupational mobility, 84-93, 290-91
Occupations: distribution of, 76-84, 312-20; held simultaneously, 77, 89-90; heritability of, 85-87; wealth levels among, 106-110, 129-43
Oettingen, 6, 238; counts of, 6, 19-21, 23, 202, 237, 261
Orphans: wealth of, 111n

Paktbürger, 41, 54
Parish registers, 37-38, 45, 53, 298-300
Pasquills, 202-204
Pentecost fair, 7, 83, 267
Pfandbücher, 244
Pflaumloch, 20-21
Philip Ludwig, count of the Palatinate, 148
Pietism, 200
Plague, 29-30, 44, 48-21, 57, 71, 114, 182
Popular disorder and discontent, 202-204, 214-20, 292
Population of Nördlingen, 3, 35-38; statistics, 299-311; trends, 52, 71-73. *See also* Births, number of; Citizenry, size of; Deaths, number of; Households; Immigration; Marriages
Prices, 25-28, 102-103; index of, 102-103, 114n, 152n, 167n, 272n, 322-23
Printing, 81, 236-37
Privy council, 13
Professionals, 141-42, 174, 176-77
Putting-out system, 205, 260-63

Reformation, 12, 21-23, 200, 222, 225
Regner, Theophilus (school rector), 226
Reichshofrat, 286
Reichskammergericht, 21
Reimlingen, 166
Religion, 10, 21-23, 216-17, 222-25, 229, 234-35, 237
Rehm (family), 191, 193; Georg Philipp (council member), 191-93, 333
Residential patterns, 10-11
Reuter, Johann (Bürgermeister), 172, 330
Ries, 4-6, 19-22, 60-62

Roman law, 208, 210
Romul, Wilhelm Friedrich (Bürgermeister), 171n, 189, 193, 332
Rothenburg ob der Tauber, 220

St. Georg's church, 9, 222
Scheublin, Tobias (clergyman), 229
Schmalkaldic War, 12, 23
Schneidt, Melchior (clergyman), 229
School ordinances, 224-26, 230-31
Schools, 223-34
Schöpperlin (family), 184; Caspar (council member), 110; Georg Wilhelm (Bürgermeister), 194, 333
Schultes: Friedrich (printer), 236; Lucas (printer), 236
Schweindorf, 21, 222
Schweyer, Matthias (weaver), 276-77, 282n
Seefried: Johann Georg (Bürgermeister), 190, 332; Theodor's widow (merchant), 268
Seng, Peter (Bürgermeister), 172, 330
Servants, 41
Shoemakers, 79-81, 95-96, 107-108, 132, 133
Social mobility, *see* Geographical mobility; Mobility; Occupational mobility; Wealth mobility
Social structure, *see* Occupations, distribution of; Wealth, distribution of; Wealth, stratification of
Soldiers, 28-34, 153-55, 214-17, 220
Stabenfest, 233
Stadtmarkung, 21
Stahringer, Johann Martin (teacher), 233
Stang, Johann Friedrich (council member), 183, 333
Streitter, Michael (council member), 102, 174, 333
Suicide, 270
Superintendent, 222-23
Swabian Circle, 4, 24, 32-34, 153, 157, 161, 166-69, 221
Switzerland: trade with, 7, 262-63, 266, 270-71, 274-79, 282-83

Tanners, 6, 79-81, 90, 107, 110, 130, 131-33, 247-48, 267
Taverners, 75, 90, 107-108, 133-35
Taxes: assessment of, 97-102; on citizens' property, 36, 97-102, 156-58; direct, 145, 156-58; evasion of, 101; indirect, 147, 153, 156, 158-59; for military purposes, 145, 156-58, 216-18, 221
Tax registers, 36, 38, 59n, 76-77, 96-97, 124n
Teutonic Knights, 6, 166, 235
Textiles, *see* Cloth production; Fine-cloth weavers; Linen weavers; Wool weavers
Thirty Years War: chronology of, 28-31; demographic effects of, 44, 48, 51, 61, 70-71; economic and social effects of, 83-84, 94, 101, 114-16, 120-25, 127-28, 135-41, 149-57, 160-61, 168-69, 182, 264, 293-94, 297; and popular disorders, 214-20; mentioned, 22, 25, 32, 34, 57, 60, 62, 82, 88, 117, 133, 174, 176, 237-38, 262
Trade and commerce, 6-7, 83-84. *See also* Italy, trade with;

Merchants; Netherlands, trade with; Switzerland, trade with
Treasury: debts of, 159-61, 167; expenditures of, 146, 147-57, 161, 162; revenues of, 146, 147, 152-61, 162
Troeltsch, Georg Christian von (Bürgermeister), 285-86
Tübingen: University of, 223, 226
Turkish Wars, 32-33, 116, 157, 220-21, 293-94

Ulm, 279, 280
Universities, 228-29
Untertanen, 22

Venice, 63
Verlagssystem, 205, 260-63
Victualing trades. *See* Bakers; Butchers; Food and drink trades; Taverners
Visitation of schools, 231-33

Walker, Mack (historian), 288-89
Wallenstein, Albrecht von (imperial general), 29
Wallerstein, 6, 23
Walls of Nördlingen, 3, 9-10
War of the Spanish Succession, 33-34, 48, 52, 125, 143, 152, 165-66
Wars and warfare in general: chronology of, 28-34; demographic effects of, 48, 70-72; economic and social effects of, 116, 137, 149-52, 157-58, 161, 168-69, 262, 292-94, 297; political effects of, 200, 220-21. *See also* French wars; Thirty Years War; Turkish wars; War of the Spanish Succession
Wealth: distribution of, 103-106, 116-25; 293-94; 324-25; of occupational groups, 106-110, 129-43; statistics of, 321; stratification of, 103-111, 289-90; total, 103, 111-16
Wealth mobility, 125-29, 290-92, 326-29
Weapons production, 81
Weavers, *see* Fine-cloth weavers; Linen weavers; Wool weavers
Wechsler, Johann Jacob (Bürgermeister), 193, 333
Weddings: regulation of, 201
Weiber, Modista (teacher), 232
Welsch (family), 184, 187; Hieronimus (council member), 171n, 190, 331; Johann Friedrich von (Bürgermeister), 174, 334; Lorenz Christoph (Bürgermeister), 194, 333; Melchior (council member), 172, 330
Weng, Georg Friedrich (Bürgermeister), 204, 332
Wernher, *see* Wörner
Westerfeld, Georg Adam (Bürgermeister), 194, 334
Westphalia: Peace of, 20n, 31, 157
Widenmann (family), 184; Georg (merchant), 246-47; Georg (council member), 101, 191, 332
Widowers, 66-68
Widows, 36, 66-68, 70-77
Witch-craze, 24-25, 206-14, 247
Women, 36, 69-70, 76-78
Wool weavers, 55, 87-88, 90, 243, 259-64, 282-83, 295; number of, 78, 81; wealth of, 107-109, 130, 131; and conflict with the Wörners, 239-40, 258-59, 264-82

Wörner (family), 142-43, 183, 239-58, 264-87; Andreas (weaver), 105n, 109-110, 239, 241-45, 252, 262, 264; Andreas (clergyman), 249-50; Catherina, 269, 272, 276-77; Daniel (weaver), 250-52; Daniel (merchant, d. 1699), 252-53, 258, 262-81, 287; Daniel (merchant, d. 1733), 142, 241, 268-85; David (weaver), 250-51; David (council member), 142, 183, 269-70, 272, 284-85, 334; Elizabetha, 241, 245; Georg (merchant), 210n, 246-48, 262; Hans (weaver), 255, 278; Hans Georg (weaver, d. 1678), 256-57; Hans Georg (weaver, d. 1724), 257; Johann Daniel (council member), 285; Magdalena, 264, 281; Melchior (weaver), 252; Michael (weaver, d. 1628), 248-49; Michael (weaver, d. 1660), 252-55; Sibylla, 256-57; Simon, 268-69; Tobias (weaver), 251; Wilhelm Heinrich (council member), 285
Wörnitz (river), 4
Wuesst; Conrad's widow, 102
Wulz, Gustav (historian), 207
Wünsch, Johann Caspar (council member), 194, 333

Zünfte, *see* Guilds
Zürich: trade with, 262, 270, 279
Zurzach trade fair, 262, 279

LIBRARY OF CONGRESS CATALOGING IN PUBLICATION DATA

Friedrichs, Christopher R 1947-
Urban society in an age of war.

A revision of the author's thesis, Princeton University, 1974.
Bibliography: p.
Includes index.
1. Nördlingen, Ger.—Social conditions.
2. Nördlingen, Ger.—Economic conditions.
3. Nördlingen, Ger.—Politics and government.
4. War and society—History. 5. Germany—History—17th century. I. Title.
HN458.N54F74 1979 309.1'43'37 79-83988
ISBN 0-691-05278-6